BRITAIN I

Für Marwan und Shaalan, noch einmal

BRITAIN IN IRAQ

Contriving King and Country, 1914–1932

PETER SLUGLETT

Columbia University Press

NEW YORK

Columbia University Press
Publishers Since 1893
New York

Library of Congress Cataloging-in-Publication Data
Sluglett, Peter
    Britain in Iraq : contriving king and country, 1914-1932/Peter Sluglett.
      p. cm.
    ISBN 978-0-231-14200-7 (cloth : alk. paper) and 978-0-231-14201-4 (pbk. : alk. paper)
    Iraq—History—1921- 2. British—Iraq—History. I. Title.

DS79.5.S575 2007
956.704'1—dc22

2006051872

∞

c 10 9 8 7 6 5 4 3 2 1

p 10 9 8 7 6 5 4 3 2 1

CONTENTS

A NOTE ON TRANSLITERATION

1. Transliteration has been kept as simple and consistent as possible; ' has been used for 'ain, and ' for hamza. No subscript or superscript marks or have been used.
2. When an Arabic word or name has a form which has been commonly accepted in English it has not been put into italics. Less common or technical terms (e.g. *muqata'a, sirkal*) are in italics throughout.
3. Kurdish, Persian and Turkish proper names, and some Arabic names which I have not seen written in Arabic but which appear in British sources, have been copied from the Police Intelligence Reports in the form in which they are most commonly found.

ABBREVIATIONS

Air   Air Ministry Files, Public Record Office, London.

BHCF   Baghdad High Commission File, National Archives of India, New Delhi.

CO   Colonial Office Files, Public Record Office, London.

DBFP   Documents on British Foreign Policy.

FO   Foreign Office Files, Public Record Office, London.

LP & S   India Office: Letters, Political and Secret, India Office Records, British Library, London.

FOREWORD

by Albert Hourani

The British ruled Iraq from the First World War until 1932, and the way in which they ruled was widely regarded as being new. They exercised authority, under mandate from the League of Nations, by means of the RAF, a network of advisers and officials in government departments, and control of the country's most important economic resource, oil, and they used this authority in order to create an administration and a political order which would in the long run be able to stand by themselves. It was generally thought at the time that the experiment was successful, and by 1930 the British Government believed itself to be in a position to assure its essential interests through a treaty negotiated between equals, and to recommend to the League of Nations that the mandate should be ended and Iraq admitted to membership.

The sense of having done well which was widespread among British officials and politicians was shared by the most influential Arab political writer of the time, George Antonius. In his *Arab Awakening* published in the 1930s in circumstances which led him to emphasize the contrast between what Britain had done in Iraq and what France had not done in Syria, Antonius wrote in warm terms of the efforts and devotion of 'an unusually capable and conscientious band of British Officials' and of Iraq's good fortune that 'in many important respects, Great Britain's interests marched with her own'.

In the post-imperial age, we are perhaps less inclined to believe that there can be a pre-established harmony between the interests of different peoples, or even that it is possible to speak of a whole people as having a single interest. Whether or not we are inclined to make judgements, we at least want explanations of the way in which policies were formed, the means by which they were carried out, and their effects on different sections or strata of society. Dr. Sluglett's careful study, based on a wide range of unpublished sources, and guided by a historian's sense of the way in which governments work and societies change, helps us to understand much better than before both the aims and the methods of the British imperial administration. The narrative of political history and the analysis of defence and security policy show clearly that it was not fortune or harmony of interests, but skilful administration, discreet but firm political action, and where necessary the use of the RAF which made it possible for the British to pass responsibility to an indigenous government so soon; and his study of tenurial, fiscal and tribal policy in Chapter 6 and Appendix II disentangles with great skill that combination of misunderstanding of the Ottoman land-system, calculations of interest, and preconceptions about the nature of rural society which led the British to support and strengthen the power of landowners and tribal chiefs.

Albert Hourani

PREFACE TO
THE SECOND EDITION

I am delighted that the book I wrote some thirty years ago on the British mandate in Iraq is available once again, and, that, through the agency of I. B. Tauris and Columbia University Press, it will almost certainly reach a wider audience than it did on its first appearance in 1976. At the same time I am saddened that renewed awareness of the importance of this not-quite-obscure episode in latter day British colonialism and modern Middle Eastern history has arisen less out of any intrinsic interest of the events themselves, but is a consequence of the continuing and broadening crisis in contemporary Iraq, which, in late November 2006, seems to be spiralling ever more horribly out of control. In many ways, the blunders and errors of judgement whose consequences resonate so loudly today are eerily reminiscent of the failings of the Mesopotamia campaign in 1914–1917, although the very much more primitive communications and other technological inadequacies meant that the mistakes of the earlier campaign were perhaps more excusable, or more understandable, than more recent ones.

Others have described, more graphically and more knowledgeably than I can, the sorry catalogue of policy miscalculations, wilful misrepresentations, lack of expertise, and downright corruption which both preceded and accompanied the ill-planned military venture whose consequences play out daily on our television screens. It is significant that it seems to have been advocated and carried out by a small group of individuals whose almost messianic fervour was not greatly encumbered by any real knowledge of the recent history and politics of the Middle East. In a review article in *Middle East Journal* in June 2006, I pointed out, not without a certain patriotic pride, that when the British government published the *Report of the Commission appointed to Inquire into the Origin, Inception, and Operations of the War in Mesopotamia* in 1917, the Secretary of State for India, Austen Chamberlain, felt obliged to resign. Chamberlain had overall responsibility for, but no *direct* involvement with, the campaign, which was initially run from Delhi and Simla by the Military Department of the Government of India. I wondered then, after the sorry chronicle of the past three years, what further dizzy heights of incompetence or atrocity would need to be attained to make Mr Rumsfeld feel obliged to do the decent thing. In the end, it would be the Republican reversal in the mid-term elections of November 2006 – rather than any obvious questioning of the wisdom of the course he insisted on pursuing – which eventually stopped him in his tracks.

In the course of revising this book in 2005 and 2006, I tried to avoid the temptation of drawing explicit comparisons between 'then' and 'now'. Readers are of course free to make such inferences as they wish, but in general it is probably best not to jump to quick and often inaccurate conclusions. For instance, there is the question of *scale*. The fact that most armed resistance to the British (and later to the new institutions of the Iraqi government) took place in the rural areas rather than in the cities meant that, certainly after the end of the First World War, civilian casualties, although none the less inexcusable, were not all that high. Secondly, Iraq had no history of sectarian-based violence. Evidently, the more educated Shi'is came to realise in the course of the 1920s that British reliance on the Sunnis meant that some of their own interests *as a religious community* could not and would not be addressed. Nevertheless, at least until the fall of Qasim in 1963, 'Sunni rule', which had been accompanied by increasing secularisation and the more or less even spread of universal education, was neither particularly fearful nor particularly oppressive, certainly not in the way it became under the Ba'th. Oil, of course, played a significant part in both operations. Under the occupation and mandate, the British wanted to make sure that the concession went to a British company, and it is almost certain in the 2000s that the United States is seeking to reprivatise Iraqi oil through the use of 'Production Sharing Agreements'.

When I heard that I.B.Tauris was prepared to consider a second edition of *Britain in Iraq* I wondered what would be the best strategy to adopt. In the end, I took heed of the kind words of Toby Dodge, Roger Louis and Charles Tripp, who all advised me to revise and update the text rather than to rewrite it. While there has been a lot of stimulating new writing on eighteenth and nineteenth century Iraq (by Christoph Herzog, Dina Khoury, Tom Niewenhuis, Meir Litvak, and Sarah Shields) and on the post-mandate period (Eric Davis, Faleh 'Abd al-Jabbar, David McDowall, Phebe Marr, Charles Tripp), there has not been a great deal on the occupation and mandate. Batatu's masterpiece appeared in 1978: in the early 1970s I had access to his 1960 Harvard thesis, which forms Book One of *The Old Social Classes*. I have tried to incorporate more of his findings and conclusions: I am always amazed at the encyclopaedic breadth and depth of his knowledge. In

Joe Stork's words: 'Hanna Batatu has constructed a masterpiece of historical literature that single-handedly catapults Iraq from the least known of the major Arab countries to the Arab society of which we now have the most thorough political portrait.' (MERIP, June 1981)

Apart from Batatu, I am indebted to Pierre Jean Luizard's *La Formation de l'Irak Contemporain* . . . (1991), and most recently to Toby Dodge's *Inventing Iraq* . . . (2003). Both books have provided important new insights into the period: Luizard's analysis of the 'revolution' of 1920 is enhanced by his access to an impressive array of contemporary Arabic material, and his profound understanding of Shi'i religio-political thought. Dodge shows how British colonial administrators understood their tasks in Iraq during the occupation and mandate, and the ways in which these perceptions shaped policy and practice, and ultimately, the form of the fledgling Iraqi polity. I have also profited from David Omissi's *Air Power and Colonial Control* . . . (1990), and Reider Visser's *Basra, the Failed Gulf State* . . . (2005). Finally, a long article on air control by Priya Satia in *The American Historical Review* (February 2006) stimulated me to clarify some of the ideas expressed in Chapter 7. My only regrets, which I could not easily address in this revised edition, are first, that I was not able to consult archival sources in Arabic (and I fear that most of these will have been destroyed during the orgy of looting in Baghdad that US forces were apparently unable to prevent in April and May 2003), and second, that I have not been able to incorporate the Arabic studies of the period, especially scholarly biographies of some of the principal figures, which have appeared over the past three decades. While *Britain in Iraq* . . . is primarily a study of British colonial policy, I should like to have paid more attention to material emanating from Iraq, both during the period on which the book focuses, and later.

*   *   *

A great deal has happened to me in the thirty years since the first appearance of *Britain in Iraq*. Both my parents died, well into their eighties, in 1995 and 1999; Albert Hourani, the kindest yet most exacting of mentors, died in 1993, having helped to plant the seeds of my later career by suggesting to Roy Mottahedeh that I might be interested in spending a year teaching Middle Eastern History at Harvard. I went back to England for a while after Harvard, determined to return to American academia if at all possible. In the autumn of 1994 I became Director of the Middle East Center at the University of Utah. Marion and I were full of hope and excitement; at last we would be teaching at the same university. Two weeks after our arrival, she was diagnosed with advanced renal cell carcinoma, from which she died some eighteen months later, in February 1996; she was 59. I am deeply conscious of the debt that I owe my sister Judith, my sons Marwan and Shaalan, Claire and Nelida, and my grandchildren, together with many friends in Salt Lake and in different parts of the world, for sustaining me through the difficult years that followed, and continuing to play such an enriching part in my life.

Since *Britain in Iraq . . .*originated as my doctoral thesis, I would like to express my gratitude to the British higher educational system in the 1960s and 1970s for financing the greater part of my undergraduate and graduate education, and to my parents' unstinting generosity in filling the gap. I don't think that either of them fully understood my fascination either with the region or the period, but their unconditional support was both exemplary and, at the time and remembered now, moving in the extreme. I should also like to salute the extraordinary energy of David Wolton, founder and prime mover of Ithaca Press, who published more than a dozen volumes in the St Antony's Middle East Monographs series (*Britain in Iraq . . .* was no. 4), as well as other books on the Middle East that might not otherwise have found a publisher. Urban legend has it that he distributed his books to London bookshops on his bicycle, but in any case it is a pleasure to acknowledge his commitment to many Middle Eastern causes, his friendship, and his unfailing good humour.

After the sadness of my first years here, I came to delight in the freedom and general unclutteredness surrounding teaching at a major state university in the United States. My colleagues here have been gracious and welcoming, and my students, once they get over the shock at the amount of work I expect from them, have often surprised me. I am grateful to the University of Utah for having rescued me from what I see, perhaps unfairly, as the excessive and enormously time-consuming administrative burdens borne by many of my British contemporaries, and more importantly for providing a structure which has permitted me to devote a considerable amount of time to my own work. I have also benefitted from the University's travel fund, and from the US Education Department's Title VI grant to the Middle East Center. Together, these funds have enabled me to attend many academic conferences, and to organise workshops here in Salt Lake City. It has been a particular pleasure to have had the opportunity to meet and maintain contact with younger scholars in the field.

Finally, I want to express my loving gratitude to Shohreh, who entered my life so unexpectedly, and with whom I have found such great happiness. Here we are, *parmi les croyants*, two exiles in Zion, the striking Iranian, the sardonic Englishman. She has brought me great fulfilment and contentment, and given me the peace of mind to write and thrive. I can never thank her enough.

Salt Lake City, November 2006

PREFACE TO
THE FIRST EDITION

This study is an assessment of Anglo-Iraqi relations and of Britain's role in Iraqi affairs during the period of the British occupation and mandate. The eighteen years which are surveyed here are among the most crucial in the country's recent history, and are of the utmost importance in understanding developments in both pre- and post-revolutionary Iraq.

The book is based primarily on British sources, and much of the more detailed research has been made possible through the use of hitherto unexploited materials now located in the National Archives of India. The papers of the Baghdad High Commission, which were taken to Bombay in 1941 and are now in the National Archives of India, New Delhi, are an invaluable source of information for the day to day working of the mandate as an instrument of government and control within Iraq. Similarly the RAF records in the Air Ministry papers contain a wealth of information on local conditions, and are particularly useful for the study of the changes in rural society and politics brought about by the advent of British rule.

The work has been divided into two sections, the first a chronological account of the eighteen years of the 'official' British connection, and the second a series of studies of aspects of policy and administration. Unaccountably, I had missed Briton Cooper Busch's *Britain, India and the Arabs 1914–1921* (University of California Press, 1972) when making my final revision of Chapter 1, but although Professor Busch covers a wider canvas, I do not think that he will disagree with my briefer survey and conclusions. Central political questions, such as the role of oil in Anglo-Iraqi relations, the Mosul frontier question, and the beginnings of the Kurdish problem, are covered in Chapters 2 and 3, while Chapters 4 and 5 discuss the years 1926–1932, with special reference to the question of Iraq's entry to the League of Nations and the attitudes to this taken by different political groups.

The remaining three chapters discuss the development of policy towards land tenure and land revenue, defence and education. The immense changes brought about by British intervention in all these fields have had striking effects on the subsequent political and socio-economic development of the country. The development of particular policies in the fields of land tenure and defence helped to ensure the concentration of political power in the hands of a small class of officers and bureaucrats, supported by local tribal or rural leaders, whose powers had been greatly enhanced by grants both of land and of wide powers of jurisdiction over their tenants and followers.

In general, Britain's role in Iraq during the Occupation and Mandate periods was to devise a system of control that could be exercised as unobtrusively and cheaply as possible. With limited resources, but with a long tradition of colonial administration behind them, the British authorities built up a system based on a subtle mixture of cajolery, blandishment and bluff. In these circumstances, where Britain had the upper hand, but could not afford too frequent or too clumsy displays of her superiority, the creation of a basically loyal if occasionally restive political authority in Iraq was vital. Hence both Britain and those who had access to political power in Iraq were forced into a recognition of their interdependence, and the relationship which had been so carefully created and nurtured in the period covered by this book, survived, almost intact, until its violent end in 1958.

I would like to express my gratitude to the individuals and institutions who have given me assistance of various kinds. I owe most to Mr. Albert Hourani, who continues to be unsparing in his generous concern and his willingness to share his profound understanding of the Middle East.

In the archival collections and libraries which I have consulted I am grateful to the staff of the India Office Library: the staff of the Public Record Office, Ashridge, Little Gaddesden, especially Mr. Franklin: to the staff of the Public Record Office in the East Room, Portugal Street, especially Mr. Donovan and the late Mr. Monger: to the staff of the National Archives of India, New Delhi, especially Miss D. G. Keswani.

In the Middle East Centre at Oxford, I should like to thank Elizabeth Monroe, and Dr. Derek Hopwood for helpful comments on parts of the text. I am grateful to Glen Balfour-Paul for his hospitality in Baghdad, and Dr. Bahadur Singh for his generous hospitality in Delhi. I should also like to thank Mrs. Mary McCormack of Bristol for her valiant efforts to improve my prose style.

Finally, my deepest gratitude goes to my parents, for having encouraged and supported me through all the stages of my education and beyond – and to Marion, for having read and fought over every word with her special mixture of affection and exasperation.

Durham, May 1976

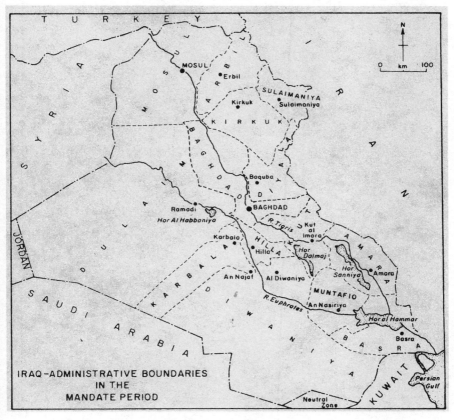

Map 1. Iraqi administrative boundaries in the mandate period

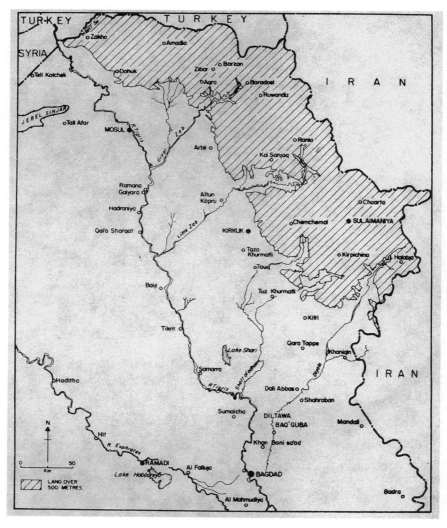

Map 2. Northeastern Iraq

INTRODUCTION

Under the late Ottoman Empire, the area which now forms the state of Iraq was divided into the three provinces (Arabic, *wilaya*: Turkish, *vilayet*) of Basra, Baghdad and Mosul. In this area lived, sometimes harmoniously, sometimes less so, Arabs, Kurds, Turks and Persians, most of whom were Sunni or Shi'i Muslims, together with communities of Christians, Jews, Yazidis and Sabaeans. Until comparatively recent times, the geography of the country had assisted the populations of the region to resist the imposition of any authority not of their own choosing. In the north, the mountains provided an almost impenetrable fortress for the Kurdish tribes, while until the latter part of the nineteenth century the desert tribal confederations, and the Shi'i tribes of the southern river valleys, especially those inhabiting the central marshlands, generally succeeded in defying the military expeditions which the Ottomans despatched to subdue them.

Whether or not 'Iraq' is an artificial entity need not detain us here, although there was no entity called 'Iraq' by the Ottomans which corresponds to the modern state.[1] Given the extensive trade and other linkages between northern Iraq and northern Syria, a more 'natural' geopolitical unit might have been one in which Mosul would have been part of what is now Syria. This would have left 'Iraq' as the former provinces of Baghdad and Basra, an arrangement which would have corresponded to the original dispositions of Sykes-Picot which lasted until Clemenceau 'gave' Mosul to Britain in December 1918.[2]

Until the time of Midhat Pasha, the capable and enlightened governor of Baghdad between 1869 and 1872, even the three main cities, Mosul, Baghdad and Basra were only under the nominal and occasional control of the authorities in Constantinople. The powers of the local representatives of the Porte hardly extended beyond the outer suburbs of the towns in which their garrisons were quartered, and the rural area was composed of a series of largely independent chiefdoms with overlapping, often shifting, spheres of control and influence. In the course of the nineteenth century, however, the Ottomans slowly extended their authority by force of arms, though their efforts at pacification were helped by significant contemporary changes in rural society and economy. With the opening of the Suez Canal in 1869, and the growth of steam transport along the Tigris and Euphrates, southern Iraq gradually became more accessible to the outside world, and as a result, growing cereals for sale or barter gradually became more attractive than rearing stock for subsistence (Sluglett, 1992). What had been an almost closed economy was greatly modified, and the surplus produce was sold to outsiders who resold either to the towns or to India and the Gulf (Hasan, 1970; Fattah, 1997). The gradual realisation that security was needed to achieve more or less regular agricultural production broke down some of the resistance to the Ottomans' attempts to pacify the country, and enabled them to bring more of the area under their control.[3]

Like other parts of the Empire, the three Iraqi provinces were governed by a tacit partnership between the Ottoman authorities and the local notables, each group knowing its own and the other's limitations.[4] By the beginning of the twentieth century this traditional mechanism was being challenged. The effects of European nationalist movements and the activities of reforming groups within the Empire itself had led to the creation first of a constitutional and then an embryonic nationalist movement in Mosul, Baghdad and Basra. But in the years between the restoration of the Ottoman constitution in 1908 and the outbreak of the First World War, young Iraqi officers and lawyers gradually became disappointed at the failure of the Committee of Union and Progress to give to the Arab provinces the greater degree of self-government for which they had hoped (Kayalı, 1997). It was these people who were to rally round Faysal ibn Husayn between 1919 and 1921: several of the officers among them had been with him in the Hijaz since 1915, and some of these had been members of the pre-war nationalist group, *al-'Ahd al-'Iraqi*.[5]

Foreign Interests in Iraq before World War I

Britain's connection with Iraq and the Gulf had grown out of its interest in protecting the route to India and trade in the Indian Ocean. Early in the nineteenth century Britain had been concerned to prevent attacks on its shipping from the Gulf coasts, and after a series of naval encounters had entered into treaty relations with the rulers of the principal shaykhdoms of the Arabian Peninsula aimed at the suppression of piracy in return for

British protection. Britain concluded a treaty of maritime peace with the tribal chiefs of Bahrain and the area now roughly corresponding to the United Arab Emirates in 1820; these treaties were extended and reconfirmed later in the century, generally including measures against the slave trade (from Africa to India and the Arabian peninsula). In 1853 the chiefs signed a Perpetual Maritime Truce (hence the 'Trucial States', as the United Arab Emirates were formerly known), and in 1892, largely to counter what seemed to be growing French interests, Bahrain and the lower Gulf emirates were obliged to sign further agreements with Britain under which they agreed not to grant or dispose of any part of their territories except to Britain, and to conduct their relations with other powers through the British government. Finally, Kuwait and Qatar, which had not been parties to the earlier 'piracy' treaties, signed similarly exclusive agreements with Britain in 1899 and 1916 respectively, largely because of their rulers' desire to escape Ottoman and/or Sa'udi tutelage.[6]

The ensuing peace enabled British and Indian merchants to trade freely with both shores of the Gulf and with southern Iraq, whose principal exports were grain and dates. The total volume of trade was small, but it was growing steadily in the years before the First World War.[7] Britain's only rival in the area, though a long way behind, was Germany, particularly after the award of the concession to build the Baghdad Railway in 1903, although there had been a long tradition of German influence over, for example, the modernisation of the Ottoman Army.[8] Foreshadowing one of the recommendations of the de Bunsen committee several years later (Nevakivi, 1969: 18–24), that the Tigris and Euphrates valleys could provide suitable accommodation for the surplus populations of India, pamphlets were written to encourage German farmers to migrate to Iraq and to use German expertise to improve the productivity of the area.[9] In view of Iraq's rapid decline in importance as an agricultural producer after the end of the First World War, it is interesting that the notion of the country as one of the 'potential storehouses of food . . . for the world' had long formed a major attraction for the European powers.[10]

In the period immediately before the First World War, another factor emerged of more permanent significance: the growing interest of Western governments and commercial interests in the oilfields of South West Persia and the potential oil wealth of the Ottoman Empire, including that of the Transferred Territories.[11] The Baghdad Railway concession had included rights over minerals in the 20 kilometres on either side of the track, though no major oil discoveries had been made in the Ottoman Empire before 1914. In South West Persia, however, the existence of oil in substantial quantities had been established since 1907, and Britain's interest in securing a steady supply for the Royal Navy prompted the British government to acquire a majority shareholding in the Anglo-Persian Oil Company in 1914 (Kent, 1993). Hence, when the Ottoman Empire seemed likely to join the war on the side of the Central Powers, the British authorities in India were concerned that German-prompted Ottoman activity might hinder trade and communications with India, and also threaten the Persian oilfields.[12] Indian Expeditionary Force 'D', with some 5,500 men, was therefore despatched to Basra, to perform a holding operation. In the beginning, 'marching deep into Mesopotamia' does not seem to have been envisaged: the force's task was simply to deter the Ottomans from suborning Britain's friends or interfering with British interests at the head of the Gulf.

The British Occupation of Iraq

However, almost immediately after the first landings at Fao, British policy underwent a complete change. The holding operation was seen to be rather a tame objective in comparison with the attractive prospect of advancing to Baghdad, and in spite of major reversals and heavy casualties, Britain found herself in overall control of the three *wilayas* by November 1918. As the army advanced, a complete civil administration was constructed in its wake, and by the end of war the territory had become organised along the lines of a province of British India. But under the changed international atmosphere which followed the Armistice, outright annexation of territory was no longer acceptable and other methods of control had to be invented.

The adjustment proved too difficult for many of the British personnel on the spot, especially the Acting Civil Commissioner, Sir Arnold Wilson, who was in charge of the Mesopotamian administration during Sir Percy Cox' absence in Teheran between 1918 and 1920.[13] Wilson's failure to understand the new climate of opinion and the new tone of London's instructions was one of the main indirect causes of the rising of 1920. British policy had to be tailored not only to serve British ends, but also to satisfy President Woodrow Wilson's ambitions for the United States and the world, expressed in terms of self-determination and equality of economic opportunity for all powers (Stivers, 1982). The system of 'A' mandates was an attempt to reconcile these two uncomfortable bed-fellows, though the actual operation of the mandate ensured that Britain's own strategic and commercial aims were given first priority.

In spite of the looser control which it implied, the new policy was a welcome relief to the British Treasury after the high cost of the Mesopotamia campaign. Especially after the air control scheme was introduced in 1922, the mandate became relatively cheap to administer. All colonies – the 'A' mandates were no exception – were supposed to pay their own way, but it was evident that some form of military occupation would be necessary in Iraq, at least for the foreseeable future. Keeping British forces there cost over £32 million as late as 1920–1921. Once the broad principles of the mandate policy had been agreed upon by the international community, its local application was left to the mandatory power. The British authorities chose to set up an Arab government, recruited largely from the Sunni dignitaries of the towns and the Sunni officers who had fought with Faysal in the Arab Revolt, backed by a network of British advisers in the ministries in Baghdad and in the headquarters of the provincial administrations.[14]

This study examines some of the major problems encountered by the British and Iraqi authorities in Iraq during the period of British occupation and mandate. Perhaps the most far-reaching of these was the lack of any sense of national unity. The diversity of the population within the three *wilayas* was more apparent than any unifying factors, while in terms of the 'traditional' commercial orientation of the three main towns, Mosul had always looked more towards Aleppo and south western Turkey than to Baghdad; Basra had long established trading connections with India and the Gulf, while Baghdad itself was a centre of the Persian transit trade. Encouraging either town, especially Basra, to surrender its traditional autonomy to Baghdad was not an easy task, although an extremely necessary one, as Basra's importance as an outlet to the sea had grown with increasing trade.[15] Outside the towns, loyalty to the new government depended largely on the persuasive powers of British police officers and the British officials 'advising' the local representatives of the Iraqi Ministry of Interior.

As well as being threatened by disruptive elements inside and outside its borders, the Iraqi government was weakened by constant shortages of money. The financial and military agreements subsidiary to the 1922 Anglo-Iraqi Treaty imposed a crushing burden on the Iraqi Treasury which was only to be relieved in the relatively distant future by income from oil. The payment of Iraq's share of the Ottoman Public Debt (Blaisdell, 1966: 177–207), the salaries of British officials[16] and the equipment and maintenance of the Iraqi army accounted for about 40% of the budget throughout the mandate. The chief sources of income were land revenue and customs and excise, and the former could only be collected on a large scale if peace prevailed in the countryside. With the general lack of enthusiasm for the government, rural tax collection often depended on threatening to bomb the more recalcitrant, and making friends with the more complaisant, of the local magnates.

Towards the end of the mandate, policies of conciliation and tax remission vis-à-vis the landlords and tribal leaders had been pursued so far that land revenue had ceased to form a significant part of national income.

The whole apparatus and style of the Iraqi government was imported from outside, and an entire network of new interdependencies was constructed in order to maintain it. The new government had also to be able to present itself as fully in control of the national state and capable of taking responsibility for the conduct of affairs. Especially during the early years of the mandate, this fiction proved difficult to maintain, since Iraqi defence forces on their own could not conceivably have held off invasions by the *Ikhwan* of Najd and threats from Turkish (or Kurdish) forces at the same time. Of necessity, the gap was filled by the British military presence. Having created the new government, the British authorities were concerned to maintain and expand its area of influence. This extension of control was strongly resisted by the local populations, particularly in the Middle Euphrates area and Kurdistan. The aeroplanes of the Royal Air Force were indispensable to the very survival of the new government, a fact which was readily apparent both to the government and to those who opposed it.[17] The Iraqi government was in no sense 'popular' or representative: it was almost entirely composed of members of the Sunni Arab urban communities, who, although in some ways more sophisticated and more educated than most Shi'is and Kurds, formed a minority, less than 25 per cent, of the total population. Much of its support came from the tribal shaykhs and landlords (both Sunnis and Shi'is) whose powers had been greatly enhanced during the course of the British occupation. This partnership survived the mandate and was only finally broken in 1958. Although its nature would change very greatly over the succeeding half century, a form of 'Sunni rule' prevailed until the American invasion of Iraq in 2003.

Britain's principal objectives in Iraq were the security of its communications with India, the Empire air route, and the protection of the Persian and Iraqi oilfields. During the 1920s, the new imperial thinking, which had come into being been in response to changes in international opinion after the war, itself underwent further modifications (Dodge, 2003a: 5–42). If British interests could be as well guaranteed by a more discreet but equally reliable form of control, it seemed unnecessary to force Iraqi governments to accept conditions which wounded their *amour propre* and were potentially damaging to their credibility. Provided the substance of authority could be guaranteed, some relaxation of the form could be made with no sacrifice and considerable advantage. Part of the problem lay in devising institutions through which British influence could be exercised discreetly, but another difficulty confronting successive High Commissioners in Baghdad was their constant need to convince officials and politicians in London, and occasionally their own subordinates, that some relaxation of control was both possible and desirable. It is rare to find the Colonial Office giving a lead in this direction, and the second High Commissioner, Sir Henry Dobbs, constantly impressed upon his superiors in London the need for greater flexibility, for a move away from the 'meticulous insistence on paper pledges' which he felt only served to complicate relations with the Iraqis.[18] In the last resort, he claimed, Britain could always produce its trump card, the threat to withdraw its forces.

The main concern of the following chapters is to show how the British authorities arranged Anglo-Iraqi relations, and the various administrative institutions within Iraq, to enable the government of the country to be carried on in a way which would best serve British and imperial interests. Writing five years after Britain left Iraq, the author of the most thorough survey of the early years of the mandate gives a useful corrective to the altruistic and humanitarian ideas often alleged to be associated with the new policy:[19]

> Nations do not vie amongst themselves for control over lands . . . primarily to give justice or to raise standards of living among the people or suppress disorder *per se* . . . If these benefits extend to the natives of the country it is because the latter cannot, in the very nature of the circumstances, help sharing them . . . It cannot be denied that individual officials and even the mother country itself are often genuinely concerned for the well-being of the peoples they have taken in charge . . . In a conflict of interests . . . it is very natural that those of the mother country should come first and that the good of the people must, in reality, be subordinated to the expected material and political returns (Ireland, 1937: 34–35).

1

FROM THE OUTBREAK OF WAR TO THE CAIRO CONFERENCE, 1914–1921

The British Occupation of Mesopotamia

On 8 October 1914, Sir Percy Cox wrote from Bombay:

> 'The expedition to Bahrain [that is, Indian Expeditionary Force 'D', subsequently IEF 'D'] starts today. Personally I have never been much in favour of this expedition to the Persian Gulf unless we were in a state of War with Turkey,[1] in which case I would strongly advocate it. The danger, in my opinion, is that we may provoke war, while the position of our ships in the Shatt al-'Arab, from an international point of view, is undoubtedly a weak one. The local authorities in Mesopotamia appear to be more hostile than those in Constantinople, and this perhaps makes the risk all the greater (Graves, 1941: 179).

Some six weeks later, installed in his new headquarters in Basra, Sir Percy wrote to Delhi that he could not see how 'we can avoid taking over Baghdad.'[2] Cox' conversion from a state of obvious reluctance to one of optimistic enthusiasm is characteristic of the heady atmosphere of the early stages of the campaign, when lack of understanding of the military realities in Mesopotamia came near to bringing the whole expedition to total disaster.

Initially the Mesopotamia campaign was launched with distinctly limited objectives:[3] the India Office in London wanted a holding operation at the head of the Gulf, the kind of exercise for which minds in the Military Department of the Government of India were well suited. Its main purpose was to deter any Ottoman activity at the head of the Gulf. But the lack of any real opposition encountered by General Delamain's force, and his advance as far as Qurna by 9 December, where he captured the *wali* of Basra and took 1,200 prisoners, increased the already growing sense of euphoria.

The temptation to advance proved irresistible, and it was not checked by any serious hesitation from behind the scenes. London had turned down Cox' suggestion of an immediate advance on Baghdad, but the possibility was not ruled out.[4] Two more brigades were despatched from India in February and March 1915, and the idea of a major extension northwards was evidently taking root in Simla. By March 1915 the Commander in Chief in India, Sir Beauchamp Duff, instructed Sir John Nixon, the new commander of IEF 'D', to submit, on his arrival in Basra, plans for the effective occupation of the Basra *wilaya* and for a 'subsequent advance on Baghdad'.[5]

The strictly military side of the campaign has been amply documented elsewhere (Wilson, 1930; 1931; Barker, 1967),[6] and will only be discussed in connection with the gradual expansion in administrative machinery which strategic gains necessitated. The speed with which the original objectives enlarged is remarkable. In Basra, Cox' first request in his capacity as Chief Political Officer was for permission to establish a civil administration; he asked for this from the Viceroy on 27 November, five days after the town had been occupied.[7] At the same time he asked to be allowed to announce that the occupation of Basra would be permanent, to allay local fears of reprisals if the Ottomans were to return. The proposal was 'peremptorily swept on one side by His Majesty's Government, on the ground that it would be utterly contrary to the agreement come to between the Allies, if occupation of any conquered country were at once announced permanent, without waiting for the final settlement to be made at the close of war.'[8]

In his telegram to the Viceroy on 27 November, Cox had specified five objectives. He was concerned to set up machinery for the management of state property and *awqaf*, the collection of land revenue and the Ottoman Public Debt, and for the supervision of the Tobacco *Régie*. Two interesting comments on these proposals were made in the India Office; Sir Edmund Barrow, the Military Secretary, wanted the administration to be 'as efficiently organised as possible, as we should contemplate the probability of a prolonged occupation' (though this could not be announced publicly), and Sir Arthur Hirtzel, head of the Political Department, minuted:

> It will probably be admitted that the government will be undertaken by the Government of India; but it is by no means certain that it will eventually prove desirable to take an Indian district as the model for it.[9]

Clearly, some sort of administration was an immediate necessity, as it appeared that the Ottoman provincial authorities had been in full retreat since the time since IEF 'D' had landed on Fao on 6 November.

It soon became clear that London and Simla had differing views on how best to proceed. From the autumn of 1914 to the spring of 1915, the India Office in London was anxious merely to consolidate a bridgehead, to gain firm control of Basra and its immediate hinterland, while the Military Department of the Government of India had more ambitious ideas, as did both political and military staffs in Mesopotamia itself. London's caution and hesitation accurately anticipated what was to come, since, time and time again, precipitate action in the field was to force agonising reappraisals on London. Also, it is quite clear from the India Office records and the report of the Mesopotamia Commission that no one in India seems to have appreciated either the true complexity of the organisational side of the campaign, or the distances involved in maintaining adequate lines of supply, let alone the delicate political implications of maintaining order in the Occupied Territories.[10]

Thus a constant theme of the campaign emerged: reluctant acceptance by London of demands by India and the Chief Political Officer of the Force for a more vigorous prosecution of the campaign.[11] Officials in the Secretariat in India seemed inclined to view the operation as a kind of frontier war, with IEF 'D' pushing ever onwards to subdue the rebel forces beyond, and it gradually became clear that the administrative expertise necessary to conduct a military campaign on this scale was almost entirely lacking. For its part, London could only endorse a series of military *faits accomplis*, though politically greater restraint could be urged.

It has already been mentioned that General Sir John Nixon's instructions of March 1915 from Simla included the formation of a plan for 'the effective occupation of the Basra *wilaya*'. Precisely what was intended by the word *wilaya* is not quite clear; it is possible that Nixon's instructions were not intended to apply to the whole province, but merely to the environs of the town of Basra.[12] However, by June 1915, General Townshend had captured 'Amara; he had reached Kut by September, and by October 1915 had got as far as 'Aziziya, only 50 miles from Baghdad. To Nixon, his subordinate must have appeared invincible, and his desire to advance as far and as fast as possible seems to have blinded him to the risks he was taking. At home, news of the continuing stalemate in the Dardanelles may have created a sense of euphoria over what seemed to be spectacular successes in Mesopotamia. On 23 July 1915, the Secretary of State for India, Austen Chamberlain, wrote to the Viceroy: 'I am glad you see no necessity for an advance to Kut al-'Amara', but by 8 October he had been converted:

'There is, it would seem, an opportunity within our grasp for a great success, such as we have not yet achieved in any quarter, and it is difficult to overrate the political (and even military) advantages which would flow from it throughout the Far East [sic] (Petrie, 1939–40: 35–37).

The actual decision to march on Baghdad was phrased more cautiously but the possible effects of such a stretching of limited resources had evidently not been calculated.[13] By December the Ottoman forces had been greatly augmented and were able to drive Townshend back first to Ctesiphon and finally to Kut, where his troops endured the bitter hardships of five months siege and ultimate surrender. As a result of this reversal, and as news of the appalling deficiencies of supply and medical provision in Mesopotamia gradually reached London, the Military Department of the Government of India was relieved of its command. On 3 February 1916, IEF 'D' became the Mesopotamia Expeditionary Force (MEF), and the War Office took full charge of operations.

Meanwhile, the process of establishing an administration for the Occupied Territories, based in Basra, had continued almost unaffected by the struggle on the higher reaches of the rivers. Local provision for sanitation and medical arrangements had been made, and a judicial department set up; the *Iraq Occupied Territories Code* had been introduced (a penal code based on Indian models) and, highly important for the future, the *Tribal Criminal and Civil Disputes Regulations*, another Indian importation modified for Mesopotamian use, had been inaugurated.[14] The initiative for this activity seems to have come almost entirely from the local authorities, especially as far as the actual details were concerned. The absence of any clear-cut or comprehensive instructions (either from India or from London) was emphasised by Gertrude Bell, later Oriental Secretary to Sir Percy Cox, in April 1916:

> Politically, too, we rushed into the business with our usual disregard for a comprehensive political scheme . . . The coordinating of Arabian politics and the creation of an Arabian policy should have been done at home – it could only have been done successfully done at home. There was no-one to do it, no-one who had ever thought of it, and it was left to our people in Egypt to thrash out, in the face of tremendous opposition from India and London, some sort of wide scheme which will, I am persuaded, ultimately form the basis of our relations with the Arabs.

And again, later the same year:

> The real difficulty here is that we don't know exactly what we intend

to do in this country. Can you persuade people to take your side when you are not sure in the end whether you'll be there to take theirs? No wonder they hesitate; and it would take a good deal of potent persuasion to make them think that your side and theirs are compatible. The elements of prevailing persuasiveness are denied to us. So we just make the best of things, say what we can, and don't do very much.[15]

Miss Bell's own ignorance of London's overall intentions is not surprising as her own chief was also working in the dark. It was only in May 1917, a full year after the secret endorsement of the Sykes-Picot agreement by Britain, France and Russia, that Skyes informed Cox of the details of its terms.[16] It is not clear whether this omission was deliberate, but it certainly illustrates the kind of difficulties under which the Civil Administration was labouring and the lack of real communication between London and Baghdad. The first broad outline of London's proposals for the Mesopotamian administration was not sent to Cox until after the capture of Baghdad on 10 March 1917.

In the absence of earlier instructions, those on the spot, recruited largely from the Indian Army and Indian Civil Service, could only set up and maintain the kind of administrative machine with which they themselves were familiar. The need, in practical terms, was acute; in 1917, only 48 out of the original 170 Ottoman officials in the Baghdad *wilaya* had remained at their posts.[17] Gradually, the type of administration familiar from the Basra *wilaya,* of direct rule of subdivisions of the province by British officers, was introduced elsewhere as more and more territory came under occupation.[18] The capture of Baghdad proved to be the watershed in the campaign; there would be a great deal more fighting before the Ottomans were defeated, but the MEF was able to advance without any serious check. By May 1917 Samarra' was captured; by September, Ramadi, west of Baghdad on the Euphrates and an important supply post for the Ottoman army, was taken. Early in 1918 General Marshall was ordered to occupy Kirkuk, 200 miles north of Baghdad, in a complicated operation designed to support General Dunsterville's quixotic adventures in Persia, but by the spring the MEF was being depleted by transfers of divisions to more important theatres elsewhere, notably Palestine and Salonika.[19] At the very end of the war, somewhat indecent haste ensured that Mosul town and most of the Mosul *wilaya* were in British hands. Arnold Wilson's account makes it clear that the city of Mosul was captured, on War Office instructions, some three days *after* the Armistice of Mudros.[20]

British Administrative Policy and Imperial Thinking

The first instructions regarding the future of Mesopotamia were issued in March 1917; their general tone did not cause the administrators on the spot to make any significant changes in their practice. But increasingly, as other pressures made themselves felt, the bureaucratic controls in place in the Occupied Territories came in for severe criticism. The problem became more acute following the entry of the United States into the war in the autumn of 1917, and more particularly after the publication of President Woodrow Wilson's Fourteen Points in January 1918. Long established and hitherto almost unchallenged assumptions of British imperial policy had to be reconciled with a whole set of new requirements. In Iraq, it was necessary to adapt the existing machinery, derived from Indian administrative models, to a new and less direct form of control, which was both unfamiliar and unpalatable to many of those called upon to operate it.

The difficulties of adjustment faced by British administrators in Mesopotamia, both before and immediately after Britain's assumption of the mandate for Iraq at San Remo in April 1920, are a reflection of far wider trends. In considering the events of the next few years, especially the crucial period between the Armistice of Mudros in October 1918 and the signature of the Anglo-Iraqi Treaty of October 1922, a broad perspective is necessary. To obtain this, some reference must be made to contemporary developments in Britain's relations both with India and with the United States; India, to understand the nature of the old methods, and the gradual questioning of them, and the United States, to understand the extent and nature of the new pressures being brought to bear.

The Administration of British India

Since the middle of the nineteenth century Britain had ruled most of India through a remarkably small number[21] of British officials, who exercised full executive authority. Except in the princely states, where the rulers had British 'advisors' but employed subordinates of their own as ministers and administrators, relatively few Indians held positions of real responsibility. Most British officials who worked in India or the Gulf area in the period immediately before the First World War believed that they alone were capable of ruling the populations in their charge, and that any significant delegation of authority would be disastrous. Particularly evident from memoirs and asides in official correspondence are expressions of fear and contempt towards the 'educated native'. Indians in particular were considered either too corrupt, or too incompetent, to rule,[22] and an elaborate moral superstructure was built to buttress this view: if educated Indians had the opportunity to exercise real power the mass of poor farmers who formed the 'backbone of the country', would suffer.

A typical advocate of this point of view was Sir Michael O'Dwyer (1864–1940) who ended a long if ultimately controversial career in India as Lieutenant-Governor of the Punjab. O'Dwyer was the mentor of two distinguished members of the occupation and mandate administrations, Colonel E.B. Howell, Revenue Secretary under A. T. Wilson, and Sir Francis Humphrys, last High Commissioner, and first British Ambassador, to Iraq. Towards the end of his autobiography, published in 1926, he quotes with approval the words of John Lawrence, Viceroy in the 1860s:

> We are here by our moral superiority, by the force of circumstances and the will of providence. These alone constitute our charter of government, and in doing the best we can for the people we are bound by our consciences and not theirs (O'Dwyer, 1926: 407).

O'Dwyer's opposition to reform was based on the fear that the self-seekers would use their new-found power to tyrannise the peasants, the kind of despotism which he saw already existing in the princely states. He had grudgingly accepted the reforms of Morley and Minto, but he thought that India was not ready for those of Montagu and Chelmsford (Robb, 2002:153–157; O'Dwyer, 1926: 155–156, 309). To men of this stamp, the notion of Britain leaving India, or Britain devolving some larger measure of power into Indian hands, was tantamount to a betrayal, the abandoning of a sacred trust. But the presence of two Liberal secretaries of state at the India Office, and gradual changes in the international climate ensured that a stand like O'Dwyer's was increasingly under attack.

Both Morley and Montagu were attracted by the notion of partnership and co-operation, of the gradual accession of Indians to positions of responsibility. This was the doctrine of dyarchy, or transferred and reserved areas of governance, which evolved in the course of the 1914–18 war.[23] This was foreshadowed in the declarations drafted by Curzon but delivered by Montagu on 20 August 1917:

> The policy of H.M. Government, with which the Government of India are in complete accord, is that of increasing association of Indians in every branch of the administration and the gradual development of self-governing institutions with a view to the

progressive realisation of responsible government in India as an integral part of the British Empire (Waley, 1964: 136).

Those on the ground, in India and Mesopotamia, had to be persuaded that direct rule was no longer a practical possibility. In the early years of the campaign in Mesopotamia, most of the officials on the political and administrative side had been seconded from the Indian Political Service. Men trained either in the Central or Presidency administrations tended to approach the political and administrative problems presented to them in Mesopotamia along the lines which they had been taught in India. It was particularly hard for them to accept what they regarded as second-rate standards.

The instructions of March 1917 indicated that Basra should continue under direct British rule and that Baghdad should be 'an Arab state with local ruler or government under British protectorate [sic] in everything but name.'[24] This was easy for the administrators to understand and apply: in contrast was the very different tone of the instructions which Cox received in August 1917:

> For the present such minimum of administrative efficiency should be aimed at as is necessary for the maintenance of order and to meet the requirements of the Force; the amendment of laws and the introduction of reforms should be kept within the narrowest possible limits. H.M. Government do not wish large or controversial administrative questions raised or referred to them until the danger of Turkish attack is passed (Ireland, 1937: 108).

Thus changes in policy towards India were rapidly combining to make the continued application of Indian methods in Mesopotamia more difficult; it would not make sense to saddle Mesopotamia with the system that was apparently to be dismantled in India.[25] However, at this stage only Sir Arthur Hirtzel of the India Office sounded the appropriate note of caution; in December 1917 he wrote to the Commercial Intelligence Section of the Department of Overseas Trade that:

> . . . (The Turkish) menace has apparently been removed. But another has taken its place, of a different kind, and one which, I think, makes it imperative for us to get to work. What I mean is that we must at least consider the possibility of a peace which will not give us the absolute political control of Mesopotamia that we should like to have . . .[26]

The United States and British colonial policy

The new 'menace' was presumably the one emerging in the shape of the first formulations of the system of indirect control later embodied in the mandate.[27] But earlier than this, there had been indications that the old world of secret diplomacy was under threat, and that any peace settlement would involve something more than a pragmatic parcelling out of territory among the victors. The prime mover of this fundamental change was President Woodrow Wilson, who was determined to see a new world order emerge in which American political and economic aims would have a more prominent place. Acceptance of this new order was part of the price which the Allies would have to pay for American support in the war.

When the United States eventually entered the war as an 'Associate Power' in the autumn of 1917, Balfour was sent to New York to confess what the Allies had been arranging amongst themselves. Colonel E. M. House, the president's confidential adviser (Viereck, 1932), described his conference with Balfour much in the tones of a prefect questioning a guilty schoolboy. For his part Balfour was anxious to cover up as much as he could for the others:

> . . . Crossing the Bosphorus we come to [Turkey in Asia]. It is here that the secret treaties between the Allies come in most prominently. They have agreed to give Russia a sphere of influence in Armenia and the Northern part. The British take in Mesopotamia and the (region which is) closest to Egypt. . . This is all bad, and I told Balfour so. They are making it a breeding ground for future war. I asked what the spheres of influence included. B.[alfour] was hazy concerning this; whether it meant that each nation had the exclusive right to develop the resources within their own sphere he was not altogether clear (Seymour, 1926: 47–48).

Balfour was lucky to get off so lightly, but it was clear that the headmaster's disapproval lingered on. Later in 1917 Wilson wrote to House:

> England and France have not the same views with regard to peace that we have by any means. When the war is over we can force them to our way of thinking.[28]

It was of course not only the Allies' attitude to secret diplomacy and future colonial settlement that upset the President; Colonel House's last two volumes of memoirs dealing with the period from the United States' entry into the war until the president's final illness, contain few direct references to Near Eastern, colonial, or mandate questions. However, Wilson's anxiety to find out what the Allies thought on such matters, his calls for clear statements of War Aims, had important side effects, such as the setting up of the 'Inquiry',[29] a group of experts to examine the sorts of questions which might emerge at a Peace Conference, and the despatch of Colonel House's peace mission to Europe in November 1917. The failure of this mission to prise any statement of war aims out of the Allies, and the confusion brought about by the Bolsheviks' revelation of the secret treaties, prompted the President to state his own aims in the Fourteen Points Speech of 8 January 1918.

It is difficult to assess the precise effect of these developments on events in Mesopotamia at the time. Certainly the Civil Commissioner forbade the local publication of the Fourteen Points, which only appeared in Baghdad on 11 October 1918. It became increasingly clear that any solution to the problem of the future of Mesopotamia had to seem to conform to the American president's high ideals.[30] Even so, later events proved that it was some time before the India Office and the Mesopotamian authorities were brought to a true realisation of the changed state of affairs. The attitude of outraged surprise is most clearly evident in Colonel Wilson's frantic tele-grams after the publication of the Anglo-French Declaration of November 1918. It is true that much of the confusion which followed the Armistice, and which came to a head in Iraq in the summer of 1920, although deriving partly from London's inability to present a clear line of action, sprang also from the difficulty of convincing civil servants, both in Baghdad and in the India Office itself that, at least overtly, Indian administrative methods and machinery could no longer be used in whatever future scheme would be drafted for Mesopotamia.

First Attempts at a Permanent Mesopotamia Policy

In the spring of 1918 Sir Percy Cox was recalled to London for consul-tation, a summons which turned out to be a prelude to his long second-ment to the British Legation at Teheran. Even at this early stage it had been agreed in the India Office that some scheme must be devised for Mesopotamia which would retain strong British influence without seeming to necessitate close British control. Before Cox' arrival in London, the Political Department of the India Office agreed that his advice would be sought on two main points:

i) Is the administrative system now being built up adapted to the contingency of the cessation of direct British control?

ii) What further means, if any, can be devised locally to secure that, whatever form the ultimate settlement may take, the main object devised by H.M. Government, viz., a Mesopotamia under British influence, shall be secured to the utmost extent that circumstances permit?[31]

Cox was also to be asked for information on certain specific points. Could any local ruler be brought to identify himself and his interests with Great Britain? What sort of personnel existed for the setting up of a local administration? How long would British troops have to support a friendly regime? How soon could trade begin again? What elements in the local population should be particularly encouraged as being most likely to direct their choice of self-determination towards a continuation of the British connection?

On his arrival in London in April, Cox dealt as far as he could with these points. He acknowledged that annexation was no longer possible, but wanted supervision of the Arab façade to be exercised by a nominated local council. He felt it was particularly vital to exclude any Turkish participation in the regime. With regard to the more detailed questions, Cox' replies cannot have been particularly heartening either to the India Office or the Eastern Committee. It is worth mentioning that the records of these meetings provide a useful corrective to the assumed polarisation of Cox and Wilson as representatives of respectively more liberal and more reactionary schools of thought: the differences between them seem to have been 'more procedural than substantive' (Kleiman, 1970: 61).

Cox considered that the family of the Naqib of Baghdad was the most suitable 'dynastic element' to rule Mesopotamia, in contrast to the family of the Sharif Husayn of Mecca, a 'figure who carries no weight in Iraq, where only the most distant interest is taken in him.'[32] Because of the uncertainty of the situation, Cox (and Wilson after him, for similar reasons) had little success in recruiting Arab personnel to senior positions.[33]

On the pressing question of troop reductions, Cox could not be optimistic, though some divisions had already been released for service on other fronts. He could also give little hope of a speedy re-establishment of British trade, though attention had in fact already been paid to creating opportunities for British commerce when the war was over.[34] As likely objects for British persuasion and influence Cox listed the Jews of

Baghdad, the notables of Baghdad and Basra, wealthy landowners and the shaykhs of settled tribes.

The meeting between Cox and the officials of the India Office and the Eastern Committee had little effect on the course of events in Mesopotamia; its real purpose seems to have been to give London a clearer picture of the state of affairs on the ground. Cox himself returned only briefly to Baghdad early in September, on his way to relieve Sir Charles Marling in Teheran. Arnold Wilson made an attempt to elicit some sort of policy statement from London, largely to see what significance he or anyone else should attach to President Wilson's Twelfth Point:

> In a rash moment I inquired by telegraph what if any significance attached to the 'Twelfth Commandment' . . . I was referred in reply to the instructions given in August 1917 that 'no large or controversial administrative questions were to be raised'. Thus discouraged I took no further steps until after the Armistice to inquire of the India Office what in their view the future might hold in store. I presumed, perhaps rightly, that if their oracles were dumb it was because their doubts were even greater than ours.[35]

Though warned privately by Hirtzel that a certain 're-orientation is necessary',[36] Wilson was given no more specific instructions, and nothing of any major consequence emanated from London until the bombshell of the Anglo-French Declaration burst over Baghdad in November. Late in September, Wilson requested the despatch of a commission to study the future of Mesopotamia, but this was simply shelved by London, and by the time it was raised again, Wilson hastily suggested a local committee; a deputation from London would, he said, be 'widely misunderstood'.[37]

Throughout 1918, the Civil Administration continued to dig itself in. Militarily, as we have seen, there was little real resistance. By placating the tribal leaders, by keeping order, and by providing a ready market for labour and foodstuffs of all kinds, the British tried to gain influential support.[38] In London too a similar note of congratulation was sounded; Lord Robert Cecil told the House of Commons that Britain had 'redeemed Mesopotamia from the state of ruin into which it had fallen under the Turks.'[39] Generally, the process of consolidation continued, and except for a set-back in Najaf in March, where a British officer was murdered, and severe reprisals taken by the authorities, little resistance took place. Minor annoyances, like billeting and the blockade, were offset for the majority of the city population by the peace and order that prevailed.

Post-War Arrangements: A. T. Wilson as Acting Civil Commissioner

It is a strange irony that the tortuous and involved McMahon/Husayn correspondence and the Sykes-Picot agreement, together with the Balfour Declaration, should have been held up to this day as the outstanding examples of Britain's perfidy to the Arabs. In contrast, the Anglo-French Declaration of November 1918, a shorter, simpler and far less equivocal document, has somehow escaped equal censure. The text of the declaration, which as its title implies, was a published document and not a secret arrangement, is short and to the point. On the issue dealt with in President Wilson's Twelfth Point, which promised 'absolutely unmolested autonomous development' to the ex-Ottoman territories, it asserted that:

> . . . Far from wishing to impose any particular institution on these lands, they (i. e. the Allies) have no other care but to secure by their support and effective aid the normal workings of the Governments and Administrations which they shall have adopted of their own free will.

Such a statement seems to present little difficulty of interpretation.

There has been no detailed examination of the precise origins of the pronouncement, when and how it came to be drafted. When A. T. Wilson protested, the India Office explained that it was issued 'primarily to clear up the existing situation in Syria which Arab suspicions of French intentions had created', implying that Iraq was somehow only included to save French face.[40] There is no obvious single explanation. The Declaration can be seen partly as a sop to the Americans, whose attempts at dictating peace terms would surely begin the moment the Armistice was signed; equally possibly it could have been an attempt on the part of the two Allies to present a common front, an appearance of solidarity in their Middle Eastern policy. This harmony, both between France and Britain, and towards their Middle Eastern clients, was of course short lived.

Wilson based his own opposition both on the dangers the Declaration presented to British interests, and the poor prospects it held out for the Iraqis:

> . . . The average Arab, as opposed to the handful of amateur politicians of Baghdad, sees the future as one of fair dealing and material and moral progress under the aegis of Great Britain . . . With the experience of my Political Officers behind me, I can confidently declare that the country as a whole neither expects nor desires any such

sweeping schemes of independence as are adumbrated, if not clearly denoted, in the Anglo-French Declaration.[41]

With hindsight it is easy to accuse Wilson of swimming against the tide, of accusing all except himself of being out of step. But his whole temperament and training were opposed to the new doctrines being put forward. More remarkable, perhaps, than his failure to grasp the reality of the situation, was, first, that he did not resign his post when asked to implement a policy he did not believe to be valid, and secondly, that in the face of his evident lack of co-operation, the India Office did not seek his resignation. For this the ultimate responsibility lay with the British government; in September 1920, at the very end of Wilson's time as Acting Civil Commissioner, the position was neatly summarised by J. E. Shuckburgh in September 1920:

> The policy pursued in Mesopotamia may have been wise or unwise, but in any case final responsibility for it rests with H. M. Government and not with their agent on the spot. If they were dissatisfied with the way their agent was carrying out their wishes, then they should have censured . . . or recalled him. By not doing so they have assumed responsibility for his views, and cannot, in fairness and decency, throw him over. If . . . Sir Arnold Wilson's policy, which was the policy of H. M. Government, was not the brilliant thing we then thought it, the fact still remains that H. M. Government was equally at fault and are bound in honour to take the blame (if blame there be) upon themselves and not to throw it upon their unfortunate subordinate officer, who *ex hypothesi* merely did their bidding.'[42]

Slow Progress towards Settlement

Looking back at the immediately post-war period in the Middle East, it seems almost incredible that two years should have elapsed between the Armistice of Mudros and the installation of Sir Percy Cox in Baghdad in the autumn of 1920 with virtual *carte blanche* to try to save the situation. The delays have been variously explained, for the period has been extensively researched and well documented from the papers and memoirs of two of the principal actors in the drama, Gertrude Bell and A. T. Wilson.

Nevertheless, the causes of the seemingly interminable wranglings and procrastinations are still not entirely clear. Had not the British government had tacit support from the United States for its claims to Mesopotamia from the very beginning?[43] Was Curzon's inability to give the India Office precise

instructions for A. T. Wilson simply a desire not to offend French susceptibilities? Exactly what was the nature of the Anglo-French dispute over
Mosul that the Bérenger/Long agreement of 1919 did not resolve? Granted
that a revitalised Turkey might make efforts to regain northern Kurdistan,
were there any signs of such moves in 1919–20? And finally, why did
Colonel Wilson constantly refuse to accept the unofficial advice pressed upon
him by Sir Arthur Hirtzel, and build up an Arab state likely to be acceptable
to the League, instead of complaining to Hirtzel in September 1919 that
'Your statement that we are going to have an Arab state whether
Mesopotamia wants it or not is the first indication I have had as to the real
significance of self-determination for this country'?[44]

Such questions are worth considering because of the effect they had in
shaping the future of Iraq. In that respect the two years were of inestimable
importance, since the delays facilitated the growth of an embryonic national
movement in Iraq whose pressure British policy was forced to recognise and
accommodate. On the British side, policy making was complicated by
divergences of opinion between the India Office and the Foreign Office, the
India Office and the Residency at Baghdad, within the India Office and
within the Baghdad Residency as well.

In fact Sir Arthur Hirtzel at the India Office was the one figure whose
attitude scarcely changed from 1916 to 1920, who recognised that
'Indianisation' would not be possible in Mesopotamia even before the
implications of President Wilson's anti-annexation pronouncements were
fully appreciated. Throughout 1919 and 1920 he wrote to A.T. Wilson in
Baghdad, emphasising time and time again that no form of veiled
protectorate would be acceptable to the League. Wilson was cut off by
education, training and experience from the new ideas in Europe; he seems
to have thought of the future of 'his state' in terms of that form of
government which all right thinking men would choose for themselves if
they were in full possession of the necessary facts, and capable of making
decisions in their own best interests. In the face of their inability to
articulate such decisions, and his disinterested responsibility for their
welfare, he saw it as his duty to decide for them. This was a further echo of
the 'Indian' belief that law and order and efficient and just administration
were entirely adequate and widely acceptable substitutes for self-
government. His point of view is well illustrated in a despatch to the India
Office in mid-November 1919:

> I believe it impossible in these days to create a new sovereign
> Muhammadan state by diplomatic or administrative means out of the

remnants of the Turkish Empire . . . For some years to come the appointment of Arab Governors or high officials except in an advisory capacity would involve the rapid decay of authority, law and order . . . any attempts to introduce institutions on the lines desired by the Sunni politicians of Syria would involve the concentration of power in the hands of a few persons whose ambitions and methods would rapidly bring about the collapse of organised government . . . the results would be the antithesis of democratic government.[45]

The problems facing the Mesopotamian authorities should not be underestimated. They were sent very general directives, which by and large they did not approve, and permission to proceed in what they considered to be a positive and constructive direction was almost invariably withheld. London's constant fear was that somehow the decisions of the Peace Conference might be wrongly anticipated. In the circumstances, since the business of the Mesopotamian state had somehow to be carried on, the Civil Administration kept to well-trodden paths.

In a telegram of 17 November 1918, Wilson continued his attack on the Anglo-French Declaration, and suggested instead that the policy that he and Cox had pursued should be taken to its logical conclusion:

I think therefore that our best course is to declare Mesopotamia to be a protectorate, under which all classes and races will be given forthwith maximum liberty. . .

On which Shuckburgh minuted on 20 November:

It is clear that the enlightened and progressive Arab in whom the enthusiasts ask us to believe is a mere fiction as far as Mesopotamia is concerned. Such progressive elements as do exist in the country are not Arabs at all but Jews and Christians. It will be a poor kind of self-determination that places such people at the mercy of an uncontrolled Arab administration.[46]

At the end of November 1918, London asked Wilson whether any suitable candidates existed for the rulership of Mesopotamia. His lengthy reply was of considerable importance for the future. He suggested that public opinion should be consulted over the selection of a candidate, and put forward four names for consideration. His attitude towards the possible candidature of a son of the Sharif was surprising, and caused some confusion in the India

Office, which had been building up a case against Husayn's second son, 'Abdullah. A member of the Sharif's family would, said Wilson:

> . . . meet with widespread acceptance in Baghdad and would probably be well received outside because all know who the Sharif is.[47] It is also considered that he would be acceptable to Shi'is on account of Sharif's widespread latitude in religious views. For reasons connected with Persian Gulf and Central Arabian politics I am however strongly opposed to it.

In view of his earlier attitudes and those of Cox, Shuckburgh was taken aback:

> Captain Wilson's present report that a son of the Sharif would command wide acceptance locally comes as a complete surprise and knocks the ground from under most of the arguments on which we have hitherto opposed the 'Abdullah solution.[48]

Wilson's own solution was to make Cox head of state with no Arab amir at all, and Gertrude Bell wrote home that 'on two points they (the Iraqis) are practically all agreed; they want us to control their affairs and they want Sir Percy as Commissioner.'[49]

London welcomed the idea of a 'plebiscite', as Wilson's rather contrived local soundings of what may be described as 'focus groups' came to be called, but quietly shelved the idea of Cox as head of state. The tone of the instructions sent to Baghdad a few days later cannot have been much to the liking of the Acting Civil Commissioner, for they reiterated the policy set out in the Anglo-French Declaration and underlined the point that it was merely a prelude to the more detailed settlement that would emerge from the Peace Conference:

> . . . it is the policy of H. M. Government to aid in establishing native governments in the liberated areas and not to impose on the populations any form of government which they dislike. Subject to those two conditions we desire to see in Mesopotamia the strongest and most settled government possible and we are prepared to give all British assistance necessary for that, including an army of occupation.[50]

In the course of the next two months, Wilson toured the country in an attempt to gauge public opinion, although, given his evident personal predilections, such activity was almost bound to be both fruitless and irrelevant. The various reports which he received from Political Officers showed a remarkable unanimity of feeling in favour of continued British control, as was only to be expected, except in Baghdad and the Shi'i holy cities. The way in which soundings were taken effectively prevented an accurate picture being presented to London, as any expression of nationalist opinion was either ignored or silenced.[51] However, at a meeting of the Eastern Committee on 24 December, Louis Mallet of the Foreign Office tried to steer opinion back to the Anglo-French Declaration; he too recognised that the existence of Faysal's Arab government in Damascus was likely to have a powerful effect on public opinion in Mesopotamia:

> If it be really the case that sentiment in favour of a purely British administration exists throughout Mesopotamia we are certainly placed in some difficulty, but I doubt if we should be wise in accepting entirely at their face value the assurances which are made to Captain Wilson by the native authorities whom he visits, and we cannot disregard the influence which it is asserted that the Emir Faysal exercises over the Arab element in Mesopotamia . . . I venture to suggest that Captain Wilson's attention be drawn to our undertaking and that he be reminded that whilst H. M. Government are resolved, in accordance with the wishes of the population, to support and assist them, they are precluded by these arguments from setting up a protectorate or protectorates in Iraq.[52]

Over the next months this question was debated at some length. Curzon consulted Cox in Teheran, who replied that although a protectorate was clearly out of the question, it would not be difficult so to order things that 'secure control of Foreign Relations and a full supervision of Administration . . . will . . . amount to a Protectorate and (give) us all we need' – further proof that his attitudes were not so very different from Wilson's. Shuckburgh agreed:

> It is generally agreed that we must not go through the official pantomime known as 'declaring a protectorate'; but it is not clear that this disability need limit to any appreciable extent the practical control we are able to exercise over Mesopotamian affairs.[53]

Even at this stage the numerous anomalies inherent in the Mesopotamian muddle were becoming more and more evident. Support for some kind of settlement involving one of the sons of Sharif Husayn would at least partially fulfill the Husayn/McMahon undertakings, but it would also irritate the French, whose annoyance at the state of affairs in Syria was palpable. In Paris in January 1919, Balfour asked for information about 'Abdullah, who seemed at the time to be the most likely candidate for the Mesopotamian throne. George Kidston of the Foreign Office wrote to Shuckburgh in a refreshingly cynical vein:

> You will understand that what is wanted is a King who will be content to reign but not govern and whose religious views are such that shaykhs may acquiesce in his rule. I have . . . suggested that if it is really desirable to get a character for Abdulla this might perhaps be obtained through Cairo. Wilson of Jedda will probably be able to say whether he steals or drinks and whether he is likely to cause trouble with the other servants.[54]

Shuckburgh and Hirtzel were evidently worried that sending 'Abdullah to Baghdad at the same time as Cox would be seen to be forcing his candidature on the Iraqis. Quite apart from the opposition that such a step might encounter within Iraq, it would form an easy target for French and other international criticism. Hirtzel was also uneasily aware of the ramifications of the situation on another level:

> If the French remain in Syria we shall have to avoid giving them the excuse of setting up a Protectorate. If they go, or we appear to be reactionary in Mesopotamia, there is always the risk that Faysal will encourage the Americans to take over both, and it should be borne in mind that the Standard Oil Company is very anxious to take over Iraq.[55]

Wilson Isolated

At this point, and throughout most of 1919, Gertrude Bell and Arnold Wilson were cooperating harmoniously; Wilson had approved Miss Bell's *Memorandum on Self-Determination in Mesopotamia*, and despatched her to Paris to represent him at the Peace Conference before he arrived. The Memorandum is of considerable interest; it was the outcome of the soundings which had taken place over the previous months.[56] Its main theme was that a continuation of British rule was desired by almost all Iraqis, and that if there was an Arab amir, he should be 'under British protection'. But Miss

Bell noted a strong movement in favour of direct British rule. The Naqib would neither consider accepting the post of ruler, nor, it was thought, give his approval to the selection of a son of the Sharif. In a veiled rebuke to London, Gertrude Bell suggested that the trouble stirred up by the constant questioning had simply had the effect of hastening the birth of a 'nationalist party with inflated ambitions', this event had 'frightened . . . the stabler elements of the community into closer co-operation with the British administration.'[57]

Though capable of considerable tenacity, one of Gertrude Bell's great strengths lay in her flexibility and her ability to adapt to changing circumstances. Whereas Wilson never really accepted that nationalism was a force which would have to be accommodated, Gertrude Bell eventually came to realise that at least some concession must be made to the fact, however unpalatable, that people prefer to manage their own affairs incompetently than to have other people manage them well on their behalf. Wilson's most articulate male colleague in the Civil Administration, his judicial adviser Edgar Bonham-Carter, whose experience was drawn from Egypt and the Sudan rather than India, came to a similar conclusion. Early in February 1919 he wrote a paper entitled *The Place of the Arab in the Administration*, which anticipated with considerable accuracy what actually happened under the mandate. Generally he felt that at this stage too little attention was being paid to Arab aspirations and foresaw that difficulties would follow if this state of affairs was allowed to continue.

It is clearly not desirable, nor do I think possible, to follow the Egyptian model and have an entirely Arab staff. But if we are to avoid a course which will take us definitely away from the goal for which we profess to set out it is essential that even at the start we should make the fullest use of Arab staff, and what is hardly less important give them a standing in the Administration. A Cabinet of Native Ministers such as exists in Egypt, who in all essentials have to act under British direction has advantages. It keeps the form of Government largely Arab, and it maintains the social and political status of the Arab and it provides a legislative machinery which should at least delay the premature introduction of representative institutions in advance of the need of the country. I should welcome the appointment of an Arab Judicial Secretary or even an Arab Minister of Justice with myself as adviser, provided he was carefully chosen and that it was clearly understood that he must either comply with the decisions of the British Government or resign.'[58]

The Administrators at the Paris Peace Conference

Early in 1919 it was felt that expert advice from Mesopotamia might be of assistance in Paris. Accordingly, preceded by his Oriental Secretary, Arnold Wilson set out from Mesopotamia for the conference. He arrived on 20 March, the very day of the famous secret meeting on the Middle East, when President Wilson first mooted the suggestion of an International Commission (which eventually emerged in the greatly watered down form of the King-Crane Commission) to report to the Peace Conference on what kind of government the inhabitants of the ex-Ottoman territories wanted for themselves (Baker 1922:1–19). The precise status of the India Office delegation (which consisted, apparently, simply of Arnold Wilson, Gertrude Bell and Montagu) was not clear; Montagu wrote plaintively to Balfour five days later:

> I really do not want to bother you, but it is extremely difficult to reconcile oneself to the fact that one's only *raison d'être* in Paris is to represent Indian interests and the Mesopotamian Government which is at the moment responsible to me when it is quite impossible to discover what is going on. We have now collected in Paris Miss Bell and Colonel Wilson. They are responsible to me. They come to me and say 'We are here. What do you want of us?' I can give them no information of what is going on. I cannot tell them what we were asked to come to Paris for.[59]

Arnold Wilson was equally unimpressed, and was disturbed by the fact that the Cairo faction, intent on advancing Sharifian claims, occupied such an important place in the British delegation (Wilson, 1931: 116). In fact, little progress towards any clarification took place before Wilson's visit to London, where he put forward his own suggestions at a meeting of the Eastern Committee on 6 April. These amounted largely to a division of Iraq into five provinces, administered by British officials with Arab advisers; municipal and district councils with appointed rather than elected members, and giving 'carefully selected Arabs of good birth and education belonging to Iraq by birth from the very outset positions of executive and administrative responsibility' (Wilson, 1931: 118).

Wilson's division of Iraq into provinces was approved in the instructions he received from London on his return to Baghdad in May 1919, but he seems to have been completely unprepared for Whitehall's insistence on different regimes for the 'Arab province of Mosul' and 'Iraq proper'.[60] Pleas for the alteration of these instructions went unheeded, presumably because of continuing Anglo-French differences over Mosul and France's interest in obtaining a share of Iraqi oil.[61]

Stalemate 1919–1920

Nearly a year elapsed between the signature of the Treaty of Versailles and the distribution of the Near Eastern mandates at San Remo in April 1920. Among other important developments in those months which were to have far-reaching consequences for the future of the area were the Greek landings in Smyrna, the American 'repudiation both of [Woodrow] Wilson and of Europe' (Nicolson 1934: 111), Curzon's resumption of full charge of the Foreign Office in London, the signature, but not the ratification, of the Anglo-Persian convention (negotiated in Teheran by Sir Percy Cox), and perhaps most significant of all, increasing friction between France and Britain over Syria, then under British military occupation, which lasted until Britain agreed to withdraw its troops in September 1919. In Iraq, as 1919 wore on and no clear cut declarations of policy came from the Residency, an acute restlessness developed, due partly to the mounting inconveniences of what seemed an endless military occupation, and partly to resentment that 'Syrians' were judged competent to run their own affairs, while Iraqis apparently were not.

On his way back from Europe in the late spring of 1919, Arnold Wilson, according to Miss Bell's account written some two years later, gave somewhat short shrift to a group of officers originally from Iraq who were occupying responsible posts in the Syrian administration:

> *Tant bien que mal* they were at that time running the whole of the military and civil administration of Syria . . . it was preposterous to tell these . . . Major- Generals . . . and trained administrators that they must be content to run municipal councils. From that day they despaired of ever getting native institutions in Mesopotamia.[62]

Faysal, then half way through his brief reign as king of Syria, was well aware of the widespread animosity with which his subordinates in Damascus regarded the regime in Baghdad:

> To those who maintain that it is impossible to constitute such a government in Baghdad owing to lack of trained men, I will say that until now not the slightest effort has been made to collect them, for most of the posts in the OET are filled by Baghdadis today.[63]

At the same time, the British Liaison Officer in Aleppo reported the candid fears of the Iraqis around him (who included Ja'far al-'Askari, Mawlud Mukhlis, 'Ali Jawdat and Naji al-Suwaydi) that the longer foreign rule continued in Iraq the more difficult it would be to set up an acceptable national government to replace it.[64] Wilson stubbornly maintained his own contention that 'to install an Arab Government in Mesopotamia is impossible and if we attempt it we shall abandon the Middle East to anarchy'.[65] His opinions were certainly shared by substantial numbers of his subordinates; J. S. Mann, a Political Officer killed a year or so later in the last days of the rising of 1920 wrote home that 'any idea of an Arab state is simply bloodstained fooling at present',[66] and in the India Office Shuckburgh commented:

> How can the local population settle down when we won't tell them what we are going to do? Colonel Wilson is bound to act on the assumption that we intend to go on governing Mesopotamia and he would be wanting in his duty if he did not take a firm line with intrigues, the object of which is to make our government impossible. We must either govern Mesopotamia or not govern it.

Patiently Hirtzel explained:

> I thought everyone knew that we were not going to 'govern' Mesopotamia in the sense in which I understand Mr. Shuckburgh to use that word and my complaint against Colonel Wilson (whose achievements for the rest I fully appreciate) is that he does not seem to comprehend the fact although he has been here and seen and heard for himself.[67]

If such differences could exist within the same department of the same office, Wilson's bewilderment three and a half thousand miles away is perhaps understandable. Yet, throughout this period it is true to say that the official voice of the India Office never gave Wilson any reason to hope that a British Indian administration would be acceptable, whatever future was to be devised for Mesopotamia. Hirtzel wrote privately with increasing urgency to Wilson throughout 1919 and 1920, pointing out that provincial and district councils would not and could not by themselves constitute an Arab state, or have the slightest chance of being approved by the League of Nations.

What we want to have in existence, what we ought to have been creating in this time is some administration with Arab institutions which we can safely leave while pulling the strings ourselves; something that won't cost very much, which Labour can swallow consistent with its principles, but under which our economic and political interests will be secure.[68]

In the end he won the day; what appeared in the 1920s had been anticipated in his proposals to Wilson immediately after the war. In fact, the battle for the minds of cabinet ministers was won long before A. T. Wilson's intransigence was pitched against the nationalists in the rising of the summer of 1920; Wilson was fighting his own masters as well as Faysal's men by then.

At the end of 1919 the British position in Mesopotamia was under attack from several directions. In Kurdistan, Shaykh Mahmud, whom the British had installed as ruler, was refusing to be as pliable as the British authorities would have liked; disaffection and discontent was widespread throughout the country, and the Sharifian officers, mostly Iraqis who had fought with Faysal in the Arab revolt and were now part of his entourage in Syria, were growing more determined to extend the benefits of their newly acquired freedom to Iraq. In Britain, the adverse political and financial effects of keeping up a 'highly organised military administration' were beginning to be noticed in official circles.[69] However, when Philip Kerr, Lloyd George's secretary, told Shuckburgh in the spring of 1920 that Parliament would not consent to incur liabilities 'in respect of Mesopotamia for more than a limited period,' Hirtzel retorted:

What the high authorities should be brought to realise is that if what they are avowedly out for is oil and other commodities they cannot have them without public security, and they cannot have public security under an Arab or any other Government without paying for it.[70]

By this time Wilson had become even more convinced that the application of the Anglo-French Declaration would entirely destroy the edifice that he and others had been constructing over the previous five years of British occupation. In his view, Kurds, Shi'is and country people would not accept the rule of Sunni officers from the towns; given such an administration they would probably be clamouring for the return of the Ottomans after a few years. Further, if the government set up by the British did not command widespread acceptance in the country, its activities as a revenue collector would be defied, and the state would become bankrupt. Apart from the anarchy which would follow, Britain would not get back any of the money it was owed for the various assets transferred to the Civil Administration. British investments stood at about £16 million, and the capitalised value of the oilfields about £50 million. If these were to be exploited for the benefit of Britain (and of Mesopotamia), stability, efficiency and good government were essential, and these conditions could not be achieved by abandoning Mesopotamia to an Arab government composed of Sunni *effendis*, whose claims to be the backbone of the country were highly dubious, and foreigners from the Hijaz whose benevolent intentions were palpably questionable.[71]

At this point Wilson's own problems were increased by the 'defection' of his Oriental Secretary. In a paper written after a visit to Damascus entitled *Syria in October*, Miss Bell seems to have understood for the first time the kind of Iraqi state which the 'nationalists' working with Faysal had in mind. The views of Yasin al-Hashimi, one of her chief interlocutors, had probably undergone some moderation for Miss Bell's consumption, but he acknow-ledged the legitimacy of the British claim to provide advisors, and accepted that a British High Commissioner (preferably Sir Percy Cox) would be needed to support and guide an Arab amir. He also agreed that Arab provincial governors should have British advisers. He would prefer one coun-try to take the mandate for both Syria and Iraq, but if this was impossible he wanted an identical educational and judicial system to be set up in the two states. He criticised current educational policy in Iraq, which was mainly concerned with building up from the bottom, with primary and technical schools:

> You may possibly create through them good farmers and good engineers but in fifty years' time we shall be no further forward in obtaining a class of highly educated men fit to take over the government of the country.[72]

While she did not entirely agree with him, Miss Bell accepted the force of much of Yasin's arguments, particularly in conjunction with his definite willingness to accept some sort of foreign tutelage; Wilson's refusal to compromise this far lost him her sympathy and support.

The Acting Civil Commissioner himself, aware of the possibility of a 'serious breakdown in 1920'[73] could see no other course than his own. Shi'i hostility was expressed by a *fatwa* issued on 1 March by the *marja'-i taqlid,* Ayatullah Muhammad Taqi Shirazi, asserting that service under the British was unlawful.[74] In addition, the nomination of Faysal and 'Abdullah as kings of Syria and Iraq by the Syrian congress in Damascus on 8 March 1920 did not pass unnoticed in Baghdad (Khoury, 1983: 90). By March, Wilson had set up a constitutional committee under Sir Edgar Bonham-Carter, which produced a plan for a cabinet-type Council of State with a majority of British members, with Arabs attached in subordinate positions; there was also to be a legislative assembly appointed on a collegiate basis from elected local councillors. In spite of the frustrations and delays caused by London's inability to make a firm declaration of intent, it seems almost incredible that Wilson could have imagined that these proposals, providing as they did for so little Arab participation, stood the remotest chance of being accepted in London.[75]

The Constitutional Committee's report arrived in England at the same time as the official statement that the mandate for Iraq had been awarded to Great Britain arrived in Baghdad, which prompted Wilson to make a flowery if suitably vague announcement 'to amplify the bald statement from San Remo'.[76] This contained no reference to any further consultation of local opinion, and a few days later Wilson was dismayed to receive instructions which called for further consultation, to be undertaken before the precise form of the mandate would be decided. He immediately requested permission to delay this announcement, or substitute for it a summary of the Bonham-Carter proposals, which he would promise to put into effect in the course of the autumn.

The situation grew more precarious as time passed, especially since Ramadan, with its attendant quickening of tempers in hot weather, fell between 19 May and 18 June. On 2 June Wilson decided to hold a meeting with the 'mandubin', a delegation of prominent notables, mostly members of the nationalist group Haras al-Istiqlal, who had approached him in the hope of eliciting a definite promise of negotiations over what was to happen next. In the course of a prepared speech at the Sarai, he referred to the British government never having deviated from either the Anglo-French Declaration or Article 22 of the League of Nations Charter. He pointed to the causes beyond his control which had combined to delay the establishment of civil government. He promised his audience a Council of State under an Arab president 'to hold office until the question of the final constitution of Iraq has been submitted to the Legislative Assembly which we propose to call' (Wilson, 1931: 255–257).

The whole tenor of Wilson's speech was not calculated to appeal to any but the most enthusiastic of advocates of British rule, and it succeeded in confirming nationalist fears. A few days later, Wilson received authority to announce Cox' impending return, but by then resentment in the country had reached a point where it could no longer be contained by such palliatives. In an outspoken telegram to London, Wilson recommended that Whitehall should make a swift and decisive choice between evacuation on the one hand and firm British rule on the other.[77] At a meeting of the Eastern Committee the next day, Curzon commented that the news from Baghdad left him with 'an unpleasant impression of Colonel Wilson's incapacity to deal with the situation'[78] and within a few weeks widespread disorder had broken out on the Middle Euphrates.

The rising of 1920 has been extensively discussed and its causes variously attributed.[79] The long delays in setting up some form of faintly representative government were of course a substantial source of dissatisfaction, and the sheer range and extent of the activities of the civil and military authorities had become a growing irritant, especially for those whose previous experience of 'government' had been either or both distant and sporadic.[80] The Sharifians (mostly ex-Ottoman officers now under Faysal's command) combined briefly with rebellious tribesmen, Shi'i *mujtahids*, and ex-civil servants to resist British rule and oppressive taxation, with the hope, at least on the part of the Sharifians, that they might succeed in establishing the kind of government in Baghdad that the French were forcing them to abandon in Damascus. In spite of the obvious dangers, and the warnings of Gertrude Bell and Arnold Wilson, the G. O. C. (Sir Aylmer Haldane) stumped doggedly off to summer quarters at Karind. The unprepared state of the army, together with confused rumours of imminent evacuation, probably contributed to the initial impetus of the rising and its long duration.

The revolt brought almost total anarchy to the countryside throughout the late summer and early autumn of 1920. Civil administration largely ceased to function outside the towns throughout most of July, August and September, and a successful outcome for British arms was by no means a certainty. Casualties on both sides were high[81] and punitive expeditions and displays of force continued well into 1921. One effect was to place the whole policy of the continued British occupation of Mesopotamia in jeopardy, especially when the extent of expenditure and commitment of manpower became more widely known. Politicians were faced with a dilemma, for although aware of the potential of Mesopotamian oil they could scarcely use it as an argument for the continued out-pouring of British 'blood and treasure' there. That explanation might have brought relief from press attacks, but it would have occasioned howls of fury from Europe and America.[82]

Aftermath of the Rising

By October the army had largely regained control, Wilson had been replaced by Cox, and it was clear that some as yet unspecified method of choosing a ruler acceptable to local opinion would be brought into play. However, until the very end of the year, when Whitehall definitely made up its mind to support the candidature of a son of the Sharif, Cox remained as much at a loss about Britain's intentions as Wilson had been, though he was readier to understand the wisdom of speedy preliminaries. Thus in October 1920, all were waiting for the oracle to speak; some far-reaching policy statement was expected, but for the time being none was given. The situation was eased by Cox' great prestige and the general sense, not entirely unjustified, that his return was an augury of some kind of definite settlement. He described his task as that of undertaking:

> . . . a complete and necessarily rapid transformation of the facade of
> the existing administration from British to Arab, and, in the process
> a wholesale reduction in the numbers of British and British Indian
> personnel employed . . . Whatever the primary feelings of many of my
> comrades may have been, indeed must have been, most of them
> gradually came round to the view that as an alternative to the bag and
> baggage policy the experiment was worth trying and not necessarily
> doomed to failure.[83]

Within a fortnight of his arrival Cox had managed to persuade the elderly Naqib, 'Abd al-Rahman al-Gaylani, to head a Council of State, thus giving a visible demonstration of his intention of setting up an Arab government. Most of those invited to sit on the Council did so, and on 11 November Cox proclaimed the Provisional Government as an established fact.[84] What he was unable to do was to announce any details about the future head of state, and this question became the chief topic of concern over the coming months.

An 'acceptable' ruler was of vital importance to the British government in the light of changed attitudes in Whitehall. In the summer of 1920, Edwin Montagu, the Secretary of State for India, had suggested that it would be advisable to reconsider the nature of Britain's relationship with Iraq, and wondered whether the mandate as it stood was the most suitable vehicle. From this there emerged the notion that a fairly cheap concession to nationalist sentiment would be to dispense with the form of the mandate while retaining its substance, and to substitute a treaty of alliance for the mandate relationship. A treaty implied contracting parties and signatories,

and the future ruler of Iraq would have an important role to play in this
arrangement.

Candidates for the throne: the selection of Faysal

Naturally, the choice of such a ruler, and the way in which he would be presented to the Iraqis, were matters of considerable delicacy. In January 1919
the India Office had opposed 'Abdullah's accompanying Cox to Baghdad on
the grounds that such obvious British support would have been tantamount
to forcing the Iraqis' hands and would thus be an easy target for international
criticism. It was therefore essential that whoever was chosen by Whitehall
should at least not be widely opposed in Iraq. With this proviso, there were
only three serious candidates: 'Abdullah, Sayyid Talib of Basra, and Faysal.
The Naqib of Baghdad, although showing a certain amount of interest in the
throne from time to time, was effectively debarred from seeking it both
because of his age (he was 75) and his close identification with Sunni
orthodoxy. He was eventually persuaded to support Faysal's candidature, and
served as Prime Minister until 1922.

After the Sharifian rout at Maysalun in July, 'Abdullah became a political
nonentity, a suitable recipient for the booby prize of Transjordan. Had Faysal
remained in Damascus, 'Abdullah, as the older brother, might well have
become King of Iraq; he was as acceptable to the Shi'is as his brother, and
seemingly also to the British, for in April 1920 Curzon had suggested
inviting him to London. The proposal was firmly resisted by the India
Office; Hirtzel commented wryly:

> . . . the idea that we shall be any the wiser when we have seen
> 'Abdullah is disproved by experience. All that will happen (as in the
> case of Faysal) is that we shall be hoodwinked by his interpreter.[85]

Sayyid Talib was a rather more serious candidate. Gertrude Bell reported
throughout the summer of 1920 that he was attempting to build up a
'moderate' party and it is certain that he was largely responsible for the
relative calm in Baghdad and the ease with which Cox was able to proceed
towards setting up a Council of State. He was financed from British funds,
as were the other candidates,[86] but his close connection with local politics
was at once an advantage and a disadvantage. As a Sunni from Basra it is
difficult to imagine him capable of mustering widespread support nationally,
and his notoriety dating back to Ottoman times did not stand him in good
stead. It seems likely that his deportation in 1921 was arranged more to clear

away an undesirable subordinate than to eliminate a serious candidate for the throne.[87]

Probably Britain still wanted a king who would be content 'to reign but not govern',[88] and Faysal seems to have been regarded in official circles as a suitably pliant instrument. Certainly when he began, almost at once, to behave in a rather un-puppet-like fashion his 'insubordination' appeared to the authorities at the time as a monstrous breach of faith and rank ingratitude. But in spite of criticisms of him both before and after his installation, Faysal seemed the only possible choice, for very much the same reasons, ironically, as A. T. Wilson had put forward in November 1918; he belonged to a family which had by now become well known throughout most of the Arab world; his tolerance in matters of religion made him acceptable to most Shi'is, and his brief reign in Syria had given him a certain reputation as a nationalist leader.[89] In spite of all this, some serious difficulties had to be overcome. Cox' instructions of August 1920 certainly implied that Faysal's candidature would be highly desirable, but it was not until the Cairo Conference, some eight months later, that the king-makers were certain of success.[90] The problem was to reconcile the various conflicting elements so that Faysal could be made acceptable to the nationalists, to those who wanted close British control, and of course to the French.

In fact, French objections followed swiftly on the publication of a rumour which appeared in *Le Matin*. The French Prime Minister pointed out that allowing Faysal to become king of Iraq would create tensions between Britain and France,[91] but a formula was evolved soon afterwards to meet such objections. Sir Eyre Crowe, the British Ambassador in Paris, told the French Prime Minister:

> [W]hether the natives of Mesopotamia demanded to have Faysal for their King or not Sir Eyre Crowe could not say, but it was obvious that if such a demand were put forward it would not be easy for the British government to turn a deaf ear to it.[92]

Faysal's own interest in securing the throne of Mesopotamia was unofficially conveyed quite quickly to the British authorities. In September 1920, Colonel Frank Balfour of the Mesopotamian Civil Administration, then on leave in London, had a conversation with General Haddad, Faysal's adviser after which he reported that 'Faysal is definitely out for Iraq and would take it as more or less satisfying his undeniable grouse against us (sc. over Syria).'[93] His acceptance was conditional on three main factors; the agreement of his brother 'Abdullah, a promise of British support, and a reasonably clear definition of his functions. In fact, London never gave any serious consideration to any other candidate, but there were important questions over how best Faysal should be packaged. He was not likely to be widely opposed, but the fact still remained that without some indication of British approval it would be difficult to muster solid support for him. The British authorities were thus faced with the problem of exactly how much open encouragement they should give their candidate, since either too much or too little could prove fatal.

In December/January 1920–21 Cox made his views clear to the India Office. He believed that a ruler should not be imposed, but found that the people whom he consulted would welcome a lead from Britain. He felt that a procedure which insisted on the adoption and election of a candidate by the (as yet unformed) National Assembly would be too lengthy and uncertain. He urged that the British government should come out clearly for Faysal as candidate:

> My belief and that of those of my staff on whose judgement I rely is that such an announcement of *fait accompli* would be a welcome relief to the majority of the people of Mesopotamia and that it would have the support of the moderate elements among the Nationalists while it would take the wind out of the sails of the young extremists who want to get rid of the Mandate altogether. After announcement of Faysal's candidature we should soon learn whether public opinion in his favour was so general as to make it unnecessary to wait for elections or whether we should allow elections to take their course and allow Faysal to canvass for himself like others.[94]

It was agreed that French susceptibilities should be overridden but that Faysal, now in London, should be made to promise not to intrigue against the French and not to make any attempts to try to recover Damascus. At that stage, in January, before the possibility of Transjordan had presented itself, Faysal felt unwilling to accept Britain's offer as it stood, unless 'Abdullah had either declined the offer or been rejected both by Britain and Mesopotamia; but he told Kinahan Cornwallis:[95]

> I would only consent to go to Mesopotamia after I had been fully informed about the form of government which H. M. Government envisaged there, and after I had satisfied myself that it was being set up in the spirit which marked our earlier deliberations. I have little doubt that it will be so, but I could accept nothing blindly.[96]

Cornwallis returned much impressed from this interview, and it was decided by the Foreign Office that Cox' advice should be followed. The installation of 'Abdullah in Transjordan and the return of large numbers of Baghdadi officers to Iraq from Syria in the spring of 1921 further increased Faysal's chances of success.

Sir Percy Cox' problems in Baghdad were not simply confined to the creation of circumstances favouring a suitable candidate for the Mesopotamian throne, or persuading unwilling ministers to take up the portfolios that they had been offered.[97] In the late autumn of 1920 there was still considerable doubt as to whether Britain would stay in Mesopotamia at all, whether British troops might not be withdrawn to Basra. This uncertainty, which persisted to a greater or lesser extent until the final delineation of the northern frontier in 1926, was particularly crucial at this early stage.[98] British press and parliamentary disapproval of continued expenditure in Mesopotamia was not slow to reach Baghdad. The British Chamber of Commerce at Baghdad sent a pungent telegram of protest to the India Office:

> British forces by their occupation of Mesopotamia destroyed the only form of government that country had known for centuries . . . evacuation at the present time will leave it without any government worthy of the name. Thus the final result of British intervention in Mesopotamia would be its complete ruin, for which ultimate responsibility will rest with H. M. Government. The Chamber fully realises the urgent need of lightening the burden of the British taxpayer and believes that this can be done with safety and honour along the lines at present contemplated and inaugurated by H. M. Government.[99]

Eventually a continued British presence was to be assured through the measures adopted at the Cairo Conference, as well as by the encouragement of a candidate for the throne who was thought likely to bring the greatest stability to the country.

The Formation of the Middle East Department of the Colonial Office and the Cairo Conference of 1921

While the negotiations over Faysal's candidature were being conducted in London, a major administrative change was taking place which was to have permanent significance for British Middle Eastern policy: the creation of a new department within the Colonial Office to deal specifically with the

Middle Eastern mandates. The formation of the Middle East Department of the Colonial Office followed the recognition that some new arrangement was necessary for running the affairs of the mandated territories, a function which the India Office could not adequately exercise and which the Foreign Office was not by its nature equipped to perform. The details of the formation of the department have been described elsewhere; it was the outcome of a long process of discussion begun as long ago as 1917, but whose form in 1920–21 owed most to the initiative and drive of Winston Churchill.[100]

As Minister of War, anxious to cut down military spending as far as possible, Churchill had mooted an economical, if controversial, scheme for controlling Mesopotamia through the use of the infant Royal Air Force.[101] By February 1921 he had been made Secretary of State for the Colonies, and by then the necessary steps had been taken towards the creation of the new Department. It contained men who were no strangers to the affairs of the area: J. E. Shuckburgh (knighted in 1922), of the India Office, was put in charge (Hirtzel preferred to stay at the India Office, where he remained for the rest of his career); other luminaries included Major Hubert Young from the Foreign Office, who had taken part in both the Arab revolt and the Mesopotamia Campaign; R.W. Bullard, former consul in Basra and Governor of Baghdad, Colonel Richard Meinertzhagen, formerly Chief Political Officer, Palestine, who was Military Adviser to the department, and, for a couple of years, at Churchill's special insistence, T. E. Lawrence.[102]

The immediate task of the new department was to organise the Cairo Conference, a meeting of high British and Arab officials in the Middle East in March 1921 to discuss the future political financial and military arrangements for the mandated territories. The main object of the conference, as described later by Churchill, was to maintain firm British control as cheaply as possible.[103] For Iraq, the air scheme was adopted (involving eight squadrons of aircraft and six armoured car companies) and the main lines of the Treaty to be negotiated with the future Iraqi government were laid down; Britain was to control Iraq's foreign relations and have what amounted to a right of veto in military and financial matters. On the question of a ruler, it was felt vital that Britain should give a lead: Faysal's candidature had become more or less a foregone conclusion, but more formal approaches to him, 'Abdullah, the Iraqis and the French were agreed upon. Discussion also took place on the subject of Kurdistan; the apparently excessive cost of administering Kirkuk and Sulaymaniya prompted Major Young to remark, somewhat naively, that their secession 'would . . . be no loss to Mesopotamia'.[104]

Various other matters, including details of financial arrangements, the assets transferred by Britain to the Mesopotamian Civil Administration, the refugee problem and the location of bases were discussed, but the main objectives were the reduction of military expenditure and the selection of a suitable ruler. It was thought likely that the turbulence in the country would soon subside after the establishment of a national government, and the RAF commitment was planned on a reducing scale from the very beginning. The Colonial Office took overall co-ordinating responsibility for these arrangements, which meant that the Air Officer Commanding in Baghdad was subordinate to the High Commissioner, in the same way as the Air Ministry in London was directed in Iraqi affairs by the Colonial Office.

It was over a year before the political arrangements concluded at the Cairo Conference were formalised in a treaty between Britain and Iraq, and three more years before that treaty was ratified by the Iraqi government. Even then, several important matters were still under negotiation, either between the British and Iraqi governments directly, or with other powers; the frontier between Iraq and Turkey was not settled by the Treaty of Lausanne (July 1923), and in fact final arrangements were made only in 1927. Thus Cairo was an expression by Britain of its future military and financial commitments in the Middle East, of the extent to which the 'imperial burden' would be lightened. It marked the beginning of a new kind of colonial policy, and formalised the end of direct British rule in Iraq. The immediate reason for the decisions taken is not hard to find: massive expenditure in Mesopotamia could not be continued in the face of so many other more pressing demands on the British Treasury. It was becoming increasingly difficult to explain either in or out of Parliament how the spending of millions on the Tigris and Euphrates contributed to the building of homes fit for heroes.[105]

2

FROM THE CAIRO CONFERENCE TO THE RATIFICATION OF THE ANGLO-IRAQ TREATY, MARCH 1921 – SEPTEMBER 1924

The three years which followed the Cairo Conference were filled with intense diplomatic activity in London and Baghdad. Signs of disharmony, and of considerable acrimony, appeared almost immediately, both the British and Iraqi governments accusing each other of making unacceptable demands and of breaking faith. The events of these years well illustrate the permanent problem facing Faysal and the Iraqi government: they were vitally bound to Britain for their very existence, yet in order to appear credible within Iraq they had to appear to oppose the more demeaning aspects of British control. However, especially in the early years, until, in fact, the end of the Mosul frontier dispute and the signature of the oil concession, it seemed that British rule had to make itself felt. Later on, when these major issues had been settled, it was possible for the British to relax their grip.

The immediate question facing the British authorities in the spring of 1921 was the somewhat comic opera matter of Faysal's 'election' to the throne. His adoption by Britain effectively precluded the possibility of any other candidate being chosen, but it was essential that public opinion in Iraq should be broadly in favour of him, and that at least he should not be seen to be widely opposed (Kedourie, 1970: 239–242). Two of the three local candidates had little chance of success, the Naqib being too old and the Shaykh of Muhammarah a Shi'i; the former was nudged into dropping his candidature and the latter was directly advised not to stand by Sir Percy Cox. The third, Sayyid Talib, presented a real challenge, and he was eventually removed by the British authorities in what appear to have been somewhat *sub rosa* circumstances.[1] With his disappearance from the scene, Faysal's success was a foregone conclusion.

Faysal's position in the period before his election was especially delicate, since he had the same time to appear to be both a 'nationalist' and to be conforming to the broad wishes of the British government. Hence he could not be seen to arrive in Iraq at Britain's express invitation, but it should nevertheless be clear where Britain stood with regard to him. For this reason there was a good deal of movement and correspondence between Baghdad, Jidda and London after the High Commissioner's return from the Cairo Conference, and nearly two months (mid-April to mid June 1921) elapsed between Cox' return to Baghdad and Faysal's departure from Jidda aboard a British mail vessel. To clarify matters Cox asked, and Churchill agreed, that a declaration of Britain's intentions should be made in England; the announcement was made in the House of Commons on June 14. The text of an officially inspired Reuter's communiqué was sent to Baghdad a few days earlier:

> In response to enquiries from adherents of the Emir Faysal the British Government have announced that they will place no obstacles in the way of his candidature and that if he is chosen he will have their support.[2]

It is difficult to judge how popular Faysal actually was at this stage. Descriptions of his arrival and reception vary: Cox' most frequently used adjective to describe local feeling is 'cordial.'[3] Many shaykhs appeared in Baghdad to welcome him, clearly stirred into this action by the knowledge that he was the candidate whom the British supported. After his speech to the shaykhs at Ramadi, 'Ali Sulayman of Dulaym and Fahad Beg of 'Anayza declared allegiance to Faysal because 'you are acceptable to the British Government'; Miss Bell reported that Faysal 'was a little surprised', though it seems highly unlikely that any other consideration would have drawn the shaykhs' support.[4] It is in fact difficult to point to any group beyond the urban Sunnis and the 'Baghdadi officers' who actively desired to place Faysal on the throne of Iraq.

Old wine in new bottles: the Anglo-Iraqi Treaty

By the time of Faysal's arrival in Iraq a new policy element had been introduced. Ireland's contention that the idea of replacing the mandate by a treaty was discussed at the Cairo Conference is not borne out by the source he cites (Ireland, 1937: 338). Although there had certainly been vague discussions about this over the previous year, it does not seem to have been until early June 1921 that Cox finally realised that the mandate in its original state was unlikely to gain widespread local acceptance. On June 4 he suggested that a statement should be made along the following lines:

> . . . the process of evolution towards national government is pro-ceeding so much more expeditiously than had been formerly anticipated . . . certain provisions of the draft Mandate framed under conditions which existed a year ago were getting out of date and that in view of the fact that there was reason to hope . . . that a permanent national Government would be established at a very early date, H. M. Government had decided to defer consideration of terms of Mandate until a new ruler had been installed and could be consulted as to the precise form of compact between the two countries, which would best serve the mutual interests of both.[5]

Gertrude Bell wrote home at the same time:

> Sir Percy has urged that we should drop the Mandate altogether and go for a treaty with the Arab state when it is constituted. It would be a magnificent move, if we're bold enough to do it.[6]

At this stage, and for a few months afterwards, it seems that Faysal genuinely believed that the substitution of a treaty for the mandate implied the creation of an essentially different relationship. The immediate task of the High Commissioner and his staff between June and August was to try to persuade Faysal, once accepted by 'popular acclamation', to consent to be crowned without this new relationship being precisely defined. Questions of his status, the position of both Kurdistan and Basra within, or associated with, Iraq, and the precise definition of Iraq's relationship to Britain would best be attended to after Faysal's accession and the formal creation of the Iraqi state.[7]

To facilitate this, the High Commissioner urged that the 'Iraqi people' should be consulted about the Council of Ministers' unanimous decision to nominate Faysal King of Iraq. Thus another 'referendum' was held, pro-ducing a 96% majority in favour of Faysal, and on 23 August he was crowned in Baghdad. The vagueness of all the parties about their relationships with each other at this stage augured uncomfortably for the future: Cox warned early in August that Faysal would expect to exercise royal prerogatives as soon as he was crowned, and urged London to give due consideration to the delicacy of the situation :

> At present nationalism in Iraq is a plant of disappointingly sensitive and

tender material. . . It is therefore necessary for us to bend every tendril to form and pattern a national state and that this may be accomplished I beg as regards Mandate that hand of H. M. Government will bear very gently.[8]

The advice was timely; Faysal nearly refused the throne because of Britain's initial insistence, eventually withdrawn, that he should declare his formal subordination to the High Commissioner in his accession speech.

The problem was, and long continued to be, one of finding a formula acceptable to both sides. This was not achieved at once, and the fierce in-fighting of the next few years illustrates the difficulties encountered in arriving at a settlement. Gradually, in the course of the 1920s, the British authorities realised that there were subtler and less openly offensive methods of exercising control than had originally been considered necessary. It was perfectly possible for the Iraqi government to exercise its authority in certain limited spheres without perpetual interference in matters of detail either from the British advisers or the High Commissioner, and it became increasingly clear that direct confrontation was more usefully avoided. In 1921, however, this particular lesson had still to be learnt. Cox, clearly under considerable pressure, pointed out that:

[T]he reservation of ultimate control to the High Commissioner must be carefully wrapped up, for as you will remember suspicion of our motives and good faith is very near (the) surface and there are always elements anxious to raise it.[9]

The initial difficulty was essentially a legal one. The British government could only define Faysal's position in a treaty, whose terms had yet to be negotiated. Until Faysal was on the throne, the negotiations could not begin, since there was as yet no party to contract on behalf of the Iraqi state. For his part, Faysal was reluctant to commit himself to an uncertain future, relying entirely on the good faith of H. M. Government.

The deadlock was temporarily broken by both sides agreeing to climb down to enable the coronation to take place. Faysal withdrew his insistence on obtaining full clarification of his powers beforehand, and the Colonial Office withdrew its insistence that he should announce his subordination to Britain in his accession speech. Faysal pointed out that the practical limitations of his own position provided a more ample security to Britain than any formal undertakings:

His attitude is practically this. He says 'Apart from my personal ideas in direction of Arab nationality I am an instrument of British policy.

H. M. Government and I are in the same boat and must sink or swim together. Were instrument to fail and in consequence they left Iraq, I should have to leave too. Having, so as to speak, chosen me, you must treat me as one of yourselves, and I must be trusted as H. M. Government trust you . . . I undertake to be guided by your advice in all matters and the mere fact of your presence here and that of Advisors should be sufficient guarantee to those whom it may concern of preservation of your interests.[10]

Eventually, it was decided that the League would be informed that Britain intended to carry out its obligations under the mandate by means of a treaty with Faysal under suitable guarantees, and Faysal was asked to sign a document promising that, until the actual signature of the treaty, he would undertake to safeguard Britain's international obligations under the terms of the mandate and its previous and current financial commitments in Iraq. Additionally, Cox was asked not to raise the matter with Faysal again until H. M., Government had communicated the matter to the League.[11] On this basis, Faysal's 'coronation' took place in Baghdad on 23 August 1921.

A few days later, London asked the British Representative at Geneva, H.A.L. Fisher, to inform the League of Nations that:

[W]hile King Faysal is clearly ready and willing to include in his treaty with H. M. Government all proper provisions to ensure that the Government of Mesopotamia shall be carried on in strict conformity with the spirit of the Covenant of the League of Nations, it is in the opinion of H. M. Government undesirable that the treaty should appear to subvert that independence which was already provisionally recognised before there was a national government in the country.[12]

In fact, owing to the non-ratification of the Treaty of Sèvres and the greatly changed situation brought about by Atatürk's seizure of power in Turkey, the League was obliged to postpone its consideration of the 'A' mandates. However, it was decided in London that the High Commissioner in Baghdad should be instructed to go ahead with the negotiations for the Treaty. In October and early November 1921, negotiations on a variety of subjects proceeded smoothly; Young, who had been deputed by the Colonial Office to help Cox conduct business in Baghdad, wrote home on 23 October:

We do not intend to let ourselves be unduly bound by any provision which is included in the draft Mandate if we are satisfied that it would really cause trouble if we insisted on Faysal agreeing to it . . . In spite of the fact that we have presented what we call the final draft of the Mandate to the Council of the League of Nations it is not too late, if it proves absolutely necessary, to suggest further alterations.[13]

In the light of the evident 'cordiality' of these discussions, and Cox' general inclination to side with the more feasible of Faysal's suggestions, H.A.L. Fisher's somewhat hardline announcement to the League on 17 November of Britain's intentions towards Iraq[14] came as a considerable shock. Cox seems to have been as unprepared for it as Faysal: on 20 November he wrote to London suggesting that either the mandate should be entirely disregarded or H. M. Government should so arrange things as to eliminate the more irritating features of the League's requirements, a 'normal treaty relationship unhampered by the Mandate', as he telegraphed to Churchill on 20 November.[15] Faysal, Cox felt, could well be spared the necessity of having to make an undertaking not to discriminate against the French. Gertrude Bell wrote home early in December:

> The word Mandate produces much the same effect here as the word Protectorate did in Egypt. Fisher's declaration to the League . . . has raised a minor hurricane. Even Faisal was taken aback – the mandate, he understood, was to be dropped and here it was reappearing in another form.[16]

First Disagreements: Faysal's opposition to the Treaty

Fisher's declaration at Geneva marked the end of the period of general agreement, and was largely responsible for the delays before Faysal's signature of the treaty. The King became deeply suspicious of the true nature of British intentions and saw the military threat from Turkey and later from Najd as part of an Allied master-plan to terrify him into submission. His already considerable suspicions of France's intentions had been reinforced by the Franklin-Bouillon agreement between France and Turkey of October 1921, which seemed to him to be an invitation to the Turks to attack northern Kurdistan. His sensitivity on these and other issues drew sharp rebukes from the Colonial Secretary:

> I have come to the conclusion that Faysal is rather too prone to raise difficult constitutional and foreign questions . . . In a few years all these points will doubtless be settled, but meanwhile why instead of fretting

and fussing cannot he live quietly and do his ordinary practical work as
a ruler . . . the enormous cost and burden Iraq has been and still is to us
is the important point for him to notice . . . All the time he takes our
money he will have to take our directions. In my opinion you ought to
cool him off with considerations of this kind expressed in your own
admirable manner. As regards the French, we will deal with them from
here. Above all do not let him work himself up against them.[17]

Faysal had made his own position clear at an interview with Young towards
the end of October. He said that he had explained to T. E. Lawrence in Cairo
that 'he would not accept the terms of the document which we (H. M.
Government) have submitted to the League of Nations',[18] but he was
prepared to accept the mandate as it stood for a limited period, during which
both parties would busy themselves with the preparation of the treaty. As
we have seen, Young also believed that the terms could be modified, but
Fisher's announcement seemed to have made this impossible. All hope that
the treaty would be easily and smoothly concluded was now lost, and both
Faysal and the Naqib proved sufficiently obdurate towards British demands
that Mejcher has good grounds for believing that it was only Faysal's
providential appendicitis in the summer of 1922 that saved the Iraqi
monarchy from premature extinction (1976: 294).

The Colonial Office does not seem to have been the prime mover in the
decision not to modify the treaty in a way acceptable to Faysal and the Iraqi
government. It appears that the Foreign Office, concerned not to annoy the
French, was principally responsible for Fisher's stand at Geneva. R. C.
Lindsay wrote in January 1922:

> [O]ur policy in Iraq is in strong contrast to the French policy in Syria
> and must be causing heart-burnings in Paris. To go to Geneva and ask
> that the draft Mandate for Iraq be modified in such a manner as to
> accentuate further the divergence between French and English Arab
> policy is I submit impossible.[19]

In a similar vein the Foreign Secretary in cabinet a few weeks later referred
to the dangers of allowing the different treatment of Syria by France and Iraq
by Britain to become over-emphasised. For this reason he also felt unable to
accede to Iraqi requests for diplomatic representation abroad.

The profound effect of this rift on Anglo-Iraqi relations can hardly be
overestimated. Typical of many similar requests was a telegram from Cox of
December 1921:

Both Faysal and the Naqib press for insertion of some words demonstrating that hated Mandate as understood is at an end. I have already explained Faysal's reasons.

Young also took up the cudgels on Faysal's behalf:

Difficulties in the way of conclusion of satisfactory arrangements about British staff, Kurdistan, military policy and financial arrangements will be greatly reduced by conclusion of main treaty on lines desired by Faysal.[20]

A month or so later, back in England at a meeting of the cabinet's Middle Eastern Committee, he stated that:

The object of both sides in all the discussions at Baghdad had been to arrive at a Treaty that would justify Faysal in the eyes of his own people while preserving the necessary position of H. M. Government *vis-à-vis* the League of Nations.

The refusal of Britain to consider modifications in the mandate at this time, largely for fear of wounding French susceptibilities, but probably also because of a degree of unwillingness to weaken the British position in Iraq any further, had far-reaching effects for the future. This was due to the ambiguity of Faysal's status and his lack of a real power base within the country, together with his natural disinclination to accept these particular terms. He was forced by circumstances into the position of having to seem to resist British demands as far as possible, since not to do so would have lost him what meagre credibility he had in the eyes of the Iraqis. It was not until the summer of 1924 that Faysal and his circle were finally forced to choose between resistance and acquiescence, and chose the latter to ensure their political survival.

The Anglo-Iraqi Treaty of 1922

Between December 1921 and August 1922 there were detailed discussions on the Anglo-Iraqi Treaty. There was to be a main treaty defining the shape of Anglo-Iraqi relations, and subsidiary agreements dealing with military and financial matters and the numbers and duties of the British officials to be employed by the Iraqi government. The treaty itself was to last for twenty years. The negotiations took place against a background of mounting opposition to the British presence, coupled with Turkish raids across the

northern frontier and Turkish aid and encouragement for the Kurds. Over
these months, British irritation with Faysal grew, as he was driven from one
subterfuge to another, either associating himself openly with avowed
opponents of the treaty or making clumsy approaches to the Shiʻi leadership
of the Holy Cities. In the end, in August 1922, a major crisis was only
averted by the *deus ex machina* of Faysal's illness, which enabled Cox to take
full power into his own hands until the King was well enough to sign the
treaty.

The contents of the treaty have been carefully analysed elsewhere (Ireland,
1937: 351–360). It covered such matters as British representation of Iraq in
foreign countries, the number and duties of British officials, British supervision of the judicial system, the adoption of the principle of the Open Door
(the system giving economic equality for all foreign states including the
United States), and repayment to Britain for the public works constructed
during the period of military occupation. The real stumbling block, however, lay in the underwriting of the treaty for Iraq by the British government, the guarantees required to ensure that it would be carried out. It was
on this provision, and the details of the separate agreements, that the treaty
almost foundered.

By February 1922 Cox was beginning to feel the strain of his negotiating
position in Baghdad. He believed that the best policy was simply to go
ahead and make an agreement with which Faysal would be content to
associate himself, in such a way that neither he nor H. M. Government
would lose face:

> Considering the impossibility of adopting any costly policy in Iraq it
> seems in view of attitude (of) British taxpayer more prudent to secure
> goodwill of Iraqis by giving them what they want than to adopt policy
> which will probably have contrary effect.

Churchill explained in March that it was now too late to abrogate the
mandate, and continued:

> All legal claim to special position in Iraq on which whole policy of
> Treaty depends would be forfeited by Great Britain if Mandate were
> abandoned.[21]

Various expedients were advanced; Churchill suggested sending Lawrence to
Baghdad to reason with Faysal; Cox demurred, but offered to come to
London either by himself or with the King.

Early in April, reports of a forthcoming conference of Shi'i clergy at Karbala' appeared in the weekly police intelligence summaries, and later in the month both the Persian and Arab Shi'i *'ulama'* met there to protest against the mandate (Luizard, 1991: 440–448). Faysal seems to have been connected with these meetings, though at this stage only indirectly: he probably hoped to gather convincing evidence of the country's hostility towards the treaty. Most of the *'ulama'* declared themselves opposed to the treaty, though not quite so trenchantly on this occasion as they were to do in the autumn.[22] The meetings did not give Faysal quite the support for which he had hoped, but they marked the beginning of a period of fairly close contact between the court and the *'ulama'* which lasted until their exile to Iran the following summer.

Constant procrastination over the treaty, caused by growing nationalist hostility, produced deep frustration and exasperation in Whitehall. In the course of angry exchanges a familiar ploy reappeared, not for the last time; the threat either to withdraw the British presence to Basra or to evacuate the country altogether, if British demands were not complied with. Churchill warned wryly: 'Faysal should be under no delusions in this matter. He will be a long time looking for a third throne.'[23] Every attempt was made to 'explain' the benevolent nature of the mandate, but officially inspired newspaper articles and announcements had little effect upon public opinion. Wholehearted support for the treaty as it stood was confined to a very few groups within the country. These were, broadly speaking, those tribal leaders whom the British had either supported or elevated in the past, or who had remained on the British side in the 1920 insurrection and who had subsequently found themselves victimised by officials of the Iraqi government; the urban notables of Basra who saw the British connection as the best safeguard of their interests, and the great majority of Christians and Jews, who looked to Britain's continued presence in Iraq for their own protection.

By the summer of 1922 the failure to come to any agreement had produced one of the frequent crises of the early mandate period. In the spring the Wahhabi raids from Najd had begun, and the King and the cabinet wished to allocate considerable sums to defend the country against this threat. The uncertainty of the intentions of both the British and Iraqi governments are reflected in a letter from the Minister of Finance, Sasun Hasqayl, threatening resignation over this issue. It is particularly indicative of the prevailing confusion, since this urbane and distinguished individual was staunchly pro-British:

> In a good cause it may be justifiable to spend beyond one's means, but the man who has to bear the odium of laying this burden upon the

community, either present or future, must be in a position to know whether the end justifies the means. I am not at present in that position. I do not know what danger has to be guarded against, or to what extent the British Government accept liability for the defence of the country.[24]

Sasun was eventually persuaded not to resign, but the Shi'i Minister of Commerce, Ja'far Abu'l-Timman, did, and it took constant cajoling on the part of Sir Percy Cox and Gertrude Bell to keep even the Naqib's hands on the reins of office. In the summer there were rumours that the one of the most influential *mujtahids* of Kadhimain, Shaykh Mahdi al-Khalisi, had issued a *fatwa* against the treaty, which would have resulted in solid opposition from all the leading Shi'is; the Euphrates leader 'Abd al-Wahid Sikkar had already persuaded most of his neighbours to refuse the mandate, and an anti-treaty *fatwa* would have had serious repercussions. The rumours were not substantiated at this stage, but they foreshadowed the major campaign by the *'ulama'* against the elections which took place in the following year.

Throughout May, June and July 1922 protests against the treaty continued. There was an important meeting between the Shamiya shaykhs and the Najaf *'ulama'* in August, during which Faysal's Shi'i go-between Sayyid Baqir ibn Sayyid Ahmad Baqir al-'Ayn announced that the king did not want the mandate and was working for its abolition. There were other meetings, public and private, in Baghdad where the leaders were Shaykh Muhammad al-Baqir al-Hilli, Ja'far Abu'l -Timman and Hamdi al-Pachachi.[25] Cox telegraphed that Faysal was untrustworthy, that he was 'crooked and insincere', and noted also that the delays were bringing most government business to a standstill.[26]

Events finally came to a head on August 23, when Cox was publicly jeered at by a crowd at the Palace on his way to offer his congratulations to Faysal at the end of his first year in office. Cox asked for, and received, an immediate apology; Faysal fell ill with appendicitis the next day, and Cox assumed full powers, packed the nationalist leaders off to the prison island of Henjam, and saw to it that the treaty would eventually be accepted. After formally submitting his resignation, and then calling together a new cabinet, the Naqib was finally persuaded to put his signature to the document on October 10, shortly before the fall of Lloyd George's coalition government in England.

Move and Counter Move: The Background to the Ratification of the 1922 Treaty

The signature of the treaty by the Naqib, as Faysal's plenipotentiary, might have been the end of the matter, but this was by no means the case: the Iraqi cabinet had only felt able to accept the treaty on condition that it would be ratified subsequently by the Constituent Assembly. This body, whose task was also to pass the Iraqi constitution, or Organic Law, had yet to be elected, and although the Treaty is dated October 1922 it was not ratified until June 1924. During this interval of nearly two years several events occurred both inside and outside Iraq which greatly changed the position and aims of the two high contracting parties to the treaty. The fall of Lloyd George's cabinet, at least partly occasioned by the threat of war with Turkey, has already been mentioned (Walder, 1969). This was shortly followed by the Lausanne conference at which Britain failed immediately to secure Mosul for Iraq, the increased Turkish pressure on the northern frontier, and the continuing anti-British and anti-treaty agitation within Iraq.

In Britain, during the early months of the Bonar Law ministry, the possibility of a complete evacuation of Iraq was earnestly considered, and a cabinet committee was formed specifically to discuss Iraq policy. It was thought that assisting Iraq to resist Turkish pressure might bring about a fresh outbreak of Anglo-Turkish hostilities for which there would be no public support in Britain. Throughout November and December 1922 the possible cession of Mosul to Turkey was seriously contemplated in both London and Baghdad. Success in western Asia Minor had made Turkish strength seem a greater menace than it actually was, and a real threat to the north of Iraq. The defeat of Britain by Turkish arms was unthinkable, but withdrawal to avoid a confrontation still remained a possibility.

The British government, wondering whether it could hold Mosul, was greatly hampered by its inability to state clearly why it should wish to do so, and a fierce 'Quit Mesopotamia' campaign was soon raging in the press. The cabinet was particularly anxious about Curzon's role at the Lausanne Conference, and feared that negotiations might break down over Mosul:

> The Prime Minister and the Cabinet, being sensitive on oil questions, were terrified lest Curzon, by taking a strong line on this matter might place them in a disagreeable position . . . He (Bonar Law) feared that Turkey might manoeuvre us into a rupture upon this question of Mosul. 'This', he wrote, 'would be the most unfortunate thing that could happen, since . . . half our people and the whole of the world would say that we had refused peace for the sake of the oil . . . If I made up my mind that we were free to leave I would certainly not be responsible for continuing to hold the Mandate.[27]

In the end Curzon succeeded in shelving rather than solving the frontier problem, by putting the matter in the hands of the League. This delay meant that the disturbances in Kurdistan continued to vex the Iraqi government, gave employment to the Royal Air Force and provoked a string of embarrassing parliamentary questions.[28]

Just before his retirement as High Commissioner early in 1923, Cox was recalled to London to appear before the Cabinet's special Iraq Committee. In the course of answers to a long questionnaire, he stated that British policy was generally popular in Iraq, except in Baghdad and the Holy Cities. He did not recommend a plebiscite for Mosul as he considered that a satisfactory peace settlement with Turkey would solve the problem. He stated frankly that the Iraqi government could not collect taxes without active British support. Evacuation from the country would be seriously prejudicial to British interests, especially the security of oil of the Transferred Territories[29] and the potential oilfields of Mosul. Cox also noted that Iraq provided an ideal training ground for the RAF, and was a vital link in the Empire air route. Finally, the High Commissioner stated, it would be especially wrong for Great Britain to violate its original pledges to the people of Basra: in his view, Britain should under no circumstances evacuate Iraq, but, if forced to withdraw, should not go farther than Basra.[30]

The change of policy resulting from this and other meetings was a 'Protocol' announcing that 'the present [i.e. 1922] Treaty shall terminate upon Iraq becoming a Member of the League of Nations and in any case not later than four years from the ratification of peace with Turkey' (quoted Ireland, 1937, 470–471), a move designed to limit future British commitments of men and money. Earlier, the British government had stated its general intentions in a Commons statement which was also designed to allay Iraqi fears:

> The Under Secretary of State for the Colonies . . . stated that after victories in Great War we were not going out of Iraq at point of Turkish bayonet. Pending conclusion of peace with Turkey we were pledged in honour not only to Allies but under international obligations not to be driven by armed forces out of (the) country. Further, we were committed to policy of setting up Arab national state in Iraq and were bound in honour to endeavour to carry that policy through and do our best for the Iraq state.[31]

The statement came in response to a plea from the new High Commissioner, Sir Henry Dobbs, for some initiative from London to ease the situation in

Baghdad, where the Iraqi government was gradually becoming paralysed because no conclusive agreement had been reached at Lausanne on the frontier between Iraq and Turkey. The situation was further complicated by Ismet İnönü's offer of independence 'to the Arabs' (which he communicated to Sharif Husayn),[32] which enjoyed a brief appeal among the less realistic elements in Baghdad. However it was some time before the British government were able to commit itself more definitely. Perhaps the reoccupation of Rowanduz by British troops on 20 April and the decision to adopt a 'Forward Policy' in Kurdistan had something to do with the timing of the announcement of the Protocol, which appeared simultaneously in London and Baghdad on 30 April and was the subject of a Commons statement on 3 May 1923.[33]

The general effect of the Protocol on Anglo-Iraqi relations was mixed, but it certainly did not result in an immediate clearing of the atmosphere. The Iraqi government's chief concern was to discover how far Britain would be prepared to assist Iraq against the Turks: would Britain continue to support Iraq's claim to Mosul under any circumstances, and how much help would be given? The real question was how much Iraq could afford to spend on its own defence and whether Britain was prepared to bridge the gap between that and actual requirements. The Protocol was welcomed by the nationalists, in so far as it placed some limit on the length of the British connection, but by this time the Iraqi government was aware of the necessity of British aid against Turkey and was alarmed at talk of its possible limitation. But the saving clause of the Protocol did not pass unnoticed:

> . . .Nothing in this Protocol shall prevent a fresh agreement from being concluded with a view to regulating subsequent relations before the expiration (of the four years).

If either the Colonial Office or the High Commission had imagined that the new arrangement would facilitate the ratification of the treaty they were to be disappointed. Preparations for the elections to the Constituent Assembly were held up by events in Turkey and Kurdistan [34] and by the *fatwas* which had been issued by the Shi'i *mujtahids* since November 1922 onwards. These delays gave time for the opponents of the treaty to marshal their forces again, so that eventually ratification was very much in the balance.

Overtures to the Shi'is[35]

It is difficult to pinpoint the chief cause of Shi'i dissatisfaction, to know whether the *'ulama'* of the Holy cities were more deeply opposed to the

Sunni government of Faysal and his followers or to the power of Britain behind the throne. At the time of the Karbala' meetings in April 1922 Faysal seems to have given serious consideration to some sort of alliance between himself and the Shi'i hierarchy against Britain; even after their 'expulsion' from Iraq in the summer of 1923 he almost immediately began secret negotiations with them over the terms under which they would be permitted to return. But while the tone of the Karbala' conference was 'pro-Faysal and anti-Treaty', the hierarchy's most powerful supporters, the dissident Euphrates shaykhs led by 'Abd al-Wahid Sikkar, were almost equally hostile to the monarchy and the Baghdad politicians. This group presented a more substantial threat and was thus especially to be feared. By November 1922 the rumours which had been circulating in the early part of the year about *fatwas* against the treaty took slightly different but more substantial form. The *mujtahids* issued interdictions against participation in the elections, and posters carrying the text of these *fatwas* were widely displayed. Their general tone was uncompromising:

> Participation in the elections or anything resembling them which will injure the future prosperity of Iraq is pronounced *haram* by the unanimous verdict of Islam.[36]

The situation was all the more serious because the *fatwas* came not only from the firebrand Mahdi al-Khalisi, but from the elderly al-Na'ini and al-Isfahani, the senior *mujtahids* of Karbala' and Najaf, and thus commanded far wider respect and obedience. It was reported from Karbala' and Ba'quba that the local election committee had tendered its resignation, and the Shi'i population seemed determined to follow the lead given by the clerical hierarchy. Faysal was quick to appreciate the implications of this development. At the end of November he wrote to Cox:

> I am fully confident that if we succeed in winning over these shaykhs and separating them from the *'ulama'* who think that they are blindly obedient to them we shall attain our desire to make a success of the elections and to ratify the Treaty without any trouble.[37]

Judging by the considerable tax arrears of various Euphrates shaykhs which remained unpaid over the next few months, the Iraqi government seems to have come to the conclusion that the only means of detaching the shaykhs from the *'ulama'* was to press very lightly in matters touching revenue.[38] As far as the Palace's relations with the *'ulama'* were concerned, there seems to have been a brief understanding between Faysal and al-Khalisi in mid-March 1923, but to little effect. The anti-election campaign, temporarily halted, started again in earnest a few weeks later, when *fatwas* against participation reappeared in Kadhimayn. The prohibitions were confirmed by al-Isfahani, al-Na'ini, and al-Khalisi, and the ban on participation in the elections was accompanied by a further *fatwa* forbidding Shi'is to assist the Iraqi government against the Turks.

In the face of this continued opposition, the cabinet decided in June that strong measures were necessary if the authority of the government was not to fall hopelessly into disrepute. After a hostile demonstration at Kadhimain on 21 June and another at Karbala' on 24 June, it was decided that al-Khalisi, undoubtedly the guiding spirit behind the hierarchy's anti-election campaign, should be deported – like many of the other Shi'i *'ulama'*, he was a Persian national – and the other leading *mujtahids* promptly left for Persia in protest. In spite of Dobbs' forecast of a 'fearsome squeal from Tehran',[39] Persian official reaction was fairly mild after the first salvoes, perhaps because of the general distraction brought about by events surrounding the rise to power of Reza Khan. It was explained that with the exception of al-Khalisi and his immediate following the *'ulama'*, had not been expelled; they were free to return whenever they wished, provided they undertook not to interfere in politics and to revoke the *fatwas* forbidding participation in the elections.

This action on the government's part solved the immediate crisis, though it naturally exacerbated sectarian hostility. The King tried to come to some friendly understanding with both Shi'i clergy and Shi'i laity, but the more influential of the leading politicians, with the general approval of the British advisors, were more concerned to put the Shi'i hierarchy in its place. Communications with Whitehall dealt with the importance of keeping clerical meddlers out of politics rather than with the more serious question of Shi'i grievances. In much the same vein, Cornwallis, the Adviser to the Ministry of Interior, wrote to Dobbs:

> Their religious beliefs alone prevent them from countenancing the Iraqi government and I believe that when they set out from Karbala' the other day they would have raised a rebellion had they had any encouragement.[40]

Throughout the mandate, in attempting to justify their frequently discriminatory policy towards the Shi'is, the Iraqi government argued that until Iraq became 'independent' the Shi'is had had no voice at all in politics, no separate courts and no publicly financed educational institutions, In general, however, the obvious imbalance of Shi'is in the cabinet, the Chamber of Deputies and in the civil service was a constantly exploitable source of irritation. More immediately important for this particular period was that Faysal was forced to abandon his attempt to broaden the basis of his support within the country, although he continued negotiations with the *'ulama'* in exile during the autumn of 1923.

The elections to the Constituent Assembly, whose task was to pass the Organic Law, or Constitution, and ratify the treaty, occupied the period between July 1923 and March 1924. The elections began on July 12 and the Assembly met for the first time on March 27. This long gap was largely due to the complex business of electoral registration and the electoral system itself, which was indirect or collegiate. Those entitled to vote, male taxpayers over 21, were duly registered, and voted for the secondary electors, one secondary elector per 250 primary electors; these then voted for the deputies. Representation for the Christians and Jews was assured by providing four reserved seats for each religion. Additionally, for the Constituent Assembly, but not for the regular Iraqi parliaments, special representation for tribesmen was provided, which had the effect of packing the Assembly with some forty tribal shaykhs.[41] The shaykhs at first formed a solid block of treaty supporters, though threats, intimidation and the passage of time gradually curbed their enthusiasm.

In the course of the autumn of 1923 Faysal's constant interference in the affairs of government, and his secret negotiations with the exiled *'ulama'* brought him into open conflict with his Prime Minister, 'Abd al-Muhsin al-Sa'dun. For his part Sa'dun had considerably annoyed the King by his refusal to ensure that Faysal's name was read out before that of the Ottoman sultan in the *khutba* in the mosques of Baghdad. [42] Relations between the two men were never particularly cordial, and throughout the mandate there were occasions on which the Residency forced the King to accept Sa'dun as premier so that the latter could act as a restraining influence. In spite of Dobbs' pleas, Sa'dun resigned, and Ja'far al-'Askari, a weaker personality but a man both friendly to and trusted by the King, was appointed to head a new cabinet. Advantage was taken of this change to distribute two portfolios, Finance and Education, to Shi'is, Muhsin al-Shallash and Abu'l-Muhaysin. The High Commissioner apparently consented to the change of cabinet at this critical moment because he felt that there were limits to the extent that Faysal could be manipulated:

> So long as his Majesty is guided with a light rein I find that he confides to me with a fair amount of frankness even his less reputable

plans which can then be criticised and discouraged; but too strict and constant opposition only drives him to deceit.[43]

The change of ministry was shortly followed by an intimation from the exiled *'ulama'*, minus Shaykh Mahdi al-Khalisi, that they would now be prepared to pronounce the elections lawful. They did not in fact return to Iraq until April 1924, by which time al-Khalisi had died of apoplexy at Mashhad.

Meanwhile the election in England of the first Labour government served for a short while to cast doubt on the future shape of Anglo-Iraqi relations, but it soon became apparent, much to the chagrin of the nationalists, that continuity would be preserved. Nevertheless, the change of government gave grounds for hope in Baghdad that the terms of the treaty and agreements[44] might be modified and added force to the arguments of those opposed to their ratification.

Delays and Uncertainties, 1923–1924

Another major uncertainty was the question of the future of the Kurdish areas. Events in Kurdistan in the summer of 1923, particularly the evacuation of Sulaymaniya and Rowanduz by British troops and the reappearance of Shaykh Mahmud, gave rise to considerable anxiety about the extent of British help that could be expected over the Mosul *wilaya*, an anxiety underlined in the Assembly's rider to the treaty ratification in June 1924.[45] The apparent weakness of British forces naturally increased these uncertainties; Dobbs pointed out late in December 1923 in a private letter to Shuckburgh that it was vital that Britain should appear to be serious and determined over the frontier situation. He urged immediate ratification of the Treaty of Lausanne, and the speedy inauguration of a conference on the frontier. This, he pointed out, would also facilitate a more rapid reduction in the numbers of the British garrison.[46]

This tense situation persisted over the next months: the major problems facing the British authorities were what to do if the Anglo-Iraqi Treaty was not ratified, and if the Mosul *wilaya* was not given to Iraq. The dilemma was only partly resolved by presenting British support for Mosul as being dependent on Iraqi support for the treaty. In fact, Dobbs told the Iraqi government in March 1924 that Iraq's position in the Mosul *wilaya* would be greatly strengthened if the treaty and agreements were accepted by the Constituent Assembly before the Mosul negotiations began.[47] By the end of the month, two days before the first session of the Constituent Assembly, the agreements were accepted by the cabinet, and Anglo-Turkish talks at Constantinople on the future of the Mosul *wilaya* were scheduled to begin in May.

Any hope that the passage of the treaty through the Constituent Assembly would be a mere formality was very soon dashed. Opposition groups gradually began to form, even among those thought to be the staunchest supporters of the British connection. The Kurds and the 'loyal' tribal leaders were soon found to be wavering in their allegiance, particularly after two pro-treaty shaykhs, 'Addayy al-Jaryan and Salman al-Barrak, were attacked and beaten up by an unidentified gang, which caused a certain amount of apprehension among their colleagues. Again, a group of tribal deputies led by Salim al-Khayyun demanded, in return for their support of the treaty, the extension of the use of the *Tribal Disputes Regulation* and increased tribal representation in the future Chamber of Deputies. Finally, the terms of the agreements subsidiary to the treaty had been more demanding than the Iraqis had expected. Nevertheless, B. H. Bourdillon, the Acting High Commissioner, considered that ratification would be possible if he could announce that the end of the treaty, four years after the signature of peace with Turkey, would also signify the end of the mandate, even if Iraq was not yet a member of the League of Nations. He hoped to bring an end to speculation and discussion by forbidding further alterations in the text of the treaty.[48]

To ease the situation, the Colonial Office agreed to inform the Iraqi government through the High Commissioner that they would ask the League to accept the treaty, protocol and agreements instead of the mandate, and that

> H. M. Government have no intention of continuing to hold after termination of the Treaty any position in relation to Iraq other than that defined by the Treaty . . . or by such subsequent agreements as may be hereafter concluded with the Iraqi government as contemplated in the Protocol.[49]

However, such assurances did not seem to have had the desired effect, and it became clear a few weeks later that an emergency policy was needed in the event that the treaty was not ratified. Dobbs thought that London's intentions in this respect should be publicly announced, but the Colonial Office demurred. Eventually, Dobbs was informed that if the treaty had not been ratified by the time the Permanent Mandates Commission met on 11 June, H.M. Government would have to get the League's consent to an as yet unspecified 'alternative arrangement':

It will be seen that formula outlined

i)   Does not commit H. M. Government to any definite course of action if Treaty, etc. are not accepted and

ii) Leaves initiative to H. M. Government and not the Permanent Mandates Commission in proposing an alternative.[50]

The Treaty in the Chamber of Deputies

By now there was every indication that a direct confrontation was approaching. After the 'Id adjournment, which finished on 10 May 1924, only 54 of the 110 deputies elected took their seats in the Chamber, two short of the number required to form a quorum. In the next few days there were noisy street demonstrations and on 29 May armed followers of Salim al-Khayyun paraded outside the Assembly building, some actually penetrating to the Chamber itself.[51] On 2 June Dobbs cabled:

> Assembly met today and a succession of speakers denounced the Treaty in unmeasured terms. I do not think that there is the slightest chance of its being accepted. I shall immediately cause Faysal to dissolve the Assembly if Treaty is rejected before I receive H.M. Government's decision.[52]

The treaty and agreements were eventually ratified in circumstances of high drama on the evening of 10 June, the day after the breakdown of the Anglo-Turkish talks in Constantinople and just in time for the meeting of the Permanent Mandates Commission, by a majority of 13 (37 for, 24 against, 8 abstentions). A compromise was inserted in the last sentence of the resolution which passed the treaty, rendering it null and void if Britain failed in its efforts to secure the Mosul *wilaya* for Iraq. However, as the Colonial Office was able to point out, Britain was no longer responsible for this, since the matter had been passed to the League.[53]

The Significance of Ratification

The ratification of the treaty was vitally important for the continuation of the mandate relationship. Since direct control had been formally abandoned in 1920 it was essential that Britain's Iraq policy should be acquiesced in by the Iraqis. British terms had not only to be accepted but to be seen to be accepted: hence the plebiscite of 1918–19, the referendum for Faysal's election, the elections to the Constituent Assembly and the ratification of the treaty in 1924. The resumption of direct control was no longer a practical possibility; the arrangement actually in force brought sharp protests from the United States at its implied economic exclusivity, and British military involvement on the northern frontier proved almost too much for British public opinion to swallow. Furthermore, closer control would have greatly increased the price to be paid for the relationship:

> [T]he success of the Iraq experiment is primarily dependent upon the extent to which Iraq may prove capable of paying for her own administration, including her defence, and meeting her obligations, including those to Britain and the Ottoman Debt Administration.[54]

By the time that the ratification question had reached crisis proportions, Dobbs was realising that there were limits to the amount of pressure which could profitably be brought to bear on the Iraqi government. He pointed out that one of the consequences of the Protocol of April 1923 was that Britain was now trying to secure the same financial settlement with Iraq in four years as had been originally contemplated in twenty, while expecting Iraq simultaneously to take responsibility for its own defence. Rather tongue in cheek he had written to the Colonial Office in February:

> It is obvious that H. M. Government are not likely to wish to weaken or destroy by excessive demands the State which they have been at such pains to set up.[55]

Clearly, the Iraqi state was not in a position to bear the crushing weight of excessive political, financial and military demands at this time. Writing about defence Dobbs stated firmly in June that:

> [I]nsistence on complicated agreements of this kind . . . had helped to bring about the present political situation by making it appear to the Iraqi public that HBM's Government is desirous of binding them hand and foot. I should prefer to settle each question as it arises . . . [56]

This 'meticulous insistence on paper pledges'[57] was the cause of many of the crises which developed over the course of the next few years. Iraqi governments were constantly asked to enter into agreements which they either could not possibly afford (such as payments to Britain and the Ottoman Debt Administration) or which they found humiliating and difficult to justify to the Iraqi public (parts of the treaty and agreements).

Ultimately most of the difficulties and disagreements affecting Anglo-Iraqi relations came either from the high cost of many of the measures which Britain insisted on the Iraqis carrying out, or from the obviously subordinate relationship to which the actual texts of the documents relegated Iraq's role. In time, some of the more visibly objectionable features of the Anglo-Iraqi relationship were to be ironed out, but this development was sufficiently long delayed to encourage the growth of deep resentments, and a determination to obstruct as far as possible anything that might be construed as a limitation on Iraqi sovereignty.

Nevertheless, the rough passage afforded the treaty does not seem to have caused more than very momentary misgivings in Whitehall: the Empire air route, the oilfields, the RAF training ground, British prestige and investments, could not be given up simply because the Iraqis did not want them. But it was important that the Iraqis should be able to be presented as desiring the continuation of the British connection. Even the fierce opposition to ratification in Iraq should not be allowed to obscure the vital dependence of the Iraqi government on Britain for its continued existence. This dependence resulted, as we have seen, from the very limited basis of the government's support within the country and the general lack of feelings of national identity.

> [C]oncerning the political life of the country it is difficult to speak. An Iraq nationality has hardly yet developed. Men feel the ties of loyalty to their tribe or their town or family more than to their country. A patriotic sense of public duty is often lacking . . . There are as yet no political parties and not even any very clear personal programmes (*Iraq Report*, 1924: 17).

It was of course vital for the government that such a sense of national solidarity be developed as quickly as possible, but its own activities did not encourage this. The government's confrontation with the *'ulama'* had lost it the active support of most of the Shi'is, and even Kurdish participation in the elections derived more from a desire to get British support for a Kurdistan free from Turkish influence than any solidarity with the Iraqi government: many Kurds still hankered after a wholly independent Kurdistan. Hence the government bought the loyalty of tribal shaykhs and landlords with tax remissions and concessions so that they would be discouraged from active hostility towards it.[58] Ultimately, the only support on which the regime could rely permanently was that of Britain, which in practical terms meant the cooperation of the RAF in dealing with hostile elements. In May 1925, after a visit to Iraq, Leo Amery, the Secretary of State for the Colonies, wrote of the RAF:

> It is due to its ceaseless vigilance that the work of political construction is able to proceed. Without its presence the novel experiment which we are conducting in the country would have no chance whatever of success . . . If the writ of King Faysal runs effectively throughout his kingdom it is entirely due to British aeroplanes. If the aeroplanes were removed tomorrow the whole structure would inevitably fall to pieces.[59]

Thus a vicious circle was created. However 'nationalist' and 'independent' the Iraqi government tried to be it was always forced into a position of subjection to Britain because of its own weaknesses. By 1924 the more permanent members of the Iraqi government realised that there was no escape, and that the only hope of amelioration lay in tinkering with the details of the Anglo-Iraqi relationship, and trusting that Britain might eventually be persuaded that greater liberality over, for instance, the Iraqi Railways or the Transferred Assets, would pay some sort of dividends. Furthermore, the more practical among the politicians were not slow to realise the more tangible rewards of co-operation which accrued from their remaining in office. Yasin al-Hashimi and Nuri al-Sa'id, former soldiers in the Ottoman Army, took advantage of their positions both to acquire lands and to pass laws either validating the transactions or securing tax exemptions, and even 'Abd al-Muhsin al-Sa'dun was not above using his office to advance his family's claims in the Muntafiq.[60] If accommodation was a distasteful necessity, it could at least be made to pay.

3

OIL, BOUNDARIES AND INSOLVENCY: POLITICAL AND ECONOMIC PROBLEMS, 1924–1926

The oil of Mosul, the location of the northern frontier of Iraq, and the financial problems and difficulties of the Iraqi government, formed the chief preoccupations of Anglo-Iraqi relations during the two years which followed the ratification of the treaty by the Constituent Assembly in June 1924. These three issues are closely interconnected, though each has its own history and background. Exploitation of Iraqi oil by any or all of the Allied powers required that Mosul should remain part of Iraq, and ensuring that Iraq would be able to defend its territory involved straining the meagre financial and strategic resources of the Iraqi government to the utmost, emphasising yet again its heavy dependence on Britain. In order to understand how these three issues impinged on one another and on the course of Anglo-Iraqi relations, the more strictly chronological framework of the previous two chapters will be set aside. We shall first examine the role of oil in Anglo-Iraqi relations, then the problems surrounding the Turco-Iraqi boundary, and finally the financial difficulties the Iraqi government incurred under the circumstances of the mandatory relationship.

Great Britain and Iraqi Oil

Although Britain's dominant role in the exploitation of Iraqi oil was probably the most enduring result of its involvement in the country's affairs, it always seemed rather bad manners to say so, largely, perhaps, because of the vigorous public denials of the connection made by statesmen at the end of the War and in the early 1920s (Monroe, 1981: 101). Until the early 1970s, few commentators explictly examined the role of oil in British policy either in the context of one of the stated objectives of IEF 'D'[1] or in the context of British efforts to secure the Mosul *wilaya* for Iraq. However, the evidence assembled by Mejcher (1976) shows beyond reasonable doubt that oil at least as much as strategic considerations dominated British official thinking towards Iraq. It is certainly true that Britain's subsequent interests in Iraqi affairs approximated very closely to the interest of the Iraq Petroleum Company. Details of the oil companies' connections with the British government are too complex to be discussed adequately in this chapter, but the inter-weaving of public and private interest is plainly discernible:

> With regard to the present situation I do not see what we can do to prevent combines and syndicates on a large scale being formed for the eventual exploitation of oil resources in any part of the world . . . I hear quite vaguely that Lord Inchcape and *Messagéries Maritimes* are the moving spirits in the new combine of which you speak. Lord Inchcape is, I understand, a member of the Petroleum Executive and also a Director on behalf of H. M. Government of the Anglo-Persian Oil Company. The Petroleum Executive, I believe I am right in saying, is largely composed of people who have a direct personal interest in oil enterprises. What can one expect, therefore when private and public interests are inextricably mixed up in a Government body of control?[2]

For a closer understanding of the events of the post-war years it is necessary to consider the evolution of British oil policy and trace the development of British commercial interest in Middle Eastern oil.

The Basis of British Oil Policy

Once oil began to be widely used by the world's navies, it was considered essential that supplies and reserves should be freely available, that the Great Powers should be able to ensure that their own access to sources would not be impeded. Hence the guidelines of British oil policy were formulated very quickly: that Britain should be in a position of political influence or control in the territories where oil was known, or equally important, thought likely, to exist, and that other powers should be excluded as far as possible, both politically and commercially, from these areas.

The appreciation of the potential usefulness of oil as a fuel for the British navy antedates the beginning of this century. Arthur Marder notes that Admiral Fisher was known as the 'oil maniac' as early as 1886 'in naval and departmental circles' (1961: 45). In the years before the First World War, when Fisher was First Sea Lord and Churchill First Lord of the Admiralty, this enthusiasm was translated into practical results.[3] In 1912 a Royal Commission was appointed to investigate the question of oil supplies in the context of naval requirements;[4] it agreed with Churchill that: 'we must become the owners or at any rate the controllers at the source of at least a proportion of the oil which we require',[5] a point of view put forward again in almost identical terms by Admiralty spokesmen at the time of the Lausanne Conference.

At this time, the great bulk of world oil supplies came either from the United States or Mexico, which was then dominated by the United States. However, smaller quantities of oil were also being produced in Rumania and Russia, and, since 1909, a small trickle from Persia, where production and marketing was being carried out by a single British company. The Anglo-Persian Oil Company (APOC) had been formed by W.K. D'Arcy to exploit the concession which he had been granted by the Shah in 1901, and the Abadan refinery produced 273,000 tons of oil in 1914, its first year of operation. It should be remembered that APOC remained the sole oil producing undertaking in the Middle East until 1927; its operations were first confined to Persia itself and then extended to the Naft-Khana fields in the Transferred Territories, where production began in 1923.

In the Ottoman Empire, numerous rival international groups had made bids for oil concessions between 1900 and 1914. Their persistence may have caused the Ottoman authorities to realise that they had powers of disposal over a commodity of more than passing value and to temporise accordingly. Eventually, in 1912, a group consisting of British, Dutch and German interests managed to combine to form the Turkish Petroleum Company (TPC)[6] which was given, in rather obscure circumstances, a concession to prospect for oil in the Baghdad and Mosul *wilaya*-s just before the outbreak of war. German interests had already obtained mineral rights over the land on either side of the proposed Baghdad railway line under the railway concession in 1903. The participants in the TPC agreed that they would not interest themselves in the production of oil in any part of the Empire 'otherwise than in association with their TPC colleagues' (Longrigg, 1961: 30). This was partly an attempt to prevent US interests gaining access to the area, France having not as yet seriously sought a foothold, and partly an attempt to force the hand of the Ottoman authorities by reducing the number of concession hunters. In April 1913 a merger between the Anglo-Persian and Turkish Petroleum Companies was proposed, which took place a year later.[7]

Prompted, as has been mentioned, by the Admiralty, the British government had for some time taken a considerable interest in Middle Eastern oil. In 1913, in the course of the Turkish Petroleum Company's negotiations with the Ottoman authorities, the Ottoman Ambassador in London was handed a statement of intent by the Foreign Office:

> H. M. Government . . . rely on the Ottoman Government to make without delay arrangements in regard to the oil wells of Mesopotamia which will ensure British control and meet with their approval in matters of detail.[8]

However, the most important expression of the British government's interest in oil was its decision to purchase 51% of the shares of Anglo-Persian a few days before the outbreak of war in 1914, a transaction which automatically gave it a substantial interest in the Turkish Petroleum Company at the same time.

All possibility of the TPC actually being able to take up its concession had to be abandoned following the outbreak of war. No prospecting was undertaken during the war itself, but surveys, whose general indications were highly favourable, were carried out in slightly *sub rosa* circumstances in 1919.[9] During the war, as is stated in the Curzon/Colby correspondence, a certain amount of oil-working had taken place to provide for the daily requirements of both the British and Ottoman armies.[10] A cabinet memorandum of June 1921, *Petroleum in Mesopotamia and Palestine*, referred to the German-worked wells at Qayyara yielding 10, 000 gallons a day in wartime, with lesser quantities being extracted at Tuz Karmatli, Qala' Naft and Zakho. The report admitted that deep drilling had yet to be undertaken, but stressed the close geological correlation between the areas north of Baghdad and the Maidan-i Naftun field in Persia:

> It is not possible to give any estimate of the potential production of Mesopotamia as this can only be determined when deep drilling has been carried out over a wide area. There is no doubt however, that this region can safely be regarded as extremely promising. The actual output of the Maidan-i Naftun field in Persia is at present two million tons per annum, and this quantity could if necessary be very materially increased from the wells already drilled.[11]

Post-War Policy

In the period after the war, the question of British control of Middle Eastern petroleum was a subject of intense concern to several departments in Whitehall. It was above all vital that no power should be in a position to deny Britain access to supplies. A Foreign Office memorandum of March 1918 had noted that this was a matter which 'cannot be treated as a purely commercial venture but must be envisaged as a national responsibility, which admits of no half-measures or ill-considered action.'[12] At a conference at the India Office later in the year, Colonel A. T. Wilson explained that:

> . . . oil is the only immediately available asset of the Occupied Territories, the only real security the Iraq administration are in a position to offer for the loan which they will undoubtedly require in the near future from the British Treasury.[13]

As we have seen in Chapter I, 'every effort was made to score as heavily as possible on the Tigris before the whistle blew', with the result that General Marshall, following instructions from the War Office, captured Mosul (thus gaining *de facto* control over the Mosul *wilaya*) some three days *after* the Armistice of Mudros.[14]

The immediate problem facing the British government was that of devising circumstances under which the oil could actually be exploited. In the world which emerged after 1918, in which the principle of 'economic equality' was paramount, no one country could be seen to dominate the trade of another, especially if the dominating country was not the United States of America. From this arose the long struggle which developed after the war for the control of the oil resources of the Middle East, especially those of Iraq. As a consequence of political control being so long disputed, prospecting and surveying had to be suspended as well. British surveyors had visited Iraq in 1919 and American companies were pressing the British government through the US Embassy in London for the grant of similar facilities. It seems eventually to have been decided that the adoption of a policy of *non possumus* to all comers was the least offensive solution, and after an India Office conference in October 1919 all prospecting and surveying in the Occupied Territories was halted. Curzon wrote to the American Ambassador:

> The provisional character of the military occupation does not warrant the taking of decisions by the Occupying Power in matters concerning the future economy and development of the country . . . we have also felt that to open the Occupied Territories to prospectors during the period of military tenure would be most undesirable as it would lead to a rush of speculators and others who, under the guise of simple

investigators, would aim at securing definite and exclusive rights or options from native landowners.[15]

Nevertheless, in spite of this self-denying ordinance, international negotiations over Iraqi oil took place on the implicit assumption that Britain would have the controlling voice over its development. In April 1919, before the signature of the Treaty of Versailles, a provisional oil agreement had been signed by the British and French petroleum ministers, Long and Bérenger. The French had handed over Mosul to Britain in December 1918 and had not received anything in return:[16] the Long-Bérenger agreement solved the problem by making over the Deutsche Bank's former 25% share in the TPC (confiscated during the war by the Custodian of Enemy Property) to French interests. This action was formalised a year later in the San Remo Oil Agreement.

These Anglo-French negotiations did not escape the notice of the American government, which protested sharply to Britain against what it considered to be the exclusive nature of the arrangements; the Americans particularly objected to the assertion in the San Remo Agreement that the company working the Iraqi oilfields should be 'under permanent British control'. The State Department pointed out that the agreement was in clear breach of the 'Open Door', the principle that all countries had equal rights in former enemy territories. Furthermore, it went on to challenge the basis of the Turkish Petroleum Company's claim by questioning the validity of the original concession. The agreement itself had been issued in the form of a grant from the Grand Vizier, rather than by a *firman* of the Sultan, and it remained in force largely because it was supported by the British government. Curzon asserted that Britain supported the claim; Colby declared that the US government did not. In a Cabinet paper early in 1922 Churchill noted:

> . . . There is some reason to believe that neither the United States nor France would be sorry to see the Turks back in Mosul in a position to give to their nationals the oil concessions which are at present claimed by H.M. Government for the Turkish Petroleum Company.[17]

He feared that continued American opposition was likely to jeopardise the whole future development of Iraqi oil. He argued that the vigour with which the TPC's claim had been supported in the past made a sudden withdrawal on Britain's part impossible, but that since the claim rested on a diplomatic rather than a legal basis, it was unwise to submit the matter to arbitration. This left two possibilities; either the Company's activities could be restricted to a limited concession area within Iraq, or the United States, and possibly also Italy, should be invited to participate in it. The latter alternative was ultimately adopted, and by 1923 provisional accommodation for United States interests had been agreed, to the extent of approximately a quarter of the Company's share capital. Little more was heard about the Open Door after that.[18]

While these inter-Allied disagreements were taking place, the business of maintaining British control over the areas in question continued, not without opposition. As has been mentioned, tensions were aggravated by the vigorous 'Quit Mesopotamia' campaign waged in the Northcliffe Press. However, by 1921, after the Cairo Conference and the installation of Faysal, the pattern of the general strategy followed over the next few years is discernible. Control of the areas in which oil was strongly suspected to exist was to be vested in Britain through the agency of the mandate. If other powers attempted to gain participation for their nationals, Britain would be prepared to surrender some part of the TPC's interest in order to maintain its political position. Until the status of the disputed territories had finally been decided, no oil prospecting or surveying was to be allowed. Lastly, any concession would have to be ratified by the Iraqi cabinet and parliament.

Inevitably, all the problems surrounding the development of Iraqi oil depended on the permanent inclusion of Mosul within Iraq. Oil and the frontier award are so inextricably mixed that it is difficult to discuss one except in terms of the other; in spite of all the denials, the Lausanne Conference was as concerned about oil as it was about Mosul. A letter from the Admiralty to the Foreign Office, written a few days before the opening of the Conference, underlines the nature of Britain's interest, and provides the key to British policy:

> ... from a strategical point of view the essential point is that Great Britain should control the territories on which the oilfields are situated ... provided this can be secured, the composition of the company or companies which work the oilfields is a matter of less importance.[19]

The Mosul Frontier and Iraqi Oil

It had been rightly anticipated that the Mosul question would prove the most intractable of all the problems of the Turkish peace settlement, and the subject was therefore postponed to the later sessions of the Lausanne Conference. Nicolson has described Lord Curzon's rhetorical and diplomatic skill in undermining the Turkish case, but he points out the great delicacy of the situation, especially in view of British fears of provoking another crisis with Turkey.[20] Of particular interest was Curzon's attempt to disclaim any connection between the oil of Mosul and the inclusion of the area within the state of Iraq. In his speech on 23 January 1923, Curzon argued that the existence of the oil was no more than hypothetical, and that in any case the TPC had invited inter-Allied participation in its activities:

> It is supposed and alleged that the attitude of the British Government to the *wilaya* of Mosul is affected by the question of oil. The question of the oil of the Mosul *wilaya* has nothing to do with my argument. I have presented the case on its own merits and quite independently of any natural resources that may be in the country. I do not know how much oil there may be in the neighbourhood of Mosul, or whether it can be worked at a profit or whether it may turn out after all to be a fraud . . . but both the British Government and the TPC itself recognise that oil is a commodity in which the world is interested and as to which it is a great mistake to claim or exercise a monopoly. Accordingly, the Company, with the full knowledge and support of the British Government, took steps, and negotiations have ever since been proceeding to associate the interests of other countries and other parties in this concern so that all those who are equally interested may have a share. If the enterprise is successful, Iraq will be the main gainer and I have no doubt that Anatolia will profit in turn. That is the substance of the oil affair which I have explained to the Conference in order that they may know the exact amount of influence, and that is nil, which has been exercised in respect of oil on the attitude which I have ventured to take up on the question of Mosul.[21]

The tentative nature of the first part of this passage was at variance with most of the information available to Curzon, especially the 1919 surveys, and the 1921 *Report on Palestine and Mesopotamian Oil,* both of which indicated the extremely high probability of the existence of oil in commercial quantities. Furthermore, the Admiralty letter quoted above, and Bonar Law's fears as expressed by Nicolson,[22] contrast strangely with the whole tenor of the Foreign Secretary's speech, as does his conversation with the Italian representative at the conference a few weeks earlier:

> I told Marquis Garroni that when we have definitely settled the question of Mosul (which we had no intention of relinquishing) we

would give them a share of the oil. And he expressed the most unbounded gratification.[23]

The conference broke up without an agreement on the boundary question, and in consequence the Mosul dispute was referred to the League of Nations a few days later. Inevitably, the TPC's prospecting operations were further delayed, but the general surplus of world oil supplies cushioned the company from any adverse effects of postponement. However, while the conference was still in session, the British government began to put pressure on Iraq in the hope of facilitating the bargaining with Turkey. It had been agreed at San Remo that the Iraqi government should be allowed an option of 20 per cent equity participation in the TPC. It was now suggested, early in 1923, that this option should be surrendered to the Turkish (or Turkish and Italian) government, in exchange for Turkish recognition of Iraqi sovereignty over the Mosul *wilaya*. The Colonial Office telegraphed Dobbs:

> You should point out that definite assurance of possession of Mosul *wilaya* is Iraq's main interest in Turkish treaty and is worth serious sacrifice . . . H. M. Government think that Iraq will benefit by showing that they are more concerned about integrity of their country than about oil dividends.[24]

At this stage, the 'sacrifice' was not required, because the conference failed to come to an agreement, but in 1924 the negotiations between the Iraqi government and the TPC reached a serious impasse on the same question, of whether Iraq should be allowed the promised equity participation or should simply be given royalties. Payment on a royalty basis left the government far more dependent on the Company, over whose affairs it would have no control, and meant that the country's oil income would be determined by the amount of production which the Company considered to be in its own, rather than Iraq's, best interests. Sasun Hasqayl, the Iraqi Minister of Finance, made every possible effort to secure equity participation but failed, due to the determined opposition of the TPC and his own government's inability to raise the necessary capital.

As a result, negotiations between the government and the Company were suspended between May 1924 and February 1925. By the latter date, it seemed that no Iraqi cabinet could be formed willing to take responsibility for granting a concession on the terms offered, and the Company was being equally obdurate. The points of disagreement seemed fundamental. For its part the Iraqi government wanted, apart from equity participation, a gold rather than sterling basis for its royalties. It wanted to retain for its disposal all lands outside the plots selected for exploitation by the Company. It wanted a sliding scale introduced so that more production would bring a higher percentage of royalties. Finally, it was not prepared to waive import duties on materials for the Company's exploratory operations for fear of massive abuse. Dobbs advised the Colonial Office that the normal tactic of forcing the Government's resignation simply would not work, since the terms were so widely unacceptable.[25] The Cabinet added more fuel to the flames by refusing to pay its contribution to the Ottoman Public Debt.

Eventually, compromises were made and accepted, closely following an episode in which Count Teleki, the Hungarian president of the Mosul Boundary Commission, offered to act as mediator between the TPC and the Iraqi government. It is not known what arguments he used with the cabinet, but an agreement was reached very shortly after his meeting with them.[26] The Iraqi demand for a gold basis was agreed to and the sliding scale for royalties introduced. A combination of these concessions, the Count's inter-vention, and a renewed awareness of the necessity of British support in the struggle to retain Mosul, seems ultimately to have had the desired effect. The cabinet's assent was obtained by Dobbs and the Company's negotiator, E. H. Keeling (though very nearly lost again after a disagreement over the Company's local selling price) and the concession was signed on 14 March 1925.

Although some prospecting was undertaken in the areas of the Company's concession in the Baghdad *wilaya* in the course of 1925, work in the richer areas of the Mosul *wilaya* had to await the award of the region to Iraq by the Permanent Court of International Justice. Final ratification of the concession by the Iraqi parliament did not take place until June 1926, partly because of the continuing uncertainties along the northern frontier, and partly because the British government, apparently intent on agreement at any price, had once more raised the spectre of Turkish participation in the Company. Eventually, a provision was inserted into the Turco-Iraqi treaty giving Turkey 10 per cent of Iraq's oil royalties for 25 years.

Nearly nine years after the end of the war, in April 1927, exploratory work began in earnest in the most promising areas, and on 15 October that year oil was found in enormous quantity at Baba Gurgur near Kirkuk. In spite of this important discovery, the general surplus of oil to world requirements ensured that development would proceed for the next few years at a leisurely pace, a fact of less concern to the company (renamed the Iraq Petroleum Company, IPC, in 1929) than to the Iraqi government. With very little production the government received correspondingly little revenue, while the value of the company as a major potential supplier gradually increased. To compensate for this lack of revenue, IPC agreed to lend the government £400,000 in 1931, in form of an advance against royalties. This solved the government's immediate financial problems, but since similar payments were made almost every year, the advances had the effect of making the government permanently dependent on the company for ordinary revenue. It was not until the early 1950s that oil receipts began to make a more substantial contribution to the Iraqi economy.

The two most enduring economic consequences of Britain's intervention in Iraqi affairs were first that Iraqi imports, at least until 1958, came mainly from Britain[27] and secondly that Iraq's oil resources were controlled by a British dominated company until the company was nationalised in 1972. British concern for Iraqi oil was more profound in the early days of the mandate than has been thought, and denials by statesmen that oil played any major part in British calculations seem to have been given exaggerated credence. This seems partly to have been due to the impression that the existence of large quantities of oil was at best hypothetical, and partly to the fact that the importance of the matter was unlikely to have been obvious at the time to contemporary administrators who wrote letters at the time or books later,[28] since they were concerned with more day to day issues. However, it is now possible to find archival evidence which suggests that the War Office, Admiralty, Foreign Office and Colonial Office had a fairly accurate idea of the oil potential of Iraq, and that it had been a matter of constant concern to high officials in England at least since the beginning of 1918.[29] Curzon's 'lusty denials' at Lausanne and elsewhere were probably essential in view of the state of international, and particularly American, opinion at the time.

The Mosul Boundary Dispute

In the preceding section, the incorporation of the Mosul *wilaya* into Iraq has been discussed in terms of oil politics, and there is clearly a close inter-relation between the two issues. The Mosul question also had other important ramifications within Iraqi internal politics and within Anglo-Iraqi relations. It seems probable that most of the Arab population of the Mosul *wilaya* was anxious for inclusion within an Arab state, and that this was also desired by the Sunni inhabitants of the Baghdad and Basra *wilaya*-s: without Mosul, Iraq would be a Shi'i-dominated state. As far as Anglo-Iraqi relations were concerned, the resolution of the Mosul question in Iraq's favour was an almost unique issue: it was sought with almost equal fervour by both the British and Iraqi governments.

One misleading line of enquiry should be dealt with first. It has been suggested that Britain was concerned, in the negotiations with Turkey over the Turco-Iraqi border, to establish a strategic frontier between the two countries.[30] Although this consideration may appear to be a sound one, the fact remains that it does not seem ever to have been seriously discussed either in the Colonial Office or in British official circles in Iraq. The similarities between the situation in Iraq and on the North West Frontier of British India are illusory, since strategy in India depended on the presence, at however great a distance, of a military force immensely superior to anything that could be sent against it. The practice of supporting local chiefs to police the frontiers and prevent cross-frontier raiding must be seen in the context of the forces of the Indian Army being able to tackle any really serious border violations which might pose a major threat to security. There was not, and would never be, any military force in Iraq sufficient to contain a serious invasion from Turkey. In a despatch of February 1924, Dobbs discussed the arguments for and against building a railway link between Mosul and Nisibin. He believed that Mosul would benefit economically from this route, and discounted the strategic risks:

> [T]he Northern frontier of Iraq is so essentially indefensible against Turkey by any force that Iraq is ever likely to raise that the latter will always have to trust mainly to diplomatic means to defend herself against the former.[31]

Even allowing for Dobbs' often-expressed scepticism of the ability of the Iraqi army, it is difficult to contradict this argument: no arrangement of the frontier would ever be able to act as a major deterrent in the face of a determined Turkish advance.

With this in view, British and Iraqi policy over Mosul is best seen in terms first of the desire to ensure that the oilfields remained on the Iraqi side of the *de facto* frontier, and secondly to maintain the integrity of the Iraqi state as British and Iraqi politicians envisaged it in the 1920s. The chief barrier to this policy, apart from the international wrangling over oil, was the opposition of a substantial number of Kurds, some of whom cherished varying, imprecise, but strongly maintained, notions of autonomy along the lines promised to them in the Treaty of Sèvres (August 1920). It was the extreme complexity of the Kurdish problem, and the new situation which came into being with the rise of the independent Turkish state, which accounted for many of the delays in the settlement of the frontier between Iraq and Turkey.

The Kurdish Question and the Mosul Boundary

Four days after the end of the war with Turkey, on 3 November 1918, the town of Mosul was entered and occupied by British troops, and the area of British occupation was held to extend over the whole of the Mosul *wilaya*. Kurdish nationalist groups in exile outside Turkey and local leaders in Kurdistan had long been asking for some sort of separate status for the area, and saw the defeat of the Turks and the occupation of Mosul by Britain as a golden opportunity to press their somewhat inchoate agenda for autonomy. In Iraq, two British officers with long experience of Kurdish affairs, Major E. B. Soane[32] and Major E.W.C. Noel, were instructed to begin immediate negotiations with local leaders. The Civil Commissioner in Baghdad had recommended to London on 30 October 1918 that a central council of chiefs for Southern Kurdistan should be set up 'under British auspices',[33] and after three weeks in the area Noel recommended the establishment of a Kurdish state extending as far north as Van in eastern Anatolia (some 90 miles north of the present Turco-Iraqi frontier).[34] In mid-November, again largely at the instigation of Noel (who had come to realise that he would not be able to influence events north of the *de facto* northern boundary of the Mosul *wilaya*), Shaykh Mahmud Barzinji, head of the Qadiri order in Sulaymaniya, a leader who was believed to be acceptable to a significant number of tribal chiefs in the region,[35] was appointed *hukumdar* of Sulaymaniya, with a substantial British subsidy, in the hope that he would be able to preside over a 'South Kurdish Confederation'.

However, the unity which the Ottoman defeat had produced among the Kurds of Turkey and Iraq was short-lived. Noel reported in the spring of 1919 that Kurdish solidarity in eastern Anatolia had been based largely on fears that the Allies would exact retribution for the displacement and destruction of the Armenians and Assyrians, and now that this no longer seemed likely to materialize, disputes had broken out among rival tribes, none of whom would accept the authority of any single leader.[36] The geography of the region, mountainous terrain with fertile valleys, together with traditional tribal rivalries, made the preservation of 'order' on British Indian lines virtually impossible. The complications of Kurdish politics seem almost endless, but the difficulties were increased by British predilections for the construction of tidy administrative units, governed by 'reliable' or subsided local leaders.

One major difficulty was that the whole concept of self-determination required general agreement in the recognition of suitable representatives for the 'Kurdish people'. The Kurdish leaders of the central area of northern Iraq, around Dohuk, 'Amadiya and Zakho, and of Barzan and Arbil, did not accept that Shaykh Mahmud's governorship of Sulaymaniya entitled him to be recognised as 'King of Kurdistan'; Mahmud was in fact unable to exercise any authority over Halabja and Panjwin, both only twenty miles from his capital. Another group of claimants, the Badr Khans, an ancient Kurdish family exiled to Constantinople since the mid-nineteenth century, may have had the ear of the British authorities there, but were no longer able to command support locally. This was also true of the Baban family, long resident in Baghdad.

The truth seems to have been that, had they been given the opportunity, the Kurds would probably have preferred to have been left to make their own administrative arrangements. They welcomed their freedom from Ottoman rule, and though there is some evidence that they would have been prepared to accept nominal British suzerainty, this can be explained more by their wishing to ensure that the Turks stayed away than by any active desire to be controlled by Britain. Further, the desire for Kurdish autonomy did not, because of traditional tribal and clan rivalries, at this stage produce any coherent movement towards Kurdish unity.[37] By May 1919 the British authorities were obliged to remove Shaykh Mahmud, who had succeeded in alienating almost all those upon whom he had relied to maintain his position in Sulaymaniya. A rival leader, Sayyid Taha of Neri, a descendant of 'Ubaydullah, the leader of the great Kurdish revolt of 1896, now appeared, claiming to be able to head an independent Kurdish state under British protection, but it was clear that he also had too narrow a basis of support to ensure him any lasting success.

Throughout late 1919 and for most of 1920 British troops were kept busy on the northern frontiers of Iraq. Revolts flared up everywhere; some were inspired by the Turks in an attempt to drive British troops out of the Mosul area,[38] and some were simply the normal Kurdish expression of distaste at the imposition of yet another outside authority. Gertrude Bell, with a somewhat limited comprehension of guerrilla warfare, considered that the only answer was to 'beat the *aghawat*', and thus to deprive the Kurds of those of their leaders who were preventing what she considered the more generally desired co-operation with Britain,[39] but Soane, writing more knowledgeably about actual conditions in Southern Kurdistan, showed greater insight:

> Generally the mass of people desire no change at all; above all they do not want a council for Kurdistan, they rejoice at being saved from Shaykh Mahmud, and clearly Shaykh Mahmud's rebellion failed because they did not support it. They, after all, know that we could not do anything if they chose to rise against us.[40]

Late in March 1920 the British cabinet authorised a public statement about the Mesopotamian mandate; Britain would accept it, and Mesopotamia would include Mosul. This decision was welcome news in Baghdad, but its significance was not at all welcome in Kurdistan. The decision antedated (by some five months) the Treaty of Sèvres, whose article 62 calls for " a scheme of local autonomy for the predominantly Kurdish areas lying east of the Euphrates, south of the southern boundary of Armenia . . . and north of the frontier of Turkey with Syria and Mesopotamia."[41] From that time onwards it has always been clear that the Kurds in Iraq have never wanted to be governed from Baghdad, but it has nevertheless always been considered essential, in terms first of British, and later of Iraqi, policy that they should be. Safeguards could be introduced: guarantees that the Kurdish language would be maintained and Kurdish officials employed, even the direct administration of Sulaymaniya by the British High Commissioner, but these paper promises were not enough. Even the most minimal attempts by Britain to secure some sort of special treatment for the Kurds were vigorously resisted by the Iraqi government.

By the spring of 1921 the situation in the area presented more problems than before: it was reported from Sulaymaniya that public opinion there would oppose 'even a conditional unity with the Iraqi government',[42] while Dohuk, 'Amadiya and Zakho would not object to incorporation within Iraq. Later in the summer, Rowanduz was occupied by Turkish troops, who were still there at the end of the year. No uniform treatment of the whole area seemed possible, but separate regimes for each area would naturally arouse other, so far dormant, issues; the Turcoman population of Kirkuk, about to vote solidly against Faysal in the referendum, was reported in June 1921 as 'solidly anti-Arab . . . though not anti-British.'[43]

It was not long before the British abandoned any serious consideration of separate treatment for the Kurds, and the idea of the wholesale incorporation of the 'Kurdish area' (south of the northern boundary of the Mosul *wilaya*) into the Iraq state was gradually adopted.[44] In September Cox telegraphed a summary of his own and Faysal's views. Faysal feared that if any sort of separate Kurdish state were to be encouraged, the Iraqi Kurds would join with their fellows in Turkey and Iran and thus constitute a permanent menace to Iraq. Furthermore, and this is the earliest specific statement to this effect, the King wanted the inclusion of Kurdistan within Iraq in order to secure a permanent preponderance of Sunnis over Shi'is in the Constituent Assembly. Cox concluded:

> To my mind it seems that it would be a reasonable course to work for
> the inclusion of Kurdish districts and their participation in National

Assembly on conditions of local assent and special supervision by
British Officers and if necessary by High Commissioner.

Churchill replied:

> I appreciate force of arguments in your 503 (above) – subject to
> proviso that Kurds are not to be put under Arabs if they do not wish
> to be.[45]

Of course, even this proviso was doomed to be relegated to the lumber room
of broken diplomatic promises. It soon became clear that it would simply
not be possible to allow free expression of opinion on the part of the Kurds
who were not at all content at the prospect of being permanently joined to
Iraq. It became essential to rule out the possibility of the creation of an independent Kurdistan, or anything which might make the Kurds believe that
this could be achieved. Cox wrote to Faysal in January 1922 that both Turkey
and Iraq would profit from agreement on this issue:

> . . . the effect of this will be that while having to abandon the
> contingent possibility of the Kurdish areas of Iraq joining a Kurdistan
> which would be definition be entirely independent of Turkey, the
> Turkish Government would also be free from the obligation of
> allowing the Kurdish areas of Turkey itself to opt for complete
> independence.[46]

In the absence of any immediate agreement with Turkey, however, the
security situation continued to deteriorate. Between July 1921 and
December 1922 eight British officers were killed on the northern frontier;
some were ambushed, and others killed on active military service; it was
clear that the Turkish authorities were giving more than tacit encouragement to the 'Iraqi Kurds'. In the early spring of 1922, a Kemalist official
was installed in Rowanduz; he was succeeded in June by the celebrated
Colonel Öz Demir, who gradually extended his authority through the *sanjaks*
of Arbil, Kirkuk and Sulaymaniya. Support for the Ankara government
remained strong in the area until the abolition of the caliphate on 1
November 1922, which alienated many devout Muslims (McDowall, 1996:
141, 142). By the autumn of 1922, the British authorities were forced to
bring Shaykh Mahmud back to Sulaymaniya from his exile in Kuwait in a
second attempt to bring order out of chaos, and to deal with the 'Turkish
threat'. Predictably, he proved no more acceptable, either to those who had

installed him or to those over whom he ruled, than he had been in 1919, since he was unwilling to confine his activities to Sulaymaniya, and was also clearly in contact with Turkish representatives including Colonel Öz Demir. Noel reported the situation there in October:

> I am up against the universal suspicion, in some cases almost amount-
> ing to a certainty, that we are determined to get the Kurds into Iraq
> by hook or by crook and that the election business is all eyewash (i. e.
> the elections to the Constituent Assembly) . . . I would point out that
> to the Kurdish mind the assurances that no Kurds will be forced into
> Iraq cannot be squared with the principle of Kirkuk *liwa* as an
> electoral college.[47]

The problems caused by the delays over the ratification of the treaty by the Constituent Assembly were compounded in the north by the general antipathy on the part of a large proportion of the population towards the whole idea of the Iraqi state. Kirkuk, as we have seen, had little enthusiasm for Iraq, and even less for Shaykh Mahmud. Furthermore, as the leading citizens of Kirkuk town pointed out, while they knew of and did not like the arrangements Britain had made for Iraq, they had no idea what Britain intended for Sulaymaniya and the rest of Kurdistan. C.J. Edmonds, the Political Officer in Kirkuk, suggested inviting representatives from Kirkuk and Arbil *liwas* to Baghdad to discuss a possible federation which might be arranged on the lines of an Indian Political Agency.[48] It soon became widely apparent to the Kurds that there was no longer any hope for Kurdish independence, but merely a very limited form of autonomy within Iraq; Kurdish disapproval of this arrangement explains the failure of the formal offer to the Kurds in December 1922:

> H. B. M. Government and the Government of Iraq recognize the
> rights of the Kurds living within the boundaries of Iraq to set up a
> Kurdish government within those boundaries and hope that the
> different Kurdish elements will, as soon as possible, arrive at an
> agreement between themselves as to the form which they wish that
> the Government should take and the boundaries within which they
> wish to extend and will send responsible delegates to Baghdad to
> discuss their economic and political relations with H. B. M.
> Government and the Government of Iraq (*Iraq Report*, 1922–23: 38).

The terms of this invitation seem to have encouraged Shaykh Mahmud to listen more attentively to the emissaries who had been visiting him with promises of co-operation from Turkey, although he was evidently losing ground in his own bailiwick of Sulaymaniya.[49] Noel and Edmonds evidently disagreed over whether to continue to support Mahmud; reports received in the Residency were both contradictory and acrimonious, and it is difficult to get a clear picture of events in the area. What does emerge is that by the end of December a band of Turkish irregulars under Öz Demir had gained ascendancy over Shaykh Mahmud; Noel reported from Arbil that Mahmud was definitely opposed to any form of Iraqi suzerainty, that he was gaining more support in Arbil and Kirkuk and that he was financing himself from the tobacco excise.[50]

Early in 1923, after the Chanak/Çanakkale crisis (Walder, 1969), and with the failure to come to any immediate settlement of the boundary at Lausanne, it was decided that a major show of force was the only way of dealing with the situation. This development was the beginning of the 'Forward Policy' eagerly sought by the RAF as a means of proving itself, which caused considerable alarm in Whitehall.[51] Local Administrative Inspectors were informed:

> In the course of the operations it is hoped . . . to extend the influence of the Iraqi government among the Kurds who are at present not subject to it, and any opportunity which presents itself . . . should be seized upon and reported at once.[52]

Sulaymaniya was bombed early in March, Rowanduz was occupied by ground troops on 22 April 1923 and Koi and Ranya shortly afterwards. It was decided that the garrisons should stay in position until the arrival of the proposed Boundary Commission, since evacuation would enable the Turks to reoccupy at once and proclaim a *status quo* in Turkey's favour. The turbulence which continued on the frontier throughout the remainder of the year was, according to the High Commissioner, due to lingering Turkish fears that the authorities in Iraq intended somehow to give independence to 'their' Kurds, thus forcing Turkey into an embarrassing position *vis-à-vis* its own Kurdish population:

> I suggest that it might considerably ease the frontier negotiations if we could give preliminary official pledge to Turkey that in the changed circumstances we have abandoned the idea of Kurdish autonomy included in the Treaty of Sèvres and that our aim is to incorporate in Iraq as far as may be feasible under normal Iraqi

administration all the Kurdish areas which may fall on the Mosul side of the frontier as the result of the negotiations.[53]

Attacks by combined Turkish and Kurdish forces continued through the autumn and winter of 1923 and into the spring of 1924. However, by the middle of the year it was apparent that British forces had the upper hand; after the re-occupation of Sulaymaniya in July 1924, Shaykh Mahmud had fled to the mountains. In a final attempt to prove themselves a force to be reckoned with, Turkish troops crossed the Hazil Su in the autumn and attacked Assyrian settlements in the vicinity of 'Amadiya and Dohuk; on this occasion the Turks were not simply encouraging irregulars, but were employing Turkish army units. The Air Officer Commanding noted that had an attack on Zakho not been frustrated by prompt action, Mosul would have been seriously at risk.[54] It seems that the Turks were determined to make the most of the delay between the appointment of the boundary commission and the plotting of the status quo frontier, which lasted from 30 September to 15 November 1924.

We have already noticed that both the British and Iraqi governments wanted the inclusion of Mosul within Iraq; it will be equally clear that the Kurdish inhabitants of the area were at best indifferent and at worst positively hostile to this aim. In general, then:

> The new Republic of Turkey insisted that most of the Mosul province was an integral part of Turkey. Britain's occupation of the Mosul province, having been accomplished after the Armistice, did not prejudice the situation, and the League's experts agreed Turkey still had an uncontested legal right to the area. Britain, which had not yet made peace with Turkey, insisted that Iraq needed Mosul, that Mosul belonged in Iraq . . . (Shields, 2004).[55]

The Turks and the Kurds took advantage of the delay in the settlement of the frontier to keep the area as turbulent as possible: the Kurds, to gain maximum advantage in terms of control, the Turks to keep as much of the area as they could under nominal Turkish suzerainty. Neither the Turks nor the authorities in Baghdad could afford to allow independence or even autonomy to be granted in the area; the Turks were fearful of the conse-quences of an unruly Kurdish state on their borders, and the Iraqis did not wish to single out areas for any form of special treatment which would limit the authority of the Iraqi government.

In May–June 1924 Britain and Turkey once more attempted to negotiate directly over the frontier, but the talks in Constantinople broke down, and the dispute was referred to the League of Nations for final arbitration. On 30 September the League appointed a three-man international commission to investigate local conditions and generally to sound out local opinion, in an effort to discover whether the inhabitants wished to stay with Iraq or go over to Turkey. Both Britain and Turkey undertook (in advance) to accept the results of the arbitration as binding. The activities of the Commission were confined to the southern, or Iraqi, side of the temporarily demarcated frontier, the so-called Brussels line.[56] The Commissioners commenced their work with a series of meetings and interviews in London in late November, and did not arrive in Iraq until early in January 1925. We have seen that Turkish pressure increased throughout the autumn of 1924; Shaykh Mahmud's activities in the vicinity of Sulaymaniya in September 1924 had occasioned the bombing of the town by the RAF in November, a decision which occasioned some unease in London.[57] The area was therefore still in a state of unrest at the time of the Commission's visit, though the coming of winter had forced an end to serious campaigning. In the course of a visit lasting from January to March, the Commission heard evidence in Baghdad, and made extensive tours of the Mosul *wilaya* under close British supervision; at one point the members threatened to resign if facilities for snap visits to areas were not made available. They did in fact manage to travel to most of the more important centres.

Essentially, the Turkish government claimed that the Kurds and the Turks were 'brothers', while the British claimed that the Kurds did not want Turkish rule. The League Commissioners tried to apply basic principles of ethnic self-determination, thinking that Arabs would plump for Iraq and Turks for Turkey, but found the actual situation far more complicated. For instance, 'Arabs who thought commerce was better before the war spoke in favour of Turkey. Turks who believed that the countryside was more secure than previously were in favour of continued British control'. There were religious Turks who disliked Kemal's secular government, Arabs who favoured union with Iraq if the British left, and Arabs who would only want to be attached to Iraq if they could have an assurance that the British would stay (Shields, 2004). The idea of a plebiscite was dropped and replaced by the Commissioners' personal impressions of the 'alleged wishes of Mosul's population' (Beck, 1981: 264).

It emerged fairly early in the Commission's visit that its members were likely to recommend, in some form or other, an extension of the British connection. Sir Henry Dobbs wrote to the Colonial Office at the end of February that he was convinced that Iraq would be awarded the Mosul *wilaya* if British tutelage could be extended 'far beyond the Protocol period',[58] that is, well beyond the previously stipulated 'four years from the ratification of peace with Turkey'. However, the Commissioners continued their interviews and tours, causing local political officers to complain of 'paralysis' of administration and the 'well-nigh impossible strain' caused by their visits.[59] The fact was that by early 1925 the more accessible parts of the Mosul *wilaya* had been under direct and effective government control for over six years, and integration of administration and services was almost total: this period of Anglo-Iraqi control had made the prospect of Turkish reoccupation seem remote, and on the whole unwelcome.[60] Furthermore, the Commission seems to have considered that the welfare of the Christian minority population of the area, and, apparently, of the Kurds, would be better served by the Iraqi than by the Turkish government. It is difficult to gauge the Commission's attitude in the matter of the exploitation of the Mosul oilfields; Count Teleki's intervention has already been mentioned, and it is a fact that the cabinet signed the TPC concession agreement at the very end of the commission's visit.[61]

The Commission published its report on 17 July 1925, very much on the lines anticipated by Dobbs. It laid down that Mosul was to be part of Iraq, subject to an extension of the connection with Britain and subject also to safeguards to preserve the character of the Kurdish areas in such matters as administrative personnel, education and language:

> The British Government is invited to submit to the Council of the League of Nations a new Treaty with Iraq, ensuring the continuance for 25 years of the mandatory regime defined by the Treaty of Alliance between Great Britain and Iraq and by the British Government's undertaking, approved by the Council on 27 September 1924, unless Iraq is, in conformity with Article I of the Covenant, admitted as a member of the League before the expiration of this period. The British Government, as Mandatory Power is invited to lay before the Council the administrative measures which will be taken with a view to securing for the Kurdish populations mentioned in the Commission of Inquiry the guarantee regarding local administration recommended by the Commission in its final conclusions.[62]

There was some delay in the acceptance of the report, since further Turkish diplomatic efforts succeeded in referring the matter for final settlement to the Permanent Court of International Justice at The Hague. However, the Commission's report was not to be reversed, and by 18 July 1926 it had been accepted by all the parties concerned. In spite of the prolongation of the

period of mandatory control which it entailed, the Anglo-Iraqi Treaty of
January 1926, which embodied the League's recommendations, was received
without serious opposition in Iraqi political circles, except among the pro-
Turkish groups in Kirkuk, Mosul and Sulaymaniya. The note of resignation
is evident in a contemporary report of Baghdad public opinion:

> Those in favour of the Treaty, on whatever grounds, use the argument
> that the Treaty is not only essential for the retention of the Mosul
> *wilaya* but is also essential for the actual existence of the independence
> of Iraq and its monarchy . . .[63]

In the Chamber of deputies, the treaty was passed unanimously on 18
January 1926; there were 58 votes in favour, and 19 abstentions, corresponding to Yasin al-Hashimi's followers associated with his *Hizb al-Sha'b*
(People's Party). A rumour reported from Hilla suggested that the British
had arranged this token opposition to avoid criticism that they had created
an artificial unanimity.[64]

The new treaty contained no specific guarantees for the Kurds, although
high sounding declarations of intent were underlined in the course of an
impressive speech by the Prime Minister, 'Abd al-Muhsin al-Sa'dun, on
21 January.[65] It included provisions for reviewing the Anglo-Iraqi Treaty of
October 1922 every four years; on the occasion of each review, the British
government undertook to consider either recommending Iraq for admission
to the League of Nations, or, if this was not judged possible, to consider
amending the military and financial agreements attached to the 1922
Treaty.[66] The first of these reviews would fall due, in accordance with the
Protocol of 1923, in the spring of 1927. It is worth pointing out that the
1926 Treaty in no way contradicts the Boundary Commission's report; both
documents stipulate that the mandate shall continue for 25 years, but
equally, both contain clauses providing for the admission of Iraq to the
League of Nations before that date. Naturally, King Faysal and the Baghdad
politicians seized on the 'escape' clause, and began at once to work for the
earliest possible entry of Iraq into the League.

Iraq's Financial Difficulties

The third major concern of Anglo-Iraqi relations in the years between
the ratification of the Treaty and the solution of the Mosul question was
the extreme gravity of the Iraqi government's financial position. We
shall discuss the very different problem of revenue raising in another

chapter[67] but for the moment we shall review the particular financial difficulties of the middle 1920s, and the various attempts to deal with them.

Between 1924 and 1926 the Iraqi government was confronted with financial demands from all sides, as well as by emergencies requiring immediate expenditure. Severe flooding and greatly increased military and relief expenditure had added to the country's financial difficulties, but these were also reflected in the poor state of the economy. This was partly due to the bad harvest which followed the floods, but also to the severe decline in the Persian transit trade. There were several bankruptcies in Baghdad, particularly among merchants trading in sugar and cheap textiles, who were unable to get rid of their stocks.[68] Foreign investment, which the country desperately needed, was not forthcoming, probably because of the continuing uncertainties in the north.

The chief formal claims on the Iraqi treasury were first, its liability under the Ottoman Public Debt Administration (Blaisdell, 1966: 193–197) and to the British government, and secondly the stipulation that 25 per cent of all revenue should be devoted to defence, under the terms of the agreements subsidiary to the 1922 treaty. The 'debts' to Britain were rather questionable: when an official British valuation of the Iraq Railways was submitted to the Ministry of Finance in 1924, Dobbs protested to London that the figure arrived at included the Sharqat line, which was of no commercial use whatsoever and had been constructed for purely military purposes during the war, and the Kirkuk, Karbala' and Khaniqin extensions which had been financed by the Iraqi government themselves.[69] The whole history of the Iraqi Railways is a remarkable example of official penny-pinching and meanness, the more ridiculous because the British government had so very little chance of obtaining redress from its penniless dependent. Much the same is true of the Transferred Assets, the stores, military equipment and public utilities left behind or constructed by the occupation authorities. Their valuation and immediate charge to the Iraqi government account meant that the country began its existence in 1921 with an immediate deficit of 95 *lakhs* of rupees (about £63,000).

The British Treasury's general disinclination to be generous towards Iraq, a country which undoubtedly represented an enormously profitable potential investment, can probably be explained in terms first of the general currency of the principle that colonial (or quasi-colonial) territories should be able to pay their own way, and secondly of the considerable and widely criticised sums spent in Iraq immediately after the war. By 1926–27, however, Iraq's share of the Middle Eastern Services' vote had fallen considerably:

Year	Expenditure in Iraq (£ million)
1920–21	32.00
1921–22	23.36
1922–23	7.81
1923–24	5.74
1924–25	4.48
1925–26	4.12
1926–27	3.90[70]

In 1926–27, £3.1 million of the £3.9 million total was spent on defence. Since the duties of the RAF in Iraq were divided in unspecified proportions between the defence of Iraq and the defence of the Empire, the figure of £3.1 million does not represent 'straight' spending on Iraq. All in all, it was surprising to many British officials in Iraq that the Treasury should need quite so much persuading:

> . . . In a contract between two parties of an uneven strength the stronger can well afford not to insist upon too sharp a delineation of rights which it knows it will be able to enforce if the time comes when it will be necessary to do so: the weaker naturally wants to insist on full paper safeguards.[71]

It was in the interests of both the British and Iraqi governments that the latter should be able to defend itself, and spread its authority from the centre into the countryside. We shall see that the major pacification operations of the RAF on the Euphrates and elsewhere in southern Iraq were more or less complete by the middle 1920s.[72] There was, of course, no question of Iraq ever being able to defend itself against a full scale invasion from outside, but the Military Agreement was supposed to end in August 1928, after which Iraq would theoretically be responsible for its own defence.[73] The preparations undertaken by Iraq inevitably involved the government in serious shortages of money, since British aid was less than generous, and the Iraqi government was incapable of finding more revenue.[74]

By the beginning of 1925 it was clear that the Ministry of Finance would be unable to balance its budget for the coming year, a situation quite unthinkable in terms of fiscal practice at the time. The Colonial Office, determined not to spend money on bailing Iraq out, commissioned Sir E. Hilton Young, M. P., and Mr. R. V. Vernon of the Middle East Department of the Colonial Office to enquire into the financial position and prospects of the Iraqi government. Their terms of reference were:

> To enquire and report to H. M. Government and to the Iraqi government what steps should be taken to ensure that it shall be possible to balance the Iraqi budget during the Treaty period and afterwards, having regard to the requirements of the country for defence and security, administration and development, the provisions of the Financial Agreement and the obligations in respect of the Ottoman Public Debt imposed by the Treaty of Lausanne.[75]

The results of the mission, which it was hoped would be able to suggest permanent solutions to the government's financial difficulties were almost wholly, if inevitably, disappointing. It could only show the country how to make the best of its meagre resources rather than suggest ways of increasing receipts by changes in taxation or more productive uses of revenue. The mission suggested economies and reductions in salaries in the lower ranks of the Ministries of Health, Education, Agriculture and, incredibly, Irrigation. It was aptly remarked in a newspaper article in May 1925 that since irrigation was the chief means by which the government might hope to increase its resources, it was sheer madness to restrict that ministry's activities.[76]

However, if the Hilton Young report's recommendations had been carried out in their entirety, the immediate problems facing the Ministry of Finance might have been reduced, since the mission also suggested measures to be taken by Britain to ease the situation. These included a loan for the Railways, a generous reconsideration of the Transferred Assets, and the liquidation of Iraq's liabilities to the British government, which included such minor irritants as Iraq's compulsory contribution to the costs of the High Commission. The recommendations, in sum, amounted to the suggestion that the Financial Agreement attached to the 1922 treaty should be dropped.

In a despatch written a few days before the passage of the 1926 treaty through the Chamber of Deputies, the Acting High Commissioner, B. H. Bourdillon, urged that the new treaty should include a provision to the effect that H. M. Government should undertake the immediate amendment of the Military and Financial Agreements:

> It is a fact that the Treaty and Agreements would never have passed the Constituent Assembly (i.e. in 1924) had it not been for repeated

assurances both verbal and written that H. M. Government would sympathetically consider amendment of the Agreements.[77]

In the event, the new treaty postponed any efforts at amendment until the spring of 1927. However, as far as the Financial Agreement was concerned, the Colonial Office was eventually able to convince the Treasury of the futility of continuing to press for money which could not and would not be found, and a policy of greater leniency in financial matters was gradually adopted, though the relatively satisfactory resolution of these difficulties was not accompanied by an equal measure of agreement on future military policy, an area of constant conflict in Anglo-Iraqi relations over the next four years.

Until 1926, no actual relaxation of Britain's financial claims upon Iraq had taken place beyond a small grant in aid to the Iraqi army, amounting to £125,000 per annum for four years.[78] Although no payments for the Transferred Assets had in fact been made, it was widely feared in Iraqi government circles that since there had been no formal renunciation, a demand would soon be presented. There was the further matter of the Ottoman Public Debt, of which Iraq's share had been assessed at £T9.5 million; Bourdillon pointed out:

> If it were not for the Ottoman Public Debt charge Iraq would be able not only to dispense with the subsidy for the Army, but also to contribute to the cost of the Levies. Turkey herself can pay nothing on account of the Ottoman Public Debt and I presume that it is now admitted that the Iraq share is quite inequitable.[79]

By a policy of quiet procrastination, this liability was greatly reduced; by the time that Iraq stopped payment, only £T1.6 million[80] had been received by the Debt Administration. As regards the Transferred Assets, London was finally prepared to see reason; writing off the 95 *lakhs* (about £63,000) was a fairly cheap piece of philanthropy, especially as the money had been spent eight or ten years before. After appeals from the High Commissioner and R. V. Vernon (formerly of the Colonial Office, by now adviser to the Iraqi Ministry of Finance) the Colonial Secretary took up the matter personally with the Chancellor of the Exchequer:

> If I could wire out to Baghdad that we are willing to waive the claim to the Transferred Assets, and if they will play up over the oil royalty [sc. the proposed 10 per cent payable to the Turkish Government for 25 years], it may just enable us to fix everything with the Turks while

they are reasonable and so save you large sums in the long run. In any case it ought to save you far more in the next few budgets than you could ever hope to get from these trifling but bitterly resented instalments of payments for these assets.[81]

The Treasury finally surrendered its claim in June, in time for the High Commissioner to be able to announce the decision at an important state banquet on June 25.[82]

Conclusion

The events between the ratification of the treaty and the final ratification of the Mosul boundary served to emphasise Iraq's continuing subordination to Britain, which was regarded as necessary if the Iraqi government was to survive in its existing form. The government seems to have become aware, even more sharply than before, of the urgency of maintaining its relationship with the mandatory power, and also, during this period, seems to have given up any serious attempts at acts of defiance. Iraq needed Mosul for its survival; only British aid, both diplomatic and military, could secure the area, keep the Turks out and keep the Kurds reasonably quiet. Again, only Britain could close the gap between Iraq's capacity for defence spending and its actual defence needs. This indispensability, seen most clearly in the context of the Mosul question, explains the acceptance of the Iraq Petroleum Company's concession on terms which were not at all favourable to Iraq, and the government's rapid and generally willing acquiescence in the new Anglo-Iraqi treaty, prolonging the mandate from four to twenty-five years. The government was neither strong nor popular, which meant that it had to look outside Iraq in order to maintain itself in power until it had devised sufficiently strong machinery of its own.

By the middle of the 1920s, therefore, it had become clear that no further serious resistance to British pressures was likely, or even possible. The remaining six years of the mandate form a period of general cooperation with Britain, in contrast to the sharp conflicts of the earlier years. This is reflected in the gradual loosening of the formal ties binding the two governments. It seems likely that Britain, now so sure of its standing in Iraq, could afford a relaxation in control. There were, of course, running quarrels from 1926 to 1932, over such matters as conscription and safeguards for minorities, but it is difficult to avoid the impression that once the major objectives had been achieved, and provided British military bases would be able to remain in Iraq for the foreseeable future, less overt and more subtle ways of controlling the Iraqi government could be employed. It should be remembered that some eighteen months after the 1926 treaty was signed, binding Britain to Iraq for 25 years unless Iraq entered the League before the expiry of the period, responsible authorities both in the Colonial Office and at the Baghdad Residency were canvassing Iraq's possible entry to the League in 1928.[83] By that time, the British authorities seem to have come to the conclusion that the machinery of constraint could be safely left under less careful supervision, since the mechanisms were beginning to work automatically. In the following two chapters we shall see how this new relationship developed, and the various political alliances and counter-alliances which it produced.

4

THE YEARS OF FRUSTRATION,
1926–1929

In January 1926, at the time of the signature of the new treaty with Britain, 'Abd al-Muhsin al-Sa'dun had been Prime Minister for some six months, heading a cabinet which included Nuri al-Sa'id as Minister of Defence, and Subhi Nashat as Minister of Finance. The government was supported in the Chamber of Deputies by a bloc associated with the Prime Minister's *Hizb al-Taqaddum*, while the 'opposition', led by Yasin al-Hashimi and Rashid 'Ali al-Gaylani, drew its support from Yasin's *Hizb al-Sha'b* and Amin al-Charchafchi's *Hizb al-Nahdha*.[1] The general policy of *Hizb al-Taqaddum* was to cooperate with Britain and pursue independence for Iraq at whatever pace Britain seemed to be dictating. In consequence, 'Abd al-Muhsin's relations with the Residency were normally excellent, which inevitably strained his relations with King Faysal. The King, while respecting his Prime Minister's competence, saw his own role in the conduct of affairs diminishing, and, seeking to provide a counterbalance, suggested to 'Abd al-Muhsin at the end of October that members of the opposition should be given under-secretary-ships at ministries, and other measures disagreeable to the Prime Minister.[2] 'Abd al-Muhsin suggested an election, which he considered would strengthen his position in the Chamber, but the King, fearing just this result, opposed a dissolution. Annoyed at the King's evident lack of support for his cabinet, 'Abd al-Muhsin decided to make the election of the President of the Chamber of Deputies a vote of confidence in himself, so that when his nominee, Hikmat Sulayman, was defeated by Rashid 'Ali, he promptly resigned from office. The opposition, headed by Yasin, suggested that Ja'far al-'Askari should be invited to return from the legation in London to head a govern-ment which would include Yasin and Rashid 'Ali, and this course was adopted.

The real reason for this change was that the King, together with Nuri and Yasin, wanted to form a cabinet which would have a greater chance of persuading the Chamber of Deputies to accept conscription, which would enable Iraq to achieve sufficient material independence from Britain to have a good chance of obtaining full League of Nations membership in 1928. 'Abd al-Muhsin would not it was felt, be able to act contrary to the known views of the Residency, which was strongly opposed to conscription, while Ja'far would be content to act as a figurehead for Nuri, Rashid 'Ali and Yasin, all of whom, with the King, were strong advocates of it. A conscript, and therefore relatively cheap, army would be within Iraq's current means, and since military self-sufficiency was considered a vital criterion for independence, a pro-conscription cabinet would have a better chance of achieving early League membership.

Conscription as a Political Issue

The role of the Iraqi army, together with the functions of the RAF, will be discussed in Chapter 7. However, the controversy surrounding the introduction of conscription had important effects both on Anglo-Iraqi relations and on the internal politics of Iraq, and it is appropriate to separate the political from the specifically military aspects of the problem. Under the arrangements in force in the autumn of 1926, the Military Agreement of 1924 would terminate at the end of 1928. At that time, in theory, Iraq would assume full responsibility for its own defence. How, in practice, could this be achieved? There seemed to be two alternatives. First, that Iraq should request Britain to continue to allow the RAF and the Levies to come to the assistance of the Iraqi government in situations where it was unable to exert control adequately through the Iraqi army. At the same time, pressure would be brought on Britain to make good the inauguration of an Iraqi air force, which had been promised under the 1924 Military Agreement but whose formation had been successfully blocked by the Air Ministry (perhaps fearing that the RAF might thereby be made redundant).[3] During the visit of the Secretaries of State for Air and the Colonies to Baghdad in the spring of 1925, Dobbs had declared:

> The experience of the past two years supports my contention that 9,000 efficient ground troops would keep internal order as an appendage to a sufficient mercenary air force.[4]

He favoured the formation of exemplar units, with technical assistance to be provided by a British Military Mission. Clearly, such an army would necessarily have been limited to the role of maintaining internal security: Dobbs did not visualise the possibility of Iraq alone ever being able to defend herself against invasion from outside, a view which did not imply an early end either to the British military presence or the British mandate.

The second alternative was that favoured by King Faysal and his close personal associates, most prominent among whom were the ex-Ottoman soldiers Nuri and Yasin. They wanted a much larger army (figures of between fifteen and twenty thousand were mentioned) together with an Iraqi Air Force. Only this, they considered, would be sufficient to guarantee the country's independence, for only with so large an army could Iraq even attempt to dispense with British military help. Yasin, who was Prime Minister at the time of the discussions in April 1925, took exception to Dobbs' scheme on two main grounds:

> . . . first, that what was most badly needed for the Iraq Army was rapid expansion which would only be got by conscription, and secondly that the Iraq people would believe the scheme to be a plan for putting their army under British control.[5]

The pro-conscription lobby gained an important ally in the person of Major-General Daly, the Inspector-General of the Iraqi army, who had arrived in Baghdad in the early summer of 1925. After a few months' exposure to the King and Nuri he seems to have become convinced of the soundness of their views. By March 1926, Daly had prepared a defence scheme for Iraq, which took account of the gradually decreasing role to be played by British forces. The scheme was designed to maintain existing defence strength, but with a greater military commitment on Iraq's part. The plans outlined were infinitely more ambitious and grandiose than Dobbs desired, and rested on principles to which he was fundamentally opposed. The Inspector-General envisaged a total of 19,000 troops, including the Iraqi army, the Levies and an Iraqi air force. Even without the air force it would cost 119 *lakhs* of rupees (£80,000), while the High Commissioner's own scheme would cost only 51 *lakhs* (£34,000).[6]

The Forces against Conscription

The largest flaw in the proposed scheme, apart from the obvious impossibility of raising the money required, was the fact that however much conscription might appeal to ex-officers of the Ottoman Army, it would meet with serious opposition from much, if not most, of the rest of the population of the country. The Sunni townsmen would officer the army, and thus be able to

assure the dominance of town over countryside, while the Shi'i tribes in the
south, and the Kurds and Yazidis in the north, would most likely not
acquiesce in the scheme for precisely that reason. In spite of the reforming
decrees of the nineteenth century, conscription under the Ottomans had been
arbitrary and brutal, and the Shi'i tribes had borne the brunt of it. Both the
High Commissioner and Colonel Kinahan Cornwallis, the Adviser to the
Ministry of the Interior, were well aware that conscription would be
strenuously resisted if it was introduced. Furthermore, as Cornwallis pointed
out, its application would strengthen the hands of tribal shaykhs, who would
be able to pay off old scores by picking tribal sections led by their rivals for
the leadership and sending them off to the army.[7] Certain areas, especially
the Euphrates below Baghdad, would have to be excluded; in fact, if
conscription were to be introduced at all the tribal areas would be better
removed from its application.

In addition to this limitation of the field of recruitment, there was
another important objection. In the same despatch, the High Commissioner
pointed out:

> It is to my mind out of the question that British aeroplanes should
> bomb Iraq tribesmen for resistance to conscription for the Iraq Army
> and should thus divert against the British in Iraq the discontent which
> will inevitably be produced by an attempt to enforce among the tribes
> a policy never enforced by the Turks. If the Iraq Army and the Police
> are likely to be strong enough by 1928 to see through a policy of
> conscription among the tribes, let them see it through.[8]

In the following month, October 1926, the Iraqi government presented
Dobbs with a draft conscription law. By submitting the draft, together with
his own comments, to the Colonial Office, Dobbs left Whitehall with little
alternative but to tackle the problem and to reach conclusions identical to
his own. Shuckburgh pointed out that the use of British troops to enforce
conscription in Iraq would meet with serious opposition from other government departments, and indeed, more generally in Britain. Conscription was
'a policy which is against all our traditions and which has never been enforced in this country (sc. Great Britain) except for one brief period . . .
during the stress of the Great War.'

He continued:

> Sir Henry Dobbs suggests a middle course. He proposes that we
> should allow the Iraqi government to proceed with their law but

should warn them in advance, that if it leads to trouble they must not expect our help. Sir Henry Dobbs apparently hopes that the Iraqi government, knowing that they cannot count on support from us, will realise that the task is beyond their powers and will drop the project. If so, well and good, but it is in the nature of a gamble and like other gambles may not come off. But in all the circumstances I can see no better alternative.[9]

The decision, that active British support would not be given, was communicated to the Iraqi government in January 1927. Although there was no official announcement, the attitude of the Residency, and, by extension, of the Colonial Office, was well known in Baghdad political circles. In the middle of May, Faysal complained somewhat naively to Dobbs that he felt that the conscription law would not command a majority in the Chamber of Deputies unless it was helped by popular enthusiasm:

> which he maintains would be created by the desired announcement that H. M. Government will at the close of the Protocol period press for Iraq's admission to the League . . . Unless he can obtain it he thinks he will have to withdraw the conscription bill. This would make it impossible for Iraq to afford troops to replace the British forces and make all discussions regarding the new military Agreement very difficult.[10]

As this conversation implies, there had as yet been no formal announcement that British troops would *not* be used to enforce conscription: Dobbs, fearing a cabinet crisis, had urged meeting Faysal's wishes thus far, and not insisting on a formal statement unless direct questions were asked in the Chamber of Deputies.[11] By mid-May 1927, with no discernible progress either on conscription or the revision of the agreements, which would enable Iraq to enter the League in 1928, the cabinet's resignation was expected daily.[12]

At this point it was rumoured in Shi'i circles that a new cabinet would contain as many as three Shi'is, provided that they agreed to support conscription. According to Ridha al-Shabibi, the King had promised him the Ministry of Education, and Muhsin al-Shallash the Ministry of Irrigation and Agriculture: al-Shabibi told the King that the country as a whole was opposed to conscription, and that none of his group, the *Hizb al-Nahdha*, was prepared to cooperate with the Cabinet.[13] On the following day, 27 May, the King again begged the Shi'i politicians to support the cabinet on the issue, but al-Shabibi told his audience at the *Nahdha*'s headquarters that

since the British were opposed to conscription they should not fall in with
the King's wishes. The *Nahdha* members agreed, and suggested further that
any Shi'i supporting the cabinet should be threatened with dire
consequences.[14]

By this time Faysal was clutching at straws. Dobbs reported to London
on 27 May that the whole matter of the cabinet's threatened resignation had
been staged by the King in order to enable the cabinet to make public their
criticisms of Britain's dilatoriness over military policy and the question of
Iraq's entry to the League. Faysal apparently hoped that this would jolt
Britain into beginning negotiations at once. Dobbs 'found it difficult to
combat in respectful terms this petulant and childish plan,' and advised the
King to refuse to accept the cabinet's resignation, informing him at the same
time of his own efforts to obtain London's approval of a policy of silence over
the exact nature of British participation in the enforcement of conscription.[15]
Four days later it was reported that the cabinet had withdrawn its
resignation:

> Public opinion in Baghdad is now convinced that the threats and
> manoeuvres of the Cabinet were merely intended to impress and
> coerce the British into agreeing to support the conscription bill and
> secure modification of the Military and Financial Agreements. It is
> said that unless the British will support the Government in putting
> the Bill into effect, it matters little whether the law is passed or
> not.[16]

On 1 June, Dobbs was told that the Iraqi government need not announce
that British assistance would not be forthcoming, and on 8 June, the last day
of the Parliamentary session, the Conscription Bill was given its first formal
reading in the Chamber of Deputies. As had been expected the Shi'i Minister
of Education, Sayyid 'Abd al-Mahdi, resigned immediately, but with the
ending of the session, the issue slipped quietly into the background for the
time being.[17]

Prelude to Deadlock: Iraq's attempts to secure League entry for 1928

Though conscription was a major preoccupation in Iraqi political circles at
this time, it was of course subsidiary to the wider question of whether
Britain would be prepared to countenance the prospect of Iraq entering the
League of Nations in 1928. Considering the matter in the spring of 1927,
Dobbs realised that supporting entry in 1928 would run the risk of oppo-

sition from the League, because of the recommendations of the Boundary Commission's report, and 'strong French opposition on other grounds.' He felt, however, that considerable progress had since been made in Iraq, and that the report thus bore little relevance to current conditions within the country. Furthermore, he believed that the relative tranquillity which now prevailed was due to the Iraqi conviction that Britain would press for Iraq's early entry to the League. He suggested that outstanding defence problems could be solved by the conclusion of:

> [A] Treaty of specially close friendship with Great Britain the terms of which will not be such as to disqualify Iraq for membership . . . (and) which Iraq would be likely to accept (which would include) . . . the stationing for some years in Iraq of a comparatively small and cheap British Air Force and a promise to train up an Iraq Air Force during that period, a renewal of the portions of the Military and Financial Agreements necessary for its maintenance there, including especially the power of refusal to lend its aid unless the policy of Iraq conforms to our wishes . . .[18]

Although the political situation in Baghdad had calmed down for the time being, Dobbs continued to be concerned at the behaviour of the King and his immediate circle. In a personal letter to L. S. Amery, the Colonial Secretary, on 14 June, he suggested that the King, Yasin and Nuri were deliberately trying to confuse the issue by putting it about that *all* British forces would leave Iraq at the end of 1928, whereas in fact it had already been agreed that the RAF would stay. They wanted to build up 'a large army free of British control, and at the same time to be helped and safeguarded by us while in the process of making this army'. Further, they maintained that such an army could only be created by conscription, and again, that the Iraqi parliament would only consent to conscription if it was told that Iraq would enter the League in 1928. For his part, Faysal realised that he needed the RAF to stay on, but believed that Britain was equally anxious to keep air squadrons in Iraq to protect the oil, imperial communications and other British interests. Hence, as the High Commissioner saw it, Faysal would make a bargain; Britain would recommend Iraq for membership of the League in 1928, and in return, Faysal would allow the RAF to stay on in Iraq for a limited period. Additionally, the King and the Iraqi government would require to be given complete control of the Iraqi army. Britain would not, whatever happened, want to leave Iraq in chaos, since this would be as inimical to their interests as to Iraq's. On the other hand, if Britain would not yield, the King and his circle might attempt to start a rising in favour of complete independence:

> What the King, Nuri and Yasin want to do is, on the one hand to rouse anti-British feeling or demonstrations sufficiently to pass conscription and frighten the British Government into relaxing all control, and on the other hand to smother the agitation when they have gained their ends and return bowing and smiling to a comfortably relaxed British alliance. The King took precisely the same position in 1922 when Cox was insulted at the Palace. The King's fortunate attack of appendicitis then saved the situation. We cannot count on appendicitis again.

The High Commissioner considered that if the RAF was to remain in Iraq after 1928, there should be no question of any relaxation of British control over the Iraqi armed forces. Thus both the Palace and the Residency considered that they possessed the trump card: Faysal believed that the British would not leave because of the oil, and Dobbs believed that Faysal could not hold his throne without a British military presence.[19]

In London, discussions were taking place on military policy, and the general question of League entry. The Chief of Air Staff, Sir Hugh Trenchard, considered that the Iraqi government already had far too much control over the Iraqi army, and also that it was labouring under the mistaken impression that independence was just around the corner. When informed by Sir Samuel Wilson of the Colonial Office that British policy was directed to just this end, 'Sir Hugh Trenchard retorted in effect that it was time that this playacting ceased. He had on several occasions been informed by several members of the Cabinet that they had no intention of withdrawing from Iraq at however distant a date provided it was possible to retain a hold on the country; the present policy was only designed to meet criticism in this country and in Iraq.'[20]

Eventually it was agreed that Britain should maintain the RAF in Iraq, train and equip an Iraqi Air Force, and maintain two battalions of Assyrian Levies as imperial troops to act as aerodrome guards.[21] On 6 July 1927, after these arrangements had been agreed upon by the British Government, Dobbs was told to communicate them to the cabinet in Baghdad, together with the assurance that Britain would support Iraq's candidature for the League in 1932, provided that the present rate of progress was maintained The Iraqi government might, if it so wished, make a public statement to that effect.[22] A few days later, Dobbs flew to London to discuss the situation with the Colonial Secretary. It was decided that amendment and revision of the 1926 Treaty could usefully be commenced, but on an informal basis until the autumn when Britain would be prepared to announce its agreement.[23] This proposal seems to have been occasioned by immediate as well as long term political considerations: Dobbs was anxious to find some means of getting Faysal away from Baghdad, where his constant interference was affecting the whole running of the administration. Accordingly, on 21 July, Faysal was told that the Colonial Secretary personally favoured revision of the treaty and agreements.[24]

Unfortunately for the tranquillity of Anglo-Iraqi relations over the next few months, Faysal seems to have taken this communication as containing the promise of a far more substantial improvement in Iraq's status than was in fact being offered: he left almost at once for Europe, under the impression that entry to the League in 1928 still remained a possibility.[25] This confusion greatly complicated matters both in Baghdad and in Switzerland (where Faysal took up residence). Political circles in Baghdad were convinced that Faysal would bring back complete independence, or something very close to it, from Europe.[26] In the course of meetings with J.H. Hall and Sir John Shuckburgh of the Colonial Office at Aix-les-Bains early in September, it became clear that Faysal imagined that he had been summoned to Europe for this very purpose:

> He declared that unless he could take back with him a revised Treaty he would not return to Iraq . . . His visit to Europe had been the subject of general discussion and high expectations had been raised. If he returned empty-handed, not only would the disappointment be intense, but he himself would suffer an irreparable loss of prestige.[27]

Over the next few months, relations between Faysal and the British government were tense and strained, as the King continued to stand firm, refusing to go back to Iraq empty-handed. In Baghdad there was rumour and confusion, and a bewildering and constantly changing variety of political groupings and alliances. In the earlier part of the year, relations between leading Sunnis and Shi'is had become more than usually tense, largely over the possible introduction of conscription. The unease and dissatisfaction expressed by some Shi'i politicians upset the 'nationalists', who feared that failure to present a united front in Baghdad for an independent Iraq would jeopardise the outcome of the negotiations in Switzerland and London.

Sunni/Shi'i Antagonism as a Political Factor, January to December 1927

After the deportation of the *'ulama'* in the summer of 1923, the Shi'i political and tribal leadership can be divided roughly into those advocating cooperation with Sunni nationalist politicians against Britain, and those who pressed for solidarity to secure specifically Shi'i objectives, such as greater representation in the government and civil service.[28] Occasionally the two groups would come into conflict, especially when the Residency seemed to be more concerned to press for Shi'i rights than the Sunni government was to grant them. Neither of the Shi'i groups nor any group of Sunni 'nationalists' ever managed to gain exclusive political power, which was normally wielded by another clique, consisting of Sunni politicians close to the King. This group, although opposed in principle to Britain's presence in Iraq, came to realise that too determined opposition to Britain might mean permanent unemployment for themselves. It is not always easy to determine, at any given moment, the position of an individual *vis-à-vis* any particular group because of the personalised nature of Iraq politics at this time, but the following broad divisions apply generally to the period under discussion:

A. Nationalist (mostly Sunni) independent: 'anti-British':

Rashid 'Ali (B), Yasin al-Hashimi (B), Ra'uf Chadirchi, Hikmat Sulayman, Jamil Midfa i, (B), Naji Shawkat, Naji al-Suwaydi, Tawfiq al-Suwaydi, Shaykh Ahmad al-Da'ud, Ja'far Abu'l-Timman (Shi'i), Muhsin Abu'l-Tabikh (Shi'i, B, C), Bahjat Zaynal, 'Ali Mahmud, Sunni lawyers.

B. Court: Faysal and immediate circle.

Nuri al-Sa'id, Ja'far al- 'Askari, 'Abd al-'Aziz al-Qassab, Jamil Midfa'i (A), Yasin al-Hashimi (A), Rashid 'Ali (A), 'Ali Jawdat, Muhsin Abu'l-Tabikh (A, C), Muhammad al-Sadr (Shi'i, C).

C. Shi'i: non-nationalist.

Amin al-Charchafchi, Muhammad al-Sadr (B), Muhsin al-Shallash, Shabibi brothers, most Shi'i tribal leaders and most Shi'i cabinet members, Muhsin Abu'l-Tabikh (A, B).[29]

The position of the Shi'i 'non-nationalists', as we may call them, was particularly vital in the conscription controversy, since their influence would be decisive. Conscription was likely to be bitterly opposed by most Shi'i leaders, who would see it as one more instance of Sunni *effendi* domination. However, while the 'non-nationalists' could do little of their own accord to adjust the continuing and resented under-representation of their sect in the cabinet and civil service, they and their supporters *were* in a position to resist conscription. United, the tribes would be more than a match for the Iraq army, and, as was well known, Britain would not be prepared to allow its troops to be used in the implementation of a policy of which the Residency so plainly disapproved. In these circumstances, instead of trying to placate these Shi'i leaders, or winning them over by suitable concessions, the Iraqi government seems to have taken no particular care to prevent what appears to have been a series of almost gratuitous offences to Shi'i susceptibilities.

The first sign of this tactlessness was a history of Islam published for use as a school textbook by the Ministry of Education. The book contained passages attacking the Shi'is and Shi'ism which were bound to cause considerable annoyance. The book was subsequently banned, and the author dismissed from the educational service, but the bitterness remained, and there was a demonstration of secondary school students against the banning and the dismissal.[30] Further trouble occurred within the Ministry when young Shi'i teacher (the poet Muhammad Mahdi al-Jawahiri), a personal protégé of the Minister of Education, himself the only Shi'i in the Cabinet, was dismissed for a poem supposedly in praise of Iran which appeared in a provincial newspaper.[31] The Minister held that all dismissals should be referred to him for sanction, but the Director-General, Sati' al-Husri, disagreed. These trivial incidents annoyed the 'non-nationalists', who believed that they were part of a calculated programme of intrigue to force the Minister's resignation.

In mid-February, the rapid growth of the professedly sectarian *al-Nahdha* party was causing some alarm both at the Palace and at the Residency. Its General Secretary, Amin al-Charchafchi, was pressing for permission to publish a newspaper to be called either *al-Nahdha* or *al-Ittihad*: an intelligence report of the time notes:

> The men at the head of the movement are showing an unmistakable desire to intensify the exclusively Shi'i bias of the party, and the High Commissioner has spoken to the King of the dangers of a Sunni countermovement being provoked if the activities of the Shi'i party became too prominent. His Majesty entirely agreed and said that the Iraqi government would refuse permission for the publication of the proposed new newspaper. He would also speak severely to Amin al-

Charchafchi and others working with him and would attempt to prevent the formation of a purely sectarian political party.[32]

Tensions rose in the provinces as well as in the capital: it was reported from Kut *liwa,* in the context of the long-standing quarrels between the Hayy *sirkals* and their powerful Sa'dun landlords that 'the flames were fanned by the general Sunni/ Shi'i tension, the judge there and the *sirkals* being Shi'is and the *qa'immaqam* and the *mallaks* all being Sunnis.'[33] The high water mark of the period, however, occurred on a specifically religious occasion, the Muharram processions at Kadhimayn.

In 1927, Muharram, the month of Shi'i processions and 'passion plays', began on 1 July. The first few days passed off without incident, but on 9 July the Acting High Commissioner was concerned at a report that the Ministry of Defence considered it necessary to send a detachment of the Iraqi army to Kadhimayn, since the local police were normally capable of controlling the crowds. Ja'far al-'Askari denied that troops had been sent. On the following day, 10 July, in the course of the religious procession, a detachment of the Iraqi army was seen to be present. Shots were fired: the crowd panicked, and a number of deaths and serious injuries resulted. Muhi al-Din, the commander of the army detachment, a protégé of Nuri al-Sa'id, fired the first shot, but was acquitted of blame at a court of inquiry. For a time serious repercussions, in the form of more riots, seemed likely, in spite of an offer of compensation from the King. There are signs that the riot may have been deliberately provoked. Apart from the unusual presence of troops, there was:

> . . . a story to the effect that on 4 July Ja'far al-'Askari's wife asked a lot of other ladies to take lunch with her at Kadhimain on the 10th and see the show. On the 8th or 9th she is stated to have cancelled the whole arrangement on the grounds that she had heard something would happen and she strongly advised the others not to visit the mosque on July 10.[34]

The acquittal, and even worse, the subsequent promotion, of Muhi al-Din, the officer responsible, was not calculated to allay Shi'i suspicions that the riot was another and more violent development in the Government's campaign. The only concession to the Shi'is which followed the incident was the grant of permission to Amin al-Charchafchi by the Ministry of Interior for the publication of *al-Nahdha,* which lost no time, in its first issue on 10 August, in attacking the cabinet, conscription, and the government's failure so far to publish the results of the Kadhimayn inquiry.[35] In fact, the paper was suspended after less than eight weeks by an order of the Council of Ministers, which occasioned angry correspondence between the Residency, the Prime Minister's Office and the Palace, where ex-King 'Ali was acting as Regent for his brother. Attempts by Cornwallis and the Acting High Commissioner to make the government lift the suspension resulted in the resignation from the cabinet first of Yasin al-Hashimi and then of Rashid 'Ali on the grounds of over-interference by Britain in the internal affairs of Iraq.[36] A further incident took place at the end of the year, in which Shi'i *'ulama'* were alleged to have been manhandled in the cellars of the mosque at Samarra'.

> No issue of any importance is expected from this incident at Samarra, but following so closely upon the suspension of *al-Nahdha* . . . the tally of Shia grievances . . . which cover a wide area, is increased by one.[37]

Predictably, the Shi'i leaders, and al-Charchafchi in particular, were subjected to swingeing criticisms when the King and his party returned from Europe with so much less than they had hoped for. Ja'far al-'Askari blamed the *al-Nahdha* group and its activities, and the King was reported as being exceedingly angry. At an interview at the Palace on 23 December, al-Charchafchi was rebuked severely by the King for having broken the oath he had sworn, to refrain from agitation in any way during the King's absence: he replied that the failure of the Government to punish Muhi al-Din, the prime mover of the Kadhimayn riot, had made further silence impossible.[38] Again:

> In conversation on 21 December Nuri Pasha stated that during the London conversations, appeals from the Shia leaders were constantly being received from the Colonial Office; these greatly weakened the position of the Iraqi delegates and influenced the British delegates in refusing extensive concessions.[39]

However, there is little real evidence to support this contention. Dobbs and the Colonial Office certainly knew of the agitation in Iraq, but the British government was animated far more by the necessity of devising a new formula for British control in Iraq than by anything more than a passing solicitude for Shi'i aspirations.

Negotiations for a new Treaty, September to December 1927

We have seen that one of the motives behind the unfortunately worded invitation sent to Faysal in July was to get him away from Baghdad, where his presence was becoming unbearable. Bourdillon, Edmonds, and Air Vice-Marshal Ellington all seriously canvassed the idea that if Faysal could not be persuaded to stop intervening in the administration, he should be made to abdicate. Edmonds noted:

> [T]he opinion is widely expressed in the most unexpected circles that the disappearance of the dangerous neurotic is after all the only solution to the present problems.[40]

Unfortunately, having managed to lure the 'dangerous neurotic' away from Baghdad it was not at first found possible to mollify him. At this stage Britain evidently did not contemplate much more than a provisional recommendation for Iraq's entry to the League in 1932, and this was not sufficient to satisfy Faysal and those close to him. Shuckburgh and Hall returned from Aix-les-Bains after their conversations with Faysal somewhat perplexed as to the best policy to pursue. However, by the end of September, the Colonial Office and the High Commissioner (who remained in London until December) had reached a new agreement which meant that Faysal would not have to go home empty-handed. A revised treaty was proposed, which would relax Britain's formal rights of intervention in the affairs of Iraq, but which would at the same time maintain firm control over everything affecting British interests and Britain's external obligations: 'in other words', as the Middle East Department's memorandum succinctly puts it, 'to retain the substance at some sacrifice of form.' This memorandum also takes due note of the fact that not only did Faysal need Britain in order to maintain himself in power but that Britain also needed a pliant and cooperative ruler in Iraq:

> For better or for worse we have chosen King Faysal as the instrument of our policy. In the eyes of the world we are identified with his regime. He may have his failings like the rest of us, but upon the whole he has served us well and there is the greatest objection to any course which would seriously antagonise him or place him in a position which he would regard as untenable. The loss of his goodwill and cooperation (to say nothing of his covert hostility) would make our position untenable. We cannot, in fact, have a contented Iraq without a reasonably contented Faysal.[41]

Furthermore, it was a fact that Britain's *formal* right to restrain the Iraqi government, or the King, had never been invoked, since the High Commissioner's power was based far more on his ability to threaten the withdrawal of British support than by anything more overt. Unfortunately for the authorities in London, Faysal also realised that nothing of 'substance' was being offered. Thus although the negotiations could begin for a new treaty, they reached deadlock almost immediately. The cause of the first difficulty was the control of the defence of Iraq. Faysal and his entourage argued that if Britain actually intended to carry out the terms of the Military Agreement in 1928, and leave Iraq at the end of that year, then, *ipso facto,* control of defence thereafter must rest with the Iraqi government. It followed that the right of the High Commissioner even to offer advice could not continue under those circumstances. Writing a few days after the first major oil strike at Baba Gurgur near Kirkuk, Dobbs believed that it would be wise for Britain to waive the stipulation that British forces would leave:

> the recent enormous commitments of the TPC and the APOC in Iraq and the discoveries of immense quantities of oil in the concessions of both of them make it now impossible to abandon control of Iraq without damaging important British and foreign interests. It was very different when the existence of oil was doubtful, as it was when the last Anglo-Iraqi treaty was discussed.[42]

Once Britain had committed herself to staying in Iraq, this implied that ultimate responsibility for defence still remained in Britain's hands. Faysal however was particularly fond of a form of words which included either 'joint responsibility' or a 'share in responsibility' for defence: Dobbs wrote to Shuckburgh on 11 November that 'he has always been a slave of this phrase and a fanatic upon it even from the time of his earliest discussions with Cox.'[43] This concession was of course unacceptable, particularly to the Air Ministry. Dobbs tried in vain for two days to convince Faysal, now in London, of the argument that the dispensation from having to accept the High Commissioner's advice was based upon the premise that Britain would withdraw all its troops: if Britain was now prepared to stay, it must retain its former powers.[44] For the time being Faysal seemed immoveable; on 18 November the Acting High Commissioner in Baghdad was informed that Faysal had decided to suspend negotiations for the treaty, and to explain this in Baghdad by reference to Britain's promise to take full responsibility for the defence of Iraq after 1928. This was followed by several days of stalemate, in the course of which Faysal vacillated between this policy, refusal to return to Iraq, and abdication.[45]

After ten days of suspense, a face-saving formula was devised. At a lunch party at Claridges on 28 November, Faysal asked Austen Chamberlain, the Foreign Secretary, whether Britain would come to Iraq's aid in the event of trouble arising *as a result* of Iraq following Britain's advice. Chamberlain replied that he was sure that Britain would not fail to do what was necessary in those circumstances: Faysal said that he would be prepared to accept that assurance and negotiations were resumed.[46] On 2 December Baghdad was informed that agreement had been reached and that the signature of the new treaty was expected daily. This took place on 14 December, and by 20 December Faysal was back in Baghdad, faced with the uphill task of convincing both supporters and waverers that something substantial had been achieved.

The task proved, as had been foreseen, not only uphill but virtually impossible. The two strong men of the Cabinet, Yasin and Rashid 'Ali, had already resigned over the *Nahdha* incident, and it was only a matter of a few days before Nuri and Ja'far handed in their resignations as well. The announcement that Britain would formally support Iraq in 1932 on the condition that all went well in the interim, that Britain would not abandon Iraq in 1928, and that ratification of the new treaty depended on a satisfactory revision of the Military and Financial Agreements, did not serve so much to conclude the events that had gone before as to open up a period of renewed and more intense disagreement and conflict between the British and Iraqi governments. Britain was prepared to be obstinate until the essential safeguards for its interests were obtained, while the Iraqi government for its part persisted in refusing to be deflected from the 'true' independence which it sought.

Stalemate: December 1927 to September 1929

On 7 January 1928, in view of the resignations, and the Prime Minister's undoubted desire to escape back to the Legation in London, Ja'far's cabinet resigned. The situation, just as in November 1922 and July 1925, called for a more or less 'nonpolitical' ministry, since neither the nationalists nor the court party would accept office under the circumstances of the latest Treaty negotiations. Only one man, 'Abd al-Muhsin al-Sa'dun, could be relied upon both by the Palace and by the Residency to form a government, and the known coolness between Sa'dun and the King had the advantage of enabling the latter to plead, if necessary, to his own supporters that the choice had been forced upon him by Britain.[47] The new ministry contained Sa'dun himself at Defence, 'Abd al-'Aziz al-Qassab at Interior, Yusuf al-Ghanima at

Finance, Hikmat Sulayman at Justice, Tawfiq al-Suwaydi at Education and Shaykh Ahmad al-Da'ud at *Awqaf.* There were two Shi'i members, Muhsin al-Shallash at Communications and Works and Salman al-Barrak at Irrigation and Agriculture, much to the dissatisfaction of Shi'i politicians, who had expected four Shi'i representatives and who had in any case never forgiven Sa'dun for his involvement in the deportation of the *'ulama'.*[48]

The most pressing problem facing the new government was the revision of the Military Agreement with Britain that had been written into the 1927 treaty. This involved questions of finance and organisation: how much money would Iraq be asked to spend, and could Iraq afford it? On 20 December 1927, Dobbs had informed the Colonial Office that the Iraqi cabinet was anxious for detailed proposals from Britain on the amount and nature of the assistance which would be given to the Iraqi armed forces to enable the Iraqi government to produce realistic budget estimates. The problem of defence arrangements had become particularly acute in the face of threats of invasion from Najd as well as pressure from the Baghdad press for an 'active' defence policy. Dobbs asked for authorisation to tell the government formally that the 'Daly scheme' must now be dropped, because of opposition to conscription: that the RAF and the two battalions of Levies would stay in Iraq and be paid for out of British funds: that surplus stores and equipment would be handed over at 10% of their book value at the conclusion of the new Military Agreement: that Britain should continue to give a subsidy to the Iraqi Army for 1928–1931, provided that there was no reduction in the number of British officers, and finally that Britain would continue to honour its pledge to train Iraqis for the Iraqi air force. It took 20 months to wheedle an agreement out of H. M. Government on these items.[49]

The situation early in 1928, therefore, was that although it was known that the RAF would be retained in Iraq for some indefinite period after the end of 1928, the precise details, and particularly the cost to Iraq, had still to be worked out. In the absence of any definite information on such matters, conscription still remained a live issue: Sa'dun was not inclined to favour its introduction, but realised that it might become an important issue in the elections.[50] To ease the Prime Minister's difficulties, and to clarify his own position and that of the Air Officer Commanding, Dobbs requested that a parliamentary question should be asked and answered in London to the effect that Britain, while doubting the advisability of conscription, would not oppose it, but would not help the Iraqi government to enforce it, nor take any responsibility if any trouble broke out in consequence. An assurance to this effect was eventually given in the House of Commons at the end of

April.[51] On the question of costs, the British government was less compliant. It insisted, as a matter of principle, that Iraq should pay the difference, about £20,000 per annum, between the costs of the RAF being stationed at home and being stationed in Iraq.[52] Dobbs pointed out, for the time being in vain, that the Iraqi government regarded such a payment as inequitable, and also that the government feared that once the principle of surplus costs was admitted, Iraq might have to pay substantial sums in the event of any large scale air operations based in Iraq. Furthermore:

> . . . there is an increasing tendency to regard British forces in Iraq as available for Imperial purposes outside Iraq, e. g., the defence of Kuwait and ensuring the safety of British personnel on the oilfields of the APOC. It will be exceedingly difficult to justify to the Iraq Parliament the principle of payment for excess costs.[53]

In fact, in the course of the year it became clear that Iraqi politicians, of whatever political complexion, were convinced that the object of British policy was to maintain Iraq in a state of dependence on Britain and not to allow it to build up the necessary forces to make the promised independence a reality.

The elections for a new Chamber of Deputies occupied the period between mid-January and mid-May. In the course of these months Faysal and Nuri did their best to secure an anti-Sa'dun chamber, hoping, apparently, to defeat the new cabinet and force the reappointment of the 'Askari cabinet with enhanced powers.[54] The new cabinet itself was in a highly unenviable position since it lacked the support of the Palace, the nationalists, and the Shi'is, and the Prime Minister could be attacked with some justification by all three groups on the grounds that he was no more than the High Commissioner's nominee. At the beginning of 1928, some three weeks after the dissolution of Parliament there was a violent demonstration against Britain and Zionism, occasioned by the visit of Sir Alfred Mond to Baghdad (Eppel, 1994: 17–20). The demonstration was ostensibly organised by Yusuf Zaynal, Hamid Dabbuni and Talib Mushtaq of the Teachers Training College, but further investigations gave strong grounds for the belief that the teachers and pupils taking part had received active encouragement from more august quarters. Yasin and Rashid 'Ali had met with Zaynal and Mushtaq a few days before the incidents, and the King was also believed to have been involved.[55] It was also reported that Nuri al-Sa'id, as Deputy Commander in Chief, had given special leave of absence to a number of his tougher personal adherents in the Iraqi army to be available to encourage voters to vote against the government candidates.[56]

At the same time, Faysal was trying to influence leaders of the Shi'i party either to oppose 'Abd al-Muhsin themselves, or to join the Palace party. To this end, Yasin and Ja'far al-'Askari were sent on conciliatory visits to leading Shi'is, including 'Umran al-Hajji al-Sa'dun, the Shabibi brothers and Naji Salih, pointing out 'Abd al-Muhsin's record of intolerance towards Shi'is. Efforts were made to encourage Ja'far Abu'l-Timman to take part in politics again, while Amin al-Charchafchi was carefully excluded from the Baghdad election inspection committee once he had announced his support for the Prime Minister.[57] However, by the time the new Parliament met in May, most of the opposition to the government had either been defeated at the polls or simply melted away. Sixty-six deputies out of a Chamber of eighty-eight could be counted upon to support the government,[58] proving almost incontrovertibly the power of the government of the day to rig the returns in its own favour. On this occasion, allegations of irregularities at the polls were received from Baghdad, Basra, Mosul and from Kut, where the election was actually declared invalid.[59]

Little progress towards the renegotiation of the agreements had been possible over these months, although Dobbs had repeatedly tried to ease his own and Sa'dun's position by asking the Colonial Office to intercede with the Treasury to make concessions in the more sensitive areas of disagreement, the RAF costs and the Iraqi Railways. It is almost incredible that the Treasury remained so obstinate for so long: as Dobbs and many other people realised, British forces would stay on in Iraq whether the Iraqis paid the difference or not. The RAF, the High Commissioner maintained, was in Iraq to protect the Abadan oil refinery and the developing Iraqi oilfields, to safeguard imperial air communications, and to be trained in terrain offering useful facilities for practice and development. Moreover, he concluded, 'the people of Iraq are as well aware of these facts as we are.'[60]

al-Wadha' al-Shadd

It was at this time, between the conditional promise and the unconditional offer of independence, that Iraqi politicians seemed to have found the anomalies inherent in the mandate especially perplexing and bewildering. The phrase, *al-wadha' al-shadd*, perhaps 'perplexing predicament', became the common shorthand to describe the situation:

When the King is impotent to work his will it is *al-wadha' al-shadd;* when the ministers are criticised, their answer is the *al-wadha' al-shadd*: when officials fail in their duty it is *al-wadha' al-shadd,* and when the cry goes up from the peasants that they are starving the fat effendi finds his conscience easy: '*Que voulez-vous, c'est l'oudha al-shadd*' . . . The belief is widespread that there is, inherent in the present peculiar 'perplexing predicament' of the country, something fundamental which is an insuperable obstacle to progress towards real independence, and that this obstacle is the *al-wadha' al-shadd* for which England is alone responsible.[61]

Perhaps the hyperbolic style of this passage is the best proof of its authenticity; the fortnightly intelligence reports (from one of which this extract is taken) were compiled by the Oriental Secretary, the member of the Residency staff officially most closely in touch with local feeling and opinion.[62] The contradictions and difficulties which confronted Iraqi politicians and leaders must have been the subject of endless conversations in Holt's office. The *Report on Iraq* for 1928 notes that this situation was imaginary and existed 'only in the minds of fervid patriots', but since this Report was not published until the autumn of the following year, by which time relations had significantly improved, the difficulties inherent in Anglo-Iraqi relations in 1928 are probably characterised fairly accurately in the passage quoted here. At that time, no proposal could be put forward by the Iraq Prime Minister or the cabinet that the Colonial Office did not seem to reject out of hand, and yet the possibility of independence was only five years away.

The whole period between the autumn of 1927 and September 1929 is marked by a sense of the impotence of the Iraqi government in the face of Britain's refusal to compromise. Hence any chance of manoeuvre was eagerly seized upon. The British Oil Development (BOD) Company's bid for a share in Iraqi oil in April 1928, which enabled the Iraqi government to delay renewing the IPC concession, was a welcome opportunity for the Iraqi government to use what bargaining power it possessed, and here at least it appeared for a time that progress might be made. Given the BOD's lack of share capital, its offer of immediate exploitation of any oil the company found, as well as the construction of a pipeline and railway linking the Tigris to the Mediterranean, was probably fanciful (Longrigg, 1961: 73–75), but it had the effect of forcing IPC to come forward with a similar construction project. The Iraqi government was content to play the two companies off against each other in the hope of raising the bidding. Of course, the IPC was eventually given the concession, and built the pipeline, but for a while, until the cabinet's resignation at the end of 1928, the Iraqi government was able to maintain the upper hand in at least one important area of conflict.

The main difference outstanding between the British and Iraqi governments at this stage was the question of defence. Britain was not, because of its imperial and commercial interests, prepared to allow Iraq to take responsibility for its own defence.[63] In October, Dobbs wondered whether it might not after all be possible for Britain to relax its control over the Iraqi army and let the Iraqis go their own way.[64] After some weeks London replied that after careful consideration:

> H. M. Government are unable to accept policy suggested . . . and are not prepared to disassociate themselves from organisation . . . of Iraq Army to extent proposed . . . you should emphasise that H. M. Government are not prepared to make any further concessions on matters of principle.[65]

If presented direct to the Iraqi government this statement would, as Dobbs knew, cause the cabinet's immediate resignation. Moved by a high regard for 'Abd al-Muhsin as well as by a desire to clear things up for his successor, Sir Gilbert Clayton, who was due to arrive early in 1929, Dobbs made a final effort to resolve the situation. He asked London earnestly to consider whether the advantages of persisting to secure all possible treaty safeguards for British forces would outweigh the disadvantages which might attend the cabinet's resignation, and suggested that it would be far better to use his own favourite weapon, the threat of refusal to allow British forces to be used in emergencies.

> There have in fact been recent signs that (the moderates) genuinely suspect that H. M. Government have changed their policy regarding Iraq because of the increased importance of Iraq as a corridor for aircraft and the discoveries of oil. I feel that we risk a final defeat of an independent Iraq 'friendly and bound by ties of obligation to H. M. Government.'[66]

This appeal was of no avail, and although agreeing to stay in office as caretakers, the cabinet resigned on 21 January 1929.

In London, the seriousness of the situation was readily apparent. It was feared that the whole basis of cooperation in which the existing arrangements depended might collapse. At the Foreign Office, Gladwyn Jebb minuted:

> The outlook is bleak. The King and Nuri want to manoeuvre us into the position of having either to acquiesce in measures which would

damage our Imperial interests or to tear down the Treaty facade from
the mandatory building. The latter is the more likely probability. But
perhaps Sir Gilbert Clayton will be able to rescue us from this
dilemma.[67]

However, in spite of the crisis in Baghdad, there were no signs that it had
spread beyond the confines of political circles in the city; the 'complete and
unprecedented' state of public security in the country was not being
adversely affected.[68] In spite of his pessimism about the chances of finding a
successor to Sa'dun, Dobbs felt at the end of January that it would be better
to wait for Clayton's arrival before pressing matters any further. The Iraqi
government apparently hoped that the incoming High Commissioner, an
old friend of the King and Nuri, might be able to find some way out of the
dilemma that would be less wounding to Iraqi susceptibilities. When they
came to realise that Clayton would not yield either, and the government was
faced with what would then certainly be regarded as a final refusal, Dobbs
believed that Sa'dun would be able to carry on as before, 'since the country
is perfectly tranquil and little interest is taken in the political crisis outside
Baghdad.'[69]

Dobbs summarised the situation in a despatch written at the end of
January 1929, three days before he left. Faysal had made Sa'dun's position
impossible by telling all the prominent political and tribal personalities that
anyone who accepted the 1927 treaty was a traitor, and in the face of
mounting pressures of this kind, the Prime Minister could not continue in
office. Faysal had told the High Commissioner that his sole aim was to
secure Iraq's entry to the League in 1932: if Britain really intended to support Iraq's candidature, let it show its determination by strengthening the
Iraqi army sufficiently for the purpose. All he asked from Britain was a
promise that unreserved support would be given for 1932, and that Britain
should withdraw from Iraqi defence affairs to a position of simply helping
the Iraqi army out in emergencies. Meanwhile, the King and his circle felt
that they had little to lose by maintaining the present stalemate.[70]

For the first two months after Clayton's arrival there was no sign of any
progress at all, and the Iraqi government took advantage of the lull to enter
the lists once more with IPC. At this stage the interim extensions of the
original concession given by the Iraqi government to the Company seemed
unlikely to be renewed, and the government had drawn up a new list of
conditions. It was prepared to extend the concession for five years, but on
the condition that a railway and pipeline survey would been made in the
course of the first two years, and that the surveys would be followed by

construction in the latter. The IPC found itself in a dilemma. First, as Gulbenkian pointed out, it was an oil company and not a civil engineering firm; while it might well be prepared to sign a concession agreement *and* arrange for a survey, it was doubtful whether the former should be made depend upon the latter. Secondly, the route of the proposed pipeline and railway was a sensitive matter: the French members of the IPC board preferred Tripoli as the point of *débouchement*, while the British members naturally wanted Haifa.

Fortunately for Britain, King Faysal also preferred Haifa, and it was agreed in London in March that if Faysal and the Iraqis wanted Haifa, they should be allowed to have it.[71] It might be difficult to convince the French that Britain was acting entirely disinterestedly in the matter, but as the Colonial Office argued, it was the mandatory power's duty to protect its charge from exploitation by sophisticated European concessionaires.[72] In the face of rumours in April that the French were starting to build a railway from Homs to Dayr al-Zawr, the Colonial Office proposed that the British Government should immediately offer an interest free loan to Iraq to facilitate the construction of the Tigris-Mediterranean railway.[73] After many delays, the railway project was dropped, but the pipeline was commenced after IPC had secured a new concession in 1931, and was eventually completed in 1934.

Dobbs left Baghdad on 3 February, and his successor arrived there a month later. During the brief interregnum there were attempts to rally public opinion behind a new combination of court and nationalist factions, in a further effort to convince politically engaged Shi'is that the interests of the country would be best served by the introduction of conscription. However, after a fervent speech by 'Ali Mahmud, a prominent lawyer and member of the newly formed *Hizb al-Watani* (patriotic party), to an audience at the Shi'i *Nadi al-Nahdha*,

> . . . an uncomfortable silence followed his being asked how the Shias would defend themselves from the Sunnis after the British had left.[74]

Soon after his arrival, Clayton found that the King and the Prime Minister had discovered a new formula, which, if accepted, would at least enable the cabinet to resume its responsibilities. The best way out of the impasse was simply to sidestep the main problem and concentrate on what were considered to be the more negotiable issues. Sa'dun and Faysal put five proposals to Clayton. First, the 1927 treaty should be done away with, and the 1924 agreements should simply be prolonged: second, that Britain should at once inform the League of the precise date at which it would be putting forward Iraq's candidature: third, that Britain should relax its attitude towards conscription: fourth, that the British government should encourage British capital to finance enterprises in Iraq, and finally that the negotiations over the Iraqi Railways should be reopened. The High Commissioner himself tended to support all these proposals except the third. He felt that the present difficulties stemmed from a suspicion and lack of confidence in Britain's real intentions on the part of the Iraqis. They could not see in particular how the prevailing military arrangements accorded with the promise to support Iraqi candidature in 1932 and believed that the conditional clause was a ploy through which this recommendation could be deferred. Hence Clayton supported the removal of the condition, and the announcement of definite support for 1932.[75] For its part, London was only able to accept the first proposal without reservation. The most crucial, the demand for an immediate application to the League would not, it was alleged, be granted since the League would not accept notification so far in advance. The furthest that London was prepared to go was:

> to inform League Council at earliest opportunity when notifying that body that it is not proposed to proceed with 1927 Treaty, and that it is H.M. Government's intention, unless in the meantime any serious check in the political or economic progress of the country has occurred, to recommend to the Council at their June session in 1932 . . . that Iraq should be admitted to membership of the League forthwith.[76]

As Clayton had expected, this disappointing answer, together with an equally dampening statement on conscription, caused Sa'dun to hand in his resignation. He promised to give full support to any ministry which might be formed, but he could no longer lead a cabinet which he considered to have no legal authority. His position, between the King, the Residency and the rest of the cabinet, was far from enviable, and it seems likely that it is his refusal to compromise in these difficult months, together with his dramatic death in the autumn, that has led to his remaining something approaching a national hero in Iraq, one of the few such survivals from the mandate period. Even Muhammad al-Sadr, who often bitterly criticised what he considered Sa'dun's anti-Shi'i policies, praised him for 'strengthening the national spirit'.[77]

Until some substantial move was made by one or other of the two sides, the only way forward was to ignore all major problems. At the end of April:

> His Majesty informed me that the Ministers had held a meeting and had decided that as they did not consider that the proposals as modified by HBMG would form a basis on which a Ministry could be formed with any prospect of the support of Parliament, they had come to the conclusion that it would be preferable to form a Ministry without making any allusion to these proposals merely on the basis of dropping the 1927 Treaty and the negotiations for the Military and Financial Agreements. The question of admission to the League would thus not form part of the Ministry's programme . . . His Majesty brought the interview to a close by saying that by this arrangement the crisis was finished.[78]

Tawfiq al-Suwaydi was disposed to accept these principles and form a cabinet at the King's request, though he came under heavy fire from the nationalists for doing so. In his memoirs he recalls that he and Nuri were both invited to the Palace: Nuri refused to take office with al-Suwaydi, though al-Suwaydi did not object to Nuri (al-Suwaydi, 1969: 129–140). Thus a cabinet was at last formed, without Nuri, Amin Zaki taking the portfolio of Defence: Yusuf al-Ghanima and the two Shi'i members retained their offices, and the newcomers to the Ministry included 'Abd al-'Aziz al-Qassab, Khalid Sulayman and Da'ud al-Haydari at Interior, Education and Justice respectively. In spite of wild talk in nationalist circles about demonstrations and even tribal risings, nothing happened at all. It is a curious feature of this period, between the beginning of 1928 and the autumn of 1929, that apart from the 1928 elections, political activity seems to have been confined to a kind of vacuum, in which the main participants were sealed off from the rest of the population. There was little of the widespread political activity among the Shi'is that had characterised the period immediately before, nor the deep hostility to the court party's government which emerged afterwards.

Thus in spite of criticisms, and in spite of its inability to break the dead-lock now in existence for almost a year, the very appearance of a government after a period of some months in which business had been largely suspended was generally welcomed outside the immediate circle of nationalist and palace politicians. In the *Hizb al-Taqaddum*, the bloc of moderates led by 'Abd al-Muhsin, on whom any cabinet had to base its majority, only seven out of fifty-four members withheld their support from the new cabinet.[79] Perhaps the continuing calm may be explained by a feeling that the

initiative now lay well and truly with Britain, since the Iraqi government
had done everything possible in the way of accommodation. For his part,
Clayton continued to press London for concessions, arguing, as Dobbs had
done, that such concessions would have infinitely greater effect if they could
be made spontaneously, rather than as the culmination of a period of
acrimonious bargaining.[80]

It was predictable that in these strained circumstances the King and his
party would not be able to contain themselves for long, and Faysal soon had
recourse to the same tactics which he had employed to undermine Sa'dun.
In the middle of June, 'Abd a-Muhsin reported to Edmonds that the King
was doing his best to destroy the al-Suwaydi cabinet. Faysal proposed a
'coalition' under Nuri: 'Abd al-Muhsin considered this unconstitutional,
especially in view of the fact that the Chamber of Deputies had recently
shown its confidence in the ministry by passing the budget by forty-five
votes to nine. Clayton took Faysal to task for his interference, but the King's
underground tactics continued. Both the court and the nationalist groups
gained additional encouragement from the hope of a Labour victory in the
British general elections (May 1929), which, as they anticipated, might
bring about a change in British policy. Meanwhile, the King was making
conditions impossible for Tawfiq al-Suwaydi: Edmonds wrote to Clayton at
the end of June:

> 'Abd al-Muhsin has little doubt that the next step would be for the
> palace (that is Nuri, the two are synonymous) to organise bands of
> roughs to insult ministers publicly, while the King would stultify the
> work of the Cabinet by refusing to assent to its decisions.[81]

The Labour victory in Britain did not, ultimately, disappoint the more
moderate Baghdad politicians, though its effect took some little time to
reach Baghdad. In June 1929 a Cabinet committee was set up under the
chairmanship of the Lord Privy Seal, J.H. Thomas, to consider development
projects in the colonies in the light of the unemployment situation in
Britain. Before considering any such project in Iraq the chairman considered
that the whole question of Britain's Iraq policy should be reviewed.
Shuckburgh noted on 1 July:

> If I understand Mr. Thomas rightly, his idea is that the question
> should be raised in its broadest form, viz., are we, or are we not, to
> maintain our present connection with Iraq?[82]

In Iraq, since no immediate pronouncement was forthcoming from London, business was suspended again. 'Abd al-Muhsin was summoned from Lebanon to try to take charge of the situation: the nationalists suggested a deputation to London: letters and telegrams of protest were despatched, and on 31 August Tawfiq al-Suwaydi submitted his resignation. Reduced to essentials, Clayton had stated very precisely what Britain and Iraq required from one another in a despatch sent to the Colonial Office at the end of July. Britain wanted security for imperial communications, the continued presence of the RAF and an assurance that all foreign officials should be British. Iraq wanted its payments for the High Commissioner and British forces suspended, its affairs to be handled by the Foreign Office rather than the Colonial Office, and an unconditional statement of support for Iraq's entry to the League in 1932.[83]

These proposals were submitted to the usual lengthy consideration from London, but eventually the new political atmosphere, and the accumulated advice from Baghdad, prevailed. On 11 September the Colonial Office informed the High Commissioner that the British government were now prepared to agree to suspend the 1927 Treaty and approach the League to admit Iraq, and nearly two years of deadlock were broken. Clayton never knew the result of his endeavours, as he died suddenly on the day that the telegram was sent from London: it was left to the Air Officer Commanding, as Acting High Commissioner, together with Edmonds as interpreter, to break the news to King Faysal three days later.[84] The King was delighted, and 'Abd al-Muhsin agreed to form his fourth and last Cabinet on the condition that he did not have 'to suffer . . . unconstitutional interference from the Palace after the new Government was in office.'[85]

September 1929 was the real watershed in Anglo-Iraqi relations, probably of more genuine significance than the actual termination of the mandate. It was at last accepted that it was possible to appear to relax control without actually doing so. The Iraqi government did not want British forces to withdraw, but it could also not be seen to be too heavily dependent on Britain. The struggle to introduce conscription had been an assertion of independence which had failed through sheer lack of support. It was necessary for Britain to make some formal affirmation of the fact that she did not intend to stay in Iraq. This was done first through promising unconditional support in 1929 for entry in three years' time, and again in 1930 by a new Anglo-Iraqi treaty which would assert that Iraq would be responsible for its own defence, but that British troops would nevertheless be stationed in Iraq. It was a paradox, but it was a paradox which was acceptable in London and also to those who counted in political circles in Baghdad. The new government in London, encouraged by the Residency and some quarters in the Colonial Office, had come to realise that the cost of continuing to irritate and disappoint the Iraqis was greater than the risk of promising them independence in 1932. The King and Nuri were beginning to lose their credibility, and since they and their group formed the only really coherent base of power within the country, they could not be seen to be ineffective indefinitely. To destroy their position in Iraq would be to destroy Britain's too.

Over the next three years, with the prospect of entry to the League in 1932 firmly established, there was time to work out the details of the disengagement, the real extent of the relaxation of control and influence that Britain was prepared to permit. The most taxing task for the British officials on the spot was to accustom themselves to playing a less active part in the administration, which was especially difficult when they were confronted by an Iraqi government apparently hell bent on policies of repression towards the various minority groups within the country, to the extent that the Permanent Mandates Commission was almost put in the position of being obliged to reconsider the whole question of Iraqi entry. The problems of the next three years, apart from the negotiation of the future details of the Anglo-Iraqi relationship, were largely concerned with the amount of 'advice' that the Iraqi government would, in these changed circumstances, be prepared to take from the Residency and the British officials. Even more than during the early part of the mandate, the line between amicable persuasion and intolerable interference was an extremely fine one.

5

PRELUDE TO INDEPENDENCE, 1929–1932

The declaration of 14 September 1929 was generally welcomed by most shades of political opinion in Baghdad, except some of the Shi'is. 'Abd al-Muhsin's new cabinet pleased the nationalists, since it included Naji al-Suwaydi and Yasin al-Hashimi, but the inclusion of only one Shi'i, 'Abd al-Husayn Chalabi, occasioned criticism, while Ja'far Abu'l-Timman remarked that only total lack of principle and blatant personal ambition could have inspired Yasin to take office.[1] On the other side, 'Abd al-Muhsin assured his anxious supporters in the *Taqaddum* Party that Yasin's inclusion had been at the express wish of the King, and that in any case it would considerably weaken the opposition to have so prominent a member of their number in the cabinet.[2]

However feasible a partnership between the court, the nationalists and the moderates may have seemed in the wave of euphoria following the declaration that Britain would support Iraq for League entry in 1932, it soon broke down. Once more the strain of trying to keep some sort of balance between the various factions proved too much for the Prime Minister. 'Everyone seems to agree,' Lionel Smith wrote to Dobbs in mid-November, 'that since his return from Beirut (Sa'dun) has been extraordinarily nervy and sensitive.'[3] He committed suicide in the evening of 13 November, and the note which he left, even in the garbled version which his colleagues presented to the press for publication, reflects the isolation in which he found himself.[4] His successor, Naji al-Suwaydi, although able to form a ministry from virtually the same personnel, also found that his position as arbiter between the court, the Residency and the various political factions gradually became intolerable. In a few months he too was obliged to confess failure and handed over to Nuri early in March 1930. Both Prime Ministers had been faced with insistent pressure from their Minister of Finance, Yasin al-Hashimi, that they should seek a major reduction in the number of

British officials. Edmonds described his amazement when 'Abd al-Muhsin presented this demand on 17 September, just after the King had asked him to form a new cabinet. Sa'dun replied that this was an attempt to reach common ground between himself, the King, Naji al-Suwaydi and Yasin. The Acting High Commissioner refused to accept this as a condition upon which Sa'dun would form a cabinet, and for a time it seemed as though the veto had been accepted. However, the cabinet was not slow to change its mind: in February, Naji al-Suwaydi attempted a rather more drastic expedient, of reducing the officials simply by excluding their salaries from the budget. The new High Commissioner, Sir Francis Humphrys, told the Prime Minister that such highhandedness could not be tolerated: he preferred a spirit of greater frankness, to avoid being forced into a position of embarrassing the government by insisting that he should be consulted before any new administrative steps were taken.[5]

As Minister of Finance, Yasin had been primarily responsible for this suggestion: Naji al-Suwaydi seems to have been pushed into it from behind rather than taking the initiative himself. At the time of his appointment in November, he had appealed to the opposition for their cooperation: both he and Sa'dun were put in embarrassing situations by Yasin's demands, which, although popular with the nationalists, had little chance of acceptance by Britain. Yasin had the King's ear, and an important following among the Baghdad politicians. Only Nuri had more influence, and in the end it was only Nuri, through having the support of the King and the Residency, and backed up by his followers in the army, who could form a cabinet from which Yasin could safely be excluded. Only Nuri had sufficient power to be able to ignore Yasin, and to be almost completely impervious to charges of collusion with Britain. For these reasons he remained Prime Minister from March 1930 to October 1932.

Nuri's term of office, which lasted over 30 months, was the longest in Iraqi political history up to this time. Nuri's ministry included his brother-in-law, Ja'far al-'Askari, at Defence, 'Ali Jawdat at Finance, and Jamil Midfa'i at Interior:[6] it was composed entirely of the court faction, and was determined to come to a lasting agreement with Britain. The cabinet's programme provided for a gradual 'transfer of responsibility from British to Iraqi hands',[7] efforts to solve the pressing problems caused in Iraq by the effects of the world depression and the fall in food prices, and the negotiation of a new Anglo-Iraqi Treaty ensuring complete independence, but 'bearing in mind at the same time the necessity for cementing friendly relations between the two countries on the basis of . . . reciprocity of interests.'[8] When negotiated, the treaty would be presented to the people at a general election.

The Anglo-Iraq Treaty of 1930

In contrast to most of the previous treaty negotiations, those of 1930 were concluded with great speed, largely because Nuri knew he had no real opposition to contend with. The more extreme Baghdad politicians, either nationalist or Shi'i, were too disorganised to combine effectively amongst themselves, and the major upheavals in Kurdistan which followed the publication of the treaty tended to play into the government's hands: Baghdad would certainly be united against attempts at dictation from Barzan or Sulaymaniya. Further, as we have seen, if the government was determined to stay in power, there was no constitutional means of dislodging it. Finally, however some of the British advisers may have distrusted Nuri's honesty and good intentions, there seemed no obvious alternative short of far stricter mandatory controls.

As a whole, the treaty and its annexes represented only limited progress towards national sovereignty. Apart from stipulations about the precedence to be given to the future British Ambassador, the employment of British officials and the stationing of a British Military Mission, the treaty declared that 'responsibility for the maintenance of internal order rests with the King of Iraq,'[9] while Britain was bound to go to the help of its ally in the event of an invasion. RAF bases, on sites to be selected by Britain, were to be maintained rent-free by the Iraqi government, and the privileges and immunities in force for British troops would continue. Armaments and aeroplanes 'of the latest available type' were to be supplied from Britain to the Iraq armed forces, on contract. The treaty, which was to last 25 years, would come into force when Iraq entered the League of Nations in 1932. Clause 11 states:

> At any time after 20 years from the coming into force of this Treaty, the High Contracting Parties will, at the request of either of them, conclude a new Treaty which shall provide for the maintenance and protection in all circumstances of the essential communications of His Britannic Majesty.

A few days after the Treaty negotiations ended, Nuri, followed soon afterwards by the High Commissioner, flew to London to begin conversations on the financial matters outstanding between Britain and Iraq, namely the Iraq Railways, Basra Port, the question of linking the RAF base at Habbaniya to the Iraqi railway system, and the transfer to the Iraqi government of the RAF's buildings and surplus stores at Mosul and Hinaydi.[10] The treaty caused little rejoicing in Baghdad, though, as usual, political circles were so divided that effective opposition was impossible.

Press criticism centred mainly on three aspects of the treaty: that it was not to come into force for two years: that it provided for a further treaty on the same terms after 25 years, and that leasing the air bases free of charge to a foreign power was not compatible with true independence. Such opposition as could be effectively channelled was directed towards supporting anti-treaty candidates in the general election: Parliament had been dissolved on 1 July, and the elections were held at the beginning of October. However, Nuri's cabinet proved as effective as its predecessors in securing the election of an overwhelming bloc of supporters, and the opposition could claim little success. Thus although the treaty was reluctantly accepted in Baghdad, there were signs among a large and powerful section of the population that they would not acquiesce so easily. As a result of their failure to gain concessions from the Iraqi government in the past, the Kurds were particularly dismayed that no guarantees of their special position in Iraq had been written into the Treaty. By 1930, Kurdistan and the Kurdish question had once more become a centrnl and volatile issue in Iraqi politics.

Kurdistan, 1926 to 1930

On 21 January 1926, three days after the passage of the 1926 Anglo-Iraqi Treaty, there was a debate in the Chamber of Deputies on the implementation of the Boundary Commission's report in so far as it affected the Kurdish areas of Iraq. The Prime Minister, 'Abd al-Muhsin al-Sa'dun, had declared roundly:

Gentlemen! This nation cannot live unless it gives all Iraqi elements their rights . . . The fate of Turkey should be a lesson to us and we should not revert to the policy formerly pursued by the Ottoman Government. We should give the Kurds their rights. Their officials should be from among them: their tongue should be their official language and their children should learn their own tongue in the schools. It is incumbent upon us to treat all elements, whether Muslim or non-Muslim, with fairness and justice, and give them their rights.[11]

In spite of this, by the time of the 1930 negotiations, virtually nothing had been done by any Iraqi government to convince the Kurds that their problems were being sympathetically considered, let alone being actively solved. Only six years earlier, the Kurds had been promised an independent Kurdistan, under the terms of the Treaty of Sèvres: in 1926 they were being offered a special regime and limited autonomy, and now, in 1930, even this had been whittled away. Nevertheless, the situation in the Kurdish areas in the spring of 1926 was generally quiet. Continued peace depended partly on the goodwill of Shaykh Mahmud, and also on the provision of some kind of local administration which would be generally acceptable to the Kurds while not veering too close to the sort of local autonomy which would offend susceptibilities in Baghdad. Most Kurds supported the adoption of Kurdish for official, judicial and educational purposes, and the employment of Kurdish officials, though some expressed a preference for the reorganisation of the Kurdish area into a single administrative entity under the supervisions of a British official.

In Baghdad, there were two schools of thought on Kurdistan and Kurdish affairs, the Arab and the British. The Arab ministers and officials at the ministries most directly concerned (generally Education, Justice and Interior) tended to dismiss the Kurdish problem as having no foundation except in the minds of the British advisers, anxious to weaken Iraqi national unity. For their part, the advisers accused the ministers and officials of deliberately ignoring the legitimate aspirations of the Kurds. Whatever the rights and wrongs of the situation, and whether or not the pledges had been forced out of a reluctant Iraqi government, the fact remained that public pledges had certainly been made, and that the Kurds were waiting for them to be carried out. There were of course practical problems, particularly surrounding the official and educational use of Kurdish: there was little written literature, and a whole series of school textbooks would have to be prepared. The language was divided into a number of dialects which differed quite widely from one another. However, as Lionel Smith remarked, such problems could be overcome: 'It is true that there is no standardized Kurdish. We must standardize it.' He suggested that there should be two secondary boarding schools in the area, one at Arbil and the other at Sulaymaniya, where the basic language of instruction should be Kurdish, but where Arabic should also be taught so that pupils could go on to further studies at an Arabic-medium institution.[12] In contrast, the Minister of Interior, 'Abd al-'Aziz al-Qassab, remarked that although Kurdish had been taught in some schools, it was of such little practical use that even the parents were not enthusiastic:

> (He) suggested that an order should quietly issue with regard to the Mosul *liwa* schools that the Arabic textbooks should be used, as being better drawn up and more suitable for the purposes of instruction, and that wherever the pupils do not understand Arabic the teacher should explain and translate to them in the Kurdish tongue. He thinks there

would be no clamour over this. New schools in the Mosul *liwa* should
have instruction in the Arabic tongue.[13]

It is difficult to disentangle any consistent 'Kurdish policy' on the part of
the Residency or the Colonial Office until 1930, when it became essential
that the Kurds should be seen to be fully integrated members of the Iraq
state. Over the four years between 1926 and 1930, Shaykh Mahmud,
technically exiled (to Iran) from Iraq, had occasional meetings and frequent
correspondence with the Administrative Inspector, Sulaymaniya, the Adviser
to the Ministry of Interior, and the Oriental Secretary to the High Commissioner. Officially, the British authorities had insisted that only a formal
dakhala (submission) to King Faysal and an undertaking to live peacefully
on the Iranian side of the frontier would satisfy both Iraqi and British
requirements. In the summer of 1927, Shaykh Mahmud came to Baghdad
and gave an undertaking in this sense, promising also that his eldest son,
Baba 'Ali, would be sent to Victoria College in Alexandria. He was to be
allowed to enjoy the income from his estates in Iraq, provided, again, that
he did not enter the country.[14] Yet in January 1928 the RAF Special Services
Officer in Sulaymaniya reported that Shaykh Mahmud was making a
prolonged tour among the Jaf tribe on the Iraqi side of the frontier, and
throughout that spring had frequent meetings on Iraq territory with the
local Administrative Inspector and the *mutasarrif*. He was put under no
restraint, never arrested, and apparently never even ordered to leave the
country. In the following year, three weeks after being reminded by Clayton
that he must keep out of politics, Mahmud was sent a present of 1000
shotgun cartridges, presumably for shooting game, paid for out of secret
service funds![15] His reply to Clayton's letter is interesting:

> Don't think that my obedience to the British Government is for the
> sake of my properties . . . our obedience is to the British Government
> however and not to Iraq. Please think of this point for a moment. If
> we were entirely obedient to Iraq, would that suit you? If you were to
> order us to be perfectly obedient in all matters to Iraq then in this as
> in other matters we should obey you. Then we should act according
> to their orders and you would not be able to blame us for the
> consequences.[16]

In November 1929, Captain Gowan, the Administrative Inspector,
Sulaymaniya, described a meeting with Mahmud at which the latter asked
for a larger subsidy,[17] and later in the month noted that the Shaykh had

complained to the *qa'immaqam* of Sharbazhar that two of his men had been arrested for theft. Gowan told Mahmud 'in future no notice will be taken of any complaints written by you to *qa'immaqams* or *mudirs* direct, but only if they are sent first to the *mutasarrif* or myself.'[18]

It is not clear how far Arab officials in Baghdad were aware of these cordial relations, but there is obviously some foundation for Arab suspicions that the British were pursuing a clandestine policy amounting at least to generous accommodation, with Shaykh Mahmud. Such suspicions may help to explain the evident hostility on the part of Baghdadi politicians and civil servants towards anything which smacked of concessions to Kurdistan, which were normally attributed to dark British designs on the fragile unity of the country. By the spring of 1927, the Iraqi government had still not shown any signs of implementing the promises given by 'Abd al-Muhsin. Bourdillon, the Acting High Commissioner, complained to the Prime Minister that there was no sign of the promised Kurdish translation bureau (which was to deal with laws and school textbooks) and that no progress had been made on the projected Decauville railway linking Kirkuk and Sulaymaniya.[19] The Government seem to have thought that it would do best not to commit itself: Edmonds remarked:

Nobody denies that the practical application of the solution to the Kurdish problem bristles with difficulties, but all efforts are concentrated on not overcoming them.

Thus, when challenged that there were no teachers in schools in Kurdistan, and the Ministry of Education replied that there were no qualified men available, Edmonds pointed out that none were being trained. Similarly, there were no textbooks for the schools, but none were being produced.[20]

Gradually, however, some sort of movement began to take shape. In April 1929 some of the more daring Kurdish deputies, including Isma'il al-Rowanduzi, Jamil Baban (Arbil), Hazim Beg (Mosul) Muhammad Beg Jaf (Kirkuk), Muhammad Salih and Sayfullah Khandan (Sulaymaniya) presented a formal list of grievances to the Prime Minister. They complained that no tangible progress had been made on the Boundary Commission's proposals, and pointed especially to the lack of educational facilities in the area, not simply in the Kurdish language, but the generally poor provision of schools and teachers. They suggested further that Dohuk should be the headquarters of a Kurdish *liwa* which would include the Kurdish *qadhas* of Mosul ('Aqra, 'Amadiya, Zibar, Zakho and Dohuk), and that the administration of Sulaymaniya, Kirkuk, Arbil and 'Dohuk' should be under a general inspectorate presided over by a distinguished Kurd. Finally, they suggested that *tapu* registration should be encouraged by waiving *tapu* fees for two years.[21]

At the same time, the police reports noted that the desire for decentralisation in Kurdistan was 'almost universal',[22] and Clayton informed the Prime Minister that he was in constant receipt of petitions and *madhbatas* from the area. The High Commissioner himself was not in favour of the proposed 'Dohuk *liwa*' or anything that smacked of separatism, but asked the Prime Minister to take urgent practical steps to remedy the deficient educational facilities in the area.[23] In the following month Cornwallis and Edmonds sent notes on the Kurdish question to the Residency, underscoring the obstructive attitude of successive Ministers of Education. They also criticised the Director of Education for Mosul, fiercely anti-Kurdish, who was also in charge of Arbil and Kirkuk. Edmonds favoured the 'Dohuk *liwa*' scheme on the grounds of administrative efficiency: on the question of officials and civil servants, he was inclined to make the Kurdish language rather than the Kurdish race the criterion for employment in Kurdish areas. As a preliminary to any major administrative reform, however, he stressed the need for the immediate reorganisation of the educational districts, and, once more, the translation bureau which had been promised since the beginning of 1926.[24]

Against this background, Britain's announcement of unconditional support for Iraqi entry into the League, issued in September 1929, caused serious concern in Kurdistan, misgivings which turned into consternation when it was known that the 1930 Anglo-Iraqi Treaty contained no formal safeguards for Kurdish interests. At the Residency, in the early part of 1930, Young was faced with embarrassing requests for enlightenment on the question of who would be available, when Iraq entered the League in 1932, to underwrite the regime which had been promised (but showed no signs of being created) for Kurdistan.[25] Reports from the north indicated a variety of developments. In Kirkuk, the local Kurdish nationalists felt that they had been cheated by Britain: they had been promised a treaty with twenty-five years' British protection, and they were now to be cut off after six. In Arbil, Kitching felt that the government's attitude was causing such discontent that British forces would be compelled to intervene. He was certain that the Iraqi government would 'cease to exist in the mountains of this *liwa* early in 1932.' None of the Administrative Inspectors or Special Service Officers considered that an organised revolutionary movement was in existence or being constructed, but all felt that positive action on the part of the Iraqi government should not be delayed any longer.[26]

As a result of these representations, and of a conference of the local British officials and the British staff in the Ministry of Interior in mid-March, Cornwallis put up a note on the Kurdish question for the new Minister of the Interior, Jamil Midfa'i, summarising what the conference had considered to be the minimum which would satisfy the Kurds. Apart from transfers of individuals, Cornwallis and his colleagues requested that the Kurdish areas should be made into a single educational inspectorate, that a Kurdish Assistant Director-General should be appointed to the Ministry of Interior, that all court proceedings where Kurds were concerned should be in Kurdish, that police and all officials in the Kurdish areas should be able to speak the language, and that Kurdish should be the official language of the provinces of Sulaymaniya, Kirkuk and the designated parts of Mosul, and one of the official languages of the town of Kirkuk. They also asked for the incorporation of a recognisably Kurdish symbol into the national flag, and, as ever, a translation bureau.[27] Following this and other pressures from British official sources, the government promised a policy centred round a Local Languages Law in a policy statement at the beginning of April 1930.[28] In spite of constant pressure from the British authorities, this law had still to be drafted by May 1931,[29] and when it eventually appeared was so emasculated as to be almost unrecognisable.

We have already seen that the omission of any direct mention of Kurdistan in the 1930 treaty had caused grave concern in the north. Cornwallis hoped that the publication of the Treaty might serve as a suitable occasion for the government to reemphasise its pledges to the Kurds, and to set in motion a proper programme which would satisfy the aspirations of the Kurdish moderates. At a meeting of the cabinet on 17 July, the ministers considered the details of the suggestions put forward by British officials which had occasioned the blanket pronouncement of intent issued three months earlier. Most of the measures requested were agreed to, including the creation of an educational inspectorate for the Kurdish areas, the appointment of an Assistant Director-General in the Ministry of Interior, with two translators directly under him, the training of police officers in Kurdish, the criterion of language rather than race as a qualification for employment in the Kurdish areas, and the principle that all judicial procedings in the area should be conducted in Kurdish.[30]

By this time, with telegrams of protest being sent to the League of Nations in considerable number,[31] the problem had ceased to be confined to Iraq and threatened to become a major embarrassment for Britain. Successive British officials had assured the League that the Iraqi government was carrying out the undertakings it made in 1926 while almost all of them had remained a dead letter, and petitions to this effect were beginning to pile up in Geneva The League had stated in January 1930 that Iraq's entry would be welcomed in 1932, but one of the conditions for entry would be that 'effective guarantees be secured for the observance of all Treaty obligations in Iraq for the benefit of racial and religious minorities'[32] and the volume of discontent in Kurdistan was a clear indication that these guarantees were not being provided. Accordingly, early in August, the Acting High Commissioner and the Acting Prime Minister, Major Young and Ja'far al-'Askari, made a tour of the Kurdish areas to emphasise the evils of separation and to demonstrate the complete unanimity of British and Iraqi policy towards Kurdistan. In the course of the tour, Ja'far made several speeches (on the lines of the cabinet decisions of 17 July) which gave the impression that these measures had already been put into effect.

The tour was not a success, particularly in Sulaymaniya, the centre of the strongest sentiments for Kurdish separatism. Guns and *picquets* of the Iraq Army had been placed on the hills above the town, and machine guns were clearly visible on the rooftops of the houses.[33] Furthermore, it was only when Young returned to Baghdad that he realised that Ja'far's statements about the Language Law, justice and officials were promises for the future rather than descriptions of what had actually been done. As a result, Young undertook to forward, with his official blessing, petitions to the League signed by several leading citizens of Sulaymaniya complaining that the Iraqi government was not implementing its policies as it claimed:

> I am telling the Regent and the Acting Prime Minister that unless I am satisfied immediately that policy which I have publicly endorsed on behalf of H. M. Government is carried out in spirit as well as letter I shall be obliged to recommend that in forwarding Sulaymaniya petition to the League, H. M. Government should explain that my announcement [while on tour in Kurdistan] was made under a misapprehension and that the Iraqi government are not in fact carrying out their programme.[34]

At the same time, Cornwallis issued a stiff memorandum to his minister, Jamil Midfa'i, who had been incensed by the Sulaymaniya petition and had removed the popular *mutasarrif*, Tawfiq Wahbi. Cornwallis pointed out that the Kurds were quite capable, if sufficiently provoked, of causing the Iraqi government the greatest embarrassment. He had always been apprehensive of trouble, in the form of some sort of Kurdish rising, but was particularly anxious that it should not arise as a result of mismanagement on the part of the Iraqi government. Although Midfa'i was angry with the Sulaymaniya leaders, he should not forget that they had telegraphed their warm approbation of the proposed Language Law when it had been mooted in April. Unfortunately the good effect had been spoilt by the Prime Minister's announcement that language and not race would be the test of employment in the Kurdish areas in the future. The choice remained: the government could either clamp down on the moderate Kurdish leaders or try to win them over. Cornwallis recommended that all the proposals which had been made should be put into effect immediately with the maximum publicity, and a number of Kurds appointed to senior positions.[35] By this time it had become abundantly clear that 'Kurdish national sentiment' had become fairly widespread among the educated classes in the Kurdish area.

By early September 1930, the Colonial Office had become aware of the gravity of the situation, and also realised that attempts to conceal the truth from the League might give rise to grave embarrassments in the future. Young was informed that H. M. Government required some concrete evidence of the Iraqi government's good faith, such as the publication of the Local Languages Law. When the Prime Minister (Nuri) returned from Europe, he should be told that the law must be published, that anyone demonstrating anti-Kurdish attitudes must be removed from the cabinet, and that the policy already given publicity should be put into immediate effect. When this telegram arrived at the Residency, Sturges noted 'this strengthens our hand considerably.'[36]

However, while London was now realising the gravity of the situation, there was little, short of the Iraqi government actually implementing the policies the policies it had promised, that could be done to avert serious trouble in Iraq. In Sulaymaniya, Tawfiq Wahbi had been removed by the Ministry of Interior in mid-August because of his evident sympathies with the leader of the Sulaymaniya moderates, Shaykh Qadir, a brother-in-law of Shaykh Mahmud. The moderates had voted in a body in July to boycott the forthcoming elections. While Tawfiq Wahbi remained in Sulaymaniya, Shaykh Qadir felt safe from outside pressures, but when he was replaced by Ahmad Beg-i Tawfiq Beg, Qadir turned once more to his brother-in-law for help.[37] Ahmad ordered the election of the inspection committee to go ahead, and a detachment of the Iraqi army was brought in to supervise the proceedings. On election day, 6 September, there was serious rioting as a result of the army's attempt to force the holding of the election. One soldier and fourteen civilians were killed, and a large number of civilians, including Shaykh Qadir, were arrested. More Kurdish petitions appeared, demanding complete administrative separation of the area from Baghdad (McDowall,

1996:176). Two days later, Midfa'i was at last persuaded to sign a memorandum on Kurdish policy to be sent to the *mutasarrifs* of the northern *liwas*, instructing them to act in accordance with the provisions of the Draft Local Languages Law which had still not been published.[38] The Acting High Commissioner telegraphed to London:

> Apart from the fact that the Iraqi government are not in the mood to reconsider concessions to the Kurds at present I consider that any actual concession, such as the publication of the Local Languages Law at this moment would be interpreted by the Kurds as a result of the violent tactics adopted at Sulaymaniya. I propose to confine myself for the time being . . . to ensuring that justice is done to those arrested as instigators of the riot and to impressing on the Iraqi government the fact that the riot at Sulaymaniya must not alter the general policy of conciliation.[39]

The immediate result of the incident at Sulaymaniya was to bring Shaykh Mahmud back into the arena of Kurdish politics. Eleven days after the riot he entered Iraq from Iran, sending his son Baba 'Ali to inform the *mutasarrif* and Administrative Inspector of Sulaymaniya of his arrival, professedly on a visit to perform condolence ceremonies with some of the Pizhder chiefs. In fact he was building up support among the Pizhder and the Avroman tribes. The Acting High Commissioner admitted that it might seem strange that no action was taken to restrain the Shaykh, but he believed that it was up to the Iraqi government to take the initiative, as Mahmud could always slip back across the Iranian frontier. The Iraqi army would have great difficulty in resisting him successfully without the help of the RAF and it was therefore desirable to wait until the situation had actually deteriorated.[40]

Mahmud did in fact return to Iran after some weeks in Iraq, but in the course of his stay he complained bitterly to the High Commissioner about the shootings in Sulaymaniya. In mid-October he wrote that the Kurds 'from Zakho to Khaniqin' were united in wanting separation from Iraq and independence under British protection. He asked that those who had been imprisoned in Sulaymaniya should be released, and also requested an extensive administrative reorganisation of the area.[41] By this time such pleas fell on deaf ears: the Residency and the British officials could not support Iraq's candidature for the League while simultaneously apparently encouraging a powerful local leader to rebel against the government's authority. Thus a message was sent from Baghdad to Sulaymaniya informing the Shaykh that the government considered him an outlaw and would under no circumstances listen to his demands. The only acceptable course would be the Shaykh's surrender and the dispersal of his forces.[42] At the end of the year it seemed extremely likely that Mahmud would be leading an uprising against the government in the spring, and petitions from Kurdistan were pouring in to the Residency in his favour.[43] Two months later the Administrative Inspector, Mosul, confirmed that most of the important *aghas* in his *liwa* had also pledged their support to Mahmud. Edmonds wondered how this threat would be dealt with: 'The Iraq Treasury is empty and I imagine that the RAF budget has been considerably curtailed since the halcyon days of Sir John Salmond when the RAF still had to make good.'[44]

In the middle of October the Residency returned to the charge, in an attempt to find out how far the 'promises' had been implemented since Young and Ja'far had made their tour in August. On the face of it, things seemed to be improving: on 24 August, Salih Zaki of Chamchamal had been appointed Assistant Director-General in the Ministry of Interior, in charge of Kurdish affairs, with two Kurdish translators; on 30 September Sayyid Nuri Barzinji had been made inspector of Kurdish schools.[45] However, the Local Languages Law had still not been published in the aftermath of the Sulaymaniya incident and it was feared in London that awkward questions would soon be asked at Geneva.[46]

Such fears were well founded. Major Young, appearing on Britain's behalf before the Permanent Mandates Commission in November, was given something of a rough passage. The chairman of the committee, pointing out the instability of the Iraqi government as indicated by the numerous changes of cabinet, also wondered whether the Mandatory was actually fulfilling its duties in respect of Iraq:

> If the British Government had definitely decided to recommend Iraq for entry into the League in 1932, then it must inform the PMC of the reasons which had led to that decision. Every time, however, that the PMC asked for these reasons, the accredited representative of Great Britain merely urged it to wait until the moment arrived.[47]

There were other serious considerations facing the Colonial Office and the Residency at this time. In December, Humphrys informed London that members of the Iraqi government were preparing their own comments on the Sulaymaniya petition, and they had pointed out to him, first, that until comparatively recently there had been no complaints from the region about the central administration, and second, that the annual reports submitted to the League by H. M. Government had underlined this. They quoted passages from the 1925 and 1926 reports, which were certainly 'economical with the truth':

> The system of employing Kurdish officials in Kurdish districts has long been accepted together with the use of the Kurdish language in the schools, and local correspondence is conducted in Kurdish if desired. In respecting Kurdish susceptibilities the Iraqi government has rightly comprehended that a united state can be built up of diverse elements and has set an example among Near Eastern Countries. Everywhere in the Kurdish areas, officials, with very few exceptions, were Kurds, and the Kurdish language was the official language of the courts and schools. The policy enunciated by the Prime Minister on 21 January 1926 has been loyally carried out by all departments and accepted by the Kurds themselves.

Humphrys continued:

> I do not know whether Your Lordship intends to transmit these comments of the Iraqi government to the League with the final comments of H. M. Government on the Kurdish question, but it appears to me that if the League are to be presented with documents which show a divergence of view between the British and Iraqi governments on the manner in which the Kurds have been handled in the past, the effect upon the League will be most unfortunate.

Some new line of argument had to be found, therefore, which the British and Iraqi governments could present to the League in an attempt to explain why, if the British authorities had painted so rosy a picture of Kurdistan in the past, such obvious signs of discontent should be appearing in 1930. Humphrys argued that a possible escape lay in arguing that the Boundary Commission's recommendations had become unworkable, because these had been made at a time when the promises of Sèvres were still very much alive in Kurdish minds. He suggested that further petitions should not be forwarded to the League until the Permanent Mandates Commission (PMC) had intimated whether or not it concurred with the Iraqi government's new policy, embodied in the Local Languages Law, which had been issued on 11 November.[48]

By now, the League was even more concerned about the situation in Kurdistan. On 22 December, the High Commissioner received the PMC's comments on the petitions which it had received so far. It recommended that the plea for an independent Kurdish government under the League should be rejected, but invited the cooperation of the mandatory to ensure that the 'legislative and administrative measures designed to secure for the Kurds the position to which they are entitled are promptly put into effect and properly enforced.' Further, it asked the British government to consider taking measures to guarantee Kurdish rights after the termination of the mandate.[49]

As Humphrys had realised, the British authorities were in an extremely delicate position. Nothing in their previous reports to the League had given the slightest sign that all was not well in Kurdistan, but they were now faced, not only with evident and widespread dissatisfaction in the area, but with the real possibility of an armed uprising. The Iraqi government claimed that this was the result of pandering to the Kurds, while the British authorities claimed that, on the contrary, it was the result of not taking Kurdish demands seriously enough. For its part the Iraqi government seems to have realised by the end of 1930 that Britain was not only anxious to be able to leave Iraq in 1932, but that failure to do so because the League judged Iraq incompetent would reflect highly unfavourably on British integrity at Geneva. Thus of all the parties the Iraqi government was in the strongest position: provided the threat posed by Shaykh Mahmud could somehow be dealt with, and that the suggestion of a League Commissioner could be headed off, it was difficult to see how it ran the risk of much more than a rebuke from the League if the Kurds were not satisfied after the end of the mandate. They also knew that because of its relations with Turkey and Iran, Britain was extremely sensitive to any insinuation that it was attempting to return to the conditions of the Treaty of Sèvres. Provided the Iraqi government could make paper concessions, and continue to procrastinate, no serious attempt to resolve the Kurdish problem seemed necessary.

Internal Affairs and Financial Difficulties, 1930–1931

At the same time as the Iraqi government was facing these problems in Kurdistan, it was confronted with a serious economic crisis affecting the whole country. At the beginning of 1930, in common with other countries which relied mainly on grain production, it could be foreseen that an acute financial crisis was approaching because of the precipitous slump in world agricultural prices. As in 1925, it seemed unlikely that the government would be able to balance the budget, and once more Sir Hilton Young was asked to visit Iraq and to advise on suitable economies. By March there was already a deficit of 25 lakhs (about £17,000) of revenue from agricultural produce, and a final deficit of between 30 and 40 lakhs (£20,000 – £25,000) was forecast.[50] In his report Hilton Young noted that although there had been an increase in production, there had been no improvements in quality; in addition, the increase had been at the expense of soil exhaustion and excessive salination, due to the widespread use of mechanical pumps without proper drainage arrangements. Furthermore, an acute agricultural labour shortage had arisen; the *fellahin*'s share of what they produced was insufficient to live on, and many had migrated to the towns in search of employment.

Hilton Young did not think it wise to meet the crisis by making permanent structural alterations either to the administration or to the economy, as this would lead to long term weaknesses. He suggested that defence expenditure might be reduced by 9 lakhs (about £6,000) and small cuts of 2 lakhs each (about £1,300) in the Agricultural and Health budgets. In fact the situation eventually called for more drastic cuts than he had anticipated: by September 1930 cuts of 10 lakhs in Public Works, 8 lakhs in Irrigation and a further 5 lakhs in Defence were deemed necessary, since the returns from Customs and Excise proved to have fallen far short of what had been forecast.[51]

On the positive side, it was recommended that the Iraqi government should pay special attention to improving the quality of agricultural produce, and concentrate on the more valuable cash crops, such as cotton. As part of a major public works programme, Young suggested the construction of two flood prevention works, at Aqar Quf and Habbaniyya, the completion of the railway extension to Mosul, and the construction of a bridge across the Tigris at Baghdad to link the northern and southern halves of the railway system. A loan should be obtained on the security of the oil revenues, which 'would provide a strong buttress for credit.'[52] However, the new oil agreement had still to be signed, and at this stage oil revenues formed an inconsiderable part of Iraq's national income.[53]

The severity of the economic crisis increased through 1930 and 1931, and serious conditions were reported from many areas.[54] Since grain prices were so low, revenue from land fell off sharply, and this development probably contributed to a major change in the method of collection of revenue summarised in the *Istihlak* Law of 1931, whereby tax was paid at the point of sale rather than on the production of grain. We shall consider the socio-economic implications of this law in more detail in Chapter 6, but it is sufficient to mention here that the change altered the whole basis of the Iraqi taxation system: land revenue gradually dwindled to under 10% of the total revenue, and the bulk of the national income was drawn from Customs and Excise, and, eventually, from oil revenue.[55]

Until a combination of these pressing financial considerations virtually forced its capitulation in 1931, the Iraqi government proved exceedingly hard-headed in its dealings with the oil company, renamed the Iraq Petroleum Company (IPC) in 1929. The second series of negotiations had begun as far back as 1927 when IPC/TPC had begun its attempt to persuade the government to abandon the plot system and to extend the time limit of the concessions.[56] By November 1929, after the government had granted two extensions, IPC informed the government of the plots which it had selected, but applied at the same time for a revision of the concession, to extend it over a wider area. As Longrigg explains, the Company could afford to proceed at a 'leisurely tempo' because of the glut in world oil supplies; this increased the Company's value, while postponing the benefit that the government would have derived from active exploitation of the oil (Longrigg, 1961: 74).

As we have seen, BOD's offer in April 1928 had shown the Iraqi government that it might be possible to squeeze better terms out of IPC. This had prompted the government's request, which IPC had been forced to consider since the spring of 1929, that any new concession should be linked with the construction of a railway and a pipeline. The Iraqi government had come round to a very serious consideration of BOD's offer, especially as the latter agreed to follow the government's preference for the southern alignment of the pipeline. By May 1930, the Colonial Office seems to have become so disillusioned with the slow progress of the negotiations with IPC that they suggested that H. M. Government should transfer its support from that Company to the BOD Company. In a useful memorandum, Rendel of the Foreign Office pointed out that this was quite impossible. The reasons given throw considerable light on Britain's *locus standi* as regards the oil of Iraq.

Under the San Remo Oil Agreement of 1920, it had been laid down that French interests should be entitled to a 25% share in any company formed to exploit Iraqi oil. Thus, under the 1928 Red Line Agreement, the Turkish Petroleum Company's concession had been divided as follows:

Company	Percentage Share	Nationality/ Constituents
1. Participation and Investments Ltd.	5.00	C.S. Gulbenkian
2. Near East Development Corporation	23.75	US: Socony Vacuum Oil Co and Standard Oil of New Jersey 50% each

3. D'Arcy Exploration Co	23.75	GB (APOC): 66%; Burmah Oil: 22% Public: 12%
4. Anglo-Saxon Petroleum Co	23.75	Anglo-Dutch: Royal Dutch: 60% Shell Transport: 40%
5. Compagnie Française des Pétroles	23.75	French: French government: 35%

Since the British government and other British shareholders had a major interest in companies (3) and (4), they were in a dominant position on the board of the Iraq Petroleum Company. If, on the other hand, the British government was to allow the BOD's claim to be accepted, the situation would be completely different. In 1930, the BOD Company was constituted as follows:

Participation	Percentage
British	51
Italian	35
Dutch	14[57]

Since no French interest was represented in the BOD the San Remo allocation would presumably have to be met out of the 51% British interest, and it was also inevitable that United States' interests would also demand a share equivalent to that which they had in IPC. Hence the only chance of breaking the deadlock lay with IPC, which would need to drop its objection to the southern alignment of the pipeline, 'in order to reach an early and satisfactory agreement with the Iraqi government.' As we have seen, by the happiest of coincidences, both British and Iraqi interests favoured the Kirkuk/Haifa route: Iraqi preference combined neatly with Britain's desire to run the pipeline over British-controlled territory.[58] At the end of June the Iraqi government confirmed that it had no intention of revising IPC's concession unless the pipeline debouched at Haifa: they had dropped their stipulation that the concession was conditional upon the construction of a railway, but under no circumstances would they budge over the alignment.[59]

At this stage the Iraqi government was in increasingly serious financial difficulties. Nuri left Baghdad for London to discuss outstanding financial differences between the British and Iraqi governments the moment the treaty had been signed; it was clear that money was needed not only for development projects, but also for dealing with the budget deficit. By 30 September agreement had been reached between Nuri and the Colonial Office on a board of management for the Iraqi Railways, and a trust for the port of Basra.[60] Later in the year, a compromise was suggested on the pipeline in the form of a bifurcation, possibly at or above Rutba, with one arm running to Haifa and the other to Tripoli, and this was eventually written in to the agreement with IPC which was finally signed in March 1931.

By this time, the Iraqi government was in really desperate need of money, and the dead rent payments (advances against future royalties) made by the Company as part of the concession were a vital necessity. The money was spent not on development projects, but turned directly over to the Treasury, so that the country became more or less dependent on dead rents or royalties for its solvency. Total oil revenue for the period 1933–1940 amounted to about £2 million per year, about one quarter of the total national revenue. The figures for 1930–1932 show how narrowly the crisis was averted:

Year	Revenue (Lakhs)	Expenditure	Deficit	Royalties from IPC
1929–1930	576.66	574.61	2.05	—
1930–1931	464.57	511.58	47.01	—
1931–1932	481.74	509.19	17.45	86.70[61]

Even with the oil revenues, there was a deficit of 17.45 lakhs (£12,000) in 1931–1932: without them, it would have been over 100 lakhs (£65,000). The previous year, 1930–1931, had seen the highest deficit in the country's 10 years' history. It is probable that the Company was able to obtain highly favourable terms from the government because the latter had very little alternative.

As a result of the new concession, instead of 24 plots of eight square miles, IPC obtained a blanket concession for the whole of the 35,000 square miles of Iraq east of the Tigris in the Baghdad and Mosul *wilayas*. The royalty rate of four shillings gold remained unchanged, though it was not honoured when sterling was devalued late in 1931. This left the rest of the country open to competition from other oil interests, and it was generally considered advisable in Whitehall that IPC should be excluded from bidding for rights in these areas: Humphrys accordingly informed the Iraqi government in May 1931 that they would be wise to exercise a veto in this respect.[62] Britain's attitude here seems to have been influenced by the stand taken by the Italian government at Geneva in the spring of 1931. The Italian Ambassador in Baghdad informed Humphrys quite frankly that:

> . . . the Italian Government were not really interested in the question of principle which they had raised, nor in the despatch of a commission of enquiry. Their main motive, apart from a desire to make their weight felt, was to extract some solid consideration for the withdrawal of their opposition, and in the course of the conversation it became clear that they have in mind a share in the development of Iraqi oil.[63]

Apparently the Italian Ambassador also feared that the British group, which was the majority shareholder within BOD, might sell out its interest to the highest bidder, presumably the IPC. In fact this was avoided, and the BOD obtained the concession for the rest of the Baghdad and Mosul *wilayas* in May 1932. Later developments, however, saw IPC eventually extend its control over the whole of Iraq: by 1935 the Italians had become majority shareholders in BOD but could not pay the agreed £200,000 yearly to the Iraqi government. In 1936 a holding company bought out the Germans and Italians on behalf of IPC, and by 1938 IPC controlled all oil concessions not only in the Baghdad and Mosul *wilayas*, but also in Basra and the Iraqi-Sa'udi neutral zone, and continued to do so until the passage of Law 80 by 'Abd al-Karim Qasim's government in 1961, under which the unexploited parts of IPC's concession area were brought back under Iraqi control.

Shaykh Mahmud and Kurdish politics, 1930–1931

At the end of 1930, British officials in the Ministry of Interior were expressing widespread misgivings over the Iraqi government's Kurdish policy. Edmonds pointed out that the signatories of the Kurdish petition to the League asking for a separate state had been treated as though they were guilty of treason; they realised that they could not hope for complete independence, but understandably stated their maximum demands to be sure of being granted the minimum.[64] After the shootings at Sulaymaniya, Shaykh Mahmud could come forward as champion of a just cause; three quarters of the Iraqi army was now in Sulaymaniya *liwa* although apparently incapable of preventing the situation from deteriorating. Further, although the Iraqi government claimed to be fulfilling its obligations, this was far from the actual state of affairs. The Kurdish Assistant Director-General in the Ministry of Interior had been given no work: the Ministry was still appointing Arab *qa'immaqams* to Kurdish areas, and the Language Law had not been applied.[65]

Some slight relief was afforded by the resignation of Jamil Midfa'i from the Ministry of Interior early in February 1931: for nearly three months the post was taken by Nuri himself, but his 'permanent' successor, Muzahim Pachachi, was a considerable improvement as far as his attitude to Kurdish problems was concerned. The League's replies to the Sulaymaniya petitioners, though communicated to the High Commissioner at the end of December, did not reach the petitioners themselves until the end of February, and in the meantime Cornwallis in particular pressed the minister to make every effort to try to dispel the distrust for the central government felt by the vast majority of Kurds. He asked him again to make sure that the government's declared policies were implemented, and made detailed recommendations for new schools and the appointment of Kurdish- speaking police and other officials.

Meanwhile, it was gradually becoming clear in Whitehall that the Iraqi government was resisting implementing the measures which Britain had promised were being put through. The Colonial Office warned that Iraq might be forced to accept the appointment of a Commission of Enquiry, or, even worse, a Resident Commissioner, if Geneva was not satisfied. The British government wished to be able to tell the next meeting of the PMC in June that the Iraqi government's declared policy had been 'carried into full effect.' Meanwhile, London asked for as much information as possible to be sent from Baghdad:

> There is I think no doubt that for some reason or other the P. M. C. have got the impression that we have been intentionally withholding information from them . . . The FO are anything but sanguine of Iraq's prospects of entry next year, and the only apparent means open to us of improving those prospects in the interval would seem to be by satisfying the P. M. C. by the weight and volume of evidence that Iraq is really fit for independence.[66]

Some of the information being presented to the League was in the form of a memorandum drawn up by J. H. Hall of the Colonial Office, commenting on seven petitions received from the inhabitants of Sulaymaniya which had been despatch after the shootings on 6 September 1930. Hall took pains to exonerate the behaviour of the army, and dismissed four of the petitions by describing them as emanating from the 'notorious rebel and bandit Shaykh Mahmud'. The memorandum fails to point out the material fact that Shaykh

Mahmud's reappearance in Kurdish politics was a direct consequence of the shootings. Two of the other petitions could also be treated cursorily since they originated from the brother of the 'bandit', Shaykh Qadir (who was in fact the leader of the more moderate Kurds in Sulaymaniya). There was no attempt to deal with any point of substance raised in any of the petitions. It is difficult to avoid the conclusion that the PMC's suspicion that Britain was 'intentionally withholding information' was entirely justified.[67]

In the spring of 1931, military action was taken against Shaykh Mahmud. By mid March he had taken control of Halabja and Khurmal and was collecting taxes in the Kara Dagh villages, with a following of about 600 men, successfully defying the Iraqi government, which had sent a force of 350 mounted police to the area. Although in overall control of operations, the Air Officer Commanding decided to leave the actual command of forces in the field to the Iraqi army: no Levies were used, and, according to his lengthy report on the operation written in October 1931, the RAF's part was not primary until March.[68] On 26 March the High Commissioner received a formal request for aerial assistance from the Iraqi government, and on the 28th the villages of Kani Kermanj, Shawazi and Bagh Anaran were bombed in order to free a squadron of police which had been hemmed in by Kurdish forces.

After a month's harrying by the army and RAF together, Mahmud indicated that he was prepared to come to terms. After some wrangling between the Ministry of Interior and the Residency, it was agreed that Interior should sign the letter which the Residency had drafted. Mahmud was informed that his life and the lives of his family would be spared, that he was to live in Iraq at a place appointed by the Iraqi government, and that he would receive an adequate allowance. On 13 May, Holt and the Shaykh met at Panjwin: Mahmud accepted the terms and was installed at Ur on 15 May:

> It is interesting to note that at the first meeting at Panjwin Shaykh Mahmud went up to an RAF officer who was present, and pointing to the wings on his tunic said, 'You are the people who have broken my spirit.'[69]

The Iraq Army was sent to Jalabagh to finish the operation, and the area was quiet until the following winter: peace was further ensured by setting up a semi-permanent Levy camp at Ser 'Amadiya, and further detachments of Levies were sent to Sulaymaniya in August.

Among the less militant Kurdish leaders, the reply of the League to the petitions was generally well received. The moderates seem to have taken the reply as indicating that the League would keep an eye on their interests. The Administrative Inspector Sulaymaniya believed that, following the reply, 'we may expect a continuance of the legitimate demand for the fulfilment of the 1926 promises.'[70] Thus Shaykh Qadir wrote to the High Commissioner:

> I have been asked by my fellow countrymen to . . . enquire whether the Mandatory power intends to carry out the terms of the resolutions . . . It is now about two months since the resolution was passed but no changes have taken place and it is presumed that Your Excellency has no objection to our making further demands to the League of Nations if this resolution is longer postponed.[71]

Five weeks later, Humphrys forwarded a copy of the letter to Nuri commenting that 'it gives an indication of the effect which has been produced upon the signatories of the Kurdish petition by the reply which has been sent them from Geneva, and shows how important it is that immediate steps should be taken to reassure them.'[72]

At the same time, Cornwallis reported that the attitude of the Minister of Interior, Muzahim Pachachi, was 'very sensible', that he had been meeting leading Kurds in Baghdad and was planning a tour of the Kurdish areas in May. Cornwallis considered that the British officials should therefore 'keep in the background until we see whether there is really a genuine desire to adopt a conciliatory policy.'[73] His tour of the Kurdish areas was evidently a success and reports from both Sulaymaniya and Arbil were favourable. However, there was still little progress in implementing the promised administrative reforms. The Kurdish Director-General at Interior was being given work of a 'general nature': the Education Officer was only an Inspector and did not have final authority in his area, and there were still large numbers of non-Kurdish speaking police in the Kurdish areas. On the other main issue, the Local Languages Law, the cabinet continued to drag its feet: in February Nuri had told the High Commissioner that progress had been halted due to the discovery that no standard form of Kurdish existed, as Lionel Smith had observed some five years previously. Eventually, after a good deal of argument, the law was passed on 19 May, but it had suffered considerable reduction in its scope by this time. Technical departments were excluded from the law: a knowledge of the Kurdish language replaced race as the criterion for employment in the Kurdish areas, and the Kurdish *qadhas* of Mosul *liwa* were to be given a year to decide upon the dialect of Kurdish which they preferred. Holt pointed out angrily:

> My own view is that the King and Nuri are determined to do their utmost to maintain the use of Arabic in these *qadhas*. If they can delay

for a few months implementing the stipulation ascertaining the wishes of the people the Mandate may come to an end before the year is up and then there will be no-one to press them to honour their pledges.

Commenting on a letter from Nuri on the application of the law, Holt pointed out that if it was interpreted as the Prime Minister chose (to imply that those in the technical services need not know Kurdish), this would mean that 'any Kurds wishing to use the public services in the Kurdish areas, e. g. to buy stamps or to be treated at the hospitals, will have to use Arabic:' he considered that the whole letter 'was a useful exposure of the Iraqi government's complete lack of good faith with regard to the treatment of the Kurds.'[74]

The British authorities in Baghdad continued to press the Iraqi government to take action, but as Holt and others had correctly anticipated, the latter took refuge in a policy of procrastination. After prolonged correspondence, Nuri admitted that 'technical services' only referred to the actual technical personnel (doctors, engineers, electricians, etc.): the administrative staffs would be recruited locally.[75] The Residency pointed out that it should be remembered that the law had not been introduced simply to legalise existing practice, but:

> as part of a programme of legal and administrative reforms "designed to rectify the situation created by the fact that of recent years the Iraqi government had somewhat fallen away from the promises given by a former Iraqi Prime Minister in 1926" (my quotation is from the minutes of the 19th session of the Permanent Mandates Commission) . . . I feel that it would be dangerous to admit any 'no change' principle . . . since I am convinced that the Iraqi government would only be too willing to avail themselves of it to restrict the application of the Law to other public services and even to education.[76]

Between January 1931 and July 1932, the British authorities in London and Baghdad were obliged to steer an uneasy course between satisfying individual powers and the League as a whole that Iraq actually was fit for independence, and nudging the Iraqi government into accepting a minority policy which it could adopt without the loss of *amour propre*. Thus Britain had to interpret Iraq's policy to the League, and the League's policy to Iraq in terms as conciliatory as possible to both parties. The Italian government in particular was thought likely to attempt to block Iraq's entry if proper attention was not paid to their interests. Hence, as late as July 1931, there was a good deal of uncertainty about the whole matter:

> Many of us here (Foreign Office) think that Iraq's ambition will be attained. Others of us feel that it is a very moot point, the more so as one or two of our late allies of the war cannot cease from asking questions about Iraq which lead us to think that they may be out to make trouble or demand a high price for their support.[77]

In the middle of June 1931, Humphrys was to appear before the PMC, to keep the Commission informed about current developments in Iraq. If Young had been faced with challenges in November 1930, his chief was given an even more critical reception on this occasion. Humphrys was closely questioned on the *Special Report . . . on the Progress of Iraq 1920 to 1931*, which had been prepared for the purpose of assisting the Commission to decide on Iraq's fitness for League entry. The burden of the High Commissioner's advocacy, on this and other occasions, was that the Commission could and should rely on the good faith and integrity of H. M. Government's promises:

> Should Iraq prove herself unworthy of the confidence which has been placed in her, the moral responsibility must rest with H. M. Government . . . The new Treaty contained no obligation to assist the Iraqi government to suppress disorder, but if such assistance was given the British Government would make its own terms. It would never agree to give assistance by means of the RAF until it was sure that such assistance was justified . . . He could assure the Commission that the British Government had no intention of becoming the tool of the Iraqi government or of suppressing risings due to bad administration and oppression.[78]

The Council's final decision was left over until November: the issue was still by no means clear.

It seems at this stage as if Britain's chief concern was to provide the League with evidence that Iraq was actively considering appropriate measures, while omitting to mention that actual implementation was not taking place. The Iraqi government were safe in the knowledge that provided they could avoid the appointment of a Resident representative of the League, they could give all the required promises of fair treatment of minorities, safe in the knowledge that they would never be obliged to implement them. Britain's position was just as cynical: although individual administrators might make every effort to see that justice was done to the Kurds, it was British policy to support League entry in 1932. The great weight of evidence showing that the Iraqi government was not fulfilling its obligations to the Kurds, and clearly had no intention of doing so, had to be hushed up rather than brought out into the open. With luck, and with the main focus of Kurdish resistance languishing under house arrest in Nasiriya, any further open confrontation would be avoided. There is no doubt, however, that both the British authorities in Baghdad and the Colonial Office in London were fully informed as to the true state of affairs.

Baghdad Politics, January to August 1931

At the beginning of the year, a new party, *Hizb al-Ikha' al-Watani*, was busy collecting supporters, and branches were formed in several provincial centres. Early in January a number of tribal leaders met a delegation from Baghdad at Karbala', where it was hoped to hold a mass meeting. All the anti-government groups, the *Hizb al-Watani*, *Hizb al-Ikha' al-Watani*, and *Hizb al-Nahdha* had declared that they would participate, but the *mutasarrif* refused to allow the meeting to take place. The opposition, already disgruntled by the 'defection' of Muzahim Pachachi,[79] were further dismayed by the failure of the Karbala' meeting, and also by their inability to secure the aid of the Karbala' *'ulama'*. Previous attempts to organise opposition to the government, or to any particular measure, had not been successful because although temporary alliances were possible, the interests of the various anti-government groups differed so widely from each other that unity soon broke down. This was still largely the case at the beginning of 1931, but it gradually became clear that this time there was some hope of organising a concerted attempt to bring down the cabinet. This aim had support from groups as far apart politically as trade union leaders in Baghdad and Basra and tribal leaders in the Euphrates. It is interesting that the opposition in 1931 was directed not so much at the iniquity of the terms imposed by Britain in the 1930 treaty and the oil concession, but against the craven acceptance of these terms by the cabinet and the Chamber of Deputies, and the cabinet's policy of stifling any criticism of its policy in the press.[80]

It is difficult to distinguish a separate role for the two main parties: generally the *Hizb al-Watani* was the old Sunni nationalist group, while the *Ikha'* was more Shi'i-centred. However, the largest of the labour unions, the *Jam'iyat Ashab al-Sana'i'* (Artisans' Association) was closely associated with the *Ikha'*: the two most prominent opposition leaders, Ja'far Abu'l-Timman and Yasin al-Hashimi, distrusted each other intensely and were attached to both parties. The main task of the leadership was to ensure that the Euphrates chiefs did not break away from the parties: in spite of their general dislike of the government, the Euphrates leaders had not forgotten what they considered to have been their betrayal by the Sunni politicians after the rising of 1920, when they had done all the fighting and the 'effendis' had reaped all the rewards. For their part, the urban leaders knew that no serious challenge could be posed to the government without at least the threat of an armed tribal rising.

At the official opening of the *Hizb al-Ikha' al-Watani* in Baghdad in March, Rashid 'Ali and Yasin addressed a meeting of about 2000 people: they called for a new government and a cabinet pledged to reconsider the political relations of Britain and Iraq. There were reports of strong 'anti-government and anti-King' feeling in Baghdad, and large scale arms purchases in the Euphrates towns.[81] The economic depression, and the government's failure to take account of it by allowing tax remissions, had particularly aggravated tribal leaders, but conditions in the country were also affecting wage earners. At the end of February there was a brief strike of railway workers, organised by the *Jam'iyat Ashab al-Sana'i'* protesting against short time working on the railways, but the management's explanation that this was the only alternative to dismissals was accepted.[82]

By the end of April the mood had become more militant. There were petitions to the King calling for the cabinet's dismissal, suggestions of boycotts of foreign goods, and attempts to organise more strikes. Requests for mass public meetings were normally refused but the parties held large gatherings at their own headquarters. A joint committee to coordinate the activities of the two parties was set up, consisting of Yasin, Rashid 'Ali, Ja'far Abu'l-Timman and Mahmud Ramiz: strenuous efforts were made to maintain friendly links with the tribal leaders, who were deeply distrustful of Yasin and Rashid 'Ali.[83] Early in June the two parties decided on a joint campaign to refuse payment of taxes, and further attempts were made to involve the *'ulama'*. However, at this stage there were signs that the movement was beginning to lose its momentum, and that it was only saved from decline by the appearance of a tangible issue which could act as a focus of popular grievance. The Municipal Fees Law, a revised scale of taxation on all tradesmen, was a serious annoyance to large sections of the urban community, and a general strike, lasting over two weeks, was successfully organised (Farouk-Sluglett and Sluglett, 1983b, 2007).

On 4 July, the King left Baghdad for Europe, leaving behind his brother, ex-King 'Ali of the Hijaz, as Regent. Early in the morning of the next day, shops were deserted, and by midday buses had almost ceased to run. All day there were street parades and demonstrations, and speeches against the Fees Law. The *Jam'iyat* called for its repeal, and over the next few days, for the release of those arrested for demonstrating. After presenting a petition to the Regent, the secretary-general of the *Jam'iyat*, Muhammad Salih al-Qazzaz, was arrested and the *Jam'iyat* compulsorily closed by order of the Ministry of Interior. Both the party headquarters were raided by the police. After a few days, food was still obtainable, but there was virtually no public transport in Baghdad. Reporting to London on 11 July, the Residency seems to have been taken unawares:

> Situation reveals surprising lack of support for present Government and unpopularity of King Faysal. Republican cries have been openly raised in the streets and Yasin has been publicly hailed as future President, while except in Government newspapers there has been no sign of loyalty to King or support for Government.[84]

For the first few days of the strike, the opposition party leaders hung back, presumably to see how widely supported it was. After five or six days, however, after a meeting at the *Hizb al-Watani* (including Ja'far Abu'l-Timman, Yasin, Rashid 'Ali, 'Ali Mahmud, Baqir al-Shabibi), it was resolved to send a deputation to King 'Ali, and letters to the *'ulama'* of Karbala' and Najaf. On 11 July, Muhsin Abu Tabikh met 'Abd al-Wahid Sikkar and Samawi al-Challub in Kadhimayn: the two latter agreed to call out the tribes around Diwaniya when the time was ripe. Meanwhile, on the same day, the demonstrations in Baghdad were becoming more violent; 50 people were arrested and there were reports from Kufa and Diwaniya that most of the shops had closed down.

By the middle of the month the strike had spread to most of the towns on the Euphrates, and was particularly serious in Rumaytha, Kufa and Diwaniya, and later on in Basra. Demonstration flights were made by the RAF over the area on 13 and 14 July.[85] On 15 July Nuri returned to Baghdad, and the capital gradually quietened down, but the disturbances in the provinces continued, especially at Basra. Reinforcements of police were ferried from Baghdad to Basra in RAF transport planes in response to an urgent request from the Administrative Inspector.[86] By 20 July order had been restored in most of the main towns, but al-Jaza'iri reported from Najaf to Muhammad al-Sadr that the tribes remained in a turbulent state.[87] In Baghdad, Nuri asked the Acting High Commissioner to consent to Yasin's removal from the capital under section 40 of the *Tribal Criminal and Civil Disputes Regulation*, but this was refused. By now things were returning to normal, and an attempt to start the strike again on 24 July in Baghdad was unsuccessful.

The strike was more remarkable in revealing the organisation of the opposition and the contempt in which the government was held than for any concrete achievements in the way of concessions. The party leaders had obviously taken charge after the first few days, and after al-Qazzaz' arrest their coordination had ensured that the strike spread to several provincial towns. Ludlow-Hewitt, the Air Officer Commanding, who was Acting High Commissioner in Humphrys' absence, considered that sending demonstration flights over Rumaytha and Diwaniya had had the necessary 'steadying effect'. However, his diagnosis of the situation was perceptive:

> I must confess to having had a certain amount of sympathy for the position of the opposition. As you know, their chance of exercising their influence in a constitutional manner within the *majlis* was virtually destroyed by the Government's manipulation of the elections. Finding themselves in a hopeless minority in the *majlis*, they resigned, believing their only means of influencing the situation to be through a press and propaganda campaign in the country.

The only way that the opposition could overthrow the cabinet was to engage in the sort of popular agitation that had taken place. Naturally, this would not simply stop at political change, but lead to tribal risings as well. In the circumstances, Ludlow-Hewitt confirmed that he would have agreed to the arrest of the opposition leaders if absolutely necessary. Accordingly he interviewed Yasin and told him that while the British government intended to take a 'neutral attitude' to domestic politics, they could not remain indifferent to any attempt to stir up the tribes, and that they would be obliged to take the 'strongest and most severe action' to prevent this sort of agitation.[88] By mid-August the situation had returned to normal. Several of those arrested during the strike had been exiled under Section 40 of the Tribal Criminal and Civil Disputes Regulation, and the *Jam'iyat Ashab al-San'i'* remained disbanded. Although the immediate crisis had passed, Young realised that the underlying causes of discontent were unaffected:

> On the one hand there is Nuri Pasha, looking perhaps to such models as Mussolini and Mustafa Kemal, and determined with King Faysal to set up an autocratic government in Baghdad. On the other hand stands Yasin Pasha, with the opposition leaders, including most of the best brains in the country, who refuse to cooperate with Nuri Pasha

and who will naturally not consent to be permanently removed from participation in the government without a struggle.[89]

On 26 September there was another raid on the *Ikha'* party offices, which seem to have had a dampening effect on the spirit of the opposition: promises of massive demonstrations on the King's return to Baghdad did not come to anything. There was a brief flurry of excitement in the middle of October, when it was rumoured that the cabinet might resign, but what actually took place was a minor reshuffle caused by Muzahim's having fallen out with his colleagues: the only important new appointments were Naji Shawkat to Interior and Ja'far al-'Askari to Defence, with Muzahim himself leaving to take over the Legation.[90]

The opposition took some time to recover from these reversals. The problem was that the spectre of the 1920 revolt was still alive: a tribal rising was so uncertain and so uncontrollable a manifestation that the British authorities and the RAF would always range themselves against one. Furthermore, the unity of the opposition was always vulnerable, particularly since some of the more prominent politicians actually did have the chance of office from time to time, and, more venal considerations apart, it might be argued that Yasin or Rashid 'Ali might have more chance of solid achievement from within rather than fighting the cabinet as perpetual outsiders. The same was true of the tribal leaders, who criticised Ja'far for associating with Sunni politicians at the same time as he was threatening to have nothing to do with Yasin if he took office. In these circumstances the King and Nuri well knew that until another and stronger threat developed, their own position was virtually unassailable.

Kurdistan and the League, 1931 to 1932

As a result of the decisions taken at the PMC in June, the British authorities were forced to continue to exert pressure on the Iraqi government to see that the Kurdish policies were actually being carried out. In September 1931 Young complained to Nuri that there were still far too few Kurdish policemen, and that Humphrys would need detailed evidence that the *Languages Law* was working effectively. The prospects were not hopeful; on the transcript of a typically evasive interview between a senior Interior official and the Prime Minister, Holt noted:

This report of Mr. Chapman's conversation with the Prime Minister strengthens my fear that the latter intends to use every dodge to avoid employing Kurds in the public services. Christians and Jews are to be called Kurds in order to make the statistics look better. The *Local Languages Law* is not to be applied to the *Auqaf* department . . . only in the kindergarten schools are non-Kurds to be replaced by Kurdish teachers.[91]

At Geneva, Britain continued to maintain the attitude taken up in the summer, that Iraqi entry should be a matter of British honour. If possible, even supplementary guarantees for Iraq to sign should be avoided. The PMC, however, was still far from happy about the Iraqi minorities. It reported that it had had 'no opportunity of observing at first hand the moral condition and internal policy of Iraq, the degree of efficiency reached by its administrative organisation, the spirit in which its laws are applied and in which its institutions function.' The Commission therefore had to lean heavily on Humphrys' declaration of Britain's moral responsibility which he had made in the course of the previous session:

> Had it not been for this declaration, the Commission would for its part have been unable to contemplate the termination of a regime which appeared some years ago to be necessary in the interests of all sections of the population.[92]

The final decision had to be left over to the full Council of the League, due to meet at the end of January 1932. As a result of the Commission's report, it was felt that the Italians might still attempt to raise the possibility of a Commission of Enquiry. At a meeting in London to discuss ways of countering this, Hall pointed out that 'if it was a question of giving the Italians anything in Iraq,' their representative might be able to 'come to an arrangement with the Iraq Prime Minister direct', since Nuri would be at Geneva, and noted further that the Iraqis were currently engaged in discussions with the BOD company. It was realised by now that guarantees were going to be required, but Hall assured the meeting that there was no danger of the Iraqi parliament refusing to ratify any such guarantee after they had been accepted by the Iraqi representative at Geneva.[93] Whether or not Nuri came to some sort of arrangement with the Italians in the corridors of the Palais des Nations is a matter for conjecture, but no objections of substance were ultimately raised to Iraq's entry.[94] On 28 January 1932 the Council of the League agreed to Iraq's admission, subject to the signature of various guarantees including the administration of justice and the general safeguarding of minority rights, with full membership to take effect after the October 1932 meeting of the League Council.

Last attempts by the Minorities: Barzan and the Assyrians

The signature of the minority declaration by Nuri on 30 May 1932 at Geneva effectively marked the end of the mandate, though there must have been some anxious moments at the Residency and in Whitehall in the spring and summer of 1932, when two final challenges to the Iraqi government's pre-independence authority appeared, the Barzan tribe and the Assyrian Levies. It had dawned on the Assyrians rather later than on the Kurds that when Britain left Iraq their small community (estimated at about 40, 000 at the beginning of 1933) would be entirely at the mercy of the Iraqi government; their main source of employment, the Levies, would gradually decline, and they would be surrounded by a generally hostile population, whether Arab or Kurd (Stafford, 1935: 41). In 1925, when the recommendations of the Mosul Boundary Commission had dashed all hope of their being able to return to their old home, the Hakkiari mountains in southeastern Turkey, most Assyrians not employed in the Levies, and many of the families of those who were, had settled in the northern part of the Mosul *liwa*. Eventually, under pressure from Interior and the Residency, the Iraqi government was persuaded to set aside part of the area around Baradost for the Assyrians, and a settlement scheme was planned to start in August 1932. However, the Baradost *qadha*, controlled by Shaykh Rashid of Lolan, lay adjacent to the lands of the Barzanis, and the latter area was still not permanently under the control of the central government.

The more important activities of the Barzani leaders lie outside our period: Mulla Mustafa, the brother of the nominal leader Shaykh Ahmad, became the centre of resistance to the Iraqi government after the arrest of Shaykh Mahmud, and the *de facto* leader of the Kurds, a position which he continued to occupy until his elimination from Kurdish politics in 1975. At this stage, the Barzanis' long struggle against successive Iraqi governments was just beginning. In the spring of 1931, reports began to reach Baghdad that Shaykh Ahmad Barzani had founded a new religion and had begun to impose it upon his subjects. By June the disturbances consequent on his missionary zeal had reached Baradost, where the preparations for the Assyrian settlement scheme were beginning. Apart from its bizarre religious overtones, the fighting appeared at first to be the kind of intertribal skirmishing almost endemic to that part of the country. However, by 11 July the Levy garrison at Billeh was replaced by Iraqi troops, presumably to act as a deterrent, but this had the effect of removing a strong armed body of experienced Assyrians from the area. In spite of what appears to have been a relatively trivial situation, Nuri suggested to Ludlow-Hewitt, the Air

Officer Commanding then Acting High Commissioner, that joint air and land operations should be undertaken against Barzan.

> As you know, these operations were turned down a month ago because the season was already too late. [Nuri] had no plan in his mind at all and is simply putting up the Barzan operations as a means of scotching the Assyrian settlement plan . . . it is definitely too late to alter the original decision of the Government and also I do not think it is safe to commit a considerable part of the Iraq Army to operations of unknown duration in the Barzan hills when the tribal situation is so unsettled in the South. I am afraid it only reveals Nuri's intention to obstruct the Assyrian settlement scheme.[95]

It is difficult to establish a definite connection between the fighting in Barzan and the desire of the government to frustrate the settlement scheme. On 9 December 1931 an Iraqi army column was sent to surround Barzan village, which was fairly close to the army post at Billeh, but it was beaten off. Air action was requested, and the RAF bombed Barzan village. For a while Ahmad desisted from further activity, but in February he was active again and defeated another army column sent out from Billeh.[96] At this point, the government decided that it was time to bring the area under proper administrative control, and a larger force was despatched in March.[97] The troops were routed by the Barzan tribesmen under Mulla Mustafa, and the situation was 'only saved from complete disaster by the support of the RAF'[98] which from then on took complete charge. The terrain, steep valleys and wooded mountainsides, favoured guerrilla activity but as usual repeated attacks by the aeroplanes on the tribesmen and their villages lost the Kurds many of their supporters. There were *pourparlers* in April and May, and on 22 June Shaykh Ahmad crossed the border and sought asylum in Turkey.

Whether or not the connection was intentional, the Barzan operation did prevent the proposed programme of Assyrian settlement being put into effect, thus increasing the tensions already caused by the prospects of imminent British departure. Like the Kurds, the Assyrians had been promised vague safeguards by the Boundary Commissioners in 1925:

> We feel it our duty to point out that the Assyrians should be granted the reestablishment of the ancient privileges which they possessed in practice if not officially before the war. Whichever may be the sovereign state, it ought to grant the Assyrians a certain local autonomy.[99]

For this reason, the British had urged the Boundary Commission to ensure the inclusion of the Hakkiari mountains in Iraq. The recommendation of some sort of special regime for the Assyrians was treated by the Iraqi government with the same degree of concern as the idea of special measures for the Kurds, but with the Assyrians the problem was further complicated by their being Christian and their close and somewhat equivocal connection with Britain through the Levies. This force, of about 2,000 men, was generally considered far more reliable and efficient than the Iraqi army by the British authorities, and had been used in conjunction with the RAF for all the operations in Kurdistan until 1930. The Levies, though a homogeneous entity, were loyal to their British commanders; they were imperial, not Iraqi, troops. Their own national allegiance was centred on the person of their patriarch, the Mar Shimun. In 1932 he was a young man in his early twenties, who had studied at school and theological college in England between 1925 and 1929 under the auspices of the Archbishop of Canterbury.[100]

As the time for Iraqi independence drew nearer, and the plans for Assyrian settlement continued to be delayed, the Assyrian Levy troops decided that they should take matters into their own hands. Accordingly on 2 June, the Levy officers presented their resignation in a body to the Air Officer Commanding. The Iraqi government, and the British government, feared that if this resignation took effect the battalions would simply make for the north immediately, and when established there, would engage in a confrontation with the Iraqi army which they would be almost certain to win. If the Assyrians could defy the Iraqi government successfully, the Kurds would be given renewed encouragement to do the same. It was also to be considered that while British troops could be used to put down rebel Kurdish Muslims, it was another matter to send them out against discontented Assyrian Christians. A few days later, Humphrys reported that the Assyrians showed no signs of not being in earnest, and the affair was taken sufficiently seriously in London to be the subject of a special cabinet meeting. Humphrys had requested that a battalion should be flown in from Egypt, to act as a deterrent; the British cabinet, most reluctantly, gave permission, but left the actual decision to the High Commissioner.[101] The troops arrived on 22 and 23 June, and Humphrys reported their 'very steadying effect': by 30 June the immediate crisis was over.[102]

In the course of these weeks, the Mar Shimun had put forward a petition to the High Commissioner, which contained his community's requests. Ideally, the Assyrians still wanted to return to Hakkiari, but if this was not possible, the Mar Shimun asked that they should be allowed to settle around

Dohuk, with an Arab governor assisted by a British adviser. The patriarch's own right to administer the *millet*[103] both spiritually and temporally should be officially recognised. He asked for an Assyrian member of the Chamber of Deputies, and for schools and hospitals in the Assyrian area. Finally he asked that these demands should be embodied in a guarantee which Iraq should present to the League, and that the guarantee should also be made part of the Organic Law of Iraq.[104] Naturally, the Iraqi government rejected the petition at once, but neither the British nor Iraqi governments could stop the Assyrians resigning from the Levies if they wished to do so.

As with the Kurds, the British authorities were caught between a desire to do some sort of justice to the Assyrians, soothing the League, and not offending the *amour propre* of the Iraqis. Humphrys knew that the most acceptable solution to the problem would be for the Assyrians to return to Hakkiari, and wondered whether the Turks might be prepared to take Barzan as a straight swap.[105] Although the Assyrians had done some damage to their cause by precipitate action, the problem of their eventual settlement had still to be solved: the Acting High Commissioner pointed out in August that although the Iraqi government was supposed to be settling the Assyrians in Baradost it was not actually doing so.[106] Tentative approaches were made to the Turks, but no progress seemed likely, and the problem was left for the Iraqi government to solve. At Geneva on 9 December the Iraqi representative turned down the proposal for a Nansen office referee to be sent to Iraq: Hall, then at Geneva, noted that opinion was strongly critical of Britain. It was alleged that there was plenty of land available and 'our denial of this fact is merely a piece of British chicanery done with the object of propitiating the Iraqi government.' Humphrys replied:

> The essence of the Iraqi government's opposition to the League Commissioner is not . . . that they fear that he would find land which they have said does not exist, but that if he came they would cease to be masters in their own house. As the King says, they would have escaped from the British mandate only to come under the mandate of a collection of cranks from Geneva.[107]

Nothing more, it seemed, could be done.[108]

The End of the Mandate

No great enthusiasm was displayed in Iraq in October 1932 when the country was finally admitted to the League. The year had been marked by the usual fruitless opposition activity, with the revival of activity on the part of various Shi'i groupings again in the spring. In May the King and Nuri quarrelled: this was resolved at the time by Nuri taking six weeks leave, since, as Humphrys pointed out, a change of government at this stage would not be looked on with favour at Geneva.[109] The King's attitude seems to have been inspired by an uncomfortable feeling that Nuri was stealing the lime-light, and Nuri had hardly had time to return home from Geneva at the end of October when he was ordered to tender his resignation. The King, according to Young and Humphrys, while acknowledging his Prime Minister's signal successes in international affairs, had become increasingly worried about the cabinet's unpopularity at home.[110] In any event a cabinet consisting mainly of civil servants was appointed under the premiership of Naji Shawkat, and Nuri left the country with the Residency speculating how well the King would manage without him.

It may seem strange that so little excitement was generated by the ending of the mandate in October, or by the earlier meetings of the League which had made Iraq's being accepted in the autumn more or less a ceremonial formality. However, those in Iraq who understood the realities of the situation, and who were not members of the very small circle to whom power was actually entrusted, realised that there was little to be jubilant about. The real extent of British influence had not been perceptibly limited: while Britain could no longer interfere overtly in internal affairs, the 1930 treaty had left it considerable latitude in matters of defence and of administration, through the retention of senior British officials at key posts in important ministries. These two matters, the position of the Ambassador and the advisers, and the relations between the RAF and the Iraqi government, were the subject of constant discussion between London and Baghdad over the last three years of the mandate.

The RAF's role after 1932

In the months preceding the negotiation of the 1930 Treaty, the position of the RAF was hammered out in negotiations between the Foreign and Colonial Offices and the Air Ministry. As far as defence against invasion from outside was concerned, Britain would certainly come to Iraq's aid: the more delicate problem of internal security was, the Air Ministry considered, too complex 'to be entrusted to the Government at Baghdad'. Eventually an Iraqi air force would be capable of taking over those duties, but it was un-likely to materialise as a fighting force for several years. In fact, the Treaty (article 5) states that 'responsibility for the internal defence of Iraq rests with the King of Iraq', but it became clear that Britain's duty to protect British imperial interests in Iraq would be susceptible of fairly wide interpretation if the situation called for it. The opposition might complain that the presence of bases in the country was not compatible with true independence, but the Iraqi government well knew that it depended on the RAF for its survival in office, and it had no alternative but to accept both the bases and the British Military Mission: Humphrys stressed at the time:

> . . .the success or failure of the new order after Iraq has been admitted to the League will largely depend upon the moral influence which the RAF will continue to exert on a people naturally lawless and averse to paying taxes.[111]

As we have seen, it was feared in some circles in England that by implication, the presence of the RAF in Iraq after the country became independent would involve British pilots acting as a mercenaries for the Iraqi government. Attempts to define the precise position of British forces after the end of the mandate soon became bogged down in semantic and logical difficulties. The preservation of internal security was the province of the Iraqi government, but the protection of imperial interests devolved upon British forces; nevertheless, a case might well occur when internal disturbances might begin in the country which were not a direct threat to British interests, but which might, if left unchecked, or if left solely for Iraq forces to deal with, prove to be so.[112]

These anomalies were not cleared up by the instructions given to the High Commissioner in the summer of 1932. Their general tone was to leave him with wide discretionary powers when he became Ambassador at the end of the mandate. The Air Officer Commanding was to be responsible to the Air Ministry and not to the Ambassador, though if the former wished to employ the RAF, this should not be undertaken without prior consultation with the Ambassador, unless this proved absolutely impossible. As far as internal security was concerned, *independent* action by the RAF was ruled out. In general:

> . . . the RAF should not be employed except upon a request in writing from the Iraqi government to the Ambassador . . . the Ambassador should satisfy himself in every case in which British interests are not directly involved that the RAF is not being used in support of governmental oppression or the introduction of unpopular innovations.[113]

The instructions are couched in the vaguest possible terms: there is no definition of 'air action', no indication of whether it implied demonstration flights or bombing raids. In fact the mere presence of aircraft proved a sufficient deterrent, as had been the experience in the general strike in 1931 and would be seen again in the Euphrates troubles of 1935, both of which can be traced to maladministration on the part of the Iraqi government. In practical terms, the position of the RAF changed very little after the end of the mandate: with the concurrence of the Ambassador and the Air Officer Commanding the government of Iraq could request its cooperation, just as they had done in the past. Furthermore, since the same man, Sir Kinahan Cornwallis, remained head of the advisory staff of the Ministry of Interior, through whom the actual requests for assistance would come, it is even more difficult to detect any substantial change in the situation.

The Position of the Ambassador and the British Advisers

In the spring of 1930, Naji al-Suwaydi's government had resigned, actually because the Prime Minister and his colleagues were not prepared to negotiate the new Anglo-Iraqi treaty, but ostensibly because the High Commissioner would not agree to reductions in the British advisory staffs. It was appreciated by the Colonial Office that it was natural and reasonable that the Iraqis themselves should wish to take on an increasing share of the responsibility for the running of the country between that time and 1932, and it was moreover likely to be a matter of interest to the authorities at Geneva to know how far a genuine transfer of power was taking place. In a note for Humphrys, his new chief, Hubert Young had outlined the difficulties of the situation: the ministers in particular realised that they could not easily dispense with British officials, but hesitated to risk the odium of too obvious reliance upon them. Young recommended that where measures were proposed by the Iraqi government that would limit the powers of the 18 holders of the 'Treaty posts' (i. e. those defined in the first Anglo-Iraqi treaty of 1922 as part of the conditions of the mandate), the High Commissioner's permission must be sought in advance. Actual intervention by the High Commissioner would only follow a request from an adviser.[114]

In the *Special Report on the Progress of Iraq . . . 1920 to 1931* there is a reproduction of the official letter sent to all British advisers, which informed them officially of Britain's intention to support Iraq's candidature for the League in 1932. The letter points out that in order to enable Iraq to enter the League in 1932:

> . . . it is desirable to accelerate the assumption of administrative responsibility by the Iraqi government so far as this is consistent with

their treaty obligations, and a progressive share in the administration
. . . [was to be assumed by Iraqi officials.]'

The High Commissioner stated that he did not intend to intervene in
'domestic matters' in circumstances where British officials were satisfied
with the proposed actions of the Iraqi government, but he would still be
kept informed of the introduction of any new administrative measures with
a view to enable him to let it be known, unofficially, 'what attitude I intend
to adopt in the event of the responsible British adviser concerned being
unsuccessful in inducing the Iraqi government to accept his advice.'[115]

This letter was intended to cover the period between 1930 and 1932, and
in 1932 the question arose of the kind of relations which should exist
between the advisers and the Embassy when Iraq became independent:

> It is true that the proposal is that (another) circular letter to British
> officials should not actually be sent to them until Iraq had been
> elected a member of the League . . . but I understand that the idea is
> that it should be secretly agreed with the King before that date and
> one can only imagine the effect that would be produced at Geneva if
> it became known that any such letter was under discussion . . . From
> the point of view of our relations with Iraq itself, the objections seem
> equally serious. I understand that the system of British officials . . . in
> Iraq is by no means universally popular . . . were the proposed letter
> to be issued, might it not, if a copy got into the wrong hands, a
> possibility which cannot be ignored, particularly in view of the wide
> circulation which it would receive, furnish such circles with a most
> dangerous and effective weapon against British officials in future and
> make the position of all British officials in Iraq untenable.[116]

It was recommended that no such letter should be sent, the course which was
eventually adopted, not without some misgivings from Baghdad. As far as
the High Commissioner's position was concerned, Young reported in
September 1932 that Humphrys paid at least one weekly visit to the King
and the Prime Minister normally paid a weekly visit to the High Commissioner. The Iraqi Ministry of Foreign Affairs had always worked closely
with the Residency, and Young urged that this should continue. Young also
assumed a close liaison between the head of the British Military Mission and
the Embassy. The Embassy, however, could no longer call for information
from British officials as of right, as the High Commission had done in the
past.[117] It seems to have been arranged in London first, that the British

Ambassador at Baghdad was in a special position in Iraq, and secondly, that when Humphrys himself left Iraq, the position should be reviewed afresh.[118] Humphrys himself asked for authority to arrange privately with King Faysal and the Prime Minister to receive informally from Cornwallis, *de facto* senior British adviser:

> . . . news of importance affecting the internal security of the country so as to be in a position to advise, in the event of the services of the RAF being requested to deal with internal troubles. Sir Francis Humphrys is confident that this procedure will be regarded as entirely natural and that King Faysal and his Prime Minister will raise no objection.[119]

Surprisingly little change was noticeable in this area either.

'No state', A. J. Balfour wrote in 1919, 'can be described as really independent which has habitually and normally to follow foreign advice, supported, if the worst comes to the worst, by troops, aeroplanes and tanks.'[120] Whatever the true nature of British power and influence after the country entered the League, it was widely believed by Iraqis that they were not the true masters of their country. Victory, of a kind, had been won, but it was a limited victory, conditional independence. Further, it had not been won by the country as a whole, but only by a small clique imposed on the country from outside, which had few claims to the acceptance, approbation or trust of the rest of the population. Having proclaimed that it would give up the mandate, Britain was determined to do so, but naturally took good care to see that its influence over the things that mattered remained as it had been before as far as possible. The end of the mandate had significance for the small group of Sunni officials and soldiers gathered around King Faysal, in giving them a freer hand to exercise control within the country, but the British authorities still retained supreme power, and the vast majority of the population still possessed no power at all.

6

TENURIAL, REVENUE AND TRIBAL POLICY

Until the last years of the mandate, the taxation of agricultural produce formed a considerable part of the revenues of Iraq. The amount of tax, and the way in which it was collected, depended largely upon the system of land tenure, which was determined partly by social and economic conditions in the countryside and partly by administrative orders from the central government. In the period when Iraq was becoming a part of the capitalist world market, major changes in the patterns of cultivation took place and new tenurial arrangements were introduced. The resulting confusion was heightened first by the Great War and the political and economic upheavals which followed, and subsequently by the world depression of the late 1920s and early 1930s.

In broad terms, the period between 1850 and 1950 was one of retrogression rather than progress for the average Iraqi cultivator. During this time a society of generally free tribesmen became transformed into one of near serfs bound to the soil, and both tribal leaders and 'new' landowners gained unprecedented legal and economic powers over their peasantry. The avowed intention of most of the legislation passed in Ottoman times was to enable individual cultivators to make legal registration of what had been only customary rights in land, and to underline the authority of the State as landlord. But whatever the purpose of the Ottoman Land Law, Midhat Pasha's 'reforms', or the later efforts of British and Iraqi officials, the effect was the widespread conversion of state land into the private property of largely absentee landlords.[1]

During the occupation and mandate period, political and tax levying authority in rural areas was given to individuals selected for their likely loyalty either to the Civil Administration or the Iraqi government. The gradual weakening of shaykhly authority which had taken place over the previous decades was arrested by giving official recognition to many of the powers which the shaykhs had long ceased to exercise in practice. By the middle 1920s an informal alliance had grown up between the Iraqi government and the larger landowners, whereby in return for their support, the landowners would be left as far as possible to their own devices.

One far-reaching effect of this policy was to put the government in a position in which it faced almost incessant financial difficulties. Forced into dependence on local leaders, it was in no position to present its chief supporters with realistic tax demands. Eventually, taxes on land fell from about 42% of government revenue in 1911 to about 14% in 1933, the difference being made up first by all round increases in customs and excise and later by oil revenues.[2] This change affected only the landlord, not the fellah, since the landlord paid less tax, but the fellah was compelled to hand over the same amount of his crop to the landlord or his agent as before.

The Main Features of the System in Southern Iraq in the Later Ottoman Period[3]

For our purposes, the most important social and economic changes in the later Ottoman period were the gradual spread of settled or sedentary agriculture, and concurrently the decline in the cohesion of the tribe as a unit. At first, agricultural production was mainly confined to the banks of canals in the vicinity of towns. Since water supplies were highly unreliable, especially before the introduction of mechanical pumps, the area under cultivation often varied from year to year. Also, the transition from transhumant stock-raising to sedentary crop-raising took place at different times in different places, depending on the kind of tribal organisation and the type of land available. Tribesmen did not necessarily abandon desert life altogether: thus a report of 1918 notes that:

> Roughly speaking on the Euphrates from Ramadi to Abu Ghuraib the lift land is cultivated by tribesmen who settle down for a few years to agriculture and then return to desert life in alternative spells.[4]

Since agricultural production necessitated relative peace and stability, the martial virtues which had been important in promoting tribal cohesion inevitably became less significant, and in consequence, the position and influence of the paramount shaykh began to wane.[5] Prowess in battle and the maintenance of a force of armed retainers became less important as occasions requiring such resources occurred less and less frequently. Hence the powers of the shaykh declined, and those of the lesser shaykhs or *sirkals*, increased.

Whereas the *sirkals* had been bound to pay dues to their shaykhs, they now became very largely independent, and were to be found paying taxes direct to the government, especially in Basra *wilaya*. Furthermore, as agriculture became a profitable activity and not simply a means of subsistence, the relationship of the tribe to the land changed. The *dira,* or tribal land, was formerly the common possession of the tribe,[6] though individuals did develop prescriptive rights (*lazma*) over particular areas, normally by oral tradition. However, since actual cultivation was most commonly based on extended family units, other tribesmen might in practice be partners of the *lazma* holder.[7] Gradually, however, boundaries, leases and conditions of tenure became issues of considerable importance as well as sources of friction under the largely free for all situation which prevailed.

In the course of the nineteenth century, and especially during the governorship of Najib Pasha (1842–1849), relations between the tribes and the authorities became closer, in the sense that Ottoman control gradually became effective over a wider area (Nakash, 1994: 33–43). The powerful Kurdish principalities of the north were reduced, and frequent expeditions to the Middle Euphrates helped to break the powers of the local tribal confederations as well as weakening the position of the Sa'dun rulers of the Muntafiq. As the process of extension of government control was almost entirely a one way one, of revenue extraction in return for very few tangible benefits, constant tribal resistance to government is hardly surprising.

While government remained weak, tax collecting was confined to the immediate vicinity of towns, but the general principle on which taxes were gathered remained the same when the 'pacified' area increased in size. Taxation was based on a percentage of the annual gross yield, which fluctuated according to the size of the crop. Local variation would depend upon the type of irrigation, the kind of crop, and the honesty of the revenue officials. A model of the revenue system would show the fellah at the bottom of the pyramid, probably owning the simple implements required for agriculture. He would normally be directed to work in different parts of the *dira* by the *sirkal*, a kind of foreman or bailiff, often a 'sub-shaykh', who 'divided the plots, fixed the dates of sowing and harvesting and occasionally advanced seed or money (Haider/Issawi, 1966:163–164).' Above him in the hierarchy came the shaykh, who might be at the head of the pyramid, and thus the intermediary between the tribe and the government (if such relations existed) or, nearer the end of the Ottoman period, might himself be subordinate to a landlord or *mallak*.

Until well into the twentieth century, the fellah seems to have been little affected by any changes in administrative organisation:

In a country where land is unlimited and cultivators few, a population of nomadic origin could not be brought to cultivate at all unless the fellah, the actual pusher of the plough, were secured at least half a share in the produce of his labours.[8]

The major source of agrarian conflict during and well after our period derived from the new relationship between the *sirkal* and the *mallak*, or landlord. Until the British came, the *mallaks* had only been able to make feeble attempts to collect their *mallakiya* (landlord dues), but after the occupation and mandate they were given official authority to collect them, which meant that the income of the *sirkals* was proportionately reduced.[9] This was most acutely felt in areas where the *sirkals* had already become accustomed to paying revenue direct to government.

Until 1831, control of Iraq was in the hands of Mamluk pashas who were more or less independent of the Ottoman authorities. The government was backed up by a corps of janissaries aided by locally hired forces which were used to maintain limited security in the vicinity of the towns. After 1831, however, most officials were appointed direct from Istanbul. To be sent to serve in Baghdad or Basra was a mild punishment to the official concerned, though appointments were usually short term, to prevent an individual building up a local power base. The result of the short duration of appointments, and the system of tax farming, was that the governor's real power over the province was very limited. He could only hope to exert control by means of a conciliatory alliance between himself and the local notables, based on mutual necessity (Fattah, 1997). Baghdad's situation as a 'frontier province' probably forced the governor to rely rather more heavily than elsewhere on the notables, but their own position, surrounded by powerful armed tribes, necessitated an equal measure of support from the Ottoman administration. The main feature of the alliance was the interposition of a number of intermediaries between the revenue authorities and the taxpayer:

It is a feature of the Turkish fiscal system that everyone from the Government downwards, leased out his rights and passed on his liabilities to someone else.[10]

Such arrangements were modified but by no means destroyed by the Tanzimat reforms initiated in the years after 1839. The principal aim of the reforms was to reassert the rights of the central government and to draw the provinces more closely under the control of the Imperial authorities. The Land Law of 1858 was one of the cornerstones of the system, upholding the rights of the Ottoman government as the owner and lessor of all land, in order to obtain at least its traditional share in the gradually increasing fruits of the soil.[11]

The Land Law of 1858

The new code set down various categories of land, of which only the largest, *miri* (state or unalienated land) need concern us here.[12] The basic premise of the code was that the (Ottoman) state was sole landlord of *miri* land, and possessed *raqaba*, ownership. It could grant out the *tasarruf*, usufruct, of tracts of land to *multazims* or *muhassils*, lessees, who could acquire leases by making bids for them at periodic auctions. This is true *miri, miri sirf* tenure, where the Government's position as ultimate owner is quite clear, and where the holding of rights was only permanent in the sense that continuity could be achieved by the same man or his heirs putting in the highest bid at the auctions, normally held every three, five or ten years. A vital feature of the 1858 law was that:

> Possession of this kind of immoveable property will henceforward be acquired by leave of and grant by the agent of the government . . . Those who acquire possession will receive a title deed bearing the Imperial cypher. The amount paid in advance (*mu'ajjala*) for the right of possession is called the *tapu* fee (Fisher, 1919: 3).

The intention here seems to have been to validate the rights of those in possession by the grant of title deeds, called *tapu sanads*. Theoretically, the *sanads* offered more or less permanent rights of possession (without the auctions, or periodic re-granting), encouraged greater investment in land through security of tenure, and enabled government and the revenue payers to deal directly with one another.

Naturally, the Land Code was far from being an act of disinterested benevolence on the part of the Ottoman authorities. As well as enabling government to assert its control over the provinces more effectively, the growing tendency towards sedentarisation and the increasing cereal production which resulted probably acted as a spur to a more vigorous revenue policy. Also, more peaceful conditions in the countryside were gradually making tax collection easier. The code was almost certainly designed primarily to match conditions in Anatolia, where the fragmentation of large estates and the creation of a body of leasehold tenants would result in breaking the power of the 'lords of the valleys'. It was felt that the possessors of *sanads*, 'a body of industrious peasant proprietors and taxpayers' (Dowson, 1932: 6) would be more ready to pay taxes to a government which had confirmed them in the possession of their lands.

In Iraq, however, such conditions only rarely applied. The code could not fit around the kind of corporate communal ownership which existed and the difficulties which followed Midhat Pasha's attempts to introduce it to the area in 1869 largely derived from the incompatibility of the two systems. Neither Islamic nor Ottoman law recognised the existence of corporate legal entities[13] which meant that leases could only be given to individuals rather than to the 'X' or 'Y' tribe. Thus in 'British Iraq' the effect of the code was to restore or even to create the authority of tribal leaders, by giving individuals rights over lands which had formerly been held in common by both leaders and followers.

The Application of the Code in Iraq

Although published in 1858, the Land Code was not applied in Iraq until Midhat Pasha became governor of Baghdad in 1869. At first Midhat attempted to force the tribes into submission by military expeditions, but in contrast to his predecessors he also took active steps to bring about a land settlement. The policy of distributing *tapu sanads*, however, produced results almost precisely the reverse of those which Midhat seems to have intended.[14] Many of those who came forward to claim *tapu sanads* were not entitled to them: fears on the part of individual *lazma* holders that rights might somehow be taken away, or that registration might facilitate conscription, or that there was no advantage, and might even be some suspicion, attached to claiming what they considered their own already, all deterred legitimate claimants from registering their rights. Hence:

> The class of *tapu* tenant thus created has always been the object of the tribesman's bitterest hostility . . . but the tribes were not always ready to be openly defiant of authority. Their leaders were often bought with the land, and the purchaser was often content at first to bide his time. When the authorities were complacent and powerful enough to enable him to recover the share due according to custom to the landlord, he recovered it or something less. When times were adverse, he came to terms with the tribal shaykh, to whom he would lease out his rights for a fraction of their nominal value.[15]

What happened, in many if not most cases, was that the tribal leaders would register the land in their own names, thus making the whole *dira* to all intents and purposes the personal property of the *sanad* holder.

However, the effects of *tapu sanads* should not be overestimated, in the sense that they were not widely distributed. After Midhat's departure the *Tapu* Department virtually ceased to function as an active land registry for the rest of the Ottoman period, and other factors contributed to narrowing its field of activity. Some 30 per cent of all land in the Baghdad *wilaya* became the personal property of the Ottoman Sultan; these, the *Sanniya*, or Crown Lands, which included the 'Amara rice estates, were managed by a special department and hence never registered in *tapu*. Further, the authorities soon realised the disadvantages of the permanent nature of the transaction; permanent alienation meant the loss of a powerful weapon of control, whereas the issue of *miri sirf* tenancies could be confined to loyal and trustworthy lessees. By the time of the British occupation the majority of the land was still held under this latter form of tenure, with *tapu* holdings in the irrigation zone confined to areas near towns, the banks of the Diyala, the Shamiya, parts of the Muntafiq, and between Fao and Qurna in the delta.[16]

Hence the 'system of tenure' prevailing in 1914 was not really a system at all, but a hodgepodge of different practices in different areas. Also, the application of the Land Code in circumstances in which it was often quite irrelevant, had created highly anomalous situations, which the British authorities accepted as the normal order of things. Although the occupation and mandate authorities took pains to assert that their policies were not innovatory, but simply attempts to follow existing practices, what was produced was a selection of those practices which facilitated the simplest and most effective system of administrative control combined with the collection of as much revenue as possible. The most important result of this policy was to create a small number of large property holders, either through land grants to individuals, or through measures designed to bolster the powers of tribal shaykhs and landlords.

Policy and Practice under the British Occupation

Between November 1914 and September 1915, British troops advanced from Fao to Kut, a distance of some 400 miles. Since most of the Ottoman administrators left with the retreating Ottoman army, the Mesopotamia Expeditionary Force found itself confronted not only with military objectives, but also with the task of the administering the occupied territories. By the autumn of 1915 there were political officers in all the important towns on the Tigris and Euphrates, as far as Kut and Nasiriya. For the first few months, revenue was not collected on a large scale, and in remoter and less pacific areas it was some years before any taxation was levied at all. Nevertheless, where British control was secure, collection began, and was undertaken with such efficiency and over so wide an area that the thoroughness of the work has been put forward as one of the major causes of the rising of 1920.[17] Although British methods did not differ in principle from those of the Ottomans, Ottoman demands had rarely if ever been met in full, since the necessary means of enforcement were lacking. In contrast, the British authorities had such powers at their disposal and did not hesitate to use them.

Revenue was inextricably linked with tenure, and here too the declared aim of the British authorities was to leave things more or less as they found them. In 1919 the Revenue Commissioner made an extremely important declaration of principle:

> We must recognise that it is primarily our business not to give rights to those who have them not, but to secure their rights to those who have them.[18]

This policy was generally adhered to, although there was by no means any general consensus that such rights as existed had been either justly or irrevocably acquired. The *Tapu* Department, the only institution for registering title in Ottoman times, was revived. In general, the guiding principle animating the tenurial, fiscal and tribal policies of the Civil Administration during the war, which were largely continued during the mandate, was to maintain what it found convenient to label 'traditional practice' and to uphold the supposed status quo. The British authorities tried to preserve a system based partly on 'tradition' and partly on the Ottoman model, the latter being thought to be not so much inherently bad as incompetently administered. Several drawbacks followed the adoption of these principles. First, Ottoman law bore little relation to many of the tenurial arrangements actually in force in Iraq, a fact for which the authorities, in so far as they were aware of it, made very little allowance. Further, even where Ottoman law was in use, its application did not antedate the time of Midhat Pasha, some forty-five years before 1914. Finally, the British authorities misunderstood both the nature of tribal organisation and the effect of Ottoman policies upon it, attributing the main cause of tribal disintegration to attacks on the system by their predecessors, rather than to natural forces arising from the process of sedentarisation.

Tribal Policy

Very broadly speaking, the authority of the shaykh in a pre-agricultural nomadic society was founded on the basis of a degree of reciprocity, a combination of prestige and consensus, in which the latter played a highly important part:

> . . . le peuple a tendance à considérer le chef comme un arbitre qu'on peut recuser, dont on peut provoquer le remplacement (Rondot, 1936: 6).

British officials considered that the fragmentation and breakdown of shaykhly authority which had taken place was due to Ottoman policies of fomenting discord between tribes and sections. Their stated aim was to restore the broken bonds, by re-establishing the 'traditional' authority of the shaykh, which would provide a basis of loyalty to the civil administration as well as simplifying the task, and reducing the cost, of rural peacekeeping. In addition to its practical advantages, the policy seems also to have been justified by the assumption of a community of interest between the shaykh and the tribe. This sense of cohesion was in fact already weak, and it had often disappeared altogether when the shaykh became not only entitled but enabled to exercise the functions of landlord and revenue collector. The most important official instrument of British tribal policy was the *Tribal Criminal and Civil Disputes Regulation*, (abbreviated to *Tribal Disputes Regulation*), first issued in 1916, governing disputes in the occupied territories in which 'either or any of the parties was a tribesmen'.[19]

The general principle animating the *Tribal Disputes Regulation* was that tribesmen who were (supposedly) accustomed to settling their differences by tribal methods, under the jurisdiction of their shaykh or *majlis*, should be able to continue to do so, and should thus be 'spared the complexities and expense' of the ordinary courts. At the time of its original issue, the Regulation was designed for immediate and specific purposes: it was considered essential that the areas through which the Mesopotamia Expeditionary Force's lines of communication passed should be in the hands of friendly tribal leaders, since total control could not be achieved by the occupation forces alone. Loyalty was paid for by subsidies for good behaviour, and, more important because it lasted long after the subsidies had ceased to be paid, official recognition of a selected shaykh as *the* shaykh, or the paramount shaykh, of the tribe. The *Regulation* enhanced the shaykh's position by giving him absolute judicial authority over his tribe, while other courts, with codes based on Indian civil and penal systems, were set up for the rest of the population. Thus the selected shaykh was confirmed in his office, became the accredited agent of the central administration, and had official power to act as judge and jury in civil and criminal matters.

The powers conferred by the *Tribal Disputes Regulation* were extremely wide, a feature presumably judged necessary for wartime conditions. No appeal was allowed from any decision given or sentence passed under the Regulation: there was no *habeas corpus*, and even the finality of proceedings resulting in acquittal was brought under question, since retrial for any offence arising out of the same facts was possible for a period of up to two years after the case had been discharged (Sections 11 and 50). As well as conferring these very extensive powers on the shaykh, the Regulation also gave wide authority to Political Officers (and, by extension, their Iraqi successors, the *mutasarrifs* or provincial governors) to decide to whom the *Regulation* should be applied. In addition, whole tribal sections could be removed to another part of the officer's area of jurisdiction, and under the notorious section 40, later enshrined in the Iraqi legal system for use against political offenders, 'dangerous characters' could be made to reside outside their home areas, a kind of internal exile, at the discretion of the High Commissioner.

The original *Tribal Disputes Regulation*, and its reissue in 1918, was framed on the assumption that overall supervision would be entrusted to British Political Officers, since the employment of Iraqis in senior administrative position had not yet been contemplated. Later, however, provision for a separate tribal jurisdiction was included in the Organic Law at the insistence of the mandate authorities, and the Regulation itself became part of the ordinary law of the land in December 1924. On this occasion suitable changes in wording were made in order to substitute Iraqi for British officials. In common with much of the administrative machinery introduced during the Mesopotamia campaign, the notion of a separate tribal jurisdiction was imported directly from India. Sir Henry Dobbs, Revenue Commissioner and later High Commissioner, and his contemporaries, were strongly influenced by the methods of Sir Robert Sandeman, Governor of Kaharistan in the North-West Frontier Provinces in the late nineteenth century. Sandeman's solution to the problems created by tribal warfare and disputes within tribes was to give official recognition to tribal chiefs and to tribal law, and to set up the chiefs, under the overlordship of the Raj, to police their own districts. The assumption was that:

> The balance of power is turned directly the headmen are given the means to entertain armed servants of their own and when supported by suitable allowances and the prestige of connection with our power

they both can and do exert themselves successfully to keep their tribes in order (Thornton, 1895: 301).

The advantage to the British authorities, both in India and in Iraq, was that such a system was extremely cheap to administer, and that leaders who were granted this form of official recognition owed their authority entirely to the central administration:

Sir Henry McMahon (Dobbs' former chief as Agent-General for Baluchistan, later High Commissioner in Egypt) pointed out that in countries where customary and tribal law exists in full force, it formed:

. . . an instrument for the suppression of crime which in simplicity and effectiveness can be surpassed by no other legal system which we can invent, for the simple reason that it is based on the character, idiosyncrasies and prejudices of the people among whom it has originated and by whom it has been evolved during long periods of time to meet their own requirements and remedy their failings.[20]

In some ways, as Dodge has pointed out, the 'romantic discourse' of a separate jurisdiction harks back to the paternalistic notion noted earlier, that the exposure of 'simple tribesmen' to the regular judicial processes would be unreasonable and unjust.[21] What does not seem to have been so easily grasped by its advocates was what however *effective* the system may have been, it provided endless possibilities for abuse. In situations where the prosecution also functioned as judge and jury, old scores could be settled and easy advantage taken. Writing about the Iraqi Kurds in the 1930s, Leach underlines this point:

Government support for the 'chief' frequently gives that individual a tyrannical authority quite foreign to the ordinary tribal system of government (Leach, 1940: 19).

Furthermore, in India, apart from its cheapness and simplicity, an important safeguard of the 'Sandeman system' had been that the overlordship of the Raj acted as the ultimate court of appeal. In Iraq, there was no appeal against decisions made under the *Tribal Disputes Regulation*; Dobbs admitted in 1926 that he was unable to comment on criticisms of its administration, since 'records of disputes settled under it never come before me'.[22]

Furthermore, whatever the intentions of its framers, the arrangement in fact created two classes of Iraqi citizen, as well as undermining the broad principle of equality before the law. As one contemporary commentator noted (and as will be illustrated below) tribesmen who committed murder were 'merely fined a small sum of money' or given a short prison sentence (Dodge, 2003b: 97). Furthermore, as time went on, the separation between the judiciary and the executive implicit in the institutions created by the mandate authorities gradually ceased to exist, and the executive simply took advantage of the *Tribal Disputes Regulation* to serve its own ends.

In November 1931, 'Abdullah Beg al-Sani', Director-General of the Ministry of Interior, was murdered at his desk in the Ministry by 'Abdullah Falih Beg al-Sa'dun. The case was clear cut, and the murderer sentenced to death. On appeal, however, 'Abdullah al-Sa'dun pleaded extenuating circumstances. al-Sani' had married the daughter of the late Prime Minister, 'Abd al-Muhsin al-Sa'dun, in the face of opposition from the Sa'dun family because of his humble birth. The murderer explained that it was his duty to avenge the family honour by killing his niece's husband, and that his action entitled him to trial under the *Tribal Disputes Regulation*. His plea was successful, and his sentence commuted to a term of imprisonment.[23] The reverse side of the coin, of 'urban', or broadly speaking 'political' offenders being submitted to the 'tribal' jurisdiction, can be seen in the treatment of those convicted for their part in the demonstration against Sir Alfred Mond in 1928, or in the General Strike of 1931. These offenders were sentenced to periods of internal exile under section 40 of the Tribal Disputes Regulation.[24]

The Practical Application of Tribal and Revenue Policy

Even in societies where the powers of local leaders remained strong, the policy of according government support to a selected chief caused discontent and unrest. In Iraq, where shaykhly powers had greatly declined, the difficulties were considerable. A report of 1917 states:

> Settled agriculture and extended civilisation have tended to disintegrate the tribe and to weaken the influence of the shaykhs. To restore and continue the power of the tribal shaykhs is not the least interesting of the problems in land administration which the (Baghdad) wilayet presents.[25]

Official attempts to reverse this policy, which implied extending the powers of the central government, met with almost embarrassing enthusiasm at the local level. In 1919 the Acting Civil Commissioner described the dilemma facing the British authorities in the context of administrative reconstruction in the Shamiya:

> The tribes accepted the new system with alacrity, showing themselves almost too ready to throw off their allegiance to their chiefs and to deal directly with civil officials in regard to revenue and other matters.

This posed an important question of principle:

> . . . ought we to aim at a 'bureaucratic' form of administration . . . involving direct control by a central government and the replacement of the powerful tribal confederation by the smaller tribal or sub-tribal unit, as a prelude to individual in place of communal ownership of land, or should our aim be to retain, and subject to official safeguards to strengthen, the authority of tribal chiefs and to make them the agents and official representatives of Government within their respective areas? The latter policy had already been adopted, in default of a better, in the Basra wilayet, and especially in the Muntafiq division: was it wise to apply it to the Baghdad wilayet? (Wilson, 1931: 76–77)

Over wide areas of Iraq, the powers of tribal leaders had become almost negligible until the Civil Administration restored or in some cases created those powers, and this policy was generally extended under the mandate. Thus in return for tax and other concessions, the shaykhs and landlords were persuaded to support the government on both local and national levels. In spite of the gradual spread of the authority of the Iraqi government from the centre to the countryside, and the use of the RAF to prevent any serious check to the process, internal security, if not to be inordinately expensive, came to be dependent on the cooperation of tribal leaders in seeing that the peace was kept and that a modicum of taxation was paid. In the financial year 1924–1925 many leading shaykhs in 'Amara were given generous tax remissions, specifically because their 'complaints were reiterated at the somewhat difficult moment of the passage of the (June 1924) Treaty and this circumstance no doubt lent them a special importance.'[26] The following example from Samawa is also instructive:

> The period of absence of Government in the area had resulted in rapid tribal disintegration. Every lilliputian leader who could raise three or four followers refused to obey his shaykh and struck out on his own.

This state of affairs is inconvenient for Government, and now a certain number of shaykhs are being recognised officially. Such men as these will be great gainers by the reestablishment of control by Government, which means that of themselves over their tribes also. Shaykhs will always, for the edification of their followers, raise loud lamentations over the question of taxes. Actually . . . they are the gainers by them. Of all the taxes they collect for Government they retain a share for themselves. Consequently the more Government is known to be pressing for taxes, the more the shaykhs can squeeze out of the cultivators and the more they get for themselves. It was very noticeable that as soon as tax-collecting began in Samawa all the shaykhs blossomed out in new clothes.[27]

Occasionally, the official choice of paramount shaykh ran almost comically counter to local socio-political realities. In 1917, 'Ali Sulayman of the Dulaym was appointed leader of the Dulaym *bayraq* (camel corps), and official chief of his tribe. His elevation was looked upon with some disfavour by other members of the Dulaym and later by the Iraqi government which was obliged to subsidise him. However, after the rising of 1920:

Several sectional leaders . . . in order to avoid being punished for acts of hostility . . . agreed to recognise 'Ali Sulaiman as their paramount shaykh . . . and to pay him the customary shaykhly dues.[28]

'Ali managed to collect these dues for two years, but by 1923, apparently with a certain amount of quiet encouragement from local *liwa* headquarters, the *sirkals* refused to pay. With the arrival of a new *mutasarrif*, 'Ali pressed for the restoration of his rights. The Administrative Inspector discovered that before British forces had occupied Ramadi, Shaykh Dhari (outlawed for the murder of Colonel Leachman in 1920) had been paramount shaykh of the Dulaym: 'Ali, it seemed, had no real claim to the office. Although he might be listed as paramount shaykh of the Dulaym in the files of the Ministry of Interior in Baghdad, in the Dulaym itself his presence was a hindrance to the work of revenue collection, since it was in fact much easier to collect taxes directly from the *sirkals*.[29] The confederation which 'Ali Sulayman was supposed to control included both cultivators and nomads. In 1926 Dobbs actually asked that the government should collect 'Ali's dues for him from the cultivators of the Ghurma Khawr canal and the *karads* (irrigation devices) alongside it. If this could be done:

He would then practically abandon his position as shaykh of the *badu* section of the tribe, which brings him no profit and no honour and a great deal of worry. But this would make him quite useless to Government . . . it is best to arrange for Government to collect a percentage of the gross produce for the shaykh . . . But this should be on condition that . . . he retains full responsibility for the *badu* in the desert . . .

Interior replied:

Although some formula must be found defining Shaykh 'Ali's responsibilities, should it be decided to collect for him a percentage of the gross produce of the Ghurma, I do not think that it will be practicable to make him responsible for all the Dulaim *badu*. The main point however is to maintain the authority of all the shaykhs and use it to reinforce the police.[30]

During Yasin al-Hashimi's tenure of office as *mutasarrif* of the Muntafiq, the British assumption that what was good for the shaykh must *ipso facto* be good for the tribe as a whole is clearly illustrated.[31] Yasin was appointed in June 1922: his predecessor had 'received on his appointment by the King in November 1921 direct orders that he was to bring the shaykhs to heel'[32] and both he and Yasin tried to work on these lines. Early in August 1922, Yasin attempted to replace the *mudir* of Batha', a tribal shaykh, Manshad al-Hubayyib, with a permanent civil servant from Baghdad, but the *mutasarrif*'s nominee was kidnapped by Manshad's tribesmen on his way to take up his post.[33] Consequently, a few days later:

. . . a few tribal nonentities, egged on by the Mayor of Nasiriya, 'Abd al-Karim al-Sabti, held a meeting . . . and decided to send a petition protesting against any tribal shaykh occupying the position of *mudir* . . . this was directed against the paramount shaykhs of the Nasiriya qadha.[34]

The shaykhs themselves now took up the struggle, complaining to the District Adviser that 'outside interests' (lesser government officials) were plotting together with the *sirkals* to fabricate false charges against them which had reached the ears of the *mutasarrif*. In spite of the well known difficulties which had been brought about by the assertion of paramountcy and the nomination of selected leaders as revenue payers in the Muntafiq, and the resulting hardship to the *sirkals*, the District Adviser summed up the position:

> My great difficulty with the mutasarrif has been to persuade him . . . that because a number of unimportant sirkals have informed him that they are opposed to their shaykhs, it does not mean that the shaykhs have not got their tribes solidly behind them. Further this is not a case of a cabal of shaykhs trying to enforce their will on Government, but the representatives of the cultivating classes determined to defend their rights which they believe are endangered.[35]

As a result of the processes initiated by the British occupation authorities during and immediately after the War, the Iraqi government became increasingly dependent upon the services and the cooperation of tribal leaders. There was a tendency either to allow powerful individuals to hold tracts of land for very little taxation, or to be indulgent with major revenue defaulters. The quarrel between 'Abd al-Wahid Sikkar and his *sirkals* shows how essentially political considerations could triumph over matters of revenue collection and equity.

In Ottoman times, the Shamiya and Mishkhab areas were ruled by the Khaza'il tribe. In order to bring peace to the area, the Ottoman authorities encouraged two tribes of cultivators, the Fatlah and the Ibrahim, to settle there. 'Abd al-Wahid Sikkar was one of the five sons of the Fatlah leader Fira'un, among whom the tribal lands had been divided after his death early in the twentieth century. A few years before the war some of the Fatlah shaykhs had fallen foul of the Ottoman authorities and the Khaza'il *sirkals* took possession, registering the lands in their names and dealing directly with government. Under the British occupation, the Fatlah leaders returned and were duly registered as the paramount family:

> On this occasion 'Abd al-Wahid was registered as cultivating all the Raqq al-Haswa estate, which, on the occasion of his flight from the Turks a few years previously had been divided up between his sirkals.[36]

For reasons which are not entirely clear (since the British had *restored* the Fatlah family), 'Abd al-Wahid was prominent in anti-British activity during the 1920 rising, and closely associated subsequently with the dissident *'ulama'* in 1922. As a result the British authorities were determined not to let him secure the title deeds of the Raqq al-Haswa, and the Iraqi government was equally anxious that he should. Thus at one time the

District Adviser, Diwaniya, made a register of all the *sirkals* of the Raqq al-Haswa with a view to registering the land in their names and so eliminating 'Abd al-Wahid, but after the Adviser had left the district the attempt was not continued. In June 1923, after protracted bargaining, a compromise was reached. The land was to be registered in 'Abd al-Wahid's name, but the *sirkals* could not be evicted without the agreement of the government. They had to recognise 'Abd al-Wahid as shaykh 'according to tribal law' but 'Abd al-Wahid himself was liable to eviction in the event of misconduct or revenue default.

This solution, however, did not satisfy the Fira'un family. Together with his brother, Mizhir ibn Fira'un, and his nephew, Taklif ibn Mubdir, 'Abd al-Wahid was determined to restore all the family land to its direct control. As a first step, Mizhir burnt down several villages occupied by subsections which had become independent of his control, and Taklif attempted to evict a *sirkal* who had long paid taxes direct to government. Both these actions were fined, but government was unable to prevent their recurrence. In May 1924, 'Abd al-Wahid himself burnt down the village of a sub-chief in the Raqq al-Haswa, and arranged for an 'official of the *Tapu* Department' to come to measure the area prior to issuing him with the deeds. The latter development was the result of 'Abd al-Wahid's influence in Baghdad, since the official did not have authorisation either from the *Tapu* Department itself or from the local administrative authorities. His arrival caused consternation in the area, and many *sirkals* attempted to treat with 'Abd al-Wahid, who made use of the bluff to carry out further evictions.

In July 1924 the local Administrative Inspector visited the Raqq al-Haswa to investigate complaints from the *sirkals*. He found that 'Abd al-Wahid had been terrorising the whole area by pretending that he was acting under government orders, and that the *qa'immaqam* of Abu Sukhayr was powerless to stop him. While the Administrative Inspector was on tour taking evidence, he was followed around by Mizhir ibn Fira'un, who threatened anyone giving unfavourable answers. The advantages derived by government from permitting this state of affairs to continue (whether voluntarily or involuntarily) were certainly not financial:

> It is noticeable that the . . . Fira'un are very heavily in debt for revenue, whereas most of the independent sub-chiefs have paid their taxes in full. Thus 'Abd al-Wahid owes nearly half a lakh of rupees; Taklif ibn Mubdir owes some Rs 10,000, while Fahim al-Muhammad, whose land he wants to acquire, has paid in full up to date.[37]

This dispute continued well after the end of the mandate, and 'Abd al-Wahid was one of the leaders of a major rising in the Mishkhab in 1935.[38] The episode illustrates the powerlessness of government in the face of local leaders with their own armed following. The government's enforced support of the shaykh's immunity was a direct result of the British policy of re-establishing, or in some cases establishing, particular individuals as tribal leaders and landlords *de jure*, and the failure to recognise the existing rights of the subtenants.

The Origins and Consequences of British Land and Tribal Policy

Sir Henry Dobbs was the initiator of the greater part of the land, revenue and tribal policy under the occupation and maintained under the mandate. As Revenue Commissioner in 1916 he had set up most of the arrangements for the Basra *wilaya* (Howell, 1922), and his tenure of office as High Commissioner from 1923 to 1929 ensured that his principles would be maintained in practice. In 1926, in a *Note on Land Tenure*, he asserted that in contrast to the practice prevailing in many parts of British India, it would be impossible in Iraq to deal directly with individual cultivators for revenue purposes because of poor communications and unsettled conditions in the country. The only method of preventing a serious decline in administration after the withdrawal of British forces (then scheduled to take place in 1928 or 1929), was to grant out large parcels of *miri* land to individuals for as long periods as possible, subject to occasional review and somewhat vague safeguards for the good treatment of the cultivators:

> Where possible the holdings of the existing tribal chiefs should be recognised by giving them perhaps a somewhat larger holding than other persons and possibly in some cases by imposing on them the task of collecting Government revenues and taking a percentage for the expenses of collection . . . the tribal landlord with tribal cultivators below him is much more effectively restrained by tribal custom from oppression and exaction than can ordinarily be managed by regular laws.[39]

In fact, such grants, together with the *Tribal Disputes Regulation*, brought about just that oppression and exaction that Dobbs professed to wish to prevent. The 'tribal custom' that was presumed to act as a sanction ceased to work effectively when authority was bestowed upon the shaykh from above, and when he was in a position to back up his demands by calling on resources outside the tribal framework. The desirability of providing stringent safeguards for the cultivators was outweighed by the advantages of securing a body of loyal shaykhs and landlords.

In 1932 the government of Iraq invited Sir Ernest Dowson[40] to survey the state of land tenure. In correspondence with Dobbs' successor, Sir Francis Humphrys, Dowson criticised Dobbs by implication:

> I do not think that either simplification or public peace or economic advantage are to be realised by a deliberate policy of establishing a series of large landowners as intermediaries . . . The recurrent troubles in the Muntafiq and along the Hai were . . . bred by a policy which . . . bore at least this general character. Where smallholders, paying, or wishing to pay their revenue direct to Government are found to exist . . . they should be recognised. Where large holders with satellite cultivating tenants are found to exist, this should also be recognised, provided that relations are healthy and subject to due record of the smaller man's reasonable rights. And where genuine tribal tenure still survives, and the land is farmed by the tribe as a whole, this again should be recognised. But I do not think that any of these varying conditions should be artificially promoted or artificially preserved.[41]

Dobbs' policy of giving well-behaved landlords long term security of tenure over the heads of their contented peasantry bore little relation to actual conditions in the countryside. It took scant account of long established *lazma* rights, of the changing status of the *sirkal*, and the concurrent decline in the 'traditional' authority of the shaykh. It was only relevant to conditions within the *liwas* of Kut and 'Amara, and even there it is clear from Batatu's findings that the extreme economic deprivation suffered in these areas was very largely the result of the system of land tenure in force.[42]

As a result of these policies, and as a result of the world agricultural depression in the late 1920s and early 1930s, land revenue declined steadily from just under half the state's revenues at the beginning of our period to just over a tenth at the end. This was not due to any overall falling off in cultivation or productivity,[43] but partly to falling prices, and partly to the government's inability to collect the money. As a result it became necessary to find alternative sources of revenue. Accordingly the rates of duty on imported goods were increased by 10 per cent in all cases, and 20 per cent in some selected categories in November 1931.

In June 1931 a radical revision of the land taxes was made by the introduction of the *Istihlak* or consumption tax. By this means, the basis of agricultural taxation was changed from a percentage of the gross produce to a tax on the surplus produced for sale. The produce for sale was taken to special centres where the duty, normally 10 per cent, was deducted. This step marked the end of all formal attempts to collect agricultural revenue from large landowners: the Iraqi government could no longer even pretend that it was going to continue to ask its most powerful supporters for cash contributions. Shortly after the end of the mandate, the absolute powers of landlords were formally enshrined in legislation. In 1933 the *Law Governing the Rights and Duties of Cultivators* was passed, defining the legal responsibilities of farm-owners, *sirkals*, and fellahin. Under the law, the fellah could be held responsible on grounds of negligence for almost any disaster that might befall the crop, and he and the *sirkal* could be evicted under a variety of circumstances that could be very widely interpreted: hence, if guilty of

> . . . an act leading to the disturbance of peaceful relations between himself and others with a view to obstructing the management of the farm, he shall be punishable by eviction from the farm by orders of the administrative official concerned according to the provisions of the Tribal . . . Disputes Regulation.[44]

A contemporary observer remarked:

> Theoretically the fellah has certain rights which are to be safeguarded, but when one considers the relative position of the two parties, should a dispute be laid before a *mudir nahiya* or *qa'immaqam*, one is obliged to regard the fellah's rights as theoretical only.[45]

One of the most objectionable features of the law was that fellahin who were indebted to a farm owner could not leave his employment until the debts were paid off. Since the fellahin could be held liable for any damage or disaster that might occur, and since the whole agricultural system depended on a system of advances from the farm owners to the cultivators, it was virtually impossible for the latter to break out of the circle of debt other than by running away from the farm. The application of this law, particularly at a time of severe agricultural depression, explains much of the considerable movement of the population from the rural to the urban areas in search of employment. The provisions of the Cultivators' Law were so extreme that even some members of the Iraqi cabinet wondered if they might not be contravening some of the clauses of the International Anti-Slavery Convention.[46]

Conclusions

The land and revenue policies pursued under the mandate resulted from the difficulties confronting the government in ruling over a country where its authority did not derive from any firm basis of consent. The British authorities solved the problem during the occupation period by creating islands of support in rural areas through land grants and conferring jurisdictional and fiscal privileges upon selected leaders. In some cases, Iraqi governments attempted to take away these privileges, but they were very soon forced into the realisation that it was only by the formation of some sort of alliance with powerful local magnates that they would be able to maintain themselves in power. A policy of conciliation was the only means through which the system of government as created could continue to function. Furthermore, when members of the permanent caucus which formed the Iraqi government themselves made incursions into agriculture, they quickly realised the advantages inherent in the tenurial arrangements and tax concessions which they supported. Hence the policy must not simply be regarded as the best means by which the King's government could be carried on, but also as being in the best interests of the clique which ruled Iraq.

The most important effects of the policies pursued bore first upon rural society in general, and secondly on revenue arrangements. As the powers and rights of landlords increased, those of their tenants declined. Fellahin and *sirkals* were bound to their landlords by a combination of debt, the *Tribal Disputes Regulation*, and the Cultivators' Law. The control of the landlord was complete, and the fellah or *sirkal* had no way of improving his position except by leaving the land. As far as the Treasury was concerned, the land and revenue policy resulted in the gradual decline of receipts from agriculture. The government was forced to look for other sources of income, and found first customs duties, and then, providentially, was baled out by the oil revenues. A relatively painless solution could be found for the economic dislocations caused by the policy: the same means were not available to resolve the long term political and social upheavals which it brought about.

7

DEFENCE AND INTERNAL SECURITY: THE ROLE OF THE IRAQ ARMY AND THE RAF

As mandatory power, Britain was responsible in international law for the defence of Iraq against foreign invasion. At the same time, British troops were stationed in Iraq to protect the route to India, and the Persian, and later the Iraqi, oilfields. This duality of roles produced a certain amount of ambiguity; a rising in Iraq, even if wholly brought about by the folly of the government, was also a threat to imperial interests, and Britain would likely intervene to uphold the government's authority. Hence Iraqis could allege that their country's defence policy was planned to serve Britain's rather than their own best interests.

Altogether, Britain's objectives in the defence of Iraq were fourfold: to protect her own interests and imperial communications, to defend Iraq against invasion, to maintain internal peace and security, and to achieve these aims as cheaply as possible. It was decided at the Cairo Conference that, in broad terms, defence should be undertaken jointly by the British and Iraqi governments, the Iraqis providing an army and the British a detachment of the Royal Air Force. The obligations of both countries were set down in the Military Agreement of 1924: Iraq was to devote a quarter of her revenue to defence and be prepared to take full military responsibility for herself at the end of 1928, although, as has been noted, that cut-off point was eventually abandoned. Britain's contribution was to hold the ring for the four years and to pay the entire costs of imperial forces stationed in Iraq, which included British or Indian battalions, armoured car companies, squadrons of the RAF and the Iraq Levies. British military commitment was planned on a reducing scale, and expenditure dropped from about £32 million in 1920–1921 to about £4 million in 1926–1927 and £0.48 million in 1930–1931.[1] Largely because the oilfields and the Empire air route were considered too important to be left unprotected, British troops did not in fact leave in 1928, or in 1932, and RAF bases were maintained in Iraq until 1958. It was also considered in the late 1920s that the Iraqi army had reached an insufficient state of preparedness to take sole charge of the country's defence.

The Iraqi army

Throughout the mandate there was considerable controversy about the size and function of the Iraqi army. To King Faysal and his circle, many of whom were former Ottoman military officers, a strong Iraqi army implied greater independence from British control, and an earlier possibility of entry to the League of Nations. Further, if the King and Nuri could gain control of a large military force, their own power within the country would be considerably enhanced. Their enthusiasm for expansion, and the opposition to it from Shi'i politicians who realised perfectly that Sunni dominance would thereby become all the more secure, was at the centre of the conscription controversy in the years after 1927.[2]

Most British officials were opposed to increasing the numbers of the army or widening its functions, partly because it would give so much more power to the 'court party', but also because the army was largely ineffective, and the government's small revenues did not permit sufficient expansion. It was allowed to increase slowly from about 3,500 men in 1921 to about 12,000 men in 1932, a figure far lower than Nuri and his friends considered adequate. The army was no more than a glorified *gendarmerie* acting as an occasional adjunct to the RAF, and Iraqi governments knew this and resented it.[3] In the early 1920s, the army was considered so wasteful that it was suggested that it should be virtually dispensed with: Sir Hugh Trenchard, the Chief of Air Staff, wanted to concentrate entirely on the Levies ('colonial troops' under British command, recruited from the Assyrian Christian community), which were demonstrably more efficient, and 'let the Arab Army remain purely as eyewash.'[4] This would have been politically impossible:

> If we are to embark on a policy of bolstering up the Levies into a permanent force, and of neglecting the Arab Army, we must realise that it entails not only a change in our military policy, but in the wider policy governing our very interest in Iraq. It also tends to lessen rather than foster the idea of an eventually independent Iraq.[5]

Thus in spite of its apparent incompetence, the army had to be maintained.

After several years of wrangling Britain was persuaded to give it £600,000 spread over four years as a grant in aid, most of which was used to pay the salaries of the officers of the British Military Mission. In general, although featuring prominently in the political bargaining of the period, the army played a minor military role until the very end of the mandate. It first saw extended active service in the operations against Shaykh Mahmud in 1930, when the ground had first been carefully prepared by the RAF:

> In these operations, the policy of the British Military Mission, that of training the Army to stand alone, was pursued to limits hitherto regarded as dangerous. The risks taken were fully justified by events, for the Iraqi leaders exercised their functions for the most part satisfactorily and the Army in consequence faces its future with a considerable access of confidence.[6]

This optimistic account, extracted from the *Report* on Iraq's progress between 1920 and 1931, written for the Permanent Mandates Commission, was not echoed in an internally circulated description of the Barzan operations two years later:

> Leadership and discipline broke down at a particularly critical stage, and the British Officers, whose function was to act only as advisers and who had no legal authority, found themselves compelled to take complete charge and to issue direct orders themselves.[7]

Hence, because of the general inadequacy of the army, the tasks of defence and internal security were largely undertaken by the RAF and the Levies. Apart from the RAF's police work in the Southern Desert against the *Ikhwan* of Najd in the late 1920s, and the operations against Turkish irregulars in the early 1920s, there were few instances, or threats, of invasion from outside, and in any case the deterrent effect of the British connection was the main bulwark against such possibilities. The main task of the RAF in Iraq was to maintain 'tranquillity' within the country, and it made use of the opportunity to prove itself capable of playing a cheap and efficient peacekeeping role. In this way it also helped to ensure its own future as a permanent independent branch of the British Armed Services.[8]

The Royal Air Force in Iraq

The first aeroplanes of the Royal Flying Corps had arrived in Mesopotamia in 1916. In the first months, their use was confined to reconnaissance and guiding artillery fire, but gradually the advantages of using aircraft in offensive operations became as apparent in the Middle East as they had become on the Western Front. In addition, the notion that aeroplanes had their uses in checking disturbances in areas considered impenetrable by ordinary troops began to gain currency. In April 1919:

> Bombing still continues to be carried out. No sooner has one area been subdued than another breaks out into revolt and has to be dealt with by aeroplane . . . all these tribal disturbances have been dealt with from the air . . . thus the Army has been saved from marching many weary miles over bad country and sustaining casualties.[9]

While Secretary of State for War, Churchill had instructed Trenchard to prepare a scheme for the maintenance of internal security for Mesopotamia by the RAF.[10] Churchill envisaged a series of landing grounds in the middle of defended areas, thus doing away with the long lines of communication which had bedevilled the campaign during the war. After a tour of the country, Sir Geoffrey Salmond, brother of the first Air Officer Commanding in Baghdad, concluded that the scheme was suitable in principle:

> It must be taken as an essential part of our position in Mesopotamia that the civil administration of this country is only possible because military force exists. The task which the RAF will be called upon to undertake is to maintain the *status quo* without imperilling the civil administration, even though the worst situation should arise, namely a general rising throughout the country, an improbable event.[11]

In spite of Salmond's predictions, the improbable did take place: the insurrection began a few months later and heavy fighting and considerable loss of life resulted. The advantages of air control, its speed, its great savings in time, personnel and expense were to become increasingly obvious over the following years. Even traditional military men were brought round: General Aylmer Haldane, Commander-in-Chief in Baghdad wrote to Churchill in June 1921:

> Indeed, I now think that had I had sufficient aircraft last year I might have prevented the insurrection spreading from beyond the first incident at Rumaitha.[12]

Others, especially the War Office and the General Staff, remained sceptical, and considered that the rising of 1920 proved their contention that there was no effective substitute for ground troops. However, in December 1920, there were 17,000 British and 85,000 Indian troops in Iraq, 'at an estimated yearly cost of £30 million' (Omissi, 1990: 24). Hence the arguments for the air scheme became even stronger, in terms both of general war weariness and of the desperate need for economy now pressing upon Whitehall. Churchill, who became Colonial Secretary in January 1921, strongly advocated the policy, first broached in detail at the Cairo Conference in March and ultimately adopted in August 1921, and scheduled to take effect after October 1922.[13] The RAF detachment was under the Air Officer Commanding, who was himself responsible to the High Commissioner and not to the Air Ministry. Apart from the savings involved, Trenchard considered that the air scheme was based on the principle that:

> . . . if the Arabs have nothing to fight against on the ground, and no loot or rifles to be obtained, and nobody to kill, but have to deal with aeroplanes which are out of their reach they are certain to come in and there will be no risk of disasters or heavy casualties such as are always suffered by small infantry patrols in uncivilised countries.[14]

However, the principles of air control were the subject of protracted controversy. The opposition put up by the War Office was largely based on lines of demarcation, but even within the Colonial Office misgivings were expressed which were to be largely justified during the period of the mandate. One official asked:

> How far would it be legitimate or desirable for British Forces to help the Arab Government put down risings or to enforce obedience? . . . suppose the middle Euphrates area revolts against the Amir and pushes out all the Amir's officials and sets up a Shia administration: is the Mandatory to help restore the Amir's authority?[15]

Churchill informed Cox in June, 1921:

> Aerial action is a legitimate means of quelling disturbances and of enforcing the maintenance of order but it should in no circumstances be employed in support of purely administrative measures such as the collection of revenue.[16]

— an injunction which was largely to be honoured in the breach. There were to be a number of bumps along the way before the Iraqi 'air scheme', although initiated in October 1922, gained final acceptance. By July 1923 the Salisbury Report, set up to examine relations between the RAF and its parent services (the Army and Navy) concluded that the defence of Britain and the empire would be better served by an autonomous RAF (Omissi, 1990: 33–34).

In practical terms, the preservation of 'internal security' was equivalent to extending the area of authority of the Iraqi government. In order to achieve this, parts of the country which were more or less anarchic and had rarely paid taxes in the past had to be pacified. To the Kurds, and to the tribesmen of the Middle and Lower Euphrates, there was little to distinguish the policy pursued by Britain and the Iraqi government from that pursued by the Ottomans. For the tribesmen, 'government' meant the twin evils of taxation and conscription, both of which they had almost succeeded in keeping at arm's length in Ottoman times. After the occupation, it became clear that the Civil Administration was determined not only to impose taxes but also to collect them, and where the Iraqi government could afford to do so without damaging local susceptibilities, it also showed energy in this respect.

Almost inevitably, bombing developed into an instrument of repression, in spite of the rather odd arguments developed at the time to the effect that it was either or both 'more humane' or somehow especially suited to the 'Bedouin mentality' (Satia, 2006).[17] As a result of several operations in Iraq in 1923 and 1924 which involved fairly high numbers of casualties, the Harmsworth and Beaverbrook presses, which were strongly opposed to further British involvement in the Middle East, seized on the vigorous 'peacekeeping' activities of the RAF as a further argument to 'Quit Mesopotamia',[18] and there were a number of embarrassing parliamentary questions. George Lansbury fulminated against 'this Hunnish and barbarous method of warfare against unarmed people' but he was not alone in his attacks on the policy:

> Lord Curzon has interested himself in this question. I gather that Lord Curzon was not satisfied that there is any real difference between bombing for non-payment of taxes and bombing for non-appearance when summoned to explain non-payment of taxes.[19]

In August 1924 the Labour Minister for Air presented to Parliament a *Note on the Employment of the Air Arm in Iraq*, apparently an attempt at a blanket answer to these criticisms. It described the circumstances under which RAF assistance could be requested, and the administrative procedures involved, emphasising that aeroplanes were only to be used if all other means had failed (although this was quite evidently not what happened in practice). The alternatives to air control were dismissed as impossibly unwieldy and expensive. The *Note* claimed that air defence was cheap, that it provided 'a method of control more effective and less costly to life and suffering', and that it enabled outbreaks to be controlled before they spread. Furthermore, when bombing was about to take place, the local population was always warned in advance by leaflets being dropped to enable them to take cover, so that 'the compulsion exercised by the air arm rests more on the damage to morale and on the interruption to the normal life of the tribe than on actual casualties'.[20] Of course, these discussions were taking place at a time when the idea that civilian populations might be 'collaterally' involved in hostilities in *wartime* was still relatively new, while the air scheme was to be a permanent feature of 'government control' in Iraq. .

Both the principles and the abuses of the system in practice are best illustrated by studying a single operation. The largest offensive mounted by the RAF in southern Iraq during the 1920s was the action taken against the Bani Huchaim confederation in Samawa *qadha* in the late autumn and winter of 1923–1924. In the autumn of 1923, the authorities attempted to collect taxes in the Samawa *qadha* for the first time for many years. There was no suggestion that there had been any serious unruliness or disorder in the area, and the fact that British Officers were able to tour freely confirms this. Glubb, who was then Special Service Officer at Hilla, discovered that there were serious water shortages in the area, largely due to the diversion of the channels by Sha'lan Abu Chon, the most powerful local shaykh who, like his associate 'Abd al-Wahid Sikkar, enjoyed virtual immunity from taxation. No irrigation official had ever visited the *qadha* and the *mutasarrif* was rarely seen. The tribes themselves were:

> . . . exceptionally poor . . . it is a regrettable fact that Government at the moment presents itself to their minds as a kind of absentee landlord which never concerns itself with them except periodically to demand revenue.[21]

Glubb suggested that it would be sensible to talk to the local leaders, listen to their grievances, and make whatever adjustments to revenue assessments were possible. At the same time, however, (as is evident from the dates of the letters) the Administrative Inspector, Diwaniyah, was recommending that punitive action should be taken for nonpayment of taxes. Units of the

Iraqi army and police were moved into position well before it was suggested that the 'rebels' should be summoned to Samawa. The letter sent by the Ministry of Interior to the Administrative Inspector stressed that the latter should be 'careful not to impose collection of revenue as the main condition since if it is found necessary to bomb them it must be for defiance of Government orders and not to increase the exchequer,'[22] just the distinction which Lord Curzon had found so hard to appreciate.

A week or so later Moore, the RAF Special Service Officer at Samawa, made another tour of the area listening to complaints:

In each *mudhif* (tribal guesthouse) we heard the same opinions and grievances that have been embodied in Captain Glubb's report . . . Albu Jayyash in particular were loud in their praise of the old days when water was fairly distributed and a man could feel reasonably safe in his house.[23]

Nevertheless, late in November, the shaykhs of several subsections of the Bani Huchaim confederation were 'peremptorily' summoned to Samawa at 48 hours' notice and required to give a deposit of money as surety of their tribes' good behaviour.[24] Two of the three shaykhs who arrived confessed that they had long lost the ability to control their tribes, an answer which, although considered unsatisfactory, was more than likely to be true. The necessary guarantees could not be found, and arrangements were accordingly made for the RAF to bomb the area so as to encourage obedience to Government. The casualties may appear unimpressive by today's standards, but over a two week period 144 people were killed and an unspecified number wounded.[25]

A few weeks after the end of the operation Glubb, perhaps the most perceptive observer of local conditions, wrote to Air Headquarters:

It is regrettable but it appears almost inevitable that aerial action should be associated with the payment of taxes. First, the tribesman thinks of Government merely as an institution which periodically descends upon him demanding money. If he sees Government applying coercion to any individual or tribe he naturally concludes that it is with the object of extracting money. Secondly, the average minor Government official seems to have much the same idea of his duties . . . the association of punitive action with the payment of taxes cannot be avoided. It can, however, be mitigated by constantly impressing on individuals that Government has no right to tax the community unless it gives something in return. I have very rarely heard an official take credit to himself for improving agriculture in his district, or public health.[26]

A further acute analysis was written by another RAF Intelligence Officer in April 1924:

> The primary cause of the recent outbreak was the growing irritation at demands for revenue which the tribes' poverty and fecklessness makes them unable to meet. That they in fact have little or no money is reported from all sources, both official and unofficial. Whether they would pay if they had is another question, but it seems at least possible that they would squander less recklessly what little they get if they saw a more tangible return for their repayment of revenue. At present many of them feel that they are merely supplying pay for some tomato eating *Effendis* in Baghdad.[27]

Soon after the operation had ended, an official report was sent to London by the Air Officer Commanding in Baghdad. In a minute on the report, the Deputy Chief of Air Staff suggested that before it was circulated to other government departments, certain passages should be omitted, amongst which was the following:

> Although the tribes had been continually lawless and disobedient it appeared necessary before punitive action was taken that some definite instance of insubordination should take place.

The tone of the minute itself is not reassuring:

> If this report as it stands were to get into the hands of undesirable people, harm might be done not only to the Air Force but also to [HM] Government . . . (the whole operation might be regarded as) . . . forcing an unnecessary and unprovoked quarrel on the people in order that drastic punishment might be carried out at a time when no definite claim could be fixed on these people and when the country was quiet and the main communications working normally, even to the extent that; Political Officers could go . . . without opposition mapping and reporting on the country . . . I think that certain paragraphs should not be sent out without further consideration.[28]

Later activities in the same area further suggest that these operations had simply been a form of exemplary punishment. In 1925, a squadron of aircraft was used to help the police in the sheep count, undertaken to collect the *koda*, or animal tax. The air diary records:

> This is the first serious attempt to exercise civil authority over the turbulent Bani Huchaim since the Samawa operations in 1923 . . . It is interesting therefore to note that small police columns with aircraft cooperation were able to operate successfully on such a scale in this area without encountering opposition.[29]

If the first offensive had been in any way successful, it seems strange that two years had had to elapse before any further attempts were made to extend government authority in the area. However, the deterrent effect had struck deep: in 1930 the RAF Special Services Officer in Diwaniya commented:

> Although only a few desperate criminals are now prepared to resist the police, whole sections of the tribes might assist their criminal relatives against the police were it not for the threat of aeroplanes bombing them. This form of punishment will always be remembered in the Samawa *qadha*.[30]

Perhaps the most serious long term consequence of the ready availability of air control was that it developed into a substitute for administration. Several incidents during the mandate period indicate that the speed and simplicity of air attack was preferred to the more time consuming and painstaking investigation of grievances and disputes.[31] With such powers at its disposal the Iraqi government was not encouraged to develop less violent methods of extending its control over the country.

Although the RAF ceased in theory to assist the Iraqi authorities to maintain peace within the country under the terms of the 1930 Treaty, the presence of British aeroplanes in the country after the end of the mandate constituted a powerful deterrent to any attempts to disturb the *status quo*. During the Euphrates rising of 1935, mostly the result, as the Embassy knew, of long standing grievances over land tenure which had been relentlessly exploited by Baghdad politicians, the intervention of the RAF was urgently requested by the Iraqi Prime Minister, the British Ambassador, and senior officials in the Foreign Office, before being turned down in cabinet.[32] Nevertheless the RAF was used during the rising to ferry munitions for the Iraqi army,[33] and aeroplanes were made ready for possible action.[34] According to the Ambassador, Sir Kinahan Cornwallis, just ending his tenure of office at the Ministry of Interior, considered that the Government was lucky to escape so lightly:

> (He) was blackly pessimistic when the tribes around Rumaitha and Suq al-Shuyukh were up, and was inclined to prophesy that Hai, Nasiriyah and Hilla must all go too. Indeed it was a close thing. He thinks that one of the chief reasons for the restriction of the revolt to the two small districts was the R.A. F. reconnaissance and the (accidental) shooting down of our aeroplanes. This persuaded the tribes that we were on the Government side. He got this from some of the shaykhs concerned.[35]

Only by safeguarding the interests of the Iraqi government could Britain ensure the continuation of her own position in the country. Political power had to lie in the hands of those who, however grudgingly or resentfully, realised their own deep dependence on the British connection. Hence in its task of preserving internal order the RAF was in reality merely propping one or other of the political groups who had combined to form the Iraqi government of the day. Its presence made it possible for these groups to exercise an authority over the country that could only be dislodged by violence, and in addition, no opposition in the end could be effective against aeroplanes. Inevitably, as Curzon had foreseen, its main effect was to terrorise the inhabitants of parts of rural Iraq into paying taxes. Without the Air Force the Iraqi government's ability to control the country would have been, at the very least, severely limited. Once again, the comment by Leo Amery, after his visit in 1925 holds good for the whole of the mandate period, and probably for some years after:

> If the writ of King Faysal runs effectively throughout his kingdom it is entirely due to British aeroplanes. If the aeroplanes were removed tomorrow, the whole structure would inevitably fall to pieces.[36]

8

EDUCATIONAL POLICY

The avowedly temporary nature of the British mandate in Iraq, and the notion that the arrangements being made were specifically designed as 'preparations for independence', were considerations which seem only rarely to have had any profound influence on determining administrative policy. Many British officials in Iraq imagined, and, indeed, as the depression of the late 1920s made the prospect of finding employment elsewhere rather remote, fervently hoped (Macdonald, 1936: 75–81), that they or at least their successors would remain in the country for the foreseeable future. This must in some measure explain the relatively small amount of effort expended outside the military sphere in preparing Iraqis to 'run their own show'.

Thus when Iraq became independent in 1932, there were, apart from a few lawyers, doctors and engineers, few technically qualified personnel, and few individuals capable of taking charge of the machinery of the state. One of the reasons for this deficiency was the paltry funds allocated to education during the mandate. It was assumed by those concerned with the direction of policy that education was to a certain extent a luxury and thus could be afforded a fairly low priority. Although the British advisory staff at the Ministry of Education stressed the importance of their work, lack of interest as well as lack of funds prevented any serious attempt to prepare for the future. Writing in 1924, when the Protocol seemed to indicate the drastic curtailing of the period of British control, Lionel Smith, Inspector-General of Education from 1923 to 1931, urged that the British authorities should show:

> . . . in some tangible and practical way that we have not forgotten the vital duty of training Iraqis, and training them quickly, to govern themselves. At present we can point to nothing of this intention on our part.[1]

The neglect of any serious training for independence can partly be explained by a lack of any sense of urgency, but as far as educational policy was concerned, it must also be seen in the context of the general attitudes to the education of subject peoples which were prevalent in the British Empire at the time (as well as attitudes towards the 'lower classes' in Britain) which were common currency among the administrators occupying advisory positions with the Iraqi government.

The dangers rather than the benefits inherent in education were most readily apparent to the experts in the various Imperial services. The fear so frequently expressed in memoirs and official notes from other parts of the Empire was that by going too far too fast a class of over-educated young people would be created for whom no employment opportunities would exist. Such young people would naturally come to form the nucleus of groups of political agitators; Bolshevism was seen or suspected everywhere. It was therefore considered unjustified and unwise to spend too much public money on education; such an investment would simply produce 'another indigenous aristocracy'[2] whose interests were totally alien to those of their fellow countrymen (cf. O'Dwyer, 1926). More telling however, were the 'misgivings as to the effects of unrestrained access to Western Learning' expressed by Sir James Currie, Director of Education in the Sudan from 1900 to 1914:

> Currie's scheme was essentially limited and practical in its aims. He sought to provide vernacular elementary schools to enable the masses to 'understand the elements of the systems of government,' a technical school 'to train a small class of competent artisans' and primary (later called intermediate) schools, to train elementary school masters 'and to provide a small administrative class for entry into the government services.' This was a scheme which would commend itself to administrators rather than to educationalists, and its implementation was slow. Its poverty of conception and meagreness of execution were partially concealed by the construction in Khartoum of the magnificent buildings of the Gordon Memorial College.[3]

In a very similar vein, we read in the *Iraq Report* for 1923:

> Whatever may be thought desirable elsewhere, in this country it is neither desirable nor practicable to provide secondary education except for the selected few. There are at present four Government secondary schools at Baghdad, Basra, Mosul and Kirkuk. But there are reasons for thinking that even this limited number may be too large and that it

might be better to concentrate on two secondary schools, each with a boarding section, one at Baghdad and the other at Mosul. These offer a four years' course and with the classes offering a two years' course, which it is proposed shortly to open in certain provincial towns, should be enough to meet the demands for secondary education.[4]

In 1932, eight years after this report was written, there were less than two thousand secondary school places in the whole of Iraq. Some comparisons with contemporary Britain may be instructive: it was only in 1902 that Britain acquired a centrally organised and financed (although locally administered) system of secondary schooling,[5] and until 1918, schooling was compulsory only until the age of 12. As far as universities were concerned, the percentage of graduates in the population of England long remained infinitesimal; 0.02 per cent (2 per 10,000) in 1861, 0.06 per cent in 1911. Such factors are likely to have been important in the formulation of British colonial educational policy in the interwar period, if only because the majority of those implementing it them had not experienced the state secondary system, but had attended instead what are still confusingly known as public, meaning private, schools. The minute percentages of university graduates in the general population, and the relative indifference towards the public financing even of secondary education shows how relatively low a place education occupied in political and social priorities in late nineteenth and twentieth century Britain, at least until the passage of the Butler Education Act in 1944.

The author of a recent study rightly points out that '[t]here are good grounds for arguing that education was never a top government funding priority in India or the colonial empire generally when compared with the need to maintain Britain's place in the balance of world power or the health of the domestic economy . . . a succession of British governments felt neither the necessity nor the compulsion to tackle the educational needs of the colonial territories properly. To have done so would have needed far more personnel and money than contemporary political priorities dictated.'[6] Another feature of colonial education at the time was the notion that the process was in some way finite, that after a certain time a saturation point might be reached. In the following year the author of the Education section of the Report questions the wisdom of continuing to admit students to the Teachers' Training College at the current rate:

. . . But it is already possible to foresee the time when all the primary and elementary schools will be completely supplied with trained teachers and no further trained teachers will be required except for replacing casualties and for staffing a small number of new schools. At the present rate of graduation from the Teachers' Training College this time should be reached in six years and it therefore becomes necessary to consider whether it might not be more expedient to introduce a progressive diminution in the numbers of the Training College thus reducing the annual output of teachers and the annual expenditure on the College while at the same time postponing the day when all the schools will be supplied with trained teachers.[7]

Fortunately, a steady increase, both in the construction of schools and in the supply of teachers, was maintained. Thus we have the familiar story: moderation, caution and the preparation of the selected few for the teaching profession or junior posts in government service. This level of educational provision was not calculated to meet with widespread approval from the Iraqis who were well aware that more advanced education had long been available, in Baghdad, Beirut and Istanbul for those who could afford it.

A feature of the educational system was a degree of uniformity of syllabus and curriculum, and a widespread focus on learning by rote, which owed as much to the Franco-Ottoman as to the British colonial educational systems. Primary school children in Baghdad were taught the same syllabus as village children in the few schools that existed in the Muntafiq. Rightly or wrongly, there was no attempt to design specifically rural educational programmes, either as a part of the regular school curriculum or as an extension to it. An attempt to link the experimental farm at Rustumiya with a programme of special agricultural education was abandoned because of lack of funds.[8] In general, all the educational investigations undertaken at the request of or with the permission of the Iraqi government between 1931 and 1958 draw attention to the rigidity and formality of syllabus and teaching methods.

The defects in the system cannot be entirely attributed to British colonial educational theory, and in this context the adjective 'Franco-Ottoman' needs a little further explanation. Modernised (that is, non-religious) Ottoman education, on which most Iraqi politicians and bureaucrats had been nurtured, was largely based on the rigid and formal methods of traditional French education, with one highly important addition. One of the main purposes of education in the Ottoman Empire had been to prepare students for a career in government service. Many Iraqis had no wish to change this state of affairs, and the strong pressures for more education which appeared in the press in the 1920s were very largely for more education to produce a greater number of potential *muwazzafin*. In countries where government is the largest employer of labour requiring even the smallest degree of literacy, this attitude is comprehensible, and it remains true that the notion of education as a passport to a desk, however humble, in a ministry, is still fairly widespread in the Middle East today. Whatever merits this system may have had, as Smith remarked in 1930,[9] the fact was that a graduate of the national schools emerged prepared for very few other careers.

Finally we should consider a slightly different aspect of the mandatory power's role m these matters. Direct British interference in the affairs of the Iraqi government varied substantially between government departments, according to how much British money or 'interest' was invested in them. Thus Defence, Finance and Interior were closely watched over by their British advisors and their deputies, and less important departments, such as Agriculture, Health and Education, were left to function very much more on their own, with less detailed day to day supervision. In practical terms this amounted to smaller budget allocations, and fewer British personnel (except in purely technical areas, such as medical specialties, agricultures and irrigation). As far as the Iraqi government was concerned, the portfolio of Education normally became the billet of the token Shi'i member of the Cabinet: very often the appointee would be a religious dignitary of Karbala' or Najaf, whose first language would be Persian rather than Arabic,[10] and it was rare for any continuity to be preserved from one short-lived cabinet to another.[11] Thus with a frequently inactive minister, and an advisor whose powers were less extensive than those of his colleagues in other ministries, Education became the department of state in which the permanent Iraqi civil servants had greatest control.[12] For most of the mandate, the Director General of the Ministry was the nationalist theoretician and educationist, Sati' al-Husri, a friend and confidant of King Faysal, who had asked al-Husri to accompany him from Syria to Iraq. al-Husri's appointment in 1922 occasioned the resignation of the British Acting Advisor.[13] It is not entirely mischievous to suggest that it is a reflection of the low place which education occupied in Britain's list of priorities that an Arab was given such wide responsibilities, but al-Husri's powers were real enough. The permanent Adviser, Lionel Smith, threatened to resign more than once over disagreements about policy.[14]

When the British occupation began in 1914, there were very few schools or qualified teachers in Iraq; the language of instruction was Turkish and since all the Muslim state schools were Sunni, Shi'is did not attend them. It was thought desirable to initiate a national educational system, and at the same time to inject funds into the more efficient of the existing missionary and denominational schools (Wilson, 1931: 174 footnote). However, little money for this purpose was forthcoming until the end of the war.

Table I

Year	Spending on Education (rupees)	Percentage of civil budget
1915–1916	6,500	0.40
1916–1917	23,530	0.74
1917–1918	35,500	0.35
1918–1919	180,000	1.08
1919–1920	886,808	1.90[15]

In 1915, Education was an appendage of the Revenue Department; Dobbs as Revenue Commissioner wrote a memorandum in February of that year, stressing the undesirability of over-hastiness in the provision of educational facilities:

> The shortage of primary teachers led him to declare that if it were not for the urgent necessity of supply of Arabs for Government service he should be inclined to advise that not a single school should be opened for the next two years.[16]

The first attempt to suggest a policy for education in Mesopotamia appears, rather incongruously, in the *Report of the Mesopotamia Trade Commissioners* of 1917. The two authors, Holland and Wilson, suggested that any programme devised should concentrate on 'vocational training rather than literary exercises', but also stressed the desirability of 'developing the existing commercial class and also of starting an experimental farm in connection with the agricultural department as soon as it is instituted.' We have already seen the fate of that well-intentioned suggestion; generally the report is concerned with the reestablishment of trade and commerce in the area after the war, and has only a small section on education. Its authors were dubious of the value of more sophisticated forms of instruction for the inhabitants of Mesopotamia: 'During the next ten years at all events it is hardly likely that any need will be felt for the institution of BA courses.'[17]

It was only in August 1918, with the appointment of a full-time Director of Education that practical steps began to be taken on a larger scale. Table I above shows that the sums allocated increased considerably after that. The director, Humphrey Bowman, had spent his previous career in the educational services of Egypt and the Sudan; his diaries and autobiography[18] reveal a competent, energetic if somewhat narrow-minded and fussy man, not always successful in concealing his impatience with and distrust of his Arab charges and Arab colleagues. His description of the events preceding his appointment as Director give an interesting sidelight on one aspect of officialdom's attitude to such a post. He had been asked to go to Baghdad as early as August 1917, but in spite of energetic pleas by both the Foreign and India Offices, there seems to have been a fairly active want of sympathy on the part of his superiors in Cairo:

> The Adjutant-General (Macready) was adamant and said my services could not be spared, though the true meaning was that in his opinion the time was not ripe for education in Mesopotamia. This was not his province, and he therefore could not say so, but this I know was what he said unofficially.[19]

Eventually, in August 1918, Bowman arrived in Baghdad. A contemporary diary entry sums up part of the policy he was to pursue in Iraq for the next two years:

> From what I can learn the Arabs are very keen on the education of their sons, and we shall have to go slow in order to prevent inferior schools with poor teachers springing up everywhere. As I always intended, I want to begin at the bottom with the good *maktab*: let primary schools come as they can be provided; but there are already some primary schools in the country and we must therefore accept these and do our best to improve them.[20]

This cautious approach was, as we have seen, based partly on theories about the students' inability to absorb more than a certain amount, and partly on a belief in the inadvisability of their doing so. Bowman quotes, with obvious approval, the ideas of Currie of the Sudan, who he says, was determined to 'limit secondary and advanced education to those who could profit by it', in order to avoid the creation of a white collar class for whom no employment would be found, that 'half-educated, unemployed class so prevalent in Egypt and India (Bowman, 1942: 88–89).' Bowman did his best to continue along these lines, confident that he would not be pressed to go faster; after a year he wrote an official *Note on Educational Policy*, which states quite firmly that:

> In spite of appeals and criticisms the Department has resolutely re-fused to contemplate secondary education until assured, firstly, that capable teachers are available for it, and secondly that the human material is sufficiently prepared to profit by it.[21]

He enjoyed the confidence and support of the Acting Civil Commissioner ('Bowman . . . a man of liberal views, much liked and of outstanding ability, with whom I frequently took counsel [Wilson, 1931: 175]') who was energetic in his efforts to persuade the Egyptian authorities not to insist on recalling Bowman to his parent service a year later. Bowman's views were widely shared; a more thoughtful but very similar note was written by another contemporary Mesopotamian official:

> Any advance in the direction of instituting a system of secondary and subsequently of higher education should be very carefully considered in the light of experience gained in other Oriental countries such as Egypt and India. The need of an educated class to carry on the work of the Government is doubtless pressing, but this need, unless supported by a real demand for secondary education for its own sake, should not be taken as a pretext for starting a large scheme of secondary education. *The supply for the service of the Government will eventually exceed the demand with the result that a discontented and partially educated class of people will be formed for whom there are no prospects of useful employment and no opportunities of securing a higher education.*[22] (my italics).

Wilson was not in fact successful in securing Bowman's retention in Iraq, and he returned to Egypt reluctantly after only two years at his post. For most of the remainder of the mandate, Lionel Smith, a former Fellow of All Souls' who had served as a Political Officer in Mesopotamia during the war, was Adviser to the Ministry of Education.[23] His pungent letters to Dobbs and Shuckburgh on educational and other issues convey something of the difficulties of his personal position, and some of the more general contradictions inherent in the mandate relationship. However, illness, indecision and a long absence in England prevented him from taking up his post permanently until 1923. From 1920 to 1922 the Advisorship was held by Jerome Farrell, who resigned over the appointment of al-Husri as

Director-General and subsequently served under Bowman when the latter became Director of Education in Palestine.

In general, reports and comments on the state of education in Iraq during the mandate made either in private to the Colonial Office or publicly in the Annual Reports to the League of Nations, convey an air of cautious optimism. It was felt that apart from the financial stringencies dictated by circumstances beyond the immediate control of the Education Department, a degree of progress was being made which could be reasonably expected to continue as long as the blandishments of Iraqi press and public opinion for greater quantity rather than quality in education were resisted.[24] An exception to this general note of modest confidence is a long memorandum written in November 1921 by Farrell, *The Education Department and its Relation to the Mandate and the League of Nations*. This document is perhaps more illustrative of its author's personal obsessions than of the state of affairs in the department, but with this caveat in mind, it also gives interesting insights into some aspects of mandate officialdom, showing how difficult it still was for some members of the administration to implement the policies forced upon them by Whitehall and the League.

Farrell firmly believed in the 'moral degeneration' of the Iraqi people, as a result of excessive indulgence in vices of all kinds. He suggested the inculcation of physical and mental wellbeing through the introduction of the Boy Scout movement, and the 'stimulation of healthy interests', especially upon the playing fields:

Nowhere in my experience [are qualities so engendered] so utterly lacking and so urgently needed as in the middle classes of the urban population of Iraq, where after the age of puberty an inveterate dignity allows to few the indulgence of more vigorous hobbies than tea-drinking and gossip in public, and in private certain unmentionable indoor sports. It is not from this soil that we can expect to grow such humble virtues as a sense of duty, self-sacrifice and sober patriotism. It is perhaps unnecessary to say that no corps of native officials and teachers exists or will exist for many years in Iraq capable of even appreciating the necessity for a moral revolution, still less of devising the means to it and carrying them to execution. The best hope lies in the response which the children have begun to give to the efforts of a few British masters and three or four native assistants whom they have inspired. I can see no remedy or even palliative except in British executive control of the Department.[25]

The scope and nature of the Agreements concluded between Britain and Iraq in the mid 1920s necessitated drastic economies, particularly on the development' side of budget expenditure. It was suggested that the allocation for Education should be reduced by 3 lakhs (£2,000) in May 1922, and by November of that year, the Economies Committee had suggested even more severe economies, (which included reducing the number of hospital beds from 1600 to 1000), and that school fees should be charged to make ends meet:

Table II

Type of School	Fees: Increases	Percentage of Free Places
Elementary: 4 lowest classes	Rs 10 to Rs 30 p.a.	Not exceeding 30 %
Elementary: higher classes	Rs 30 to Rs 50 p.a.	Not exceeding 20 %
Secondary: all classes	Rs 30 to Rs 75 p.a.	Not exceeding 15 %[26]

Fees – it is the familiar story – had been in force theoretically, but not actually collected, during the Ottoman period. Also at this time, small but irksome payments for books and stationery were instituted. With an air of injured surprise, the 1922–1923 *Report* states:

> As the Turkish regulations had been more honoured in the breach than in the observance, the change, in theory a step towards free education, was greeted with considerable protest.[27]

One result of the economies of the early 1920s was that the much cherished scheme for the institution of a special college for the sons of shaykhs was forced into abeyance, and in fact was never to materialise.[28] The various economies adopted did in fact reduce spending on education in 1922–1923 to 18.15 lakhs (about £12,000), which occasioned hostile press comment throughout 1923. Education policy had been laid down by Bowman in 1919 and 1920, and though these new economies affected the number of schools, teachers and pupils, there were few changes in policy or attitudes to education. The familiar emphasis on primary and elementary (or intermediate) education with a very few secondary schools (although these rose to fifteen in 1930) was maintained. The government was under continual criticism for its dilatoriness in this respect:

The whole nation is deeply disappointed by the small progress which has been made during the past few years in the development of the education of the country. The number of pupils in the primary schools is only a very small proportion of the children of the country, while the facilities for secondary education are depressingly inadequate. Only about 3% of the boys from the primary schools go on to secondary schools; what happens to the others? Are they refused admission? There are only two technical schools in Iraq. The Government has a heavy responsibility in this regard.[29]

The language of instruction, and the religious education provided in a school, was decided in accordance with the language or denomination of the majority of the pupils, though in all cases Arabic was used in the higher classes. The curriculum was heavily weighted towards the teaching of classical Arabic, and towards learning by rote, perhaps influenced by the fact that there were, in 1925, an estimated 6,925 pupils still attending *mulla* schools, where education was conducted along traditional Qur'anic lines. In the ministry itself, as has already been mentioned, British control was probably less rigid than in any other government department. Partly as a protest against this, and partly because of a conviction that the mandate was being mismanaged generally, Smith submitted his resignation in July 1924. He was to withdraw it subsequently, but his letter of resignation expresses with great clarity some of the feelings of unease which were shared by his more thoughtful contemporaries:

> I have resigned because I believe that by continuing in my present post I should not be acting fairly either to the Iraqi government or to myself . . . And as my successor, if I have one, will presumably be appointed with the concurrence of the Colonial Office, I think that the Colonial Office should know some of the reasons for my resignation and for my recommendation that my position should not be filled.

He felt that his inability to ensure that the advice he gave was actually put into practice had the effect of making his position impossible. In view of the recently shortened period of 'tutelage', Smith felt that a tiny budget, 'a succession of reactionary Ministers' with little experience of or interest in Education had brought him to a point from which he could no longer continue.

In my opinion no self-respecting person could hold the position of Adviser in Education except under these conditions:

1) That there should be some prospect of expansion in Education:

2) That there should be a return to a system of more effective control of Education by the British:

3) That a definite policy for Education, suited to the requirements of the country, should be formulated by the Ministry of Education and accepted by all British Advisors in Iraq and by H. M. Government.

1) and 3) are to my mind the most important, but 2) is also highly desirable because it would guarantee in some measure the interests of Education against the caprices of Ministers of Education. Without these conditions the work of an Advisor in Education is reduced to little more than advising how one rupee can be made to do the work of two.

He ended with a summary of his views and recommendations:

1) It is a mistake for us not to keep continually in mind that what we are trying to do in this country is a thing that has never been tried in history, I mean to introduce self-government of the most up-to-date kind into a country which has practically speaking no unity, no patriotism, no political instincts or traditions, no education and no actual wealth:

2) Education in this country has been stationary, is stationary and ought to be advanced:

3) The shadow of British control without the substance is useless. It is just as expensive to the Iraqis and it does not give them what they pay for: expert assistance. And they know it.

4) We must have an educational policy accepted both by the Iraqi government and by the British Advisors. None of these propositions seems to me incapable of realisation. The second is perhaps the most difficult on account of the increasing budget of the Ministry of Defence. But assuming that British military support is to be withdrawn at the end of the Protocol period and that therefore a strong native army is essential, it is also I think true that there is just as much danger of disruption from

within. And against this danger a sound and adequate educational system is the best safeguard.[30]

There were in fact no changes of direction in educational practice. It is true that although allocations to Education were small, they did gradually increase over the mandate period; average annual expenditure for those years was some 25.10 lakhs (about £17,000), 5.3% of the budget. The following table shows what was in fact achieved over the period in increases in schools and pupils. The financial year 1921–1922 has been chosen as a 'base' because of the disruptions caused by the 1920 rising, and 1919 and 1935 have been included since we have the budget allocation and estimated population totals for both these years.

Table III

Primary	Boys' Schools	Boy Pupils	Girls' Schools	Girl Pupils	Estimated Population
1919	??	??	??	??	2,848,000
1921–1922	84	6,743	??	??	??
1925–1926	190	16,599	31	4,035	??
1929–1930	247	24,885	44	6,003	??
1935	??	??	??	??	3,605,000

Secondary	Schools	Pupils	Annual Education budget allocation as percentage of total budget
1919	??	??	1.08
1921–1922	??	??	3.30
1925–1926	5	583	4.59
1929–1930	15	1,863	6.42
1935	??	??	10.00[31]

During the mandate the number of girls at State schools doubled, that of boys quadrupled. The table above does not include figures either from the *mulla* schools or the independent denominational schools. In 1925–1926, a year for which there are complete details of numbers in all primary schools inspected, the numbers are as follows:

Table IV

Schools	State	Denominational	Mulla	Total
	20, 654	12, 900	6, 925	40,479[32]

It is clear from these tables that more schools were opened over the period, and that more children attended them. The Iraqis welcomed this increase in educational facilities and indeed clamoured for more; the Ministry was hard pressed to satisfy popular demand, and judging from the volume of criticism, frequently failed to do so. By the time he was firmly established in his post Smith wanted a 'liberal educational policy, based on the needs and wishes of the country as a whole . . .'[33] to be put into effect. By 1935 Education received a tenth of the national budget, ranking third below Defence and Police, and immediately above Interior. Occasionally we find references to the encouragement of either practical or vocational training, or to attempts to reduce the numbers of subjects in the school leaving certificate, but what we do not find are radical changes in the syllabus, either during the period of the mandate, or, it would seem, afterwards.[34]

After the foundation of the Turkish Republic in 1923, and its adoption of the Latin alphabet in 1925, several expert commissions were invited to suggest educational reforms to the new Turkish government. At least four reports, with sensible and feasible suggestions, were presented by distinguished foreign educationalists between 1924 and 1933. Very few of these recommendations were put into practice. In Iraq, the Monroe Commission of 1931 put forward equally sensible suggestions, which were equally ignored. In both Iraq and the new Turkey thoughtful and reforming educationalists were faced with very similar problems. Education was largely confined to city dwellers and largely directed towards government service or the teaching profession. The teacher himself would be an *effendi*, for whom assignment to a small provincial town would be at best a stepping stone to higher things, at worst a punishment to be endured. The bright child from the remote village, sent to a secondary school in a larger centre, might well not wish to return. Also, the provision of vocational training for skilled artisans and manual workers was not given high priority as manual labour of any kind was not thought to be a fit occupation for anyone sufficiently educated to contemplate anything else. Skilled workers were normally Indians, other foreigners, or members of the minorities. Against this background, and with the added problems of finance and scarce personnel, the difficulties of making substantial educational changes were enormous. Informed comment pointed towards a complete renovation of the system, but these changes were not desired either by those able to implement them or by the body of articulate public opinion. Three reports, written in 1931, 1949 and 1958 criticised the Iraqi educational system in the same terms, occasionally almost verbatim.[35]

Just before the end of the mandate, in 1931, the Iraqi government invited Professor Paul Monroe, of Columbia Teachers' College, to prepare a report on the state of education in the country. His commission of enquiry included two other teachers from the college, and one of his former graduate students, the future Iraqi Prime Minister Fadhil Jamali (Jamali, 1934). After three months in Iraq they drew up an impressive list of recommendations, mostly to the effect that the school curriculum was largely irrelevant to the needs of Iraqi society. Particularly, there was no attempt to cater for the fact that a very large majority of the Iraqi population lived either a nomadic or a rural existence. Hence they suggested peripatetic schools for the tribes, and special courses designed for a rural environment to be taught in village schools. The Commissioners were concerned that school work should be more closely linked with life outside school; they suggested the introduction of commercial and technical courses for urban schools, and the gradual abolition of learning by rote. Also, they urged that better personnel should be encouraged to enter the teaching profession by making teaching comparable in salary and status with other branches of government service. The Monroe Commission stressed diversity, and considered education as one of the chief means towards the achievement of 'stability' within society:

> One great problem is unavoidable. Any social group will produce a greater number of youths of essentially intellectual ability than is demanded or can be profitably used. To prevent an oversupply, which finally becomes a menace to the very stability of the society they are trained to maintain, it is essential that very many, perhaps the major part of youth trained for leadership should be interested in and devote themselves not to government service, or to professions, but to industry, commerce, agriculture and the production of wealth upon which modern society is based. This in fact becomes the most difficult task of nationalist education, particularly in the secondary grades (Monroe, 1932: 42).

Other parts of the report make it clear that the authors were well aware of the difficulties involved. They expressed the familiar fear that over-concentration on secondary and higher education would bring about a situation where 'the professional occupations are overcrowded while the national life is menaced by educated men who cannot make a living and in consequence make trouble' (Monroe, 1932: 167).

For our purposes, the main interest of the report lies in its recommendations for a more generally relevant system of education, which were not generally adopted.[36] Eighteen years later, the situation seems to have changed very little; 'teaching in the public primary schools is principally a matter of presenting facts, and demanding that they be memorised (Matthews and 'Akrawi, 1949).' Matthews and 'Akrawi also criticised the rigid bureaucracy of the Ministry of Education, especially the fact that a headmaster's independence was so circumscribed:

> Consequently a great deal of correspondence goes on between the schools and the administration asking for money for anything that cannot be covered by the miscellaneous expenditure fund. School equipment, books for libraries, furniture, stationery, all come from the central or provincial educational authorities and no principal is allowed to spend money on these items (Matthews and 'Akrawi, 1949: 128).

They commented also on the continuing emphasis on uniformity, the importance attached by the Ministry to a class being given the same lesson at the same time on the same day as any other class in the same level. In spite of the relatively large sums which had been devoted to education (12.9 per cent of the budget in 1938–1939, 7.8 per cent in 1944–1945, and 8.6 per cent in 1945–1946) they were not sure that educational progress had kept pace with population growth.

Matthews and 'Akrawi's report on Iraq forms a chapter in *Education in the Arab Countries of the Near East*, a survey commissioned by UNESCO in 1949. Nearly ten years later. Malcolm Quint wrote a short sociological survey of an Iraqi village, in which he included his view of the function of the school there:

> The school teaches, in effect an alien curriculum, suitable for Baghdad, for which it was designed. I call the curriculum alien since it has no real relevance or meaning to the village children. Their world is limited to the immediate neighborhood of the village, still closer to the world of Ur and Babylon than it is to our modern world. Yet the school attempts to bridge this vast gap and to prepare the students

for life in this other world, which does not as yet exist for them. The school by teaching the three Rs, history, geography, hygiene, P.E., and even English attempts to equip the students for a world which is meaningless. Hygiene classes, for instance, teach the village boy that if he brushes his teeth, gets exercise, a balanced diet, and keeps clean, etc., he will be healthy. This sort of lesson makes a great deal of sense for a boy who lives in New York or Iowa, or Baghdad, but bears no relationship to life in Umm al-Nahr, where animal dung is used for fuel, where barefoot peasants walk through fields infested with hookworm, and where the only drinking water available is almost certain to be contaminated (Quint 1958).

Especially in view of these three comments, it is difficult to sum up the effect of the mandate on Iraqi education. The only progress made was purely quantitative and there were grave difficulties in the way of making real changes either in syllabus or in teaching methods. The 'dangers' of education were readily appreciated by the British authorities, and the relatively small sums allocated in the Iraqi government's budgets were an indication both of this and the feeling that in any event education was something of a luxury. The philosophy of the mandate as a 'preparation for independence' does not seem to have stimulated more than a very few individuals to be concerned that so little practical training was being provided for this very eventuality. Furthermore, as in many other departments of government, old Ottoman traditions died hard. Fundamental change was frustrated by the educated classes themselves, who continued to cherish the notion that education should continue to be a guarantee of government employment for their children. It is probably true to say that the mandate authorities helped to extend and amplify and in some ways improve the existing system, and added the teaching of English to the syllabus, but they had over all insufficient interest, time, money or support to make sweeping changes in either the content or methods of education.

9

THE MANDATE AND ITS LEGACY

Early in 1931, following indications on the part of the Permanent Mandate Commission of its unease about the situation in Iraq, the British authorities at the Residency compiled a report outlining the main events of the period between 1920 and 1931. Not unexpectedly, the report was optimistic in tone: the authorities were concerned, perhaps desperately concerned, to stress the positive achievements of the mandate. Before being sent to London, a draft copy went to the Ministry of Interior for Sir Kinahan Cornwallis' comments:

> Your statement . . . that it is beyond question that progress in general has been maintained is one to which I think few people would subscribe. I see instances of bad administration every day. In fact, half our time at the Ministry is spent not only in pointing out mistakes but in fighting definite acts of injustice. .. What is going to happen when our influence is removed? My own prediction is that they will all fly at each other's throats and that there will be a bad slump in the administration which will continue until someone strong enough to dominate the country emerges or, alternatively, until we have to step in and intervene.[1]

In a sense, both Cornwallis' predictions, the 'strong man' and 'British intervention' were fulfilled, and he himself, as British Ambassador in 1941, found himself in charge of the latter. However, his comment is misleading in one important respect. British influence was not removed, simply employed more covertly and less directly. Once the main objectives of British policy had been secured, the necessary control could as well be exercised from behind the scenes.

By 1932, the security of British interests in Iraq seemed guaranteed. The exploitation of Iraqi oil (still at a very early stage) was firmly in the hands of IPC, an international consortium in which Britain held a majority share.[2] The empire air route was secured by RAF bases and (by this time) a reasonably discreet military presence – four RAF squadrons (each with 12–16 aircraft), an armoured car company and two battalions of Assyrian Levies employed as aerodrome guards. In the wider region, the situation in Palestine, though beginning to give cause for concern, had not yet taken on the negative dimensions it would acquire (in Arab and international politics) after 1936: in Syria, the Anglo-Iraqi Treaty of 1930 was widely held up as a model of the kind of instrument which would, ideally, regulate Franco-Syrian relations. In Baghdad, a small group of politicians and officials entirely dependent on the British connection had been installed in office, and provided they did nothing which could be interpreted by the British as unfriendly, their positions were fairly secure.

However, in any balance sheet for the mandate, most of the Iraqi people outside the small circle of government, in so far as they were affected by its activities, were the losers. The government was not carried on for their benefit, but for the benefit of the Sunni urban political elite, within a framework created and supported by the British authorities. It is profitless to blame the British mandatory authorities for failing to ensure that the Iraqi government concerned itself with the wider interests of the nation, or made efforts to reconcile rather than to exacerbate the tensions within the state: to do so would be to misunderstand the nature of imperialism. But many of the shortcomings of the state of Iraq during and even after the monarchy can be traced to the mechanisms and institutions founded at the time of the British occupation and continued under the mandate: tribal policy, land policy, a political system which could not function independently of British backing, inadequate safeguards for the minority groups, even the policy of working through a network of police informers on whose reports so much of this work has been based.[3]

The ideals of the mandate, and the ends it actually achieved, were far apart. Britain left Iraq in 1932 because it was felt possible to take the risk, rather than because of a belief that a particular state of preparedness for independence had been reached: writing after the General Strike of 1931, Edmonds analysed some of the causes of discontent:

> The general impression left on the mind is that the bases of the Iraqi state are still not as broad as one would wish: it dangerously resembles a pyramid balanced on its point. The Government is – I suppose

inevitably – in the hands of a limited oligarchy composed essentially of Sunni Arab townsmen really representing a very small minority of the country. It is therefore easy for any agitator to play on the racial, religious or personal prejudices of anybody who is not an Arab, or a Muslim, or if a Muslim not a Sunni or a townsman, or educated: when to these is added a proportion of the very class from which the oligarchy is drawn, the list is indeed a formidable one.[4]

Since they had created this state of affairs, the British authorities were naturally disinclined to change it. Even after the end of the mandate, the embassy was more concerned to cover up for the Iraqi government than to deplore their sins of commission: after the Assyrian massacre in the summer of 1933, Sir Francis Humphrys recommended that Britain should do her utmost to forestall the despatch of a League of Nations Commission of Enquiry:

> . . . my belief is that the orchestra at Geneva should be prevented and not merely discouraged from starting a tune the last bars of which are likely to be played solo by a British bugle.[5]

'In a conflict of interests . . . it is only natural that those of the mother country should come first . . . '[6]

British's attempts to deal with these problems, though often pursued by individuals of considerable integrity and devotion, were largely failures because the solutions were not ends in themselves. When it was clear that British interests would no longer be at risk, and when the necessary mechanism to protect them had been perfected, it was time to withdraw, and the *mission civilisatrice,* the mandatory power's ostensible role, was quietly abandoned. In the course of the 1920s, Britain came to realise that less expensive and less overt means of control could be devised to serve the same ends. After the Mosul *wilaya* had been awarded to Iraq in 1926, and the first agreements signed with the Turkish/Iraqi Petroleum Company, there was a perceptible slackening of British control. Similarly, the terms of the 1930 treaty, and the second round of oil concessions in 1931, all enabled Britain to make her formal departure.[7]

At the time, as Albert Hourani indicates in his generous introduction to the first edition of this book, even as severe a critic of British Middle Eastern policy as George Antonius considered Britain to have 'done well' in Iraq. But the seventy odd years which have elapsed since Antonius delivered his verdict[8] have not been especially kind to Iraq: the country has been under either martial law, military occupation, military government or totalitarian dictatorship for the greater part of the period since the mandate ended. The first military coup in the Middle East took place in Baghdad in October 1936, and ushered in five years of military government, which only came to an end with a 'second British occupation' at the end of April 1941.Some degree of normalcy returned to politics after Nuri al-Sa'id's three consecutive premierships (October 1941 to June 1944), which were followed by the relatively liberal regimes of Hamdi al-Pachachi (June to August 1944: August 1944 to January 1946) and Tawfiq al-Suwaydi (February to May 1946). After that, however, the remaining twelve years of the life of the monarchy were characterised by governments resorting to varying degrees of repression, especially during *al-Wathba*, the outburst of opposition to the 'Portsmouth Treaty ' at the beginning of 1948, and the declaration of martial law after the huge demonstrations in Baghdad in November 1952 (Farouk-Sluglett and Sluglett (2001): 16–46, Batatu (1978): 545–670). The last elections in Iraq before those of 30 January 2005 were held on 17 January 1953, although hardly in circumstances which gave much confidence in the strength or viability of the democratic process.[9]

Hence, while it makes little sense to 'blame' the British mandate for the atrocities committed by Saddam Husayn, or the French mandate for the excesses of Hafiz al-Asad, it seems reasonable to ask why the political structures introduced by Britain failed so signally and so rapidly in Iraq. Of course such failures are an almost endemic feature of post-colonial history; the dismal record of most post-independence African countries is more the norm than the comparatively upbeat experience of India. In addition, as has already been mentioned at the beginning of this chapter, the end of the mandate neither signified nor was perceived as a significant watershed: Britain continued to exercise substantial power behind the scenes, and genuine independence was not achieved until 1958.

The shortcomings of the Mandate

The middle class is the 'class in transition' *par excellence* in the Third World, and its nature and composition varies substantially over both time and space. The Iraqi middle class expanded enormously during and after the mandate/colonial period, largely in response to the secular requirements of the colonial state. Furthermore, since the 'colonial status' of the mandates was professedly temporary, there was a determined attempt to recruit locals (rather than British colonial officials) to administrative and judicial positions. The mandated territories needed a fairly large bureaucracy/civil service in the broadest sense of the word (school-teachers, typists, bank clerks), as well as an army, and since both civil and military employment required a certain basic level of technical competence, admission was perforce often on grounds of merit rather than simply by birth or influence.

By the mid-1930s, perhaps earlier, elements of a 'modern middle class' had come into being in all the present and former mandated states. At this stage, few *ideological* political parties had come into being, and the kinds of groupings which participated in, for example, the Iraqi political arena, were largely fortuitous and *ad hoc* combinations of like-minded individuals. Broadly speaking, the main goal of the politically conscious members of the population was national independence, that is, freedom from the tutelage of Britain. In Iraq, with its highly heterogeneous population (70 per Arab, 25 per cent Kurds, but where 65 per of the Muslim population was Shi'i and where Sunni Arabs formed only some 15 per cent of the population), Arab nationalism had a fairly hard row to hoe, largely because it had little appeal to Kurds or Shi'is. In spite of the Ba'th's later claims to the contrary, the ethnic and sectarian composition of Iraq make it difficult to imagine that this ideology, with its generally Sunni Arab vision of the Arabo-Islamic world, was the 'doctrine of choice' of a population whose composition was more than half Shi'i and at least one fifth Kurdish. Well into the 1950s and into the first couple of years of the post-revolutionary state (after 1958), it was the Iraqi Communist Party, with its agenda of national independence and social reform, that was by far the most significant element in the political opposition.

State structures[10]

Partly because of their top-down nature, the political-constitutional structures put in place by the colonial powers did not long survive the powers' departure. Compared with the shambles and/or the repression which came into being after the termination of the British or French connection, it is perhaps not surprising that the rather rudimentary parliamentary regimes of the mandate period (installed somewhat less impressively in Syria than in Iraq) should long have continued to arouse a degree of nostalgia among those old enough to remember them. However, the political system was not the only part of the structure overthrown by the 'revolutionaries' of the 1950s and 1960s. The 'failure of the bourgeoisie' which the various coups implied can be regarded as a consequence of its inability to play its 'historic role' as an accumulator and investor of capital, and thus to shoulder its 'proper' economic and political responsibilities. The various coups and revolutions, and the lack of any meaningful resistance to them, were also the result of a widespread sense of disenfranchisement and a lack of 'empowerment' *vis-à-vis* the state on the part of the burgeoning ranks of the lower middle and middle classes.

As far as Iraq is concerned, these are relatively uncharted waters, and formal statistics and censuses, where they exist, can only tell part of the story. In the same way as poverty excluded much of the population from the market economy, most Iraqis were also excluded from the political arena, partly by their isolation in the rural areas where many of them lived, and partly by the electoral rules originally imposed by Britain, under which the right to vote was given only to males who earned enough to pay a certain amount of tax. Some of the results of this were that elections were regularly and notoriously gerrymandered, and that political office was rotated between a fairly small group of individuals. These individuals were sometimes, and sometimes not, organised, as has been mentioned, in what were called political parties, but which in fact consisted of 'so and so and his supporters'.

Thus in mandatory Iraq (as in Syria and Egypt) social forces were not greatly engaged with the state and, in addition, no political organisation (with the possible if rather dubious exceptions of the Egyptian *Wafd* and *al-Kutla al-Wataniyya* in Syria) either bothered to obtain, or was able to obtain, any broadly-based national constituency. This was true even of *al-Ahali*, (and its successor, the National Democratic Party) a 'social-democratic' Iraqi political organization founded by admirers of the general principles adumbrated by the British Labour Party, which enjoyed great respect for its disinterested social concern but had little effective influence between the 1930s and the late 1950s. The lack of engagement resulted in the extreme vulnerability of the state when its colonial protectors had departed, or, to use a more neutral if more elusive term, its *relative autonomy*, that is, the sense in which the state was not firmly rooted in society and was thus 'up for grabs' to the highest or, more relevantly, the most militarily effective, bidder (Ayubi, 1995: 98)

Tentative Conclusions

The process of state formation in Iraq in the inter-war period was too forced and rapid to allow for stable class formation. Reality belied expectation, in the sense that the liberal political and economic structures which the mandate seemed to promise were little more than a façade. High tariff barriers were imposed both within and between neighbouring states (Peter, 2004), which, together with the limited size of the domestic market, acted as brakes on economic development. The majority of the population continued to work in agriculture under conditions which became increasingly oppressive in direct proportion to the colonial powers' success in creating a 'stable' regime of large private landlordism, with the result that rural to urban migration became the most significant demographic feature of the 1950s and 1960s.

Similarly, 'political freedom' functioned only as a form of glorified cronyism, and was extended only to a privileged few. The majority were excluded from political participation, a situation which became increasingly intolerable with the expansion of the new middle class through education and through bureaucratic, educational or military employment. The foundations of the institutional structures created by Britain in Iraq (and by France in Syria) were too fragile to be capable of peaceful reproduction or renewal, which meant that it was relatively easy for the state to be captured by well-organised or even fortuitously positioned armed groups, generally from lower middle class rural or urban backgrounds, acting on their own initiative (Batatu 1978 and Batatu 1999). For a couple of years after 1958, both the 'national bourgeoisie' and the professional middle classes were courted by the new military rulers of Iraq, only to be bypassed by the Ba'th when they were no longer needed to run the state. Under the Ba'th, loyalty to the regime soon became more important than competence (both military and civil), which led to the gradual depoliticisation of the middle classes (and indeed of most of society) and to their general alienation from the state. The result, *pace* Migdal (1988) was both a weak state and a weak society, with the forces of coercion and repression taking charge and acting largely on their own behalf.

For a while, in spite of the absence of political freedom, Iraq's oil income enabled the regime to purchase a fair degree of acquiescence from its population. Had Iraq not invaded Iran and Kuwait (and it is difficult to regard either adventure as an 'objective necessity') it might well have continued to enjoy the level of prosperity which it experienced until the early 1980s. In any case, there was no sustained or systematic attempt to build a social compact which would identify the state with the interest (or future) of a particular class (using *class* in the simple sense of 'substantial numbers of people with similar socio-political interests'). Thus as far as most of the population was concerned, Iraq's political history seems ultimately that of the largely passive endurance of an increasingly horrifying series of military coups and dictatorships. One major consequence was a deep sense of alienation and depoliticisation; participation in politics either became opportunistic, if in the service of the state, or in opposition to it, immensely, even irresponsibly, dangerous.

In general terms, the gradual transition to some vaguely recognisable form of democracy that has been the hallmark of politics over the last couple of decades in, say, Latin America,[11] has barely affected the Middle East. In the region as a whole, the only remotely democratic state is Turkey; Israel's claims to a similar appellation are belied by the fact that while its own citizens certainly enjoy the benefits of a democratic society, the three million Palestinians whom it rules have, to say the least, rather fewer rights. In many ways, some of the most significant states in the Middle East are in danger of becoming "failed states," in that there is every possibility of violence and anarchy if the extremely fragile existing order is not soon replaced by more profoundly socially rooted political systems.

Any consideration of the rationale for the longevity of the Ba'thist regime in Iraq (which was already in place well before the first edition of this book appeared in 1976) leads almost inevitably to the question of the factors that maintained it (and comparable regimes in the region) in being for so long. First, it had an extraordinarily elaborate internal security system, a bewildering number of separate agencies which kept an eye on one another as well as on their fellow citizens.[12] Secondly, such regimes could, at least in the past, offer some material rewards to their supporters, although, as has been noted falling oil prices throughout much of the 1980s and 1990s, and the fact that there has been virtually no economic development in the Arab world over the past three decades meant that much regime largesse had to be curtailed, and that its recipients dwindled in number, thus somewhat reducing the regimes' support base. Thirdly, a, if not the, major reason why a corrupt, despotic and tyrannical regime was able to hold on to power in Iraq while its counterparts in other parts of the world were overthrown or allowed to fail was that it long seemed convenient, especially in the 1980s and 1990s, that it should. Thus Iraq was supported by both the United States and the Soviet Union in its war with Iran; neither wanted the Islamic Republic to prevail. Britain, France and the United States were eager to provide Saddam Husayn with the sophisticated weaponry with which he invaded Iran in 1981 and Kuwait in 1990. Again, in the spring of 1991, when more vigorous US action could almost certainly have overthrown Saddam Husayn, who was simultaneously facing Shi'i insurrections in the south and Kurdish insurrections in the north, it seems to have been decided (presumably at Sa'udi and Turkish prompting) that a weakened Ba'th regime was preferable to the uncertainty that might result. But let us return to the 1930s, when the age of innocence was not quite over.

Just after the end of the mandate, an RAF Special Service Officer recorded a conversation between himself and a young man, 'new to the country . . .

enjoying a few days leave from the oilfields . . . at a quiet dinner party in Baghdad':

> ' . ... surely the real reason for our attacking Germany through here was to consolidate our position as regards oil. I suppose the Government was looking for the future. India must have wanted to extend its sphere of influence in the Gulf. Wasn't that the real reason?'

> 'No one ever mentioned those things at the time. I don't think the armies who fought were very interested in oil. If they fought for anything, wasn't it for something better than acquisition?'

> 'Do you mean Brave Little Belgium, a World Safe for Democracy, and that sort of thing, sir?'

> 'Something like that.'

> 'Oh, come now, sir. Isn't that rather an academic line?'[13]

APPENDIX I:

A NOTE ON SHI'I POLITICS

In September 1927, C. J. Edmonds wrote, in the course of a *Note on the Political Situation*:

There is a fundamental difference between the Shia and the ordinary minority position. The Shia, aware that they are both more numerous and better armed than the Sunni Arabs, know that they could destroy the present Government if British forces were not behind it, though they could not replace it without British help.[1]

Not only were the Shi'is 'more numerous than the Sunni Arabs', they were more numerous than all the other groups in the country combined. Unofficial censuses, taken in 1920 and 1931, show that the Shi'is formed some 55% of the population, the Sunni Arabs 22% and the Kurds 14%.[2] Nevertheless, under Ottoman rule, British occupation and mandate, Iraqi monarchy and republic, the Shi'is have never played a part in politics or government in any way proportional to their numbers in the country. This brief chapter is an attempt to trace the more important activities of the Shi'i political leaders, tribal, religious, and 'urban', from the late nineteenth century until the conscription agitation of 1927, against the background both of the internal politics of Iraq and the course of Anglo-Iraqi relations.

In the period before 1914, the position of the traditional Shi'i political leaders, especially the tribal shaykhs, had been undergoing a slow decline, largely though the gradual, if sporadic and uneven, 'conquest of the countryside' by the Ottoman authorities. Most of the great tribal leaders had ceased to be unquestioned sources of authority; their power over their tribes had dwindled as fragmentation accompanied the process of agricultural and pastoral settlement. In the more intensively cultivated areas, the *sirkal*, or sub-chief, generally paid revenue directly to the government rather than through the tribal shaykh. The *'ulama'* in the Holy Cities had been twice cowed by the Ottomans, in 1843 and 1852–1854,[3] although, especially under 'Abd al-Hamid II, the Ottomans had pursued more conciliatory policies towards the Shi'i religious establishment for much of the latter part of the nineteenth century.[4]

Generally, Shi'is in the Ottoman Empire occupied a position somewhat analogous to that of Roman Catholics in England before 1829. They were excluded from public office, and unable, except in internal matters in their own centres, to use their own code of law: such institutions of public education as existed at this time were based on Sunni teaching, and thus unacceptable to Shi'is. However, the position of the Shi'is of Iraq differed in four important respects from that of their co-religionists elsewhere in the Empire. First, they were close to the four Holy Cities, the *'atabat,* second, they were the object of the solicitude of some quite wealthy Indian Muslims (and thus of some general interest to Britain),[5] and finally, they were in constant contact with Iran. The latter factors combined to isolate Najaf and Karbala' in particular from centres of Sunni power and make them more or less independent enclaves in which the Ottomans tended not to intervene unless provoked.

Because of the nature of Shi'i religious belief, the *'ulama'* occupied a particularly vital place in the Holy Cities. Najaf, Karbala' and Kadhimayn were not only religious seminaries but also the centres of a living religious organisation, in the sense that the *mujtahids,* individually or collectively, could pronounce authoritatively on current political or religious developments affecting Shi'is; the *mujtahids* were the guardians of the day of a living tradition. They were consulted, or gave their views spontaneously, on a wide variety of issues (Algar, 1969; Keddie, 1966). Apart from the expeditions to destroy the powers of the clans of Karbala' and Najaf in the mid-nineteenth century which have been mentioned above, the Ottoman authorities do not seem to have exerted particularly forceful control over the Holy Cities; Karbala' was the headquarters of a *sanjak* containing itself and the *qadhas* of Hindiya, Najaf and Razaza, but in general, the Ottomans seem to have exercised a relatively light hand.[6] In December 1914, almost certainly provoked by the British invasion of southern Iraq (Ende, 1981), four of the leading *mujtahids* of Karbala' signed a *fatwa* in support of the Ottoman call for *jihad* which had been issued by the (Sunni) *Shaykh al-Islam* on 12 November 1914. However, Ottoman requisitioning and conscription caused immense irritation, and eventually brought about risings in Karbala' and Najaf which ousted the Ottomans from both cities. By 1915–1916 autonomous regimes had been instituted by the townspeople, and tactful overtures, together with payments of subsidies, had been made by the political staff of the Mesopotamia Expeditionary Force.[7]

In Sir Percy Cox' instructions, received after the capture of Baghdad in March 1917, the Shi'i Holy Places were 'to form a separate enclave not under direct British control.'[8] However, later in the year, probably because Najaf in particular had become a notorious loophole in the official blockade of supplies to the Ottoman army, Political Officers were sent both there and to Karbala'. At the end of January 1918 Gertrude Bell visited both cities, and noted in a letter to Sir Valentine Chirol that the situation, though calling for tactful handling, was generally quiet; there were at that time no signs of serious resistance to the British authorities.

> It's the Shias of the *saiyid* class who know that they would have the least to gain by the return of the Turks: the alienation of the Shias has been a great asset to us and has meant for instance that we have never had any serious religious feeling to contend with in Karbala' and Najaf (Burgoyne, 1961: 76).

Similarly, British policy was to appoint 'loyal' leaders on the Euphrates to act as revenue collectors and judges over their tribes, giving them fiscal and jurisdictional privileges far exceeding those they had known under the Ottomans.

The Najafis, however, did not take as readily to the imposition of British control as the authorities seem to have expected, though it is likely that the difficulties encountered there derived from a power struggle between the *'ulama'* and the rest of the community which had begun long before any Political Officers arrived. There was a series of disturbances at the end of March 1918, and a young officer, Captain Marshall, was killed. Fines were levied and exemplary punishments made, some eleven people being publicly executed for their alleged complicity in Marshall's murder. The fact that the *killidar* of Najaf was prominent in expressing his gratitude to Major Frank Balfour, the Military Governor of Baghdad, for the prompt action taken against the rebels suggests that Marshall's murderers may have attempted to curb the powers of the clergy within the city during their own brief period in power (Wilson, 1931: 74–76).

In general, however, opinion within the Holy Cities did not show itself particularly well-dosposed towards continued British rule during the soundings known as the 'plebiscite' of late 1918 and early 1919. Large numbers in Najaf, Karbala' and Kadhimayn declared themselves deeply opposed both to the British occupation and to a British-sponsored Arab administration. Other groups in Najaf wanted an Arab government with no foreign amir, whereas a more extreme group in Karbala' threatened those asking for any form of non-Muslim government with severe reprisals. Since the declarations were signed by members of the population selected by either the Political Officers or the Acting Civil Commissioner himself, it is not especially remarkable that so little enthusiasm could be found either in the Holy Cities, or in Baghdad, for any kind of British controlled regime.[9]

During the long period of uncertainty between the end of the war and the establishment of the provisional government in 1920, an embryonic national sentiment developed in Iraq.[10] An important feature of those years was the emergence of a brief but vital unity between the main Sunni and Shi'i political and interest groups. A Shi'i association, *Haras al-Istiqlal al-Watani* (Guardian[s] of National Independence)[11] led chiefly by the Kadhimayn *'alim* Muhammad al-Sadr and the Baghdad merchant Ja'far Abu'l-Timman, joined forces with members of *al-'Ahd al-'Iraqi,* a society composed largely of Iraqi Sunni officers, many of whom had either deserted from the Ottoman army or been released from British P.O.W camps in India to join Faysal in the Arab revolt, and with other Iraqis who had retreated with the Ottomans to Mosul, notably Hamdi al-Pachachi and Yusuf al-Suwaydi. The first visible sign of this alliance was the attendance of the *'ulama'* of both sects at the mourning ceremonies for the late premier *mujtahid* of Karbala', Mirza Muhammad Kadhim al-Yazdi, in the spring of 1919. Although al-Yazdi's successor, Mirza Muhammad Taqi al-Din al-Shirazi, was an elderly recluse, his son Muhammad Ridha was actively anti-British and took advantage of his father's position to publicise his views.

In February 1920, in a letter to Sir Valentine Chirol, Gertrude Bell wrote that although a tenuous alliance between the Sunnis and the Shi'i *'ulama'* definitely existed, she doubted its durability. In addition, the less traditional and more intelligent younger townspeople now had little respect for their religious elders (Burgoyne, 1961: 127–128). However, this alliance would be vital if there was to be any question of involving the tribal leaders, since the younger nationalists, especially the Sunnis, would have been incapable of achieving this by themselves. On 22 June 1920, ten of the Karbala' *'ulama',* including Muhammad Ridha ibn Mirza Muhammad Taqi al-Din al-Shirazi, were arrested and sent to Henjam for circulating a letter purporting to originate from Muhammad Ridha's father, urging the defence of Islam against 'the infidels'. By this time the nationalists, led most prominently by al-Sadr, were corresponding directly and through the *'ulama'* with tribal leaders urging rebellion. The talks between the Acting Civil Commissioner and the nationalists had not produced the desired results; there was no sign of the self-determination promised by President Wilson and in the Anglo-French Declaration, nor of the formation of any national assembly.

The rising, as has been described,[12] continued sporadically in the remoter parts of the country until the early spring of 1921. By the late autumn of 1920, however, the more prominent leaders, including Muhammad al-Sadr, Ja'far Abu'l-Timman, Shaykh Ahmad al-Da'ud and Yusuf al-Suwaydi, had fled across the desert to Mecca, to return in the summer of the following year as members of the Amir Faysal's suite (Ireland, 1937: 326). By October, British forces had managed to regain control of the greater part of the country, and their task was facilitated by the arrival of Sir Percy Cox and the immediate inauguration of what seemed at first to be a more widely acceptable form of government. Significantly, Cox refused to accede to the requests of 'Abd al-Wahid Sikkar of the Fatlah and Marzuq of the Humaydat that the *'ulama'* should be empowered to act as intermediaries to arrange a truce on behalf of the tribes; instead the tribal leaders were forced to 'come in' to local administrative headquarters in person.

Whether by accident or design, the regime introduced after the 1920 rising took little account of the Shi'i leadership, and, perhaps less understandably, equally little account of the fact that the Shi'is accounted for over half the population of the country. Until January 1921, when al-Taba'taba'i was given the Ministry of Education, no Shi'i had been offered a portfolio in the national government. To point out that many leading Shi'is were Persian subjects simply evaded the problem. The selection of Faysal, and the institution of the mandate administration served to drive a further wedge between Sunni and Shi'is; Faysal's government was very quickly forced to the realisation that not only was cooperation with Britain preferable to cooperation with the Shi'is, but that there was no real alternative. Hence Shi'i interests were almost always relegated to second place, except, as in the conscription crisis of 1927–1928, where they happened to coincide with British interests.

In the first few months of his reign, in the course of the early negotiations over the Anglo-Iraqi Treaty, Faysal attempted fairly successfully to maintain cordial relations both with the *'ulama'* and with al-Sadr and Abu'l-Timman. In Karbala' and Najaf, in the course of the 'referendum' for Faysal's election, the *'ulama'* had signed the official *madhbata*, though, ominously, a leading *'alim'* of Kadhimayn, Shaykh Mahdi al-Khalisi, made his acceptance of Faysal dependent on the rapid freeing of Iraq from external control and the convocation of a National Assembly within two months of the coronation of the King. In other places too, the fairly widespread lack of opposition to Faysal in these early months seems to have stemmed from the belief (which the King himself seems to have shared) that Iraq really was going to be given a measure of independence. By November 1921, however, when Fisher's announcement to the League became public knowledge in Iraq, the new regime became suspect. At a meeting in Yusuf al-Suwaydi's house on 20 November the company formulated four demands which they intended to present to the King:

> Convocation of the National Congress without delay.
>
> Withdrawal of Ministerial and Divisional Advisers.
>
> The appointment of a Minister of Foreign Affairs.
>
> The functions of the High Commissioner should be confined to those of a diplomatic representative. In default of compliance with these demands a declaration would be made deposing His Majesty.[13]

By 10 December, Muhammad al-Sadr was in correspondence with Badr al-Rumayyidh, the Ramadi shaykh whose tribesmen had fired the first shots in 1920, and widespread dissatisfaction was reported from the Middle Euphrates.[14] In the winter of 1921 and the spring of 1922 the deadlock over the Treaty continued, and rumours flourished of the opposition leaders being in touch variously with Persia, the Kamalists, and the Kurds in an attempt to forge an effective anti-British alliance. At this stage, Faysal was eager to amass as much support as possible, and gave covert support to nationalist agitation. It was clear, however, that a *quid pro quo* would be demanded for any widespread cooperation from the Shi'is. At the Karbala' conference of April 1922, supposedly convened to work out how best to defend the country against a possible invasion from Najd, Shaykh Mahdi al-Khalisi's demands touched Faysal's own government as much as the British presence in Iraq:

1) That the British should recognise complete independence with no mandate.

2) The immediate convocation of the National Assembly.

3) Half the cabinet to be Shi'is.

4) Half government officials to be Shi'is.

5) Declaration of a *jihad* against the Wahhabis.[15]

The range of these demands indicates that the problem had shifted from the simple objective of getting rid of British influence. By early July 1922, Ja'far Abu'l-Timman, who had been appointed Minister of Commerce in March, resigned: Gertrude Bell described the situation in Baghdad:

On Monday morning all the anti-Mandate lot went to Kadhimain to
consult their oracle Shaykh Mahdi al-Khalisi who told them that as
H. M. had not fulfilled the conditions of his election to the throne,
namely that he would preserve the independence of Iraq, their oath of
allegiance to him was null and void . . . Turning his attention to the
Iraqi government he observed that before it existed the English
governed the land: they still governed it, with a pack of spendthrifts
superadded (6 July 1922: Burgoyne, 1961: 277).

Eventually, in August, a hostile demonstration by nationalists against Sir
Percy Cox in front of the royal palace forced the issue: Hamdi al-Pachachi
and Ja'far Abu'l-Timman were sent to Henjam, and the High Commissioner
advised al-Sadr and al-Khalisi to leave at once for Persia if they wished to
avoid arrest. Only the King's providential appendicitis saved him from
deposition.

For a time, Sir Percy Cox' decisive action calmed down the agitation,
though the next two years in Iraqi politics were largely concerned with
attempts to ease the terms of the Treaty and Agreements. In the autumn of
1922, al-Khalisi had managed to persduade the elderly and conservative
*mujtahid*s al-Na'ini and al-Isfahani to sign a *fatwa* forbidding Shi'i participation in the coming elections. In February 1923 further arrests and
deportations were made; Amin al-Charchafchi, 'Abd al-Rasul Kubba and
Saiyid Muhammad Mahdi Basir al-Hilli were sent to Henjam following
critical articles in *al-Nahdha*, the newspaper of the Shi'i association of the
same name. In March a brief reconciliation was reached between the King
and al-Khalisi, but the latter withdrew on finding himself almost completely isolated from the rest of his colleagues. By May, arrangements were
being made for *madhbatas* against the Treaty signed by the *'ulama'* and other
leaders to be sent to Geneva and Lausanne; their tone reflected the demands
made at Karbala' the previous year. By this time, however, a significant
development had taken place, in that al-Sadr had advised his followers that
provided that demands for Shi'i participation were met, he would be
prepared to advise them to vote in the elections. Later in May, Yasin al-
Hashimi, then in opposition to the government led by 'Abd al-Muhsin al-
Sa'dun, attempted to urge Abu'l-Timman, just back from several months'
confinement on Henjam, to return to politics, but without success.[16] Finally,
at the end of June, after pressure from the British authorities at the
Residency and in the Ministry of Interior, and from his own cabinet, Faysal
was reluctantly forced to the conclusion that the *'ulama'* would have to be
silenced. Fortunately for their opponents, the *'ulama'* were almost all Persian

subjects: al-Khalisi and several members of his family were deported, and al-Na'ini and al-Isfahani were asked to leave. al-Khalisi never returned, but the two latter *mujtahids* were allowed to re-enter Iraq on condition that they revoked their anti-election *fatwas* and undertook not to take an active part in politics in the future.

At the time of his illness Faysal was forced to realise that while he might sympathise with demands for more complete independence, he could not be seen, particularly by the British but also by his own cabinet, to endorse these demands if that meant associating himself with the Shi'i leadership. Even more so after August 1922, it became abundantly clear to Faysal that non-acceptance of the terms laid down by Britain would mean either abdication or deposition. Also, whatever the King's personal predilections may have been[17] his ministers did not welcome support from the Shi'i hierarchy, a group whom they well knew by then to be as hostile to them as to the British. Finally the 'Sharifians', like their leader, realised how dangerously near to the wind they had been sailing; official circles in England as well as sections of the British press had canvassed the possibility of leaving Iraq altogether in the course of 1922 and 1923, and the publication of the Protocol brought home the fact that the British would not be available to prop up the regime for ever. Faced with threats, real or imaginary, from Najd and from Turkey, it became necessary to rely even more heavily on British support.

It is difficult to gauge the immediate effect of the deportations on the various different interest circles in Iraq. The 'urban' Shi'i politicians were for a while nonplussed: some of the tribal shaykhs, notably 'Abd al-Wahid Sikkar and Samawi al-Challub, had been closely associated with al-Na'ini and al-Isfahani and were clearly deeply affronted at their treatment. A group of moderate shaykhs told the RAF Special Service Officer at Hilla that while they realised that the *'ulama'* were at fault for interfering in politics to this extent, 'that knowledge in no way counterbalanced the feeling that their removal was a heavy blow at the religion of their sect.'[18] Dobbs was delighted:

> Present is unique opportunity through which the Shia Holy Cities can be purged of predominance of Persian influence which has been exercised for years to detriment of true Arab interests with the object of prolonging anarchy amongst . . . the tribes. There might never be recurrence of so favourable an opportunity.[19]

A more detailed summary of the situation is contained in a contemporary intelligence report:

It is interesting at this stage to speculate as to why the '*ulama* have seen themselves so particularly hostile to the King and to the elections. They seem to be moved by several motives. First they desire a weak government which would allow their ignorant theocracy to rule the tribes and to exploit them ... They fear that if the elections take place and an elected assembly sits to ratify the British Treaty and to validate the measures of the Provisional Government, then the King and the Iraqi government will be able to claim that their authority is based on the will of the people and will gain in strength and no longer have to defer to the '*ulama*. They believe that the Turks would be better for their interests because they would inevitably be weak. Secondly, they feel that, if the Iraqi government continues as at present constituted the Shias will have no influence in it. The Electoral Law was so formed that the elections must be hopelessly gerrymandered in favoured of the Sunnis. Thirdly they have some personal dislike of the King which is rumoured to be due to His Majesty having sworn to them at the beginning of his reign to follow a policy which he has found impossible.[20]

The second and third grounds for the hostility of the '*ulama*' seem to have been correctly analysed, but the picture of credulous tribal leaders being pushed on to precipitate action by their religious leaders needs a little modification. Apart from the direct encouragement given to tribal leaders in 1920 by the '*ulama*' it was frequently the case that the tribal leaders themselves sought *validation* of their anti-British or anti-government activities from the clergy rather than simply accepting their dictates. Perhaps it is more accurate to say that before 1923 the '*ulama*' would tend to encourage rather than discourage concerted action on the part of the tribal leaders: it is rare to find them actually instigating such action.

Throughout the rest of the mandate the same pleas were heard from the Shi'is for more cabinet and civil service representation; promises were made but rarely kept. For the next few years, however, the Shi'i opposition ceased to be an active source of danger to the regime, and by the time of the next serious revolt, in 1935, the Iraqi army had become sufficiently powerful to crush all but the most powerful combination of tribal forces. Again, it was only in 1927, when the interests of the Shi'i shaykhs in resisting conscription coincided with Britain's interests in trying to discourage it, that Shi'i grievances once more became a major factor in Iraqi politics.

The new leadership that emerged after the deportations was more flexible, and thus less united, than its predecessors had been. It is important to remember that the whole spectrum of Iraqi politics was personalised to an extent that is often baffling: few individuals can be credited with the pursuit of consistent principles, and the various permutations and combinations changed backwards and forwards through paths which are frequently impossible to trace.[21] In the broadest possible terms, Shi'i politicians and tribal leaders can be divided into those who would be prepared to cooperate with the Sunni 'opposition' and those who would not, but again, these divisions lack permanence.

Thus, in 1924, al-Sadr joined Yasin al-Hashimi, Naji al-Suwaydi and Shaykh Ahmad al-Da'ud to attempt to influence the Euphrates shaykhs not to vote the treaty through the Constituent Assembly. Abu'l-Timman, on the other hand, gloomily advised his colleagues that there was no point in opposition, since the British would get their way in any case.[22] He refused to involve himself in politics for several years, partly because of the futility of opposition, and partly because of his distrust of the Sunni politicians with whom he would have been obliged to work. Generally, al-Sadr seems to have advocated a policy of alliance with those Sunni politicians who tended to oppose the 'King's Party' (generally 'Ali Jawdat, Nuri al-Sa'id and Ja'far al-'Askari): this group consisted normally of 'Ali Mahmud, 'Abd al-Ghafur al-Badri, Rashid 'Ali al-Gaylani, Yasin al-Hashimi, Rifa't al-Chadirchi, Bahjat Zaynal and Mawlud Mukhlis. On the other hand, the members of the Shi'i *Hizb al-Nadha* (Renaissance Party), led by Amin al-Charchafci, which included the *'alim* Muhammad Husayn Kashif al-Ghita' and the tribal leaders 'Abd al-Wahid Sikkar, Sha'lan Abu Chon, Samawi al-Shallub, Saqban al-'Ali and Salman al-Dhahir, after some bitter experience of cooperation with Sunni politicians, were more inclined only to seek alliances with other Shi'is.[23]

These alignments, however, frequently failed to survive political crises, especially when Rashid 'Ali and Yasin al-Hashimi simply used opposition support to persuade either the more conservative members of the 'King's party' or even the more independent minded 'Abd al-Muhsin al-Sa'dun of the necessity of the presence of either or both of them in the Cabinet: once in office their supporters looked in vain for the reforms and improvements they had promised. A further complication in the maze of political alignments was provided by those (largely Sunni) tribal leaders or landowners whose position and influence had been created or maintained by British favour. Notable here were 'Ali Sulayman, 'Abadi al-Husayn, Muhammad al-Rabi'a and Muhammad al-Salhud, all of whom supported Britain actively or passively in 1920, and who constantly clamoured for direct British rule, which they insisted would protect their 'rights' more effectively than the government of King Faysal.

In 1920, a brief 'pan-Islamic' unity had secured the cooperation of the Holy Cities, the nationalist leaders of the two major sects, the tribal leaders and the 'Sharifians' against the British. When it became clear to the Shi'is that their other partners in the alliance were prepared to compromise with Britain in order to gain positions of power and authority for themselves, they naturally complained of betrayal, and of having sacrificed Shi'i lives and property simply to install a group of foreigners and upstarts aided and abetted by Britain.[24] Hence, after the rising, the leaders of the Shi'i hierarchy maintained their hostility towards Britain, but made their cooperation with the Iraqi government conditional on their own grievances being addressed at the same time. Tactically, however, the Shi'i hierarchy remained at a permanent disadvantage, since they had so few sanctions in their hands apart from the rather extreme threat of armed insurrection. After the major air and police campaign against the Bani Huchaim in the winter of 1923/24 it was evident that the British authorities would not tolerate any opposition to the Iraqi government which would upset the *status quo*.[25]

A further difficulty facing the Shi'i leadership was the lack of suitable or acceptable candidates for ministerial office or government employment. This deficiency was greatly exaggerated by their opponents, but the result was that only three Shi'i politicians, Ja'far Abu'l-Timman, Muhsin al-Shallash, and Salih al-Jabr, held important cabinet posts until the end of the Second World War, which precluded the training of a body of suitably experienced Shi'i ministers. Furthermore, since the Shi'is had rarely participated in secular education under the Ottomans, they did not have the pool of ex-Ottoman officials to draw on which was available to their Sunni contemporaries. Hence an important outlet for much Shi'i agitation came to consist in their appealing to the British to preserve their rights. This process is increasingly discernible, on a variety of levels, in the years after 1924.

In April 1925 the Prime Minister, Yasin al-Hashimi, who, with Nuri al-Sa'id, was a fervent advocate of a stronger and larger army, urged Muhammad al-Sadr to exert his influence in the Government's favour. Yasin and Nuri were deeply opposed to the proposals of the High Commissioner and the Colonial Secretary, which amounted to increasing the number of British officers serving with the Iraqi army, and continuing to vest executive control in a British Inspector-General. They wanted al-Sadr to raise protests and agitation among Shi'i tribal leaders and nationalists, but al-Sadr could find no tribal leader prepared to cooperate; fearing that conscription would deprive them of their own corps of armed retainers, they were quite content that the British should continue to command.[26] Exactly the same reaction greeted Ja'far Abu'l-Timman in 1927 when he was urged by the pro-conscription party, in the interests of national independence, to encourage the religious hierarchy at Karbala' and Najaf to consider conscription favourably. Again, it was the Shi'i tribal leaders who were foremost in protesting against the withdrawal of British Administrative Inspectors from the districts in 1930.

By 1927, the less radical Shi'is, including the followers of Amin al-Charchafchi (the *Nahdha* group) seem to have realised that it might be possible to use conscription as a bargaining counter. Deputations were sent to the King to try to obtain satisfaction for the usual Shi'i demands, especially a higher proportion of places in the civil service.[27] Later in the year, it was reported from Kadhimayn that:

> 'Abd al-Husayn Chalabi said at the house of Sayyid 'Abd al-Husayn al-Yasin that Nuri Pasha had told him that the conscription bill was intended to secure complete independence to Iraq and that it was the duty of all Iraqis to support it. He said that the quota would only be 20, 000 and that the government would be grateful for the assistance of the *'ulama'*. Sayyid 'Abd al-Husayn al-Yasin commented that the *'ulama'* were quite prepared to assist, but they required it to be stipulated that half of Government appointments should be held by Shi 'is.[28]

When it was realised that the government was not going to yield to these demands, the Shi'i leaders turned almost unanimously to Britain to look after their interests, especially after the riots at Kadhimayn riots in July 1927 and a similar incident at Basra gave rise to widespread fears of an organised anti-Shi'i movement:

> It is said that the Government (Nuri, Ja'far al-'Askari, Yasin and Amin Zaki) were making plans to weaken the power and prestige of the tribal chiefs and prominent Shias. It is also said that the reason for this is that they are desirous of enriching themselves by the purchase of lands from displaced shaykhs and landlords.[29]

And, later in the year:

> An arrival from Najaf states that the Shia agitators there have apparently come to know that the Government is fully aware of their activities and that he has been instructed to explain to the British that the activities of the party (not named) were in no way anti-British or

directed against British interests. Were they given the slightest sign that they had the practical sympathy of the British Government they would hoist the British flag and throw out the foreigners.[30]

A far cry from Shaykh Mahdi al-Khalisi.

A few days after the Kadhimain riots, the Acting High Commissioner, B. H. Bourdillon, wrote to the Colonial Office:

> A leading Shia said to me a few weeks ago: 'We know we are uneducated and cannot at present take our proper share in the public services. What we want is British control, to save us from Sunni domination, until our sons are educated. Then we, who are the real majority will take our proper place in the government of the country and shall not need British control.'[31]

For its part, the Iraqi government could not afford to make major concessions to the Shiʿis. It paid off the noisier and more powerful shaykhs with tax remissions and beneficial land legislation, frightened the *ʿulamaʾ* into silence, and paid attention to the urban politicians as and when the need arose. Britain could not have installed the Shiʿis in power, just as the Sunnis could not admit them to power afterwards. But though the Shiʿis could not be dealt with by either party when strong and united, they could be used by both when weak and divided. The result of this political equation has been that the Iraqi Shiʿis were largely excluded from playing a major part in the government of their country, both individually and collectively. With the Sunnis in power, the British could control the country through them; with the Shiʿis in power there could have been no British mandate.

APPENDIX II:

TENURIAL AND TAXATION ARRANGEMENTS IN 'AMARA *LIWA* UNDER THE MANDATE

'Amara has few officials, being the most orderly *liwa* in the country. It has one of the smallest police force in the country, no army and no irrigation authority.[1]

The report from which this extract has been taken was written in 1931, eleven years after the beginning of the mandate. It does not mention what might seem to be the most salient feature of the organisation of 'Amara *liwa*, the exceptionally high concentration of landholding. 'Amara was an area of vast estates with very little individual *lazma*:

Table I

Size and number of agricultural properties in seven Liwas in 1930[2]

	1–64 acres	65–319 acres	320–640 acres	Above 640 acres
Arbil	7418	528	500	–
Diyala	4092	–	546	–
Baghdad	162	220	120	360
Dulaim	2344	109	121	3
Hilla	452	364	98	82
Diwaniya	8378	–	155	69
'Amara	–	10	5	50

In addition, the richest landlords in the *liwa* were very wealthy indeed: 16
of them paid rent in excess of 25,000 rupees a year, and five of them a great
deal more:

Falih al-Saihud	304,775
Muhammad al-'Araibi	281,143
Majid al-Khalifa	432,644
Shawi al-Fahad jointly with Salman al-Manshad	611,230[3]

Throughout the mandate these huge holdings were controlled almost
exclusively by their landlords, and the whole *liwa* was only very lightly
affected by the activities of central government. Those who held the tax
farms of these great estates, or *muqata'as,* had total authority over their
tenants, first under the terms of the *Tribal Disputes Regulation* and subsequently under the 1933 Cultivators' Law. Strategically the area was highly
sensitive; it lay on one of the main through routes between Baghdad and the
sea, and bordered Iran, a potentially unfriendly state. Further, the frontier
was not marked by any insurmountable natural obstacle, so that when sheep
tax, or conscription, was enforced in either Iraq or Iran, it was perfectly
possible for the tribesmen living on either side to move over to the country
which suited them best.[4]

During the First World War the great estates of the *liwa,* whose leases
had been subject to periodic auction under the Ottomans, were assigned by
the occupation authorities on a semi-permanent basis to the landlords in
possession, on the understanding that they would be left alone in return for
'good behaviour'. These arrangements were justified at the time on the
grounds that the British forces' lines of communication passed directly
through the area, and that the cooperation, or at least the passivity, of the
local rulers was more important than revenue. In fact no taxation whatsoever
was collected from the *liwa* until 1922.

Strategic and other related arguments were used to explain the continuation of a policy of non-interference throughout the 1920s. Unlike the
arrangements in force in other parts of Iraq, where taxes were levied on the
actual quantity of the crop, calculations in 'Amara were based on consolidated
fixed assessments, and both animal and cereal taxes were collected from the
muqata'a holders, who were thus landlords and tax-collectors at the same
time. In return for the privilege of tax-collection, they were entrusted with
total administrative powers on their estates.

The existence of this tribal administration makes it unnecessary to appoint mudirs in charge of *nahiyas*. All that is required in tribal areas is a representative of Government who can convey orders to the shaykhs and see that they are obeyed. This duty is conveniently carried out by the *raises* of the *baladiyahs* in villages situated among the tribes.[5]

Furthermore, the system continued under the mandate, because of the assumption, on the part of the British, of an identity of interest of landlord and cultivator with the desirability of maintaining the *status quo*. The advantages of a body of shaykhs and landlords who owed their powers entirely to the enhancement of their position by the British authorities soon became clear. The advantages were shared; the 'special circumstances'[6] of the 1924 treaty brought further concessions to the 'Amara taxpayers in return for their support. From that time on an alliance was formed between the landlords and the effective rulers of Iraq, both British and Iraqi, which endured until the revolution of 1958. This alliance did not pass un-challenged, however, as the Ministry of Finance under the mandate showed itself unwilling to acquiesce in these arrangements and made several attempts to put matters in the *liwa* on a more businesslike footing. These efforts caused an almost continuous conflict between the Ministries of Finance and Interior and the High Commission, each advocating a greater or lesser degree of supervision of the 'Amara *muqata'as*. The result, broadly speaking, was that Interior and the High Commission prevailed over Finance; it was held to be more expensive and more trouble than it was worth to disturb the 'Amara landlords.

In June 1915, after the British had captured 'Amara town, all the local land records were apparently taken from the municipal building and thrown into the Tigris by members of the Norfolk regiment.[7] The reason for this fit of exuberance has not been recorded, but its effect was to make it almost impossible to piece together the tenurial arrangements in force in the area at the time. It was known that the 'Amara lands had only recently been designated *miri*, since they had been part of the Crown Lands (*Sanniyya*) Administration until 1909 (Jwaideh 1965: 326–336). 'Amara town itself was a recent creation which had grown up haphazardly around the Ottoman cantonment. Originally, the province had formed the *dira* of the Bani Lam tribe, but in the course of campaigns culminating in a serious defeat in 1910, they had been conquered by and made tributaries of the Albu Muhammad. In late Ottoman times the area had been divided into large holdings which were auctioned to the highest bidders approximately every three years, the

land tax and the land being auctioned at the same time. This procedure was
designed both to weaken the shaykhs and to show the government's hand; it
created the principle of a rigidly collected government share, and helped to
cause hostility and rivalry among the shaykhs and *rentiers* bidding at the
auctions.

> On the British Occupation the Turkish policy underwent a complete
> reversal, the tribal shaykh receiving the full support of Government.
> Such a policy stands above criticism by reason of its remarkable
> success in ensuring security for the British lines of communication.
> But with the coming of the Armistice it ceased to be justified.

The auctions ceased, and the holdings were assigned to 'reliable' resident tribal
leaders. The landlords continued to carry out administration in the area,
strengthened by the *Tribal Disputes Regulation*, which meant that the vast
majority of the inhabitants of the *liwa* were denied the protection of the ordinary
courts. Further, no tax at all was collected from the area until 1922, in spite of
the fact that some of the landlords were known to be exceedingly wealthy:

> A definite example will help to show that the cost of collection is in
> point of fact appallingly high and that the economy of staff, both
> revenue and administrative which is claimed for the 'Amara system,
> does not in fact exist. Shaykh Muhammad al-'Araibi, the holder of the
> Chahala *muqata'a*, after paying in all his revenue, had in his hands six
> lakhs of rupees. This sum would be sufficient to meet the whole cost
> of the administrative, police and revenue budgets of the 'Amara *liwa*
> and still leave the shaykh two *lakhs* per annum for his services as
> administrator, tax-collector and farmer.

The landlords were not only extremely wealthy, but all-powerful, since there
was no external supervision of the authority they exerted over their tenants.
The same report mentions that:

> Today the actual proportion to be taken, as well as the fact that it was
> limited to the crops only, has been lost sight of, and the 'Amara
> shaykh now drives the hardest bargain he can with his *sirkal*, and also
> claims the government share on brushwood, grazing, etc.[8]

In time such treatment would kill the goose that laid the golden eggs, but
the process was slow, partly due to the surplus labour created by the sharp

rise in population between 1920 and 1947, and even more to the legislation introduced in the early 1930s which turned the situation decisively in the landlords' favour. They no longer had to pay much tax and had an even more secure hold over their tenants and *sirkals* than before. The *Istihlak* Law and the Cultivators' Law enabled the 'Amara shaykhs to maintain their positions with even less interference from government.

Their tenants were of course very much less fortunate. Imprisoned in a cycle of perpetual indebtedness, they were in bondage to their overlords. The *sirkals* and fellahin borrowed from the *muqata'a* holders at high rates of interest to obtain advances on seed and tools. Debts mounted so high that there was no chance of the cycle being broken by actual repayment, and the only possible escape was flight from the land. Even as early as 1924 this situation was known to the authorities; Dobbs himself was moved to deplore the prohibition against a *sirkal* owing money to one shaykh transferring himself to another:

> His Excellency understands that the prohibition . . . was introduced at the instance of the shaykhs who alleged that they could not otherwise recover their revenue from the *sirkal* for the purpose of paying it to Government. Sir Henry Dobbs is very doubtful whether the shaykhs have not plenty of other methods of enforcing payment. In any case the prohibition puts far too much power into the hands of the *muqata'a* holders who can always make out that their *sirkals* are indebted to them and His Excellency strongly advises that the prohibition should be cancelled.[9]

This recommendation was not heeded, nor was any serious attention paid to Dobbs' plea that landlords should only be given long leases on condition that they gave equally secure conditions of tenure to their *sirkals* and fellahin. Leases were granted out on very long terms as before, and no safeguards were insisted on for the cultivators. Later in 1924 a committee was proposed to revise the tax farms of the area for the following year, but it never met,[10] and for a time the Finance Ministry despaired of ever obtaining realistic tax returns from the area. Suggestions for fundamental change were countered by arguments that there were insufficient administrative personnel available and that a violent reaction would be sure to follow. The use of military forces to control such an outbreak would, it was claimed, swallow up all the savings in cost which the changes were supposed to bring about.

Throughout his time as High Commissioner, Dobbs showed himself implacably opposed to any changes in the 'Amara *muqata'a* arrangements. As

Revenue Commissioner in 1915–1816 he had been responsible for setting up the terms under which the *muqata'as* were held, and was firmly convinced that they should remain in force. Even tentative suggestions from Interior that it was time to introduce the normal administrative apparatus into the area were vigorously countered:

> His Excellency would be glad to know . . . whether the policy of the Iraqi government is to split up large *muqata'as* in this *liwa* and create a large number of petty shaykhs. Since the Tigris is the principal line of communication between the sea coast and Baghdad and less precarious than the railway His Excellency is sure that the Iraqi government appreciates the great importance of maintaining peace along the line and of not disturbing without due consideration a system which has hitherto conduced to peace.[11]

Later, in the course of 1926, Finance made a determined effort to obtain more money from the *liwa*:

> The true sign of Government, as distinct from the present realities, should be security of tenure for shaykh, *sirkal* and peasant. . . . The more we insist on revenue and direct administration considerations prevailing over the tribe, the more we must be prepared to face the obligations of normal government, including those of adequate personnel.[12]

Characteristically, Dobbs took up the cudgels in a detailed reply. Finance had suggested that the larger *muqata'as* should be split up and given either to smaller shaykhs or town (*ahali*) landlords, on the grounds that this would facilitate more realistic tax collection. The High Commissioner argued that there was complete peace on the Tigris, that the area was 'notoriously the easiest to manage in the whole of Iraq', since the shaykhs' positions were subject to periodic regranting, and there were so few of them that they were easy to control. He did not want this 'admirable system destroyed without good reason': the present tax yields were fairly high because administrative expenses were so low. The best policy, expressed in terms which are by now familiar, was to let sleeping dogs lie:

> The High Commissioner cannot without dismay compare this new arrangement (of *ahali* lessors) with that of an estate under a tribal chief, related by blood to the majority of his sub-lessees, resident on his own

estates, restrained by a number of tribal sanctions and traditions from oppression or extortion, knowing intimately the affairs of his tribal cultivators and impelled by every consideration to be an indulgent landlord. The creation of new small estates under unsympathetic lessees may increase the gross revenue as long as it is not pushed too far, but if adopted prematurely as a permanent policy and largely extended, it is bound, the High Commissioner believes, to create such social and agrarian discontent as will more than swallow up in the increased costs of administration the additional revenue so obtained.[13]

It seemed especially important both to the High Commissioner and the Advisor to the Ministry of Interior that the process of tribal disintegration in the *liwa* should not be unduly or artificially hastened.[14] As we know, the fallacy here was that the authorities had themselves interfered in the natural process by deliberately shoring up the system. By giving more widespread powers to the landlords and tribal leaders than they had ever enjoyed in the past, they had created circumstances which made the tribal system seem far more robust than it actually was. Furthermore, dire consequences, in the shape of armed rebellions which the Iraqi government could not hope to be able to contain, were always held up as the inevitable results of interference; similar warnings greeted contemporary attempts to introduce conscription. Thus the High Commissioner was able to exercise covert powers of veto; in 1927 interior again suggested that some of the local *raises* should be made *mudirs* of *nahiyas*, and that taxes should be collected from them. Dobbs replied that:

> . . . the proposal appears to be an unnecessary and extravagant one, and if it results in disorder in the *liwa*, His Excellency will expect the Iraqi government to deal with the situation without help from his officers.[15]

Occasionally, the Ministry of Finance managed to press successfully for a review of the rents of the *liwa*. A committee in 1927 recommended small increases, and occasional dispossessions,[16] but the new totals represented a net increase of only 2.59 *lakhs*, composed of:

Increases	3.13
Decreases	0.54
Net	2.59

The basic policy of non-intervention continued. In view of this, the serious situation at the end of the 1920s seems surprising, for by 1928 repeated and vociferous complaints of inability to pay were being heard from some of the richest men in the liwa.[17] 'Failures' of several prominent shaykhs were reported in August of that year, and the next seasons saw the process continuing. By 1929, after seven years of admittedly intermittent and unenthusiastic revenue payments, the discrepancy between tax demands and tax receipts was wider in 'Amara than anywhere else in the country. Receipts generally were low in 1929; it was a year of bad harvests, and the beginning of the great slump in agricultural prices, but the discrepancy in 'Amara was nearly 10 *lakhs*, while the largest elsewhere, Baghdad *liwa*, was only 2.5:

Table 2[18]

Liwa	1925		1929	
	Assessment	Return	Assessment	Return
'Amara	25.37	24.37	29.41	19.23
Diwanlya	23.98	23.73	16.93	16.15
Hilla	17.40	17.51	12.28	10.98
Baghdad	14.65	13.53	11.20	8.78
Diyala	12.34	12.51	7.87	7.61

It is significant that in spite of the High Commission and the Ministry of Interior's relative indifference to the tax potential of the *liwa*, neither department had ever denied its actual wealth.

In examining the situation in these last years of the mandate, we should be aware that the 'plight' of the *liwa's* taxpayers cannot always be accepted without question. Their experience in previous years had taught them that they were unlikely to be bullied or cajoled into payment, so that their situation could as well indicate lack of the will to pay as lack of the ability to do so.

> The effect of a slump in grain prices is particularly marked in the 'Amara area where a serious situation has arisen. Last year (1929) owing to slackness on the part of the administration in the collection of revenue the holders of the 'Amara *muqata'as* were allowed to fall into arrears. With the usual improvidence of the Arab they spent what they should have paid into the Treasury. Now that grain prices have slumped many of them find it impossible to pay what they owe while those that can pay are refraining from doing so in the hope of general remissions being granted.[19]

However, a few months after this report was written a stern *mutasarrif* had threatened the major defaulters with eviction, and most of the money was miraculously found and paid into the authorities.[20]

Elation in the Ministry of Finance was nevertheless short-lived. Troubles began in earnest again early in 1931 when Finance attempted to substitute direct collection of animal (*koda*) tax from individuals for lump sum collection from the *muqata'a* holders. Interior pointed out the disadvantages of this practice in view of the current system, since:

> . . . the lessees have undertaken certain duties, protection of bunds, surrender of criminals, compensation of victims of disorder etc. in exchange for certain profits supposed to accrue to them from the lump sum method. If you deprive them of these assumed profits you cannot expect them to perform the extraordinary duties not normally demanded from those who pay taxes directly assessed . . . By making immense areas economically untenable, you land Government with the expense of ensuring law and order and the maintenance of bunds, whose length is measured in hundreds of miles.[21]

Convinced that Finance's attempts to interfere were misconceived, Edmonds was despatched by Interior on a commission of enquiry into conditions in 'Amara *liwa*.

> 'The first impression that 'Amara gives is that the administration exists primarily, one would say almost solely, as a sort of mincing machine for squeezing money out of the *liwa*. There is no doubt that the *muqata'a* holders, some of whom were very rich men, in 1924 are today either ruined or seriously in debt. 'Amara seems to have been bled dry.'[22]

He discovered later that even the 1924 figures were misleading:

> . . . in 1924 also the nominal demand bore no relation to the Government share and 'Amara's capacity to pay, and that Government also recognized the fact and wrote off nearly 10 *lakhs*.[23]

Buried inconspicuously in the middle of the report lies the real answer; the progressive impoverishment of the soil of the area through over-cultivation. We know that the effect of falling prices was felt elsewhere in Iraq, and Table II above shows that the revenue demands were in most cases scaled downwards to adjust to these changes; by 1931, however, the real dangers inherent in the 'Amara system had come to the surface, and, if it had not been for the passing of the *Istihlak* Law, it seems probable that the whole arrangement of consolidated fixed assessments would have had to have been reconsidered; the wide powers of the *muqata'a* holders very nearly caused their downfall.

At this point a particularly important aspect of the 'Amara arrangements should be reconsidered:

> Today the actual proportion to be taken (from the *sirkal* or fellah) as well as the fact that it was limited to the crops only, has been lost sight of, and the 'Amara shaykh now drives the hardest bargain he can with his *sirkals* . . .[24]

Since there were no sanctions to stop him, there was nothing to prevent the landlord extracting as much as he possibly could from his tenants, *except* the sheer incapacity of the soil to continue to bear crops at the same rate. As far as taxation was concerned, the *muqata'a* holder's capacity to pay was equally limited by the amount he received from his tenants, and on the basis of a fixed assessment he was likely to be in difficulties in years of bad harvests and low grain prices, even though, as seems most probable, his holding had been under-assessed in the first place. To maintain a high income under the taxation system in force until 1931, the landlords of 'Amara would have had to have been prepared to invest heavily in agricultural improvements. Instead, the fields were constantly over-irrigated by mechanical pumps, a form of speculation which brought high yields for a few years followed inevitably by soil exhaustion, since fallowing was hardly ever practised.[25]

Furthermore, the fellahin and *sirkals* of the *liwa* worked on an almost exclusively sharecropping basis; there were no individual smallholdings in the *liwa* at all, and we have seen that the landlords lost no opportunity of taking a proportion of all the produce of their estates. There was no incentive for the cultivator either to diversify or to increase production, for he could only benefit to the extent of a fraction of his labour, and the rewards for this extra effort did not seem worthwhile. The only equitable solution to the problem would have been to bring the apparatus of financial, administrative and organised irrigation control as applied elsewhere in Iraq to 'Amara. Even the Advisor to Finance was forced to admit defeat in a note to the Minister:

> I fully realise and sympathise with Your Excellency's desire to apply the law in 'Amara on the same lines as it is elsewhere, but laws cannot

be applied unless the machinery exists to carry them out. This *liwa* is, I suppose, the most tribal in organisation and the most devoid of communication of all the *liwas*; it is also the one in which the administrative organisation is the weakest. This situation cannot be changed in a day – the Persian frontier cannot be closed by word of mouth, and the economic attraction to cross the frontier is strong [26]

In the circumstances, Hogg felt that finance and administration should for the time being be left in the hands of the shaykhs. It was difficult to make piecemeal alterations to a system which had by then been in force for over fifteen years.

It remains to consider how it came about that the *muqata'a* holders retained their wealth over the following years. The only possible explanation lies in the increased population, and the new taxation arrangements brought about by the *Istihlak* Law. Tax was now confined to sales on surplus produce, a system which enriched the landlords but barely affected their tenants, who continued to go on paying their dues as before. Thus the landlords collected the same sums as before from their heavily indebted *sirkals* and fellahin but paid out a far smaller proportion of it to the Treasury. The Cultivators' Law, formally restricting the movement of indebted tenants, and defining closely the duties of *sirkals* and fellahin, further strengthened the hand of the landlords.

Thus the *muqata'a* holders' position was virtually unassailable; although their tenants might run away, there were plenty of others to take their place.[27] The Second World War increased demand for rice, the main crop of the *liwa*, which sent prices up again. After the war, the unpopularity and isolation of the Iraqi government forced it to fall back on traditional sources of support; the 'Amara shaykhs became prominent in the Senate and the Chamber of Deputies, and the Regent himself married the daughter of the Amir Rabi'a, one of the great 'Amara landowners.

The 'Amara landholding system was the deliberate creation of one man, Sir Henry Dobbs, whose long period of service in Iraq ensured that the machinery he had forged would not be tampered with. In effect, he replaced a system of leasing and tax-farming by one of complete ownership in all but name. The sole function of the state in 'Amara *liwa* was to receive the land and *koda* taxes, collected by the *muqata'a* holders of their agents from their own estates. By this means, free cultivating peasants were legally transformed into the bondsmen of their landlords, whose 'traditional' authority, as we have noted, had depended on a degree of consensus and agreement that the landlords were now able to dispense with. The 'Amara shaykhs thus came to have administrative, financial and finally wide political powers; all these gave them a vested interest in the status quo, and their great power gave the Iraqi government an equivalent interest in keeping them loyal. Only the total overthrow of the state which the mandate had created would destroy this relationship permanently.

NOTES

Introduction

1 See Jabar (2005). At the time of the Mesopotamia campaign, (southern) Iraq was referred to as 'Turkish Arabia' in British official correspondence.

2 Balfour reconstructed the scene from memory in a note written some nine months later: 'I [Clemenceau] therefore asked the Prime Minister [Lloyd George] what modification in the Sykes-Picot agreement England desired. He replied "Mosul". I said "You shall have it. Anything else"? He replied "Palestine." Again I said, "You shall have it." DBFP, Series I, Vol. IV, Document 242 of 11 August 1919, pp. 340–341, quoted Monroe (1981): 50. See p. 261 note 61 below.

3 There have been several outstanding recent publications on Ottoman Iraq. See 'Abdullah (2001): Çetinsaya (2006): Dina Khoury (1997); Nieuwenhuis (1982); Shields (2000), and the forthcoming work of Christoph Herzog, Edouard Méténier and Thomas Lier. For the history of the Gulf and Sa'udi Arabia, see Anscombe (1997) and Al Rasheed (2002).

4 Hourani (1968), Fattah (1997), and Philip Khoury (1990).

5 Notably Nuri al-Sa'id, Yasin al-Hashimi, Ja'far al-'Askari, Jamil Midfa'i, Mawlud Mukhlis. See the theses of 'Atiyah (1968), Nadhmi (1974) and Sakai (1994).

6 For Britain's relations with the Gulf shaykhdoms see Crystal (1995); for Britain and Kuwait see Sluglett (2002): 783–816.

7 See p. 249, note 34.

8 E.g. see Lewis (1968): 82. In addition, the Anglo-Kuwaiti Agreement of 1899, under which the Shaykh undertook on behalf of himself and his successors 'not to cede, lease [or] sell . . . any portion of his territory to the Government or subjects of any other Power without the previous consent of Her Majesty's Government . . .' was at least partly prompted by Britain's awareness of German interest in Kuwait as a possible terminus for the Baghdad railway. See Sluglett (2002).

9 e. g. *Mesopotamien: das Land der Zukunft: seine wissenschaftliche Bedeutung für Mitteleuropa*, Berlin, 1906. I am grateful to Marion Omar Farouk for this reference.

10 Sir Mark Sykes to Sir Arthur Hirtzel, 16 January 1918, Sykes Papers, FO 800/221. cf. W. Ormsby Gore, speech in House of Commons 10 March 1920: '[We] are going to undertake the gigantic task of restoring to production the 14,000,000 acres that once formed part of the cultivable area of Mesopotamia which was once the granary of the world . . .' Quoted Wilson (1931): 241–242.

11   The area transferred by Iran to the Ottoman Empire as a result of the activities of the International Boundary Commission of 1913, on which Arnold Wilson, the future Deputy Civil Commissioner in Mesopotamia, had served. See Marlowe (1967): 71–85.

12   Although it appears that Ottoman military activity was greatly exaggerated, and that, to a very great extent, London's declaration of war on the Ottoman Empire was based on faulty intelligence. See P. Morris, 'Intelligence and its interpretation: Mesopotamia 1914–1916', in Andrew and Noakes (eds.) (1987): 77–101.

13   In July 1918, Lord Curzon, the Foreign Secretary, asked Cox to replace Sir Charles Marling at the Legation in Teheran. He stayed there between 15 September 1918 and 11 June 1920, negotiating an Anglo-Persian Agreement in August 1919 which was submitted to, but famously not ratified by, the *majlis*. For details see Graves (1944): 248–264, Olson (1980), and Adelson (1995): 188–189.

14   Under the terms of the *British Officials Agreement* annexed to the 1922 Anglo-Iraq Treaty, senior posts in the Ministries of Justice, Finance and Interior were reserved for British officials. The last Adviser to the Ministry of Interior, A. I. Ditchburn, was still serving in 1950; the last Adviser to the Ministry of Justice, H. I. Lloyd retired in 1949, and the last Chief Justice, Sir John Prichard, in 1951.

15   Visser (2005) shows that in the 1920s some influential Basrawis wanted their city and its immediate hinterland to be under direct British rule (that is, to have a status somewhat analogous to that of Kuwait) rather than to become part of the state of Iraq.

16   In 1924, these salaries amounted to 30 lakhs of rupees (= approximately £20,000) – rather more than the total expenditure of the Ministry of Education in any year between 1921 and 1927.

17   This policy did not augur well for the future, since it tended increasingly to become a substitute for more 'conventional' forms of administration.

18   High Commissioner, Baghdad, to Secretary of State for the Colonies, Despatch, Confidential 'D', 18 October 1923, CO 730/42/52434.

19   The origins of the mandate system are discussed in Mejcher (1976); and more recently in Dodge (2003a): 11–15.

Chapter 1

1   War was actually declared some four weeks later, on 5 November 1914.

2   Cox to Viceroy, 23 November 1914, quoted Ireland (1937): 63.

3   According to Lieutenant-General Sir Edmund Barrow of the Military Department of the India Office, these aims were fourfold: to check Ottoman intrigue; to encourage the local Arabs, particularly the shaykhs of Kuwait and Muhammarah, to rally to the British side; to safeguard Egypt (given out as the Force's ostensible destination); and to secure the free flow of oil from Abadan. India Office Minute, 26 September 1914, "The role of India in a Turkish War", quoted in *Report of the Commission Appointed to Enquire into the Origin, Inception and Operations of the War in Mesopotamia* (subsequently *Mesopotamia Commission Report*), Cmd. 8610, 1917. p.12.

4   'We are not disposed to authorise an advance on Baghdad at present . . .,'

Secretary of State for India to Viceroy, 27 December 1914. *Mesopotamia Commission Report*, p. 20.

5   *Mesopotamia Commission Report*, p. 16.

6   The strategic side, and the arguments over the way in which the campaign was prosecuted are discussed in detail in Busch (1971) Chapter III, 'Britain's War in Iraq, 1916–1918' pp. 110–163.

7   Chief Political Officer, IEF 'D' to Viceroy, 27 November 1914, India Office, Letters, Political and Secret, 10 (LP & S 10) 4097/14/4726.

8   *Mesopotamia Commission Report*, p 15.

9   *Ibid.*

10 These deficiencies, and the appalling state of the medical services in 1915 and 1916, are discussed in some detail in the *Mesopotamia Commission Report . . .*, pp. 63–95.

11 '. . . there appeared not one single point to be urged in favour of a forward policy in Mesopotamia, always assuming the army there had the capacity to mount one'. Busch (1971): 117.

12 For similarly vague terminology ('portions of Syria lying to the west of the districts of Damascus, Homs, Hama and Aleppo') *see Report of a Committee set up to consider certain Correspondence between Sir Henry McMahon and the Sharif of Mecca in 1915 and 1916*, Cmd. 5974 of 1939.

13 'Expert opinion was therefore unanimous on the point that to take and occupy Baghdad with the existing forces would be an unjustifiable risk and that for the task of holding Baghdad General Nixon should have a reinforcement of two divisions. There was however a concurrence of expert opinion that Nixon's existing force was sufficient in the first instance to take Baghdad.' *Mesopotamia Commission Report*, p 24.

14 See Wilson (1930): 64–78, 143–69; Ireland (1937): 74–95, and Chapter 6 below.

15 Gertrude Bell to her father, 27 April 1916 in Bell (1927): 374–375; to her father, 15 July 1916, in Burgoyne (1961): 43; cf. Storrs (1937): 161; Klieman (1970): 6–7.

16 Monroe (1981): 36. Policy on the 'other side of the Arabian peninsula' was the responsibility of the Foreign Office and the Arab Bureau. See Westrate (1992).

17 Cox, Baghdad, to India Office, 20 April 1917. LP & S 10 4097/14 (1917)/1661

18 The administrative unity of the two *wilaya*-s was not achieved until October 1918.

19 This account derives largely from Barker (1967): 385–457.

20 'Every effort was made to score as heavily as possible on the Tigris before the whistle blew'. Wilson (1931): 11, 17. Cf : 'I disapproved strongly of Wilson's efforts after the Armistice to continue the war so that Mosul might be in our hands before the bargaining began at the Peace Conference.' H. St. J. Philby, *Mesopotage*, unpublished mss., St Antony's College, Oxford, p 308.

21 'On the eve of the Second World War . . . For a population of 353 million, the Indian Civil Service (ICS) had a maximum strength of 1,250 covenanted members . . .' John W. Cell, 'Colonial Rule', in Brown and Louis (1999): 232.

22 'However well-educated and clever a native may be, and however brave he may have proved himself, I believe that no rank we can bestow upon him can cause him to be considered the equal of a British Officer'. Lord Kitchener, quoted Pannikar (1953): 150.

23   See Wolpert (1967), and Edwin Montagu's speech on the Indian budget of 8
     August 1913: 'There are in India millions who do not, cannot, and probably
     never will aspire to a share in the government of their country . . . We measure
     their lands, we administer justice to them . . . But all this is to them but as a
     phase in the eternal scheme of things . . . What I ask is that where the
     machinery . . . suited to the twentieth century is introduced . . . let every effort
     be made to simplify, to adjust, to explain . . . If we make co-operation and
     devolution our guiding principles, I am sure that we are on the right lines.'
     Waley (1964): 57.

24   '. . . Basra with Nasiriyah, Shatt al-Hai, Kut and Badrai as its northern limits
     to remain permanently under British Administration . . .' Secretary of State for
     India to Viceroy, Foreign Department, Simla, 29 March 1917, quoted Ireland
     (1937): 36–37.

25   'We are really making concessions to India because of the free talk about liberty,
     democracy, nationality and self-government which have become the common
     shibboleths of the Allies [June 1917, PS] and because we are expected to
     translate into practice in our own domestic household the sentiments which we
     have so enthusiastically preached.' Ronaldshay (1928) 163–64.

26   Sir Arthur Hirtzel, India Office, to W. H. Clark, Foreign Office, Private,
     31 December 1917. FO 368/1999/1071.

27   Mejcher (1976): 110–116, dates the beginning of the articulation of the 'A'
     Mandate policy in detail by Sir Mark Sykes as December 1917–January 1918.
     At the same time, George Beer, of Colonel House's 'Inquiry' team, was
     developing a remarkably similar theory, embodied in President Wilson's notions
     of Trusteeship; see 'The Future of Mesopotamia (dated 1 January 1918)' in Beer
     (1923): 411–29. In this paper, Beer proposed protection of the natives from
     exploitation; equality of access for all nations to the economic development of
     the country, and 'concentration of responsibility on to Great Britain'. See also
     Stivers (1982), and Dodge (2003a).

28   President Wilson to Colonel House, 18 July 1917. Quoted Seymour (1926): p. 54.

29   *Ibid.,* Vol. III, p. 174. The 'Inquiry' resembled the wartime 'Garden Suburb' in
     Downing Street.

30   An India Office Memo of 31 January 1918 suggested that the general trend of
     the war and 'the U. S. President's notions of self-determination' had brought
     about a situation where Britain would have to act towards Mesopotamia as a
     'candidate towards its constituents' (B. 277 in LP & S 10 2571/17/1918).

31   India Office Printed Memo B.281, 3 April 1918, LP & S 10 2571/1917/18. A
     little earlier (January 1918) Sir Reginald Wingate, Sir Henry McMahon's
     successor as High Commissioner in Cairo, had suggested making a compromise
     with Sharif Husayn of the Hijaz in order to obtain his assent to 'a definite
     modification of McMahon's unfortunate pledge in the light of the actual facts
     and his acceptance of the principle that we should have the right to continue
     administration in both *wilaya*-s with the object of gradually building up self-
     government in both.' (B. 273 of 30 January 1918 LP & S 10 2571).

32   The Naqib, 'Abd al-Rahman al-Gaylani (1845–1927), was also the head of the
     Qadiri Sufi order.

33   'The population, from the cultivator to the well-to-do merchant or landowner,
     infinitely prefers to be handled by a British officer who of course employs Arab

subordinates . . . I may mention that whereas I have done my utmost to employ experimentally any inhabitants of this country at all likely to be suitable, this laudable endeavour finds no favour at all with the local inhabitants concerned.' Cox, Memorandum of 22 April 1918. IO, LP & S 10 4722/18/5064. Of course the 'local inhabitants' were naturally unwilling to commit themselves before being give a firm indication that the Ottomans would not return.

34 See *The Economic Situation in the Persian and Mesopotamian Markets* by Captain G. Lloyd, MP (FO 368/1650/199753, September/October 1916), and the *Memo* by Captain Fitzgerald to the Department of Overseas Trade, 4 January 1917 '. . . by prompt action and co-operation of existing firms we may ensure the establishment of British trade in Mesopotamia so firmly that competition by foreign firms may be unappreciable if not altogether non-existent.' (FO 368/1827/64629). Generally Britain's commercial pre-eminence in the Gulf and Mesopotamian markets before the war was undisputed, although overall figures were not high:

Total £ million		British Share	British percentage
1906	8.20	6.47	79
1914	12.84	9.60	76

The Mesopotamian campaign is estimated as having cost £200,000,000, or 20 years of '1914 trade': LP & S 10 1283/1913/19/5/8193.

35 Wilson (1931): 99. I have not been able to trace this correspondence in the India Office records.

36 See Ireland (1937): 150, and Marlowe (1967): 134.

37 Political, Baghdad, to Secretary of State for India, 27 September 1918: L P & S 10 2571/17/1918/4252: Secretary of State for India to Political, Baghdad, 2 November 1918; Political, Baghdad, to Secretary of State for India, 23 November 1918: LP & S 10 2571/17/4872, 5179.

38 'I hear that the shaykhs were very much impressed by the fact that the Commander in Chief stood up to receive them. They said that no Turkish vali had ever done more than loll in his chair when they paid their respects.' Gertrude Bell to her father, 19 September 1918, quoted Burgoyne (1961): 95–96.

39 House of Commons debates, 23 July 1918, quoted Wilson (1931): 99. See also 'Corruption, Fragmentation and Despotism: British Visions of Ottoman Iraq', in Dodge (2003a)

40 Secretary of State for India to Political, Baghdad.29 November 1918 (quoted Ireland (1937): 151), and Secretary of State for India to Viceroy, 28 October 1918: copy of telegram from Secretary of State for Foreign Affairs, to H. M. Ambassador, Washington 23 October 1918: '. . . it has become essential to make some public declaration in order to allay the suspicions and misgivings of the Arabs and Syrians which may be dangerously exploited by our enemies: it has therefore been decided to issue an Anglo-French Declaration . . .' See also Nevakivi (1969): 80–81.

41 Political, Baghdad, to Secretary of State for India, 16 November 1918, quoted Marlowe (1967): 136–137.

42 Minute of 22 September 1920, L P & S 10, 4722/18/1920/8/7145.

43 See Stivers (1982): Woodrow Wilson's adviser George Beer rejected the idea of

an international protectorate in favour of a 'concentration of responsibility on Britain'. Beer (1923): 421, 423–24.

44   Wilson to Hirtzel, 12 September 1919: LP & S 10, 4722/18/1919/3/6202.

45   Political, Baghdad, to Secretary of State for India, 17 November 1919, with minutes of 3 January 1920: LP & S 10 4722/18/1920/8573.

46   Political, Baghdad, to Secretary of State for India, 17 November 1918; minute by J.E. Shuckburgh, 29 November, 1918. General Officer Commanding, Baghdad, to War Office, 19 November 1918: LP & S 10 4722/18/1918/1/5104.

47   Compare p. 18 above: '. . . the Sharif of Mecca, a figure who carries no weight in Iraq, where only the most distant interest is taken in him.' (Sir Percy Cox, Memorandum of 23 April 1918).

48   Political, Baghdad to Secretary of State for India, Telegram, 24 November 1918, and Minute by J. E. Shuckburgh 26 November 1918: LP & S 10 4722/18/1918/ 1/5200. However, for further somersaults, see Political, Baghdad, to Secretary of State for India, 29 November 1918: 'Najaf and Karbala' and the Shias at large who form the majority of the country have not made their views known, but it may be confidently anticipated that they will throw their weight into the scale against a son of the Sharif or indeed any possible candidate for the Amirate': LP & S 10 4722/18/1/5373. Wilson (1931): 109, quotes part of this telegram but omits this passage.

49   Gertrude Bell to her father, 28 November 1918, in Bell (1927): 463.

50   Secretary of State for India to Political, Baghdad, 28 November 1918: L P & S 10 4722/18/1918/1/5244. The original draft, sent to Lord Curzon for his approval, ends: 'There will be no annexation and as far as can be seen at the moment no formal protectorate.' Curzon added (in his sprawling handwriting): 'There will be no annexation and as far as can be seen at the moment no *formal declaration of a* protectorate.'

51   'Seven Arabs were deported from Baghdad for their activities in connection with the plebiscite. The declaration of the chosen representatives of the Baghdad Muslims, far from being accepted as the official declaration as originally intended, was dismissed as being unrepresentative of the politically and economically important inhabitants of Baghdad . . .' Ireland (1937): 173.

52   Eastern Committee, 24 December 1918: L P & S 10 4722/18/1919/1/37.

53   Minute by J.E. Shuckburgh, 4 January 1919 on Cox (Teheran) to Foreign Office, 24 December 1918: LP & S 10 4722/18/1919/1/16.

54   George Kidston, Foreign Office, to J.E. Shuckburgh, 25 January 1919: LP & S 10 4722/18/1919/1/516.

55   Hirtzel, Minute of 1 February 1919: LP & S 10 4722/18/1919/1/551.

56   The full text of 22 February 1919 is reproduced in Wilson (1931) 330–336.

57   Though she wrote later: 'In the light of experience it may be doubted whether any such enquiry carried out under official auspices would have been likely to elicit answers which might serve to guide the questioner.' Bell, *Review . . .*, 127.

58   Bonham-Carter, Baghdad, 5 February 1919: LP & S 10 4722/18/1919/1/1463.

59   Montagu to Balfour, 25 March 1919: FO 800/215, p. 369.

60   Secretary of State for India to Political, Baghdad, 9 May 1919 quoted Ireland (1937): 186. None of the various councils was in existence by 29 October 1919. Meeting of Inter-Departmental Committee, 10 November 1919: LP & S 10 4722/18/1919/3/7546.

61   Apparently the French Foreign Ministry was aware of the oil potential of Mosul
      before 1914. French claims to the Kirkuk oilfields featured in the Sykes-Picot
      negotiations, largely to sweeten the pill of a British-supported Hashimite Arab
      state, but also because, in 1916, the British were anxious to have France to act
      as a buffer between themselves and the Russians, who were to have eastern
      Anatolia (also under the terms of Sykes-Picot). See Fitzgerald (1994), 702. The
      eventual *quid pro quo* for France's cession of Mosul was the Bérenger/Long oil
      agreement of 18 March 1919, under which Britain assigned the former German
      23.75% share in the Turkish Petroleum Company (later the Iraq Petroleum
      Company) to France.
62   Gertrude Bell to her father, 30 January 1921, in Burgoyne (1961): 202–203..
63   Faysal to Clayton, 24 May 1919, L P & S 10 4722/1918/19/23649
64   Naji al-Suwaydi had been invited to Baghdad in June to 'advise' Colonel Wilson
      on an Arab government. He was so dissatisfied with his reception that he re-
      turned to Syria almost at once. See Despatch, 57, Chief Political Officer,
      Egyptian Expeditionary Force to Foreign Office, 8 June 1919 enclosing Brayne,
      British Liaison Officer, Aleppo to CPO, EEF, 7 May 1919: LP & S 10 4722/
      1918/19/2/3912.
65   Political, Baghdad to Secretary of State for India, 11 July 1919: LP & S 10
      4722/18/.1919/4/4264.
66   Mann (1921): 182: letter to Major Cumberbatch, 15 December 1919.
67   Minutes by Shuckburgh (9 August 1919) and Hirtzel (11 August 1919) on L
      P & S 10 4722/18/1919/2/4264.
68   Reproduced in Marlowe (1967): 182–83.
69   See the minutes of the Interdepartmental Committee, 10 October 1919: 'There
      was now in existence in Mesopotamia a highly organised military administration
      . . . which did not give to the local population the opportunity for sharing in their
      own government which they had the right to expect from the Anglo-French
      Declaration . . . [Lord Curzon] did not suggest that this administration had done
      badly . . . but it was inordinately expensive and he would be glad to see it come
      to an end as soon as possible': L P & S 10 4722/18/1919/3/7546.
70   Minute by Hirtzel, 1 April 1920 on Kerr to Shuckburgh 31 March 1920; L P
      & S 10 4722/3/18/1920/2326.
71   Condensed from Wilson to Hirtzel, 12 September 1919, and Political, Baghdad
      to Secretary of State for India, 15 September 1919: L P & S 10 4722/18/1919/
      2/8253.
72   *Syria in October*, 11 October 1919: L P & S 10 4722/18/1919/2/ 8253. See also
      Chapter 8.
73   Political, Baghdad, to Secretary of State for India, 18 January 1920: L P & S 10
      4722/18/1920/2/487.
74   For the development of the role and function of *marja'-i taqlid* in the nineteenth
      century, see Litvak (1998); for this episode in March 1920 see Luizard (1991):
      386, and Political, Baghdad, to Secretary of State for India, 18 March 1920: L
      P & S 10 4722/18/1920/2/2211.
75   India Office Memo B. 342 by H. R. C. Dobbs on the proposals of the Bonham-
      Carter Committee, n.d. (June or July 1920).
76   Secretary of State for India to Political, Baghdad, 4 May 1920: LP & S 10 4722/
      18/1920/3/3326; Wilson (1931): 248–49.

77 Political, Baghdad, to Secretary of State for India, 9 June 1920, L P & S 10 4722/18/1920/5/4935.
78 Eastern Committee, Meeting of 10 June 1920; LP & S 10 940/19/1920.
79 See Vinogradov (1972); for the most detailed treatment see Luizard (1991): 381–422, and Nakash (1994): 66–72.
80 See Chapter 6. It is important not to underestimate the effects of British land and revenue policies, which, although purportedly based on Ottoman practice, differed in that they were actually carried through.
81 There were over 2,000 British casualties, missing, or prisoners and 8,450 Iraqis: Ireland (1937): 273.
82 In Britain, press hostility to the continued occupation of Iraq lasted well into 1922. See *The Times*, 16 August 1920, 6 November 1920: *The Near East*, 12 August, 1920. See also T. E. Lawrence's letter to *The Times*, 22 July 1920: 'The people of England have been led in Mesopotamia into a trap from which it will be hard to escape with dignity and honour . . . The sins of commission are those of the British civil authorities in Mesopotamia . . . who were given a free hand by London . . . They contested every suggestion of real self-government sent them from home. A recent proclamation about autonomy circulated with unction from Baghdad was drafted and published in a hurry to forestall a more liberal statement in preparation in London.' See also a leader in *The Times*, 6 September 1920: 'The principal cause of the rising in Mesopotamia is that after the Arabs had been firmly promised that they should control their own affairs under advisory guidance, the British authorities proceeded to act as though we meant to take over the whole country lock, stock and barrel.'
83 Sir Percy Cox in Bell (1939): 527–578.
84 This proclamation is reproduced in full in Ireland (1937): 287.
85 Note by Sir Arthur Hirtzel, 19 April 1920: L P & S 10 4722/18/1920/6/3888.
86 Gertrude Bell defended the expenditure: 'He's bound to play a big part in the future and till that time comes we've got to try and keep him out of mischief.' Gertrude Bell to her Father 30 August 1920, Burgoyne (1961): 160.
87 'Unless Sayyid Talib takes office under the Amir and gives proof of loyal service the High Commissioner will probably have to exile him. He is too capable, energetic and intriguing a character to be left at a loose end'. Minute by R.W. Bullard, 4 March 1921 on Intelligence Report of 30 December 1920: CO 730/1/9829.
88 See page 26.
89 See page 24.
90 Laid before Cabinet, 5 August 1920. These included the appointment of Faysal as ruler; foreign affairs in the hands of the Mandatory Power, and the British representative in charge of the garrison. LP & S 10 5876/1920/20/5876.
91 'Il est certain que l'Emir Faysal n'oubliera pas son règne ephémère de Damas et qu'il cherchera à renouer des intrigues dans cette dernière ville.' Alexandre Millerand to Lord Curzon, 17 August 1920: LP & S 10 5876/20/1920/6582.
92 Minute of a discussion between M. Millerand and Sir Eyre Crowe, 24 January 1921: LP & S 10 5876/20/1921/603. cf. Churchill to Lloyd George (from Cairo) 14 March 1921: 'In response to enquiries of adherents of the Emir Faysal, the British Government have stated that they will place no obstacles in the way of his candidature as ruler of Iraq and that if he is chosen he will have our support.' E 1090/4/91: FO 371/6350.

93 Note of a conversation between Colonel Frank Balfour and General Haddad in September 1920: Balfour papers, Sudan Archive, Durham, Box 303.

94 Telegram 148S to High Commissioner, Baghdad, to Secretary of State for India, 2 January 1921: E 277/100/93: FO 371/6349.

95 The former Director (1916–1920) of the Arab Bureau, one of the original instigators of the Arab Revolt in 1916 and a long time supporter of Faysal.

96 Colonel Kinahan Cornwallis: report of an interview with the Emir Faysal, 7 January 1921: E 553/100/93: FO 371/6349.

97 Gertrude Bell to her father, 24 October, 1 November 1920 (Bell, 1927: 568–570).

98 'the civil and military authorities are agreed that "whereas withdrawal to line indicated might be possible two years' hence, proposition is not a practical one for the present purpose."' Minute by E.S. Montagu, 24 December 1920, in E 318/100/93; FO 371/6349.

99 High Commissioner, Mesopotamia to Secretary of State for India, Telegram. 15339 of 29 December 1920. E 172/100/93: FO 371/6349.

100 He put this forward in August 1920. See Gilbert (1975): 507–530, and Ireland (1937): 310–311. Churchill made the setting up of the new department a condition of his accepting the Colonial Office; see Gilbert (1975): 523. For earlier efforts at rationalisation, and for the antecedents of the department, see: Lord Robert Cecil to E.S. Montagu, 5 September 1918, FO 800/207; *Mesopotamia; Administrative Record under British Occupation*, dated 20 August 1919, India Office Memo B 328. (Copy in Air 5/224).

101 In January 1921, Churchill's suggestions of substantial troop reductions in Mesopotamia aroused the ire of General Haldane and a threat of resignation on the part of Sir Percy Cox (Gilbert, 1975: 514–515). See Chapter 7 below.

102 'My object with the Arabs was to make them stand on their own feet. The work I did constructively for W.S.C. in 1921 and 1922 seems to me in retrospect the best I ever did.' Lawrence to Robert Graves, 3 August 1927 in Graves and Liddell Hart (1938): 113.

103 'The first consideration is the reduction of British military commitments in Mesopotamia. No local interest can be allowed to stand in the way of an immediate programme for reducing the British army of Occupation. Whatever may be the political status of the country under the Mandate it is out of the question that forces of anything like the present dimensions should be supported by the British taxpayer.' Winston Churchill, speech at Cairo. See FO 371/6343 for the full text of the proceedings of the Cairo Conference, and Churchill's article, 'Mesopotamia and the New Government', *Empire Review*, July 1923, pp 691–698.

104 Meeting of the third Palestine and Mesopotamia Committee, 14 March 1921; FO 371/6343.

105 On 17 February 1921, the Undersecretary of State for War told the House of Commons that the cost of maintaining the British Army in Mesopotamia was £2,300,000 per month. E 2219/100/93: FO 371/6349.

Chapter 2

1 Sayyid Talib's removal is said to have been occasioned by his threatening an armed uprising in the course of a private dinner party, attended by, amongst

others, Percival Landon of the *Daily Telegraph*. It seems that he was detained and subsequently deported after leaving a tea engagement with Lady Cox at the Residency a few days later. See Burgoyne (1961): 214, 17 April 1921; for further details see Haifa al-Nakib, 'A critical study of Saiyyid Talib al-Nakib in the setting of his time and environment', Leeds University M.Phil, 1972–1973.

2 Predictably, the announcement was followed by angry reactions in the French press, which was especially critical of the fact that Faysal's candidature was being announced while the League had decided to defer consideration of the 'A' and 'B' mandates. Hardinge, Paris to Secretary of State for Foreign Affairs, Despatch 1824, 19 June1921: CO 730/9/32250.

3 [I]t appeared . . . from Basra that Faysal received a most cordial reception . . . little cordiality was shown at Karbala and Najaf . . .At Hilla reception was however cordial.' High Commissioner to Secretary of State for the Colonies, Telegram 250 of 1 July 1921: CO 730/3/33044. 'Mosul has sent a deputation promising him no less cordial a reception than he received here.' High Commissioner, Baghdad, to Secretary of State for the Colonies, Telegram 280 of 9 July 1921: CO 730/3/34418.

4 Bell (1927): 615. cf. Telegram 529 of 27 September 1921 in E 10985/369/93; FO 371/6359.

5 Sir Percy Cox to Winston Churchill, Telegram, Private and Personal, unnumbered, 4 June 1921: CO 730/2/27917.

6 Gerrtude Bell to her father, 5 June 1921, Burgoyne (1961): 218.

7 c. f. Churchill: 'There is too much talk about "Mandates", "mandatories" and things like that. All this obsolescent rigmarole is not worth telegraphing about. It is quite possible that in a year or two there will be no Mandates and no League of Nations. Something quite different may have taken their place. Do let us get the practical salient points of the policy in our minds:

    (i)   To get another large wave of troops out of the country and so reduce the expenditure to the British taxpayer.

    (ii)   To get Faysal on the throne as quickly as possible.

    (iii)   To make whatever arrangements are most likely to conduce to the above objects with regard to Basra (about which I have a perfectly open mind) and Kurdistan (about which the only principle is that we do not put Kurds under Arabs).' Minute, 9 July 1921, on CO 730/3/33549.

8 High Commissioner, Baghdad, to Secretary of State for the Colonies, Telegram 376, 10 August 1921: CO 730/4/40185. His successor, Sir Henry Dobbs, was equally insistent in impressing on the Colonial Office the importance of not imposing too heavy a hand.

9 High Commissioner, Baghdad, to Secretary of State for the Colonies, Telegram 379, 11 August 1921: CO 730/4/40742

10 High Commissioner, Baghdad, to Secretary of State for the Colonies, Telegram 397, 17 August 1921: CO 730/4/41616.

11 High Commissioner, Baghdad, to Secretary of State for the Colonies, Telegram 427, 26 August 1921: CO 730/4/42913; Secretary of State for the Colonies to High Commissioner, Baghdad, Telegram 364, 2 September 1921: E 10046/100/93: FO 371/6353.

12 Colonial Office to Cabinet Office, 29 August 1921. Letter 43326 in E 9854/100/93: FO 371/6352.

13 Young to Shuckburgh, 23 October 1921: CO 730/16/55863.

14 'It will be understood that the proposed treaty will serve merely to regulate the relations between H.M. Government, and Mandatory Power, and the Arab Government of Irak. It is not intended as a substitute for the mandate, which will remain the operative document defining the obligations undertaken by H.M. Government on behalf of the League of Nations.' *Official Journal*, League of Nations, Nos. 10–12 (1921), p. 1217–1217, quoted Ireland (1937): 338.

15 High Commissioner, Baghdad, to Secretary of State for the Colonies, Telegram 699, 20 November 1921: E 12960/100/93: FO 371/6354.

16 To her father, 4 December 1921, Burgoyne (1961): 253

17 Private and Personal, Winston Churchill to Sir Percy Cox, 29 November 1921. Although Churchill was anxious that Cox should keep reminding Faysal of his client status, most of the expenditure incurred in Iraq at this time was spent on financing the army of occupation, and paying for the Iraqi Railways and the salaries of British officials. Further, most of the debts incurred by the Iraqi government at this stage resulted either from British control of government expenditure, or from the handing over to Iraq of surplus British military equipment or public works installations supplied or constructed for the needs of the army of occupation. These 'Transferred Assets' produced an immediate deficit of 95 *lakhs* (c. £63,000) on the Iraqi government account.

18 The facts seem to be as follows:

1) Allenby to Curzon (Lawrence to Churchill) from Cairo 15 April 1921 re Lawrence's interview with Faysal: 'He will accept Mandate condition if he is allowed in his first public statement in Iraq to add qualifying clause accepted by H. M. Government by which modifications in Mandate may be made, after ratification of Organic Law by negotiation between duly constituted Government of Mesopotamia and British Government.' E 4509/100/93: FO 371/6350.

2) Churchill (London) to Lawrence (Cairo) 19 April 1921: 'Faysal may be assured by you that in his first public statement in Iraq he may be allowed to say that H. M. Government agreed that after ratification of the Organic Law modifications may be made between duly constituted Government of Mesopotamia and H M. Government.' E 4700/4531/93: FO 371/6365.

19 Minute by R. C. Lindsay on E 1032/33/93, 30 January 1922, FO 371/7770.

20 High Commissioner, Baghdad, to Secretary of State for the Colonies, Telegram 815, 20 December 1921: CO 730/8/63366; High Commissioner, Baghdad, (for Major Young) Telegram 817, 21 December 1921: CO 730/8/63225.

21 High Commissioner, Baghdad, to Secretary of State for the Colonies, Telegram 163, 27 February 1922: CO 730/20/10151; Secretary of State for the Colonies to High Commissioner, Baghdad, Telegram 182, 16 March 1922: CO 730/20/10405.

22 Baghdad, Abstracts of Police Intelligence, April 1, 8, 15, May 27, June 10, 1922.

23 Minute by Churchill, ? April 1922, CO 730/21/18047.

24 Sasun Effendi to Sir Percy Cox, 8 April 1922, National Archives of India, New Delhi, Baghdad High Commission File (subsequently BHCF), Folder 23/14/1, 'Resignation of Sasun Effendi'.

25 Baghdad, *Abstracts of Police Intelligence*, June to August 1922.

26   Sir Percy Cox to Mr. Churchill, Private and Personal, 29 July 1922: CO 730/
      22/37397; Report of the Iraq Economy Committee, Baghdad 17 August 1922:
      CO 730/23/43331.
27   Nicolson (1934): 330–31, cf. Curzon to Lady Curzon, 1 January 1923: 'I found
      Bonar longing to clear out of Mosul, the Straits and Constantinople, willing to
      give up anything and everything rather than have a row: astonished at the
      responsibility I have assumed at Lausanne and prepared for me to back down
      everywhere.' Ronaldshay (1928): 332. See also Chapter 3.
28   Question on the costs of the Mesopotamian Garrison, 20 February 1923;
      Question on Treasury payments to the Arab forces in Mesopotamia, 27 February
      1923; Question on number of bombing expeditions against Arabs in Iraq ('this
      Hunnish and barbarous method of warfare against unarmed people'), 12 April
      1923: CO 730/51/8179, 9523, 16039.
29   See page 3.
30   Cabinet Committee on Iraq, I.R.Q. 30, 5 February 1923.
31   Secretary of State for the Colonies to High Commissioner Baghdad, Telegram
      116 of 3 March 1923: CO 730/46/11818.
32   'Ismet's message containing Turkish offer of independence to Arabs was received
      here. . .but at the request of Faysal publication has been withheld. Faysal has
      now received telegram from Husain stating that he has telegraphed Ministry of
      Foreign Affairs Angora expressing satisfaction with Turkish intentions towards
      Arabs which he accepts without reserve. Faysal is . . . telegraphing Husain
      saying that as Mosul is essential to Iraq Turks will if their offer is genuine
      naturally give up their claim to it . . . Air Officer Commanding and I fear that
      the Turkish offer may cause a revulsion of feeling amongst the Arabs here when
      it becomes known and that they might think that they can dispense with British
      support'. High Commissioner, Baghdad, to Secretary of State for the Colonies,
      Telegram 114 of 14 February 1923: CO 730/38/8324.
33   Cox was concerned about the effect that the announcement of the Protocol
      might have on the Turks, suggesting that there was a danger that they might
      abate their claim for the time being and raise it again in four years' time. High
      Commissioner to Secretary of State for the Colonies, Telegram 230 of 13 April
      1923. CO 730/39/18816.
34   The Colonial Office had apparently imagined that the elections would have to
      be delayed until the frontier question was settled. However, Dobbs was
      informed on 7 June 1923: 'We have no desire to place obstacles in the way if
      you and the Iraqi government are satisfied that elections can now be held with
      real prospect of success. We shall on the contrary be glad to see Constituent
      Assembly formed as soon as possible. Following is one point to bear in mind,
      i.e. that case of Iraqi government in event of Mosul boundary question being
      referred hereafter to arbitration may be to some extent weakened by Kurdish
      vote against participation in elections. . .' Secretary of State for the Colonies to
      High Commissioner, Baghdad, Telegram 261 of 7 June 1923: CO 730/48/
      28506.
35   Luizard (1991): 449–470.
36   Abstract of Police Intelligence, 10 November 1922. Quoted in Delhi, BHCF
      File 23/15/1, Vol. I, 'Propaganda and Activities against Participation in Iraq
      Elections'.

37 King Faysal to Sir Percy Cox, 30 November 1922, *loc. cit.*

38 The High Commissioner intervened early in 1923 to prevent the registration of 'Abd al-Wahid's lands in the names of his *sarkals*: 30% arrears were reported in the Kut and Hayy areas in mid-February, but 'Abd al-Wahid's lands were further protected, and 18 *lakhs* of rupees taxation (about £12,000) remitted in April. Intelligence Reports 31 January, 14 February, 1 April and 14 April: CO 730/38/10607, 13500; CO730/39/20387, 23176. See also Chapter 6.

39 Minute of 28 June 1923 by Dobbs on Adviser, Ministry of Interior to *mutasarrif*, Karbala', Telegram 10122 of 28 June 1923. Delhi, BHCF 23/13/1 Vol. I., 'Propaganda and Activities against Participation in Iraq elections.'

40 Cornwallis to Dobbs, Secret and Personal C/1428, 18 July 1923. Delhi, BHCF File 23/15/1 Vol. I, 'Propaganda and Activities against Participation in Iraq Elections'.

41 In Hilla and Dulaym *liwas* the number of tribal voters swamped those from towns and villages:

	Tribesmen	Townsmen
Hilla	40, 000	13, 000
Dulaym	37, 319	7, 208

'If the shaykhs know how to use the political power which has been given to them by the registration *en masse* of their tribesmen the Assembly will present a colour curiously different from any part of the former Ottoman Empire, where the intelligentsia of the towns completely overrode the agrarian population. Shaykh 'Ali Sulayman, to take a remarkable instance, has registered over 12,000 tribesmen which means that if the final number of primary electors including 'Anah may be taken at about 50,000, he controls about half the division. Besides this he has a seat in the Assembly as tribal representative.' Intelligence Report, 1 November 1923: CO 730/43/54840.

42 Apparently the *khutba* was being still read in Baghdad (though not in other towns) in the name of the sultan-caliph. Later Faysal and his father Husayn were mentioned jointly. (See High Commissioner to Secretary of State for the Colonies, Secret Despatch of 22 November 1923: CO 730/43/60034). When Faysal's name was first mentioned in the *khutba* after his coronation, a prominent nationalist is said to have remarked that King George V's name would have been more appropriate. Abstract of Police Intelligence, 27 August 1921. The question was reported as having been resolved in the Intelligence Report of 7 February 1924. CO 730/57/7995.

43 High Commissioner, Baghdad, to Secretary of State for the Colonies, Secret Despatch of 22 November 1923, CO 730/43/60034.

44 High Commissioner, Baghdad, to Secretary of State for the Colonies, 24 January 1924, Telegram 54 The Iraqi government asked to be allowed to send a delegation to London; Major Young minuted his annoyance at 'this rather impertinent proposal.' CO 730/57/3931.

45 See below.

46 Dobbs to Shuckburgh, Private and Personal, 27 December 1923: CO 730/55/1235 (included with 1924 papers).

47 High Commissioner, Baghdad, to Secretary of State for the Colonies, Telegram 129, 11 March 1924: CO 730/58/11898.

48   Acting High Commissioner, Baghdad, to Secretary of State for the Colonies, Telegram 211 of 17 April 1924: CO 730/58/18923.

49   Secretary of State for the Colonies to High Commissioner, Baghdad, Telegram 181 of 26 April 1924: CO 730/58/19150.

50   Secretary of State for the Colonies to High Commissioner, Baghdad, Telegram 213 of 14 May 1924; Secretary of State for the Colonies to High Commissioner, Baghdad, Telegram 218 of 19 May 1924: CO 730/59/22744, 23489.

51   There were unsubstantiated rumours that Salim al-Khayyun was working for the exiled Sayyid Talib. Intelligence Reports, 15 May, 12 June 1924: CO 730/59/25048, 60/29844. High Commissioner, Baghdad, to Secretary of State for the Colonies, Telegram 312 of 23 June 1924: CO 730/60/29934.

52   High Commissioner, Baghdad, to Secretary of State for the Colonies, Telegram 282 of 2 June 1924. Minute by H.W. Young, 7 June 1924: CO 730/60/26555.

53   Secretary of State for the Colonies to High Commissioner, Baghdad, Telegram 249, 16 June 1924: CO 730/66/29037.

54   Shuckburgh to Dobbs, demi-official, 24 January 1924: CO 730/64/3166.

55   Sir Henry Dobbs to Sir John Shuckburgh, demi-official, 7 February 1924: CO 730/71/8246.

56   High Commissioner, Baghdad, to Secretary of State for the Colonies, Confidential Despatch 'B', 10 June 1924: CO 730/60/29840.

57   'My own view is that it would be far better to secure a somewhat more loosely worded agreement, the working of which will, as a matter of fact, be quite as satisfactory as our present arrangements are, than to force the Iraqi government now *jurare in verba magistri* and to be faced with the possibility of having to evacuate Iraq because we have, after angry discussions over verbal points, failed to secure the passage of the agreement through the Constituent Assembly.' High Commissioner, Baghdad, to Secretary of State for the Colonies, Confidential Despatch of 18 October 1923: CO 730/42/52434.

58   See Chapter 6.

59   CP 235 (25), 11 May 1925: CO 730/82/22162.

60   For Yasin's acquisitions, see Kedourie (1970): 268– 69. Both Yasin and Nuri returned to Iraq with nothing: 'The state of affairs which permits the State Domains Department to dish out lands wholesale to politicians and the like while ignoring the requirements of the Government itself is highly anomalous. Only quite recently, as you may have heard, the large estate of Abu 'Ausaj has been granted to four politicians including Nuri al-Sa'id and Mahmud Ramiz.' Edmonds to Holt, DO C/2100/63/12/8 of 25 June 1929. Delhi, BHCF, 'Personalities', File 27/411, Salim al-Khayyun. For Sa'dun, see 'Situation on the Shatt al-Gharraf 1927–30'. Air 23/121. This concerns the struggle between the Mayyah sarkals and the Sa'dun landlords in Hayy *qadha*, Kut *liwa* . 'The *mallaks* (landowners) 'Abd al-Razzaq al-Sa'dun, Muhammad al-Sa'dun, 'Abd al-Karim al-Sa'dun, 'Abd al-Rahman al-Sa'dun) all had the assistance of their brother 'Abd al-Muhsin al-Sa'dun a couple of years ago in getting reinstated on some of the *muqata'as* (which are registered tapu lands) on which they live as landlords.' (RAF) Special Service Officer, Nasiriyah to Air Headquarters, I/'N/4, 7 August 1927.

Chapter 3

1   See pages 8–9 and p. 246, note 3. In retrospect, the only one of the stated

objectives of IEF 'D' that could be described as an unqualified success was that it did manage to maintain the flow of oil from the Anglo-Persian Oil Company's refinery at Abadan.

2　G. Kidston, Foreign Office, to Sir George Clerk, then attending the Paris Peace Conference, 29 July 1919, Balfour Papers, FO 800/217.

3　Churchill was First Lord of the Admiralty from October 1911 to May 1915; Fisher was First Sea Lord between 1904 and 1910 and again between 1914 to 1915.

4　At this stage the wider commercial use of Persian oil does not seem to have been given much consideration: 'The APOC urge that as fuel oil cannot be remuneratively shipped from the Persian Gulf to markets west of the Suez Canal in competition with oil produced from Russia and Rumanian oilfields, the only likely outlet for Persian oil, other than the Admiralty, is with the Indian Railways.' Admiralty to India Office, 26 March 1912. L P & S 10 3877/1912/1/4743.

5　W.S. Churchill, speech in House of Commons, 17 July 1913, quoted in *Agreement with Anglo-Persian Oil Co. Ltd. with an Explanatory Memorandum and the Report of the Committee of Experts on their Local Investigations*, Cmd. 7419, 1914.

6　These interests were:

Company	Capital	Nationality
Royal Dutch Shell	£20, 000	Anglo-Dutch
National Bank of Turkey	£28, 000	British
Deutsche Bank	£20, 000	German
C. S. Gulbenkian	£12, 000	Ottoman

7　The Company was constituted as follows:

Participating Company	Capital	Nationality
Anglo-Persian	£80, 000	British *
Deutsche Bank	£40, 000	German *
Anglo-Saxon	£40, 000	Anglo-Dutch

* Mr. Gulbenkian's 5% was divided between the APOC and the Deutsche Bank.

8　Quoted in Secretary of State for Foreign Affairs to Ambassador, Constantinople (Sir Gerard Lowther), Despatch No. 239 of 5 June 1913; India Office, L P & S 10 3877/1912/1913/1/2222.

9　In the spring of 1919 General Sir John Cowans arrived in Mesopotamia to negotiate for oil concessions, accompanied by two geologists, Messrs. Noble and Evans. According to one Foreign Office source, quoted in India Office correspondence, Cowans was acting on behalf of the Shell Company, though George Kidston of the Foreign Office noted in the letter quoted on page 66: 'The despatch of General Cowans to Mesopotamia was, I understand, a job put through by the War Office about which neither we (i.e. the Foreign Office) nor the India Office was consulted.' Cowans left Baghdad on 10 May 1919, after his presence had been noted by employees of Standard Oil. Noble and Evans stayed on, apparently continuing their surveying operations. See L P & S 10 2249/1915/1919/2, pp 2191,1733, 4002, 5206.

10　*Correspondence between H. M. Government and the Government of the United States of*

America Respecting Economic Rights in Mandated Territories, Miscellaneous No. 10, 1921, Cmd. 1226.

11 Cabinet Paper E 25, Memorandum by the Minister in Charge of Petroleum Affairs, 30 June 1921; E 7613/382/93: FO 371/6361.

12 Foreign Office Memorandum, 14 March 1918, L P & S 10 249/1915/1918/1/996.

13 See Paper B.322 (September 1918), L P and S 10, 2249/2915/1919/1/4145. In his autobiographical account Sir Arnold Wilson seems a little ingenuous: 'The daily press in Europe and the USA was during the latter part of 1919 and the whole of 1920 full of reference to the fancied connection between the reputed oil deposits of Mesopotamia and the acceptance by Great Britain of the Mandate, and nothing that British statesmen could do or say availed against the attacks and innuendoes appearing in the daily press of Europe and the USA.' Wilson (1931): 216.

14 See page 12.

15 Lord Curzon, Foreign Office, to Ambassador Davis, November 1919, L P & S 10 2249/1915/ 1918/2/7380.

16 See Baker (1922) 1–20.

17 Churchill wrote in 1922: 'H. M. Government, though they maintain that the Turkish Petroleum Company's rights are sound, admit that they were not acquired by the procedure which governed the acquisition of ordinary concessions in Turkey before the War, and it is not possible to say what the result of arbitration would be.' Cabinet Paper C. P. 3832, *Iraq Oil,* circulated by the Secretary of State for the Colonies, 13 March 1922, CO 730/28/7703.

18 See Gerig (1930): 131–141. The possibility of Anglo-American co-operation in the development of Iraqi oil had been mooted as early as 1921. In November of that year Calouste Gulbenkian had an interview with Sir William Tyrell at the Foreign Office, in which he stated that the current Franco-American oil alliance against Britain was being financed by Standard Oil, and that it would be to Britain's advantage to come to early terms with the Americans. Sir Eyre Crowe, commenting on this interview ('This is a most remarkable communication') noted his own belief that ' . . . the Colonial Office are not at all averse to letting the Americans into Mesopotamia.' E 13144/382/93: FO 371/6363. Minutes of 24 and 25 November 1921.

19 Admiralty to Foreign Office M/43677/22 of 6 December 1922, enclosed in Admiralty to Colonial Office, 7 December 1922. CO 730/27/60792.

20 See page 53.

21 Speech by Lord Curzon at Lausanne, 23 January 1923. CO 730/46/4849. In reply to this speech, the Turkish representative Ismet Inönü suggested that the future of the area should be decided by a plebiscite. Beck (1981): 260.

22 Nicolson (1934): 330–331.

23 Note by Lord Curzon, 16 December 1922. FO 839/10 (Lausanne Conference).

24 Secretary of State for the Colonies to High Commissioner, Baghdad, Telegram 1 of 2 January 1923. CO 730/51/635.

25 High Commissioner, Baghdad, to Secretary of State for the Colonies, Telegrams 112 and 113 of 23 February 1925: CO 730/73/9364.

26 Reported in High Commissioner, Baghdad, to Secretary of State for the Colonies, Telegram 120 of 2 March 1925. CO 730/73/10185. See also Barnes and Nicholson (1980): 398–399.

27   The provenance and value of imports were as follows:

Year	Value (dinars)	%age British	%age U.S.A.
1912–13	3.5 million	49	9
1952–58	92.0 million	33.3	15

Muhammad Salman Hasan, 'The Role of Foreign Trade in the Economic Development of Iraq 1864–1964: A Study in the Development of a Dependent Economy,' in Cook (1970): 346–372.

28   See Edmonds (1957): 398, quoted in Monroe (1981): 103–04, and compare J.S. Mann to Gilbert Murray, 21 May 1920: 'I do not think that any political or military officer cares a blow who gets the (oil) wells as long as we get a decent frontier which doesn't break up tribal or other divisions . . . Yes, it is all a tragedy. But we'll beat the oil people yet . . . ' Mann (1921): 263–64.

29   See Sykes to Hirtzel, 16 January 1918, Sykes Papers, FO 800/221.

30   Monroe (1981): 103: Edmonds (1957): 398. For a more recent (and more nuanced) statement see Olson (1991): 149.

31   High Commissioner, Baghdad, to Secretary of State for the Colonies, Despatch, Confidential 'A', 28 February 1924, E 4351/1560/93: FO 371/10108.

32   Author of To Mesopotamia and Kurdistan in disguise : narrative of a journey from Constantinople through Kurdistan to Baghdad, 1907–1909, with historical and ethnographical notices of the various Kurdish tribes and of the Chaldaeans of Kurdistan, London, John Murray, 1926. For a detailed exposition of Britain's Kurdish policy, and its many transformations, see Olson (1991): 52–90.

33   Political, Baghdad, to Secretary of State for India, T. 9267, 30 October 1918. Air 20/512.

34   Noel to Civil Commissioner, Baghdad (undated and unnumbered, but between 23 and 27 November 1918), Air 20/512.

35   His father, Shaykh Sa'id, had been killed in highly suspicious circumstances after having been invited to Mosul by the Ottoman authorities in March 1909. See McDowall (1996): 97, 118–119.

36   Noel to Civil Commissioner, Baghdad, No. 54 of 24 April 1919, Air 20/714.

37   See 'A Note on Northern Kurdistan', by G. L. Bell, 8 March 1920: Air 20/513.

38   It is worth remembering that Turkish/Kurdish relations, which were poor if not downright hostile for much of the twentieth century, were fairly cordial until the outbreak of the Shaykh Sa'id rebellion (which the Iraqi Kurds did not join) in February 1925.

39   See note 37.

40   E.B. Soane, 'Note on the Political Situation in Southern Kurdistan,' April 1920, Air 20/513.

41   However, by this time, and even more so by the end of 1920, the 'growing strength of the Turkish nationalist forces' made it increasingly unlikely that article 62 would be implemented. Olson (1991): 54. Sèvres also made provision for an Armenian state, thought likely to be under United States' mandate. In spite of Woodrow Wilson's evident enthusiasm for the idea, it was clear by the spring of 1920 that the US had no intention of taking it, so that an Armenian state in eastern Anatolia ceased to be a possibility; see McDowall (1996): 131. British attempts to convince the Americans to 'take Armenia' had begun in December 1918; see Stivers (1982): 30, 44, 49–57

42   H. Goldsmith, Political Officer, Sulaymaniya to High Commissioner Baghdad, 14 May 1921. P/1072/1/E. Delhi, BHCF, 'Events in Kurdistan', 13/14/Vol. I.

43   High Commissioner, Baghdad, to Secretary of State for the Colonies, Telegram 201 of 21 June 1921; Kirkuk Report, 11–25 June 1921 (Political Officer, Kirkuk, to High Commissioner, Baghdad) No. 8. BHCF Delhi, 'Events in Kurdistan', 13/14/Vol. I.

44   Much against the better judgement of many British officials in the Kurdish area. See *Kurds, Arabs and Britons: the memoir of Wallace Lyon in Iraq, 1918–1944* (Fieldhouse, 2002)

45   High Commissioner, Baghdad, to Secretary of State for the Colonies, Telegram No. 503 of 20 September 1921: Secretary of State for the Colonies to High Commissioner, Baghdad, Telegram 423 of 3 October 1921. E 12182/43/93: FO 371/6347.

46   Sir Percy Cox to King Faysal, 4 January 1922. Delhi, BHCF, 'Events in Kurdistan', 3/14/ Vol.II

47   If Kirkuk *liwa* was designated as an electoral college, this implied that it was part of Iraq. E. Noel, Sulaymaniya, to B. H. Bourdillon, Baghdad, 10 October 1922. Delhi, BHCF, Events in Kurdistan, 13/14/Vol. II.

48   C.J. Edmonds, Kirkuk, to B.H. Bourdillon, Baghdad, K 847 of 26 October 1922, Delhi, BHCF, 'Events in Kurdistan', 13/14/Vol.II.

49   By March 1922 some officials in London had become convinced that 'the Turkish nationalists have the Kurds in their pockets'. Olson (1991): 80.

50   Noel, Arbil, to High Commissioner, Baghdad, 21 December 1922. Delhi, BHCF, 'Events in Kurdistan', Vol. II.

51   It is significant that correspondence captured later in the year revealed Turkish plans to penetrate as far south as Khaniqin, 70 miles south of Sulaymaniya and only 80 miles north east of Baghdad. See Minute by J. E. Shuckburgh, 30 April 1923 on CO 730/48/23813, and High Commissioner, Baghdad to Secretary of State for the Colonies, 10 May 1923, CO 730/40/24591.

52   High Commissioner, Baghdad, to Administrative Inspectors, Mosul, Kirkuk and Arbil, Telegram 188/S of 6 April 1923. Delhi, BHCF, 'Events in Kurdistan', 13/14/ Vol. III.

53   High Commissioner, Baghdad, to Secretary of State for the Colonies, Telegram 543 of 1 October 1923. Delhi, BHCF, Events in Kurdistan, 13/14/ Vol.III.

54   High Commissioner, Baghdad, to Secretary of State for the Colonies, Secret 'A' of 28 May 1925, enclosing Air Officer Commanding's report 'Operations on the Northern Frontier of Iraq, September – November 1924', CO 730/75/25923.

55   cf. 'The Mosul vilayat, [the British Government] claimed, was naturally, economically and ethnographically part of Iraq:' Lloyd (1926). As far as the Turkish government was concerned, Mosul had been included in the Turkish National Pact of 1920 (essentially a rejoinder to the Treaty of Sèvres) and for that reason could not easily be relinquished. Beck (1981): 256.

56   Arrived at by a sub-commission of the League in Brussels in October 1924; it eventually became the permanent frontier.

57   Sulaymaniya was attacked by Shaykh Mahmud on 7 September 1924: See Intelligence Report, 18 September 1924, CO 730/62/46069. It was bombed on 7 November: see High Commissioner, Baghdad to Secretary of State for the Colonies, Telegram 574 of 8 November 1924, CO 730/63/53102.

58 High Commissioner, Baghdad, to Secretary of State for the Colonies, Despatch, Secret, 26 February 1925, CO 730/72/10992. For the text of the Protocol, see page 55.

59 Cf. C.J. Edmonds' Diary, 5 March 1925. CO 730/72/12194: 'Report of the British Assessor to the Frontier Commission 19–22 March 1925', enclosed in High Commissioner, Baghdad to Secretary of State for the Colonies, Despatch, Secret, 26 March 1925. CO 730/74/15900: Arbil Report, March 1925, enclosed in High Commissioner, Baghdad to Secretary of State for the Colonies, SO. 817 of 9 April 1925. CO 730/74/17892.

60 Though there is some evidence of intimidation: 'The Tohalla family are patrolling the town in groups with strict instructions that should they meet any of the Turkish representatives of the Frontier Commission they should assault him Anyone who shouted for the Turks when the Commission arrived was set upon and beaten up'. Abstract of Police Intelligence, 31 January 1925.

61 See page 74.

62 Quoted Ireland (1937): 406–407.

63 Abstract of Police Intelligence, 9 January 1926.

64 Abstract of Police Intelligence, 6 February 1926.

65 See page 124.

66 Article III of *Treaty between the United Kingdom and Iraq, signed at Baghdad 13 January 1926.* Cmd. 2587, 1926.

67 See Chapter 6.

68 See the Economic Reports for July, October, November and December 1925. CO 730/76/35730, CO 730/79/49541/54917, 57327.

69 High Commissioner, Baghdad, to Secretary of State for the Colonies, Telegram 244 of 8 May 1924. CO 730/59/22213.

70 See *Hansard*, 18 February 1926. The £3.9 million (actually £3,893,400) was divided as follows:

Defence (RAF)	£3,112,900
Grant in Aid – Iraq Levies	617,000
Grant in Aid – Iraq Army	135,000
Other (including moiety of expenses of High Commission)	28,500
	£3,893,400
(For comparative purposes) Cost of RAF in Egypt and Sudan, 1925–26	£1,170,000

CO 730/101/3532.

71 Acting High Commissioner, Baghdad, to Secretary of State for the Colonies, Despatch Secret 'C' of 7 January 1926. CO 730/92/1535.

72 See Chapter 7.

73 B. H. Bourdillon to Sir John Shuckburgh, Private and Personal Telegram No. 12 of 6 January 1926: 'It is of course not known to Iraqi government that subsidy up to 1931 was contained in Air Ministry scheme.' E 244/44/93: FO 371/11457.

74 'Full allowance must, I respectfully submit, be given to the stage of self-

government now reached in Iraq. It is not possible, with an elected parliament and a friendly but insecure Government that needs not only careful and tactful handling but also considerable support . . . to force through measures for higher taxation.' Acting High Commissioner, Baghdad, to S/S Colonies, Despatch Confidential 'C' of 7 January 1926. CO 730/92/1531. See Chapter 6.

75   *Report of the Financial Mission Appointed to enquire into the Financial Position and prospects of the Government of Iraq*, Cmd. 2438, 1925. The letter of appointment is dated 3 March 1925: See CO 730/82/9925.

76   *al-'Iraq*, 6 May, 9 May. Intelligence Report, 14 May 1925. CO 730/75/23974.

77   Acting High Commissioner, Baghdad, to Secretary of State for the Colonies, Despatch Secret 'C' of 7 January 1926. CO 730/92/1535.

78   See King Faysal to Acting High Commissioner, Secret, 30 December 1925 enclosed in Acting High Commissioner, Baghdad, to Secretary of State for the Colonies, Secret 'A', 30 December 1925. CO 730/92/872.

79   Acting High Commissioner, Baghdad, to Secretary of State for the Colonies, Telegram 39 of 22 January 1926. CO 730/92/2026.

80   i.e. 1.6 million gold Turkish liras (= *livres turques d'or*). *Report on the Progress of Iraq 1920–1931*, p. 127.

81   L.S. Amery, Private and Personal, to W.S. Churchill, 29 April 1926. CO 730/ 93/9075.

82   Intelligence Report, 6 July 1926. CO 730/105/312.

83   'You need not be alarmed about our 25 years' mandate. If we go on as fast as we've gone for the last two years, Iraq will be a member of the League before five or six years have passed, and our direct responsibility will have ceased.' Gertrude Bell to her father, 13 January 1926, Bell (1939): 747.

Chapter 4

1   *Taqaddum* = progress, *Sha'b* = people, *Nahdha* = renaissance. The *Taqaddum* Party was the bloc of moderates who could be relied upon to support more or less any measure the Government put forward, the *Sha'b* were on the whole anti-Government and anti-British, while the *Nahdha* stood in the main for Shi'i interests. See Appendix I for a more detailed analysis.

2   S. O. 2671, Bourdillon to Shuckburgh, 4 November 1926. Delhi, BHCF, Cabinet Formations, File 23/14/5; Formation of a Cabinet under 'Abd al-Muhsin Beg al-Sa'dun July 1925–November 1926.

3   The Iraqi Air Force eventually came into existence in 1931, when five pilots were sent for training at RAF Cranwell. There were constant complaints in the 1930s about Britain's failure to supply aeroplanes and other equipment.

4   Minute by Dobbs on Memorandum from Adviser, Ministry of Defence, to High Commissioner, M. D/C/76 Confidential of 28 March 1925. Minute dated 26 April 1925. CO 730/82/24432.

5   Despatch, Secret, High Commissioner, Baghdad, to Secretary of State for the Colonies, 16 April 1925. CO 730/74/19004.

6   High Commissioner, Baghdad, to Secretary of State for the Colonies, Despatch, Secret of 16 September 1926, enclosing Major-General Daly's memorandum of 7 March 1926. CO 730/95/18538.

7   Adviser, Minister of Interior, to Secretariat of H. E. the High Commissioner, C/ 2341/8/3 of 22 August 1926. Delhi, BHCF, Military, File 4/69 Vol. I, Conscription.

8   High Commissioner, Baghdad, to Secretary of State for the Colonies, Despatch, Secret, 1 September 1926. CO 730/95/17572.

9   Minute, dated 18 November 1926. CO 730/96/19851.

10 Report of a conversation with King Faysal, 13 May 1927. Enclosed in High Commissioner, Baghdad, to Secretary of State for the Colonies Secret 'D', 3 May 1927. Delhi, BHCF, Military, File 4/69 Vol. I, Conscription.

11 High Commissioner, Baghdad, to Secretary of State for the Colonies, Telegram 229 of 18 May 1927, CO 730/108/40008.

12 See Delhi, BHCF, Cabinet Formations, File 23/14/7, Cabinet Crisis, May–June 1927.

13 Abstract of Police Intelligence, 28 May 1927. For a more detailed discussion of the Shi'i position and Shi'i politics generally at this time, see Appendix I.

14 These supporters included Muhsin Abu Tabikh, Salman al-Yasiri, Mizhir al-Fira'un, Naji al-Salih, 'Abd al-Wahid Sikkar, 'Abadi al-Husayn. All these were reported as pro-conscription in Abstract of Police Intelligence, 18 June 1927. It is bewildering to follow the two latter shaykhs' allegiances: 'Abd al-Wahid supported conscription until mid-September, when he joined the *Hizb al-Nahdha*; (see Appendix I), while 'Abadi al-Husayn had had an interview with Bourdillon at the Residency three weeks before the report above associating him with the pro-conscription lobby in which: 'He asked me straight out about conscription. He said that the Shi'is outside were under the impression that H. M. Government were opposed to conscription and were very pleased in consequence.' Note by B. H. Bourdillon, 20 May 1927. Delhi, BHCF, Military, File 4/69 Vol. 1, Conscription.

15 The telegram concludes: 'I regret to say that Faysal did not appear to be convinced . . . He is very *tête montée* owing to the glorification of him in Lawrence's book and has apparently set his heart on an early visit to London.' High Commissioner, Baghdad, to Secretary of State for the Colonies, Telegram. 241 of 27 May 1927. CO 730/108/40008.

16 Abstract of Police Intelligence, 31 May 1927.

17 Secretary of State for the Colonies to High Commissioner, Baghdad, Telegram 183 of 1 June 1927. Delhi, BHCF, Military, File 4/69 Vol. I, Conscription. High Commissioner, Baghdad, to Secretary of State for the Colonies, Telegram 262 of 10 June 1927, CO 730/108/40004.

18 High Commissioner, Baghdad, to Secretary of State for the Colonies, Despatch, Secret, 31 March 1927. CO 730/119/40199, Part I.

19 Dobbs to Amery, D.O. S.O. 1334, 14 June 1927. CO 730/120/40229, Part II.

20 Report of a conversation between Sir Samuel Wilson and Sir Hugh Trenchard at the Colonial Office, 28 June 1927, CO 730/120/40299, Part II.

21 A British-officered force recruited from Assyrian refugees from western Iran and south-eastern Turkey, most of whom had arrived in Iraq after the British capture of Baghdad in March 1917.

22 Cab 38(27) 4 July 1927: Secretary of State for the Colonies to High Commissioner, Baghdad, Telegram 232, 6 July 1927. CO 730/120/40299, Part II. By the end of September, no public statement had been made in Baghdad, and it was widely assumed in Iraq that substantial changes, even admission to the League, were still being negotiated. See *Iraq: Suggested Treaty Revision*, Middle East Department of the Colonial Office, 28 September 1927, CO 730/120/40299 A, Part I.

23   The Colonial Secretary gave his personal sanction to these discussions since full British Cabinet approval was impossible to obtain before his summer tour.

24   Secretary of State for the Colonies to Acting High Commissioner, Baghdad, Telegram. 258 of 21 July 1927. CO 730/120/40299, Part II.

25   On the way to Europe, King Faysal stopped at Cyprus to visit his father, ex-King Husayn of the Hijaz. The Governor of Cyprus, Sir Ronald Storrs, reported: 'In the course of a long conversation this morning Faysal confided his intention of 'abdicating' unless he got a satisfactory agreement in Switzerland, where he thinks he is going to meet Dobbs or Shuckburgh. The remark was clearly released for me to pass on, which I do for what it may be worth. After lunch we taught him and Zayd golf croquet, a great alleviation.' Storrs to Ormsby-Gore, 10 August 1927. CO 730/120/40299, Part II.

26   Abstract of Police Intelligence, 20 August 1927.

27   *Conversations with King Faysal at Aix-les-Bains, 5 to 7 September 1927*. Report by Sir John Shuckburgh, printed by the Middle East Department of the Colonial Office, September 1927. C0730/120/40299, Part II.

28   See Appendix I and Luizard (1991).

29   These groupings are not intended to be anything more than a rough guide to the positions of the more important political figures. Not all of them can be accommodated: 'Abd al-Muhsin al-Sa'dun, for example, is difficult to classify with any of these groups, and many of the tribal leaders such as 'Abd al-Wahid al-Sikkar and 'Abadi al-Husayn follow complicated courses of action much as has been indicated for Muhsin Abu'l-Tabikh.

30   Abstract of Police Intelligence, 8 January, 5 February, 19 March 1927.

31   Fortnightly Intelligence Report, 26 April 1927.

32   Fortnightly Intelligence Report, 15 February 1927.

33   Fortnightly Intelligence Report, 5 July 1927. For further details see Air 23/121. The dispute continued until the following spring, the Government taking up the cause of the *mallaks*, who were substantially sided by their powerful brother, 'Abd al-Muhsin al-Sa'dun. For details of Sa'dun's part in the affair, see p. 258 note 60.

34   See generally Delhi, BHCF, Miscellaneous File 34/83/1, Riot at Kadhimain on 10 July 1927. The quotation is from Edmonds to Bourdillon, D.O. SA 12 July 1927. cf. a similar incident at Basra where soldiers attempted to interfere with the Muharram procession: Special Service Officer, Basra, to Air Headquarters, Baghdad I/799 of 17 July 1927. Air 23/432.

35   Note of 10 August 1927 in Delhi, BHCF, Press and Propaganda, File 29/93, *al-Nahdha*.

36   Cornwallis to Acting High Commissioner, SA/97 of 23 October 1927, protesting against the suspension of *al-Nahdha* without Cornwallis' permission: Acting High Commissioner, Baghdad, to Secretary of State for the Colonies, Telegram 524 of 28 October 1927, reporting Yasin's resignation: High Commissioner, Baghdad, to Secretary of State for the Colonies, Telegram 611 of 20 December 1927, reporting Rashid 'Ali's resignation. Delhi, BHCF, Press and Propaganda, File 29/93, *al-Nahdha*.

37   RAF Special Service Officer, Baghdad to Air Headquarters, I/Bd/39, 14 November 1927. Air 23/432.

38   Apparently Amin al-Charchafchi and Fakhri al-Kammuna had taken this oath: see Fortnightly Intelligence Report, 6 August 1927.

39 Intelligence Report, 21 December 1927: Abstract of Police Intelligence, 17, 24 December 1927. al-Charchafchi's attitude also lost him the support of other Shi'is, notably Ridha al-Shabibi and Ja'far Abu'l-Timman who considered that 'touting for British support was directly opposed to the idea of national freedom.' See RAF Special Service Officer to Air Headquarters I/Bd/35 of 22 December 1927. Air 23/432.

40 'Note on the Political Situation to 27 September 1927', by C. J. Edmonds enclosed in D.O. 2032 Sturges to Shuckburgh, 1 October 1927. CO 730/123/ 40465.

41 See *Iraq: suggested Treaty Revision*, Memorandum prepared in the Middle East Department of the Colonial Office, 28 September 1927. CO 730/120/40299 A Part I.

42 Memorandum by Sir Henry Dobbs, 18 October 1927. CO 730/123/40465. The strike at Baba Gurgur was on 15 October.

43 Memorandum for Sir John Shuckburgh, 11 November 1927. CO 730/120/ 42088A Part II.

44 Report of a meeting between King Faysal and Sir Henry Dobbs, 17–8 November 1927, CO 730/120/40299 A Part II.

45 Secretary of State for the Colonies to Acting High Commissioner, Baghdad Telegram 414, 18 November 1927. Note by Dobbs for Shuckburgh, 24 November 1927: CO 730/120/40299A, Part II.

46 *Memorandum of events subsequent to the breaking off of discussions with King Faysal on 18 November,* 29 November 1927.

47 Or even to encourage them to oppose the Prime Minister: Faysal was reported to have told Amin al-Charchafchi to work ostensibly with 'Abd al-Muhsin, but in fact to take orders from Yasin, and work against 'Abd al-Muhsin, if he wished to secure his rights. Abstract of Police Intelligence 28 January 1928.

48 Neither of the two Shi'is was closely connected with the *Hizb al-Nahdha*. See Abstract of Police Intelligence, 14 January 1928.

49 High Commissioner, Baghdad, to Secretary of State for the Colonies, Telegram 612 of 20 December 1927. CO 730/125/40626.

50 High Commissioner, Baghdad to Secretary of State for the Colonies, Telegram 14 of 8 January 1928. Delhi, BHCF, Cabinet Formations, File 24/14/8, Formation of a Cabinet under 'Abd al-Muhsin al-Sa'dun.

51 Dobbs to Shuckburgh, DO. SO 259 1 February 1928. CO 730/128/58003; *Hansard*, 23 April 1928. See *Iraq Times*, 25 April 1928.

52 The total cost to Britain was divided as follows:

	1928–1929	1929–1930
RAF	232,000	185,000
Levies	225,000	200,000
Indian Battalion	63 000	—
Grant in Aid to Army	75,000	75,000
Moiety of High Commission expenses	25,000	25,000
	620, 000	485, 000

Trenchard to Shuckburgh, 31 October 1927. CO 730/125/40607.

53 High Commissioner, Baghdad to Secretary of State for the Colonies, Telegram 211 of 10 April 1928. CO 730/129/58011.

54 Fortnightly Intelligence Report, 18 January 1928.

55 See High Commissioner, Baghdad, to Secretary of State for the Colonies, Telegram 82 of 9 February 1928: Secret Police Report, Wilkins to Dobbs, 12 February: Smith (Inspector-General of Education) to Dobbs, 19 February: D. O. R. O. 49, Dobbs to Faysal 20 February, suggesting that it was unwise to bring political offenders before the courts, but recommending their exile under section 40 of the *TCCDR*. Delhi, BHCF, Interior, File 7/17/144. Anti-Zionist Demonstration on the occasion of the visit of Sir Alfred Mond to Iraq, 1928. It is of some interest that this incident was the first of its kind in Iraq.

56 Fortnightly Intelligence Report, 1 February 1928. One of these was Muhi al-Din of the Kadhimain riot.

57 Abstracts of Police Intelligence, 18, 25 February 1928.

58 Fortnightly Intelligence Report, 23 May 1928.

59 Baghdad:Abstract of Police Intelligence 12 May 1928: Basra and Mosul: Fortnightly Intelligence Report 23 May 1928: Kut: See A.I. Kut to Adviser, Minister of Interior S/543/91 of 3 June 1928, which contains reports of 'fantastic' exaggerations in the lists of primary voters submitted to the election committees: ' . . . of these irregularities some have been caused by the practical impossibility of applying the letter of the law to a purely tribal area such as this division: others can only be described as deliberate.' Enclosed in High Commissioner, Baghdad, to Secretary of State for the Colonies, Despatch Secret 'B' of 16 June 1928. CO 730/130/58139.

60 High Commissioner, Baghdad, to Secretary of State for the Colonies, Telegram 423 of 18 August 1928. CO 730/134/58400. See Chapter 7.

61 Intelligence Report, 26 September 1928: cf. Ireland (1937): 368.

62 Gertrude Bell was Oriental Secretary from 1916 to 1926: she was succeeded by Captain Vyvyan Holt who served from 1926 to 1947.

63 For the 'orthodox' policy see Secretary of State for the Colonies to High Commissioner, Baghdad, telegram 423, 25 October 1928: 'The ultimate control of the defence forces of Iraq, whether British or Iraqi, must remain in British hands as long as final responsibility for the defence of the country rests with H. M. Government.' Clayton Papers, University of Durham, Box 472/13.

64 High Commissioner, Baghdad, to Secretary of State for the Colonies, Despatch Secret 'B' of 20 October 1928. CO 730/134/58400.

65 Secretary of State for the Colonies to High Commissioner, Baghdad, Telegram 633 of 31 December 1928. CO 730/134/58400.

66 High Commissioner, Baghdad to Secretary of State for the Colonies, Telegram 633 of 31 December 1928. CO 730/134/58400 Part II.

67 Minute on High Commissioner's Telegram 524 of 16 October 1928 by G. Jebb (Foreign Office) 18 October 1928: E5000/133/93, FO 371/13035.

68 High Commissioner, Baghdad to Secretary of State for the Colonies, Despatch Confidential 'B', 4 December 1928. Clayton Papers, University of Durham, Box 472/13.

69 High Commissioner, Baghdad to Secretary of State for the Colonies, Telegram 48 of 29 January 1929.Delhi, BHCF,Cabinet Formations, File 23/14/8. Formation of a Cabinet under 'Abd al-Muhsin Beg al-Sa'dun.

70 High Commissioner, Baghdad to Secretary of State for the Colonies, Despatch, Secret 31 January 1929. Delhi, BHCF, Military, File 4/69 Vol. II Conscription.
71 Cab 12 (29), Meeting of 20 March 1929. CO 730/146/68354 I 'B'.
72 Cabinet Paper C. P. 125 (29) 24 April 1929. CO 730/146/68354/I 'B'.
73 Draft Memorandum, Colonial Office, 29 April 1929. CO 730/146/68354 I 'B'.
74 Abstract of Police Intelligence, 16 February 1929.
75 High Commissioner, Baghdad, to Secretary of State for the Colonies, Tgms. 110, 111 of 14 March 1929, printed in C. P. 103 (29) CO 730/139/68015 Part II.
76 Secretary of State for the Colonies to High Commissioner, Baghdad, Telegram 108 of 25 March 1929. CO 730/139/68015 Part II.
77 Abstract of Police Intelligence, 16 March 1929.
78 Note of an interview with King Faysal 24 April 1929. Delhi, BHCF Cabinet Formations File 23/14/9: Cabinet of Taufiq Beg al-Suwaidi.
79 Ma'ruf al-Chiawuk, Nuri al-Sa'id, Ahmad al-Da'ud, Naji Shawkat, Isma'il al-Rawanduzi, Jamil al-Rawi, Jalal Baban.
80 High Commissioner, Baghdad, to Secretary of State for the Colonies Despatch, Secret 'B' , 13 May 1929. Delhi, BHCF, Cabinet Formations, File 23/14/9, Cabinet of Taufiq Beg al-Suwaidi.
81 Note of an interview with 'Abd al-Muhsin al-Sa'dun, 17 June 1929: enclosed in C.J. Edmonds to Sir Gilbert Clayton, 17 June 1929. Delhi, BHCF, Cabinet Formations File 23/14/9: Cabinet of Taufiq Beg al-Suwaidi.
82 Note by Shuckburgh, 1 July 1929. CO 730/148/68043.
83 High Commissioner, Baghdad, to Secretary of State for the Colonies, Despatch, Secret 'B' of 22 July 1929, CO 730/148/68444 Part I.
84 Secretary of State for the Colonies to High Commissioner, Baghdad, Telegram 264 of 11 September 1929: Acting High Commissioner, Baghdad to Secretary of State for the Colonies, Despatch, Secret 'A' of 23 September 1929. CO 730/148/68403.
85 High Commissioner, Baghdad to Secretary of State for the Colonies, Telegram 323 of 16 September 1929. Delhi, BHCF, 'Cabinet Formations', File 23/14/10: Formation of Cabinet under 'Abd al-Muhsin Beg al-Sa'dun.

Chapter 5

1 Abstract of Police Intelligence, 29 September 1929.
2 Abstract of Police Intelligence, 5 October 1929.
3 Smith to Dobbs, 15 November 1929, enclosed in Dobbs to Shuckburgh, 1 December 1929 (Dobbs had retired by then). CO 730/148/68444, Part II.
4 As sent to London in High Commissioner, Baghdad to Secretary of State for the Colonies, Telegram 401 of 14 November: 'The nation expects service and the British do not agree. I have no helper, and the Iraqis, who claim independence, are weak and incompetent and very far away from independence. They are also unable to appreciate the advice of a man of honour like myself. They call me a traitor to my country and a servant of the British. What a calamity this is, I am a most sincere martyr to my country.' Doctored versions of the letter, edifying the Iraqis and condemning the British, were circulated to local newspapers. See Delhi, Personalities File 27/598, 'Abd al-Muhsin al-Sa'dun.
5 Report of a conversation with Naji al-Suwaydi by Sir Francis Humphrys,

6 March 1930. Delhi, BHCF, Cabinet Formations, File 23/14/11, Cabinet of Naji Beg Al-Suwaydi.

6   With Jalal Baban, Jamil al-Rawi and 'Abd al-Husayn Chalabi at Justice, Communications and Works and Education respectively.

7   High Commissioner, Baghdad, to Secretary of State for the Colonies, Telegram 172 of 26 March 1930: Delhi, BHCF, Cabinet Formations, File 23/14/12: Cabinets of Nuri al-Sa'id.

8   Fortnightly Intelligence Report, 31 March 1930.

9   For the limitations on this responsibility, see pages 156–158.

10 *Treaty between Great Britain and Iraq signed at Baghdad on 30 June 1930*. Cmd. 3797, *Accounts and Papers*, 1929–1930, Vol. XXXIV.

11 *Proceedings of Chamber of Deputies*, 21 January 1926. Delhi, BHCF, Events in Kurdistan, File 13/14 Vol. V. As mentioned earlier, the text of the treaty contained no specific guarantees for the Kurds. McDowall (1996):170.

12 Note on the position of the Ministry of Education as regards Kurdish Schools, by Lionel Smith, 5 May 1926: Delhi, BHCF, Education, File 5/4/8 Vol. 1, Kurdish Education.

13 Dobbs to Cornwallis, DO SO 1372 of 25 June 1926: Delhi, BHCF, Education, File 5/4/8 Vol. I, Kurdish Education.

14 A. I. Sulaymaniya C/252 to Adviser, Ministry of Interior of 1 June 1927: Delhi, BHCF, File 13/22 Vol. II, Shaykh Mahmud.

15 Clayton to Shaykh Mahmud, No. 5049 of 5 May 1929, Delhi, BHCF, File 13/22 Vol. II, Shaykh Mahmud.

16 Shaykh Mahmud to Clayton, 27 May 1929, Delhi, BHCF, File 13/22 Vol. II, Shaykh Mahmud.

17 A. I. Sulaymaniya to Adviser, Ministry of Interior, C/1263 of 4 November 1929: Delhi, BHCF, File 13/22, Vol. III, Shaykh Mahmud.

18 A. I. Sulaymaniya to Adviser, Ministry of Interior, C/2/7/1, 4 January 1930: Delhi, BHCF, File 13/22, Vol. IV, Shaykh Mahmud.

19 Bourdillon to Ja'far al-'Askari, D. O. P. O. 104 of 7 March 1927. The railway, which would cover a distance of about 80 miles, would have cost between 80,000 and 100,000 rupees (£12,000–£15,000). Delhi, BHCF, Events in Kurdistan, File 13/14 Vol. V.

20 Edmonds to Holt, D.O. S.A. 232, 9 May 1928: Delhi, BHCF, Events in Kurdistan, File 13/14 Vol. V.

21 Letter to Prime Minister of 4 April 1929. Delhi, BHCF. Events in Kurdistan, File13/14, Vol. VI.

22 Abstract of Police Intelligence, 26 April 1929.

23 Clayton to Sa'dun, D.O. P.O. 139 of 20 April 1929: Delhi, BHCF, Events in Kurdistan File 13/14 Vol. VI.

24 Cornwallis to Clayton, S.A. 321 of 12 May, enclosing Edmonds' memo of 11 May 1929: Delhi, BHCF Events in Kurdistan, File 13/14 Vol. VI.

25 Minute by H. W. Young, 21 January 1930: Delhi, BHCF, Events in Kurdistan, File 13/14 Vol. VII.

26 Administrative Inspector, Arbil, to Adviser, Ministry of Interior, S/123 of 11 February 1930: Administrative Inspector, Kirkuk to Adviser, Ministry of Interior, S/78 of 10 February 1930: Delhi, BHCF, Events in Kurdistan, File 13/14 Vol. VII.

27   The paper includes the estimated percentage of Kurds in the various *liwas*:

Arbil   78.6
Kirkuk   49.5
Mosul   70.0 (the *qadhas* of Zakho, Zibar, 'Amadiya, 'Aqra and Dohuk)
Sulaymaniya   90.0

Adviser, Ministry of Interior, to Secretariat containing paper for Minister of Interior, C/1183/27/3, 3 April 1930: Delhi, BHCF, Events in Kurdistan, File 13/14, Vol. VII.

28   Communiqué issued by Iraq Prime Minister, 8 April 1930: Delhi, BHCF, Events in Kurdistan, File 13/14 Vol. VII.

29   Amin Zaki to Humphrys, 30 May 1931: Delhi, BHCF, Education, 5/1/103, Local Languages Law. The writer also complained about government neglect of Kurdish education. In 1927, the Government spent 1% of the revenues of Sulaymaniya, 3% of Arbil, 38% of Baghdad, and 18% of Karbala' on education.

30   Council of Ministers to Secretariat, Confidential 2080 of 17 July 1930, Enclosed in High Commissioner, Baghdad, to Secretary of State for the Colonies, Secret 'B' of 23 July 1930: Delhi, BHCF, Events in Kurdistan, File 13/14 Vol. VIII.

31   There are three thick bound volumes of Kurdish petitions covering the period 1930–1931. Delhi, BHCF, Kurdish Petitions, File 13/14/B, Vols. I–III.

32   Meeting of Council of the League of Nations, 13–16 January 1930, League of Nations, *Official Journal*, February 1930, pp 142–143.

33   RAF Special Services Officer, Sulaymaniya to Air Headquarters, I/S/I of 12 August 1930. Delhi, BHCF, Events in Kurdistan, File 13/14 Vol. VIII.

34   Acting High Commissioner, Baghdad, to Secretary of State for the Colonies, Telegram 381 of 18 August 1930: Delhi, BHCF. Events in Kurdistan, File 13/14 Vol. VIII.

35   Cornwallis to Jamil Midfa'i 19 August 1930, enclosed in Fortnightly Intelligence Report, 2 September 1930.

36   Secretary of State for the Colonies to Acting High Commissioner, Baghdad, Telegram 333 of 2 September 1930: Minutes by R.S.M. Sturges 3 September. Delhi, BHCF, Events in Kurdistan File 13/14 Vol. IX.

37   Précis of Events 1 June to 4 December 1930, Air Headquarters, undated and unsigned. Delhi, BHCF, Events in Kurdistan, File 13/14, Vol. IX.

38   Note on Promises made to the Kurds, by R. S. M. Sturges, 10 October 1930. Delhi. BHCF. Events in Kurdistan, File 13/14, Vol. VIII.

39   Acting High Commissioner (Brooke-Popham) to Secretary of State for the Colonies, Telegram 411 of 8 September 1930: Delhi, BHCF, Events in Kurdistan, File 13/14, Vol. IX.

40   Acting High Commissioner, Baghdad to Secretary of State for the Colonies, Despatch, Secret of 26 September 1930. Delhi, BHCF. Events in Kurdistan, File 13/14 Vol. IX.

41   Shaykh Mahmud to Acting High Commissioner, 17 September, 2 October, 1930: Delhi, BHCF, Shaykh Mahmud, File 13/22, Vol. III

42   Adviser, Ministry of Interior to Administrative Inspector, Sulaymaniya, C/3872 of 15 November 1930: Delhi, BHCF, Shaykh Mahmud, File 13/22, Vol. I.

43   Note by Sturges, 17 October 1930: Delhi, BHCF, Events in Kurdistan, File 13/14, Vol. X.

44   Administrative Inspector, Mosul to Adviser Ministry of Interior, S/711 of 13 December 1930: Note on Kurdish Policy by C. J. Edmonds, 17 November 1930: Delhi, BHCF, Events in Kurdistan, 13/14, Vol. X.

45   'Note on Promises made to the Kurds', by R. S. M. Sturges, 10 October 1930: Delhi, BHCF. Events in Kurdistan, File 13/14, Vol. VIII.

46   Secretary of State for the Colonies to High Commissioner, Baghdad, Despatch Secret 'A' of 23 October 1930: Delhi, BHCF, Events in Kurdistan, File 13/14, Vol. X.

47   Permanent Mandates Commission, 19th session 10–11 November 1930: CO 30/152/78076.

48   High Commissioner, Baghdad, to Secretary of State for the Colonies, Despatch, Secret 'A', 19 December 1930: CO 730/157/78315. *Iraq Report, 1925*, pp. 222–223: *Iraq Report, 1926*, p. 14.

49   Secretary of State for the Colonies to High Commissioner, Baghdad, Telegram 488 of 22 December 1930. High Commissioner, Baghdad to Secretary of State or the Colonies, Telegram 623 of 31 December 1930: Delhi, BHCF, Events in Kurdistan, File 13/14, Vol. X.

50   High Commissioner, Baghdad, to Secretary of State for the Colonies, Despatch CO 1280, 27 March 1930. CO 730/156/78275.

51   Brooke-Popham to Shuckburgh, D.O. S.O. 983, 9 September 1930: CO 730/156/78275.

52   'Report on Economic Conditions and Policy' and 'A Note on Loan Policy' by Sir E. Hilton Young: E 6048/42/93, FO 371/14509, printed June 1930.

53   Oil revenue between 1927 and 1929 (from Anglo-Persian's fields in the Transferred Territories) was as follows:

1927	1928	1929
£1,050,000	£1,650,000	£1,850,000

Report . . . on the Progress of Iraq, 1920–1931, pp 90–91.

54   See Appendix II for conditions in 'Amara.

55   There was a general increase of 10% customs on all imports, and 20% on clothes, arms, ammunition, clocks, watches, alcohol, cars, tobacco and imported foodstuffs (except sugar, tea and coffee) in November 1930. Fortnightly Intelligence Report, 10 November 1930.

56   That is, the 24 x 8 square mile plots laid down under the terms of the TPC concession of 1925.

57   By 1931, when negotiations were proceeding for the West of Tigris area, the Company's composition had changed:

Participation	Percentage
British	46
Italian (AGIP)	30
Franco-Swiss	12
German-Dutch	12

58   Memorandum by G.W. Rendel, 26 May 1930. E 2654/51/93, FO 371/14511.

59   High Commissioner, Baghdad, to Secretary of State for the Colonies, Telegram 296 of 24 June 1930: E 3419/51/93, FO 371/14511.

60   *Notes exchanged with the Iraq Prime Minister embodying the separate Agreement on*

Financial Questions referred to in the second exchange of Notes appended to the Anglo-Iraq Treaty of 30 June 1930, Cmd. 3627, *Accounts and Papers* 1930–1931, Vol. XXXIV.

61   Ireland (1937): 437.

62   High Commissioner to Prime Minister, P. O. 85 of 1 May 1931: E 3580/5/93, FO 371/15307.

63   Hall (Colonial Office) to Sterndale-Bennett (Foreign Office), 31 July 1931: E 3993/5/93, FO 371/15308.

64   Note on Kurdish policy by C.J. Edmonds, undated, November 1930: Delhi, BHCF, Events in Kurdistan, File 13/14, Vol. X.

65   Cornwallis to Young, DO SA 627 10 December 1930. Delhi, BHCF, Events in Kurdistan, File 13/14 Vol. X.

66   Secretary of State for the Colonies to High Commissioner, Baghdad, 19 February 1931. Telegram 108: Flood (Colonial Office) to Humphrys, Private and Personal, 20 February 1931. Delhi, BHCF, Events in Kurdistan, File 13/14, Vol. XI.

67   Memorandum by J. H. Hall, 20 February 1931: Delhi, BHCF, *Events in Kurdistan*, File 13/14, Vol. XI.

68   There is a certain amount of confusion about the role played by the RAF in these operations. In his report, Air Vice-Marshal Ludlow-Hewitt was obviously anxious to give the impression that the Iraqi army were running things themselves, and were only helped out by the RAF when things became really difficult: 'I advised that air action against the rebels should only be taken if the Iraq Army was actually being attacked and was in need of assistance.' The impression given is that, apart from demonstration and reconnaissance flights, the RAF was not seriously employed until the final phase of the operations. This was no doubt to give the impression that the Iraq Army was capable of conducting an expedition of this kind. Compare, however, the account of the Barzan operations the following year. A.V.M. Ludlow-Hewitt, Report on Operations in Kurdistan to May 1931, 16 October 1931, CO 730/163/88069, and see p. 184. See also monthly summary of air operations, November 1930, where the bombing of Panjwin, Shaykh Sadiq and Risha' (5 January 1931) and Dalash (24 January 1931) are described. Air 5/1292.

69   Report on Air Operations, May 1931, Air 5/1292.

70   Administrative Inspector, Sulaymaniya, to Adviser, Ministry of Interior, C/284/27/3 of 15 April 1931: Delhi, BHCF, Events in Kurdistan, File 13/14, Vol. XI.

71   Shaykh Qadir to Sir Francis Humphrys, 31 March 1931: Delhi, BHCF Events in Kurdistan, File 13/14, Vol. XI.

72   High Commissioner to Prime Minister, P. O. 87, 9 May 1931:Delhi, BHCF, Events in Kurdistan, File 13/14 Vol. XI.

73   Cornwallis to Young, DO SA 62 of 26 April 1931: Delhi, BHCF, Events in Kurdistan, File 13/14 Vol. XI.

74   Minute by Holt, 2 June 1931 on Prime Minister to High Commissioner 2251 of 30 May 1931: Delhi, BHCF, Events in Kurdistan, File 13/14 Vol. XI.

75   Prime Minister to High Commissioner, Confidential, 27 July 1931: Delhi, BHCF, Events in Kurdistan, File 13/14, Vol. XII.

76   Minute by Holt, 26 June 1931, Delhi, BHCF, Events in Kurdistan, File 13/14, Vol. XI.

77   Lancelot Oliphant (Foreign Office) to Sir George Clerk (Ankara). Private and Personal 31 July 1931: E 3671/3137/93, FO 371/15323.

78   Permanent Mandates Commission, 20th session, 18–19 June 1931.

79   Pachachi, formerly a prominent member of the opposition, had accepted office as Minister of Communications and Works on 5 January 1931.

80   On 25 January the Council of Ministers banned *Nida' al-Sha'b* for publishing an article by Dobbs in the *Daily Telegraph* criticising the 'Palace-Residency Alliance', as well as another article from the *Daily Herald* which alleged that the government of Iraq was accepting bribes from Sir John Cadman, the Chairman of Anglo-Persian. Fortnightly Intelligence Report, 4 February 1931.

81   Fortnightly Intelligence Reports, 3 March, 18 March 1931.

82   Fortnightly Intelligence Report, 4 March 1931.

83   Abstract of Police Intelligence, 11 April, 29 April 1931.

84   Acting High Commissioner, Baghdad, to Secretary of State for the Colonies, Telegram 304 of 11 July 1931: Delhi, BHCF, Interior, File 7/4/22 Part II, General Strike in Baghdad in Protest against the Municipal Fees Law.

85   Monthly report of air operations, July 1931: Air 5/1292.

86   Administrative Inspector, Basra, to Ministry of Interior, Telegram 991 of 17 July: Delhi, BHCF, Interior, File 7/4/22, Part I, General Strike.

87   Abstract of Police Intelligence 21 July 1931.

88   Ludlow-Hewitt to Humphrys, SO 961, 23 July 1931 (Humphrys was in London): Delhi, BHCF, Interior File 7/4/22, Part I, General Strike. The situation has close parallels with the rising of 1935. See pages 191–192.

89   Acting High Commissioner, Baghdad to Secretary of State for the Colonies, Despatch, Secret, of 14 August 1931: CO 730/170/88369.

90   High Commissioner, Baghdad to Secretary of State for the Colonies, Telegram 366 of 19 October 1931: CO 730/160/88016.

91   A. J. Chapman (Interior) to Secretariat, C/1139 of 26 September 1931: Minute by Holt, 29 September 1931: Delhi, BHCF, Events in Kurdistan, File 13/14, Vol. XII.

92   Permanent Mandates Commission, 21st Session, 10 November 1931.

93   *Record of a meeting at the Foreign Office to consider the P. M. C.'s report to the League Council on the release of Iraq from the Mandatory Regime, 14 December 1931*: E 8219/93/93, FO 371/16028.

94   The BOD Concession was signed in May 1932.

95   Ludlow-Hewitt to Humphrys, SO 961, 23 July 1931: Delhi, BHCF, Interior, File 7/4/22 Part I, General Strike.

96   'When I was in Mosul and Kirkuk last February the "defeat" of the Iraq Army was freely talked of.' Minute by G. W. Rendel, Foreign Office, on E 1820/617/93, FO 371/16045.

97   Operations summarised to this point by P. J.Dixon on E 1820/617/93, FO 371/16045.

98   Summary of Air Operations, March 1932, Air 5/1292. See also Chapter VII.

99   Permanent Mandates Commission, 7th session, June 1925.

100 Lambeth had maintained a friendly interest in the (non-Uniate) Assyrians since the establishment of the Archbishop of Canterbury's Mission: see Wigram (1929) and Coakley (1992).

101 Apparently this was the first 'international' operation involving the transport of troops by air.

102 High Commissioner, Baghdad to Secretary of State for the Colonies, Telegram 199 of 11 June 1932, CO 730/177/96602.

103 The 19th century Ottoman concept of 'religious community', under which the religious leader had spiritual and temporal authority over his people. This particular point was an important feature of the quarrel between the Mar Shimun and the High Commissioner before the massacre a year later, in the summer of 1933. See Stafford (1935).

104 Forwarded to the Colonial Office on 18 June 1932; High Commissioner Baghdad to Secretary of State for the Colonies, Despatch, Secret: CO 730/177/96602.

105 Suggested to the Foreign Office in Hall (Geneva) to Rendel, 26 September 1932: E 4981/23/93, FO 371/16035.

106 Ludlow-Hewitt to Humphrys, 8 August 1932: E 4226/23/93 FO 371/16035

107 Hall to Humphrys, 9 December 1932; Humphrys to Hall, 15 December 1932: E 6569, E6913/23/93, FO 371/19037.

108 ' ... there is no doubt that more resolute pressure by the High Commissioner before 1932 might have compelled Iraqi governments at least to put laws on the statute book which satisified the pledges made by the British and which the Iraqi state was committed to fulfil. They did not.' Fieldhouse (2002): 42.

109 High Commissioner, Baghdad, to Secretary of State for the Colonies, Telegram 185 of 1June 1932: Delhi, Cabinet Formations, File 23/14/12, Cabinet of Nuri al-Sa'id.

110 Counsellor, Baghdad, to Secretary of State for Foreign Affairs, Despatch 1060 of 3 November 1932: Ambassador, Baghdad, to Secretary of State for Foreign Affairs, Despatch 1093 of 17 November 1932: Delhi, BHCF, Cabinet Formations. File 23/14/13, Cabinet of Naji Shawkat Beg.

111 High Commissioner, Baghdad, to Secretary of State for the Colonies, Despatch, Secret, 8 July 1930: E 3728/41/93, FO 371/14507.

112 Report of an Interdepartmental Committee (FO, CO, AM) 22 October 1931: E 5316/3226/93, FO 371/15324.

113 Enclosed in Secretary of State for the Colonies to High Commissioner, Baghdad, Despatch Secret 28 July 1932: E 3846/894/93, FO 371/16045.

114 Note by H.W. Young, 18 December 1929, enclosed in High Commissioner, Baghdad to Secretary of State for the Colonies, Secret of 19 December 1929: E 670/41/93, FO 371/14503.

115 *Special Report on the Progress of Iraq ... 1930–1931*, pp. 290–292.

116 Rendel to Hall, 14 July 1932, E 3070/2576/93: FO 371/16047.

117 Acting High Commissioner, Baghdad to Secretary of State for the Colonies, 1 September 1932. CO 730/177/96600; Secretary of State for the Colonies to Acting High Commissioner, Baghdad, 20 September 1932. E 4767/9/93: FO 371/16031.

118 Simon to Hoare, 6 August 1932. E 4196/249/93: FO 371/16041.

119 E 4224/249/93: FO 371/16041.

120 *Documents on British Foreign Policy*, Vol. IV, p 344. See Thornton (1963): 168.

Chapter 6

1 Karpat (1968). See also Farouk-Sluglett and Sluglett (1983a); for a more general discussion see Farouk-Sluglett and Sluglett (1984).

2 Sa'id Himadeh, 'Taxation in the 1900's', in Issawi (1975).

3 This account of land tenure is only concerned with the irrigation zone of Iraq.

4 Administrative Report, Revenue Board, Baghdad 22 March to 31 December 1918, FO 371/3406/139231.

5 'Settled agriculture and extended civilisation have tended to weaken the power of the shaykh.' See Note 2 above and Sluglett, 'al-Muntafik in recent times' (1992).

6 Authorities differ here: 'No clear evidence suggests that land was ever considered the corporate property of an 'ashira. Rather, informants say, segments of the 'ashira always claimed certain sections of land, and within the segments individual men and their sons claimed the right to farm individual fields. Dowson reports that in general shaykhs assigned landholdings to their tribesmen.' Fernea (1970: 97). Prescriptive rights (*lazma*) were more highly developed in some areas than others (see the next note); in the Daghghara region described by Fernea, rights to particular pieces of land were of comparatively ancient origin. This would not apply to regions where although tribal lands were extensive the area under cultivation formed only a small fraction of the whole.

7 In 'Land Problems of Iraq', (London University Ph.D thesis, 1942 [selection extracted and edited by Issawi (1966)], Saleh Haider classified areas of Southern Iraq as follows:
a) areas where tribalism remained strong: Muntafiq, Diwaniya, 'Amara, Dulaym
b) areas where individual holdings predominated: Samarra', Dujayla, parts of Hilla
c) areas where the tribal system had largely disappeared: most of Basra *wilaya*, Karbala', Baghdad and environs, Diyala.

8 *Muntafiq Report*, 1919, p 7. CO 696/2. 'half a share' would not have wide application outside some parts of the Muntafiq area.

9 See here *Situation on the Shatt al-Gharraf*, 1927–1931 in Air 23/121 and note 74, pages 263–264.

10 Lt. Col. E. B. Howell, *Note on Land Policy*, Baghdad 9 May 1919, enclosed in India Office to Foreign Office, Letter P. 4804 of 10 November 1919. FO 371/4150/127807.

11 Increasing because grazing was gradually being replaced by crop cultivation.

12 For a comprehensive description of the land categories see Haider (Ph.D thesis, 1942), and Farouk-Sluglett and Sluglett (1983a).

13 A law of 1 March 1914 permitted ownership by corporate bodies, but this was in practice confined to buildings belonging to State companies or municipalities.

14 See Haider /Issawi (1966); Jwaideh (1963); Warriner (1986); Longrigg (1925): 306; Farouk-Sluglett and Sluglett (1983a).

15 See note 10 above, Lt-Col. Howell.

16 Dowson summarised the position: 'Under the regular operation of the Land Code all state lands held and used by the public should be possessed in *tapu* tenure. But no systematic grant of *tapu* tenure was made . . . when the code was introduced. Consequently *tapu* tenure was the occasional and imperfectly realised privilege of the few instead of the regular tenure of State Land it was intended to be. In many cases grants in *tapu* tenure were no doubt made to those best entitled to enjoy its rights and best able to discharge its obligations. But as a rule grants were made without any satisfactory investigation of conflicting claims.' Dowson (1932): 19.

17 Revenue collection in the Muntafiq division amounted to Rs 33,557 (about

£20,000) in 1915–1916, Rs 135,139 (about £8,400) in 1917–1918, and Rs 1,661,823 (about £104,000) in 1919–20. *Muntafiq Report*, 1921, p 31. CO 696/ 4. 'Efficiency of collection is undoubtedly greater than under the Turks but this seems scarcely fair ground for attack . . . It must be remembered that efficiency in collection includes and is inseparable from, a more equitable distribution of the burden.' Such admirable notions of fair play seem to have fallen on barren soil in the Middle Euphrates. Political, Baghdad, to Secretary of State for India, Telegram 724 of 21 July 1920.LP & S 10 4722/18/1920/8/5732.

18 See note 10 above.

19 A tribesman is defined as 'member of a tribe which has been accustomed to settle its disputes in accordance with tribal custom.' The 1918 version of the Regulation is printed in the *Special Report . . . on the Progress of Iraq 1920–1931*. For a somewhat comparable situation, see the introduction of the Berber *dahir* by the French authorities in Morocco in 1930, which established customary tribunals specifically for the Berber population: see Brown (1976): 198–202, and Hoisington (1978): 443–448.

20 Dobbs to Pulley (Interior) D. O., S. O. 2140 of 28 September 1924. Delhi, BHCF, Justice File 8/4 Vol. I.

21 See page 14, and Dodge (2003b): 84–100.

22 Dobbs to Cornwallis, DO 15353, 16 December, Delhi, BHCF, Justice File 8/4, Vol. I.

23 See Delhi, BHCF, Interior, File 7/17/168, Murder of 'Abdullah Beg al-Sani'.

24 See Delhi, BHCF, Interior, File 7/17/144, Anti-Zionist Demonstration on the Occasion of the Visit of Sir Alfred Mond to Iraq in 1928 and File 7/4/22, General Strike in Baghdad in Protest against the Municipal Fees Law, 1931. cf.: 'It must have been very galling for the Opposition leaders to discover that the executive could arrest and exile to distant parts of Iraq unwelcome agitators in Baghdad and Ba'quba under powers conferred by the Tribal . . . Disputes Regulation, devised by Sir Henry Dobbs in 1916 to compose tribal differences in the marshes of 'Amara.' *The Near East and India,* 21 August 1931.

25 Administrative Report, Revenue Board, Baghdad 22 March to 31 December 1918, FO 371/3406/139231.

26 *Revenue Report*, 1925, pp 25–26. CO 696/5.

27 RAF Special Service Officer, Samawa, (J. B. Glubb) to Air Headquarters, D. 582 of 23 December 1923. Air 23/445.

28 *Dulaim Revenue Report,* January 1924. Delhi, BHCF, Interior, File 7/22/15, Shaykh 'Ali Sulaiman.

29 Dulaim Report, 27 August to 13 November 1924. Delhi, BHCF, Interior, File 7/22/15, Shaykh 'Ali Sulaiman.

30 Dobbs to Cornwallis, 17 October 1925, D. O. S. O. 2607: Cornwallis to Dobbs, 21 October 1925, DO C/36791. Delhi, BHCF, Interior, File 7/22/15, Shaykh 'Ali Sulaiman.

31 In the words of another contemporary administrator, British policy was 'a veiled rule through the natural chiefs whom the native soil had evolved, namely the tribal shaykhs'. Thomas (1931): 24.

32 High Commissioner, Baghdad to Secretary of State for the Colonies, CO 528 of 17 August 1922, with enclosure, *Report on the Unrest in the Nasiriya Division*, by District Adviser, Muntafiq. CO 730/23/43319.

33 al-Hubayyib had been a supporter of the British authorities during the 1920 rising, and maintained frequent contact with the Residency during the Mandate. See Delhi, BHCF, Personalities, File 27/728, Manshad al-Hubayyib of the Ghazzi at Ur.

34 Fortnightly Intelligence Report, 1 September 1922. CO 730/24/48131.

35 See p. 246 Note 40. Cf. Major Pulley, Political Officer, Hilla to Civil Commissioner, 6 August 1920, referring to conversations with prisoners captured during the rising: ' . . . they are miserably oppressed by their sub-shaykhs, who seem to me to be like feudal barons. Many of them were small men of no account until we made them powerful and rich.' LP & S 10 4722/18/1920/8/6035.

36 Note by RAF Special Service Officer, Hilla (J. B. Glubb) 19 July 1924. Air 23/447.

37 *Ibid.*

38 See Chapter 7, pages 191–192.

39 *Note on Land Tenure* by Sir Henry Dobbs, enclosed in High Commissioner, Baghdad to Secretary of State for the Colonies, CO 894 of 21 July 1926. CO 730/94/15136.

40 Formerly Director-General of the Survey of Egypt, Financial Adviser to the Egyptian government and the author of studies of land tenure in Palestine and Transjordan.

41 Sir Ernest Dowson to Sir Francis Humphrys, 15 January 1932, enclosed in E 3588/3588/93. FO 371/16049.

42 See Appendix II and Batatu (1978): 132–152.

43 The area under cultivation increased from 'Probably less than 100,000 *donums* in the 1860s to about 1,613,000 *donums* in 1913 to 9,258,000 *donums* during the second world war . . . ', and the value of imports rose from ID 3.5 million in 1912–1913 to ID 7.6 million in 1933–1939. Hasan (1970): 346–372. During the mandate, the numbers of mechanical pumps increased from 143 serving 190 square kilometres in 1921 to 2,031 serving 7,380 square kilometres in 1929. (Dowson (1932): 29). These figures suggest first, increased production, and secondly, increased personal wealth. Neither factor is reflected in the total returns from taxation, which, apart from animal taxes, declined steadily over the period largely for the reasons which have been explained above. See the tables in *Special Report . . . on the Progress of Iraq 1920–1931*, p 83.

44 Article 49; see the *Iraqi Government Gazette* of 30 July 1933. A copy appears in FO 624/1/428/1.

45 Note on the Law by the Inspector General of Agriculture, Nov. 1933 enclosed in Ambassador, Baghdad to Secretary of State for Foreign Affairs, Despatch No. 807 of 22 December 1933. FO 624/1/428/7.

46 Ambassador, Baghdad to Secretary of State for Foreign Affairs, Despatch No. 807 of 22 December 1933.FO 624/1/428/7.

Chapter 7

1 Costs from *Hansard*, 18 February 1926, CO 730/101/3532 and Trenchard to Shuckburgh, 31 October 1927, CO 730/125/40607, and *Special Report on the Progress of Iraq 1920–1932*, pp. 47–48.

2 See Chapter 4, pp. 95–105 and Appendix I.

3   *Ibid.*
4   Trenchard to Shuckburgh, 9 December 1921, CO 730/8/61008.
5   Colonial Office minute of 28 November 1921 by C.J. Howard on High
     Commissioner, Baghdad, to Secretary of State for the Colonies, Telegram 707 of
     23 November 1921: CO 730/7/58553.
6   *Special Report on the Progress of Iraq 1920–1932*, p 47.
7   Monthly summaries of air operations, April 1932: Air 5/1292.
8   See Cox, 'A Splendid Training Ground . . . ' (1985): 157–184, Clayton,
     'Deceptive Might' (1999: 280–293) and the more detailed treatment by David
     Omissi (1990: 18–38). Omissi considers that the RAF's ability to provide cheap
     and effective policing for Iraq was vital in ensuring its survival as an indepen-
     dent unit, given the widespread imperative to save money (on military as on
     other spending) in the years after 1918. The air scheme, enthusiastically
     supported by Churchill, was viewed with some scepticism after the rising of
     1920, which it was felt proved that there was no effective substitute for ground
     troops. But see p. 185 note 12.
9   War Diary, 31st Wing R.F.C. April 1919: Air 1/2207.
10   Secretary of State for War to Chief of Air Staff, Memorandum of 29 February
     1920, RAF Scheme of Defence for Mesopotamia, Air 20/526. T. E. Lawrence
     claimed that he had suggested the idea to Churchill: see Graves and Hart
     (1938): 112.
11   Note (undated, but Spring 1920) by Sir Geoffrey Salmond: Air 20/526.
12   Sir Aylmer Haldane to W.S. Churchill, 26 June 1921: Air 8/34, p. 12.
13   See C. P. 3240, 17 August 1921: Air 8/34. Omissi adds the useful detail that
     subsidies were to be paid to the rulers of the states on or near Iraq's borders (Ibn
     Sa'ud, Sharif Husayn, the Imam of Yemen) in return for undertaking not to
     disturb the peace in Iraq. In addition, RAF squadrons were stationed in
     Transjordan. Omissi (1990): 25, 27–28.
14   Trenchard to Shuckburgh, 29 July 1921: CO 730/15/37682.
15   Minute by R. W. Bullard, 4 March 1921: CO 730/2/9565.
16   Churchill to Cox, Private and Unnumbered Telegram, 7 June 1921: CO 730/2/
     27278.
17   'The natives of a lot of these tribes love fighting for fighting's sake,' Trenchard
     assured Parliament [in 1930]. 'They have no objection to being killed.'
     (Trenchard's maiden speech to the House of Lords, 1930, (quoted Satia, 2006:
     37).
18   See *Daily Mail*, 27 January, *Daily Express*, 29 January, *Evening Standard* 30
     January 1924, collected in CO 730/64/4566.
19   Minute by H.W. Young, 2 March 1923 on Air Officer Commanding, Baghdad,
     to Secretary of State for Air, Telegram 130A of 22 February 1923: CO 730/45/
     10674.
20   Cmd. 2217 of 1924. 'The British contemplated using gas bombs in Iraq, [the
     Italians were to do so in Abyssinia in 1935–1936] although in the end they
     shrank from this course.' Omissi (1990): 206. Churchill's biographer is more
     ambiguous (Gilbert, 1975: 810), and Priya Satia suggests quite plausibly that
     the notion that Churchill actually favoured using gas derives from
     misunderstanding on the part of later writers of an evidently ironic aside by
     T.E. Lawrence: 'By gas attacks the whole population of offending districts

could be wiped out neatly; and as a method of government it would be no more immoral than the present system' (Satia 2006: 35 note 82). Omissi discusses the ethical opposition to air policing (on the general grounds that it could not discriminate between combatants and non-combatants) on pp. 150–183. Following Derek Sawyer, Satia notes the widespread characterisation in Britain of General Dyer's massacre at Amritsar in April 1919 as being a form of 'moral education' for the subject population, who evidently inhabited a 'different moral universe'. Satia's broader premise that notions of the feasibility and 'humanity' of the air scheme derived in part from British romanticising about 'Arabia' and 'the desert' (to simplify a more complex argument) seems ultimately unconvincing, not least because most RAF operations took place in the settled parts of lower Iraq and in Kurdistan. See also *Charlton* (Charlton: 1931), an autobiographical account by an RAF officer stationed in Iraq who resigned over the policy.

21 RAF Special Services Officer, Hilla (J. B. Glubb) to Air Headquarters, D. 495 of 18 November 1923: Air 23/443.

22 Adviser, Ministry of Interior, to Administrative Inspector, Nasiriya, C/2667 of 19 November1923, enclosed in Air 23/443.

23 RAF Special Services Officer, Samawa, to Air Headquarters, S/1 of 27 November 1923: Air 23/443.

24 Report on Operations against the Bani Huchaim, Air Officer Commanding, Baghdad, to Secretary of State for Air, 12 December 1923: Air 5/344.

25 Monthly summary of air operations, December 1923: Air 5/1287.

26 RAF Special Services Officer, Hilla to Air Headquarters, enclosed in C/162 of 20th January 1924. Adviser, Ministry of Interior, to Secretariat. Air 23/445.

27 RAF Special Services Officer, Diwaniya to Air Headquarters, B/D/2/1 of 29 April 1924: Air 23/446.

28 Report on Operations against the Bani Huchaim, Air Officer Commanding, Baghdad, to S/S for Air, 12 December 1923: Minute by Deputy Chief of Air Staff, 5 January 1924.

29 Monthly summary of air operations, September 1925: Air 5/1289.

30 RAF Special Services Officer, Diwaniya to Air Headquarters, 1/D/15 of 23 August 1930: Air 23/112.

31 For instance against the Yazidis in 1925, Shaykh Mahmud in 1930, and Barzan in 1932.

32 Cabinet Conclusions Cab 28 (35) 17 May 1935: E 3081/1583/93, FO 371/18953.

33 Ambassador, Baghdad to Secretary of State for Foreign Affairs, Despatch 295 of 29 May 1935: E 3601/1583/93, FO 371/18953.

34 'Arrangements were made for aircraft and armoured cars of the RAF to be ready to take part in operations in the event of H. M. Government deciding that intervention was necessary.' Monthly summary of air operations, May 1935: Air 5/1292.

35 An RAF aeroplane was shot down in the course of a reconnaissance flight over Rumaytha on 8 May. Private, Clark Kerr, Baghdad to Rendel, 30 May 1935: E 3592/2434/93, FO 371/18954.

36 CP 235 (25) *Visit of the Secretary of State for the Colonies to Iraq*, 11 May 1925: CO 730/89/23385. See above p. 66.

Chapter 8

1   Smith to Dobbs, D.A. Advr/33/19/151 of 15 July 1924: Delhi, BHCF, Education, File 5/1/37. A.L.F. Smith.

2   Edwin Montagu, 26 November 1917, quoted Waley (1964): 145.

3   Holt (1961): 119–120.

4   *Iraq Report, 1923–1924*, p. 206. cf. 'Captain A. L. Smith (Lionel) came to dine. We had a long and satisfying talk about the Education of Arabs. I'm not quite happy about what we're doing: nor is he. It's all very well to say that we mustn't start secondary schools till we have really first rate material both in teachers and pupils, but we really can't wait for that. We must get a move on and be content with second best, for the people here are so immensely keen to be provided with higher education and if we hold back they will think we are doing it on purpose to keep them back. You have to look at it from the point of view of politics as well as education.' Gertrude Bell to her father, 9 May 1920, Bell (1939): 487.

5   'The traditional view was that secondary education should not be vocational nor an extension of elementary schooling, but middle-class, and thus not to be publicly funded or controlled.' Stephens (1998): 101.

6   Clive Whitehead, *Colonial Educators: the British Indian and Colonial Education Service 1858–1983*, London, I. B. Tauris, 2003. p. xiii.

7   *Iraq Report,* 1925–1926, p. 132.

8   *Iraq Report,* 1924–1925, p. 210.

9   Lionel Smith, Note on the Present State of Education in Iraq, 30 August 1930, Delhi, BHCF, Education, File 5/1/1, Vol. 1I.

10 Though Gertrude Bell's comment in 1921 is directed against the Turkish 'Izzat Pasha Kirkuli: '[Hikmat Sulayman] is the man I want to get as Minister of Education in our Cabinet for Sir Percy has succeeded in moving to Public Works the former incumbent who can't read or write Arabic.' Gertrude Bell to her father, 7 February 1921. Burgoyne (1961): 204.

11 The average life of a cabinet under the mandate was 8 months. See Khadduri (1960): 370–372.

12 'In the substitution of Iraqi for British control the Ministry of Education was ahead in 1922 of all other Ministries and Departments, including even Auqaf. The experiment was regarded with misgiving by those best qualified to form an opinion, but the result has shown that those misgivings were not on the whole justified. Several of the Iraqi Directors of Areas and very many of the heads of schools . . . have shown great ability.' *Special Report . . . on the Progress of Iraq 1920–1931,* p. 225.

13 'No Arab can be found combining the necessary financial and administrative capacity with high educational qualifications and the essential inaccessibility to corrupt considerations in the appointment of officials and teachers.' Jerome Farrell: see CO 730/14/17717. 6 November 1921.

14 Smith seems to have had a high regard for al-Husri's integrity: 'His unremitting efforts to secure efficiency and a high standard in teachers and pupils naturally aroused opposition and it is a deplorable fact that his retirement was largely the result of his failure to obtain even the moral support of those who at heart approved his policy and appreciated his value. No other Iraqi combines his enthusiasm, his experience and knowledge of education systems, and his fearlessness.' *Iraq Report*, 1927–1928, pp 154–155. cf. Smith to Young,

6 January 1931, BHCF, Education, File 5/1/45, Sati' Beg al-Husri. For al-Husri's life and work, see Cleveland (1971), and Tibi (1981).

15   Figures from Ireland, (1937): 126.

16   H.R.C. Dobbs, *Notes on Education*, 5 February 1915, quoted Ireland (1937): 125.

17   Holland/Wilson Report, 15 June 1917. LP & S 10 4097/14/1917/7/4623.

18   Bowman's diaries are in the private paper collection at St. Antony's College, Oxford. His autobiography is Bowman (1942).

19   Bowman Diaries, 17 February 1918.

20   Bowman Diaries, 23 August 1918.

21   Note on Educational Policy by H. E. Bowman, 12 August 1919. LP & S 10 1454/19/1919/6227. The sentence quoted here is reproduced almost verbatim in Wilson (1931): 175.

22   Observations on Educational Policy in Mesopotamia by A. Boyd Carpenter, 19 October 1919. LP & S 10 1454/19/1920/23.

23   'There is no-one so experienced and efficient that we could hope to obtain . . . his departure will be regarded as proof that we are not prepared adequately to assist the course of education in this country.' Political, Baghdad, to Secretary of State for India, 18 June 1920, Telegram 7843. LP &S 10, 4097/14/1920/6/5776.

24   See *Work and Progress of the Education Department in the School Year 1920–1921,* in High Commissioner, Baghdad to Secretary of State for the Colonies, 7 August 1921. CO 730/5/48574.

25   Department of Education, Baghdad, 6 November 1921. This memorandum was a reply to a circular from H.W. Young, who was on deputation in Baghdad from the Colonial Office. The circular, which was sent to all advisers to ministries, was concerned with such questions as the number of British officials likely to be required over the coming years in each department, and how that department regarded its own function in fulfilling the provisions of the Mandate. See CO 730/14/17117.

26   High Commissioner, Baghdad to Secretary of State for the Colonies, Despatch, Confidential, of 8 November 1922, enclosing report of Economies Committee. CO 730/24/57536.

27   *Iraq Report, 1922–1923*, pp. 166–167.

28   'A residential school for the sons of shaykhs has been included in and afterwards cut out from every Budget since 1920. The need for combining tribesmen and townsmen for political purposes into one harmonious whole is now stronger than ever. An educated aristocracy among the tribes would do much to reconcile them to a more modern form of Government.' *Iraq Report, 1924*, p. 214.

29   *Nida al Sha'b,* 21 May 1926, quoted in Fortnightly Intelligence Report, 26 May 1926. CO 730/105/312. Later in 1926, approval was requested for an extra 2 lakh grant to education, and the appointment of a further 70 teachers. Dobbs wrote to London: 'I have not cared to interfere in the allocation of funds to the Education Department within the limits prescribed in the budget estimates as there is an important weight of opinion in Iraq that the education services are being starved and although I realise the dangers of progressive increases in establishment I did not wish to object to reasonable expenditure on social services which it appeared the Government could easily afford.' (Letter CO 993, 5 August 1926) A Colonial Office Minute on this letter by W.J. Bigg reads:

'There seems to be a distinct danger of going too fast in educational matters.' (24 August 1926). CO 730/95/15981.

30   Dobbs commented that he was well aware of the small size of the allocations: 'The reason why more funds are not available is that every penny has to be spent on the army. We can't get out of that position, so there is no prospect of educational development unless the financial arrangements are modified in favour of Iraq.' Smith to Dobbs, D.A. Adw/33/19/151, 15 July 1924, Delhi, BHCF, Education File 5/1/37. A. L. F. Smith.

31   Figures from: *Special Report on the Progress of Iraq 1920–1931*, p. 232; Hasan (1958): 339–352; Education Budget for 1935 *in Iraq: Annual Report for 1935*. Ambassador, Baghdad to Secretary of State for Foreign Affairs, No. 56 Confidential of 31 January 1936. E 851/851/93: FO 371/20010.

32   *Iraq Report, 1925–1926*, p 142. Some of these schools were given small grants in aid by the Ministry.

33   *Iraq Report, 1923–1924*, p 167.

34   *Iraq Report, 1926–1927*, pp. 124–125; *Iraq Report, 1927–1928*, p. 154; *Iraq Report, 1929–1930*, p. 139.

35   Monroe (1932); Matthews and 'Akrawi, (1949); Quint (1958).

36   Monroe himself seems to have found favour in Whitehall; the following is an extract from a letter in reply to an enquiry about whether to invite Monroe to an educational conference: 'His report on the present educational system in Iraq and his recommendations for the future were in my opinion an admirable piece of work. A great deal of what he had recommended had been advocated for years, without effect, by Lionel Smith. Professor Monroe's proposals for tribal education are perhaps scarcely practicable at the moment, but for the rest, the vast majority of his recommendations could undoubtedly be adopted by the Iraqi government with great benefit.' J.H. Hall, 1 May 1933. E 2218/446/93.FO 371/16911.

Chapter 9

1   Cornwallis to Young, 22 March 1931. Enclosed in Humphrys to Shuckburgh, DO 414 of 27 March 1931. CO 730/167/88231.

2   See Chapter V above, p. 197: again, the main participants were Standard Oil (US), Compagnie Française des Pétroles (F), Anglo Persian (GB) and Anglo-Saxon (GB/NL).

3   c.f. Montagu to Chelmsford, 8 March 1919. 'And then I shall never be satisfied myself until some investigation is made of the methods and powers and the use of the C. I. D. The statements I have heard since I have been connected with India about the shadowing of innocent people, about records, about the whole activity of the Department and the use made of it by the Government . . . make me think that an impartial investigation of its activities . . . is very much . . . needed.' Quoted Waley (1964): 199.

4   Note by C.J. Edmonds, 10 October 1931, enclosed in High Commissioner, Baghdad to Secretary of State for the Colonies, Despatch, Secret of 28 November 1931: E 5732/3715/93: FO 371/15324.

5   Ambassador, Baghdad, to Secretary of State for Foreign Affairs, Telegram 348 of 11 September 1933. E 5331/7/93: FO 371/16889.

6   See above, page 7.

7   For the chronology of this change of heart, see Dodge (2003b): 36–41.

8   The first edition of Antonius' *The Arab Awakening: the story of the Arab national movement* (London, Hamish Hamilton) was published in 1938.

9   'martial law was not abolished until [December 1953] . . . and several party leaders who had been detained were not released until after the elections were held on 17 January 1953.' Khadduri (1960): 285.

10 I have discussed these matters at greater length and in the context of a comparison between the Iraqi and Syrian mandates in 'The Urban Bourgeoisie and the Colonial State: the Iraqi and Syrian Middle Classes between the Two World Wars' (Sluglett, 2005).

11 'With the 1989 democratic elections in Brazil and Chile, all Latin American countries, with the exception of Cuba, had elected constitutional governments, marking a significant transformation in the region away from military authoritarianism. . . . These transitions from authoritarian rule make the region an important component of the 'third wave' of democratization . . . which had begun in Portugal in 1974 and quickly spread to Spain, Greece, Latin America and other authoritarian countries in Asia, Africa and Eastern Europe' (Foweraker et al., 2003: 34).

12 Some idea of the complexity and scope of these organisations can be surmised from the various documents captured in Iraq which are now being catalogued by the Iraq Memory Foundation in Washington DC.

13 Macdonald (1936): 300–01.

Appendix I

1   *A note on the Political Situation to 27/9/27* by C.J. Edmonds, enclosed in DO 2032, Sturges to Shuckburgh, 1 October 1927: CO 730/123/40465, paper 49.

2   Here it may be worth noting in parentheses first, that these were informal censuses, and second, that when official censuses were instituted in 1947, they did not, following Ottoman practice, show religious/sectarian affiliation beyond Christian, Jewish, Muslim, Sabaean and Yazidi. Delhi, BHCF, Miscellaneous, Census of Nationalities by Divisions, File 34/172. 1920 figures: Print no. 270 of Civil Commissioner of 10 March 1920. 1931 figures: DO c/1206 Chapman (Interior) to Holt, 8 October 1931.

3   For a fascinating insight into the politics of mid-19th century Karbala', see Cole and Momen (1986).

4   But see Deringil (1990). For discussions of the role of the *mujtahids*, see Algar (1969); Litvak (1998), and Luizard (1991).

5   See Cole, (1986). For the Oudh bequest to Karbala' and Najaf, which began in 1850 and came under British control in 1903, see Litvak (2000): 69–89. For the effect of the war on these payments, see Ende (1981).

6   Longrigg (1925): 313. For signs of greater vigour on the Ottomans' part, see Selim Deringil (1990): 45–62; Litvak (1998), and Çetinsaya (2006).

7   See Atiyah (1973): 96, 324. Although there was little pro-Ottoman feeling, it is doubtful whether the two towns, together with the Hayy and the Euphrates tribes, would have provided the necessary basis for a 'Mesopotamian Revolt'. See Graves and Liddell Hart (1935): 60.

8   Secretary of State for India to Viceroy, Foreign Department, 19 March 1917, quoted Ireland (1937): 97.

9   *Self-Determination in Mesopotamia* . . . see pp. 50–52 above.
10 See Farouk-Sluglett and Sluglett (2007).
11 'Atiyah, Ph.D thesis, 1968, p. 400.
12 See pages 33–36.
13 Abstract of Police Intelligence, 26 November 1921. The company included Shaykh Ahmad al-Da'ud, Ja'far Abu'l-Timman, Ali Bazirgan, Rashid al-Khuja, Muhammad al-Sadr and members of the al-Suwaydi family.
14 Abstract of Police Intelligence, 10 December 1921.
15 Abstract of Police Intelligence, 8 April 1922.
16 Abstract of Police Intelligence, 23 February, 10 March, 3 May, 10 May, 26 May 1923.
17 'King Faysal himself went to extreme limits of complaisance and even of humiliation in previous negotiations with al-Khalisi to induce him to withdraw from agitation against Iraqi government and latter only forced to do so by al-Khalisi's illegal opposition to the elections . . . It was in fact notorious that next step contemplated by al-Khalisi was issue of decree proclaiming deposition of King.' High Commissioner to Ambassador, Teheran, Telegram 108 of 7 July 1923. Delhi, BHCF 23/15/1.
18 RAF Special Services Officer, Hilla, 30 June 1923: Delhi, BHCF 23/15/1.
19 22. High Commissioner to Secretary of State for the Colonies, Telegram 361 of 11 July 1923: CO 730/41/35272.
20 Intelligence Report of 5 July 1923. CO 730/40/37008.
21 Hikmat Sulayman and Ja'far Abu'l-Timman are exceptions here as men of principle.
22 Abstract of Police Intelligence, 5 April, 19 April, 1924.
23 See pages 102–105.
24 cf. 'An arrival from Najaf states that the Shia agitators there . . . realise that they had made a great error in 1920 and that the only result of their losses in men and money had been that the bands of adventurers and upstart Iraqis who had instigated the rebellion (and carefully kept out of it themselves) have seized power, while genuine Iraqis, Sunnis and Shias of good family in many cases are oppressed for revenue and refused their fair share in the government of the country.' Abstract of Police Intelligence, 1 October 1927.
25 See Chapter 7 pages 191–192.
26 Abstract of Police Intelligence, 18 April 1925.
27 Note by Squadron Leader Buss, (?) April 1927: Air 23/432.
28 Abstract of Police Intelligence, 3 May 1927.
29 Abstract of Police Intelligence, 23 July 1927.
30 Abstract of Police Intelligence, 1 October 1927.
31 Secret, B. Acting High Commissioner to Secretary of State for the Colonies, 15 July 1927: CO 730/124/40488.

Appendix II

1   Note by C.J. Edmonds 3 March 1931. Delhi, BHCF, Interior File 7/24/24 Vol.II (hereafter referred to as Delhi, 'Amara, Vol. I or II)
2   Admiralty Handbook, Iraq and the Persian Gulf, p .477
3   Ministry of Finance to High Commissioner, W.4373 of 16 August 1926: Delhi, 'Amara, Vol. I.

4   See Cornwallis to Humphrys, DOSA/55 of 11 September 1932: Delhi BHCF Interior File 7/24/43, *Situation in 'Amara Liwa*. Cf. also *Economic Disintegration in 'Amara Liwa in August 1932*: E 3627/3627/93, FO 371/16049.

5   'Amara Administrative Report, 1922, Revenue Section: Delhi, 'Amara, Vol. I.

6   See p. 244.

7   Administrative Inspector, Kut and 'Amara *liwas* to Adviser, Ministry of Interior, No. 1132 of 21 September 1923: Delhi, 'Amara, Vol. I.

8   Administrative Inspector, Kut and 'Amara *liwas* to Adviser, Ministry of Interior, No. 1132 of 21 September 1923: Delhi, 'Amara, Vol. I.

9   High Commissioner to Ministry of Finance, No. 8943 of 3 July 1924: Delhi, 'Amara, Vol. I.

10   Finance to Interior, W.1110 of 1 July 1924 gives the committee's brief: a minute of 25 June 1925 by Sturges of the Residency states that it did not meet, Delhi, 'Amara, Vol I.

11   High Commissioner to Ministry of Interior, No. 7095 of 30 May 1923: Delhi, 'Amara, Vol. I.

12   Internal Note, Ministry of Finance, S.H. Longrigg to R.V. Vernon, 24 May 1926: Delhi, 'Amara, Vol. I.

13   High Commissioner to Finance and Interior, No. 6558 of 8 June 1926: Delhi, 'Amara, Vol. I.

14   'It would be unwise to hasten by Government action a process of disintegration which is taking place gradually and naturally through force of existing conditions . . . ' Interior to Finance, Confidential C/1686/62/5/3 of 3 July 1926: Delhi, 'Amara, Vol. I.

15   High Commissioner to Adviser, Ministry of Interior, 14 May 1927: Delhi, 'Amara, Vol. I.

16   Not always to great effect. In 1928 the Administrative Inspector at 'Amara noted: 'The Aston Committee recommended that [Mahmud al-Muhammad Sa'id] be deprived of his *muqata'a* on the grounds of incompetence. Instead of this he was given his own *muqata'as* and the adjoining one at a *badl* less than that assessed by the Committee. His failure is not a surprise.' Adviser, Interior to High Commissioner, C/211 of 22 November 1928: Delhi, 'Amara, Vol. I.

17   Report on 'Amara liwa for August 1928, Administrative Inspector, 'Amara, n.d.: Delhi, 'Amara, Vol. I.

18   Note by C.J. Edmonds to Adviser, Ministry of Interior, 3 March 1931: Delhi, 'Amara, Vol. II.

19   Fortnightly Intelligence Report, 23 June 1930.

20   Administrative Inspector, Basra to Adviser, Ministry of Interior, C/226 of 6 September 1930: Delhi, 'Amara, Vol. II.

21   Edmonds (Interior), to Swan (Finance), DO C/69 of 1 February 1931: Delhi, 'Amara, Vol. II.

22   Note by C. J. Edmonds to Adviser, Ministry of Interior, 3 March 1931: Delhi, 'Amara, Vol. II.

23   Note by C.J. Edmonds as postscript to Note of 3 March 1931, dated 9 March 1931. Edmonds noted that there had been a remission of 9.73 *lakhs* (about £6,500) in 1924, but we know that political considerations had triumphed over financial ones in this case. Delhi, 'Amara Vol. II. See also Iraq Revenue Report, 1925, pp 25–26: CO 696/5 and p 244.

24 Administrative Inspector, Kut and 'Amara *liwas*, to Adviser, Ministry of Interior, No. 1132 of 21 September 1923: Delhi, 'Amara, Vol. I.

25 See pp 257–258. For salination, see Fernea (1970): 38–40, and Poyck (1962).

26 Note by Adviser for Minister of Finance, 22 December 1931: Delhi, 'Amara, Vol. II.

27 See Hasan (1958): 339–352. Batatu's Harvard doctorate notes that a quarter of the population left 'Amara between 1930 and 1947, and more generally that 'the provinces where the concentration of land-holding was more extreme seem to have suffered the most.' See John Battatu, (sic) 'The Shaykh and the Peasant in Iraq', (Harvard Ph.D. Thesis 1958), pp 157–60, and Batatu (1978):119–152.

BIBLIOGRAPHY

This book is largely based upon British archival material, mostly on correspondence to and from the High Commission in Baghdad. The most important categories are the India Office Files for the period between 1914 and 1921, and the Colonial Office, Foreign Office and Air Ministry files for the mandate period and after. A further source, which has proved especially useful for the detailed operation of the mandate, and local politics and administration in Iraq, has been the file of the Baghdad High Commission, located in the National Archives of India in New Delhi. Other primary sources used were private papers and diaries of former officials in the Private Paper Collections of the Middle East Centres of the Universities of Oxford and Durham (Sluglett 2004a).

The only Iraqi materials easily available are secondary sources, although, when I visited Iraq in 1976 (after the first edition of this book had been published), I was shown a collection of material from the Ministry of Interior between 1920 and 1932 in the Iraq National Archives (*al-Markaz al-Watani li-hifz al-Watha'iq*) in Baghdad; It seems most likely that this collection was extensively looted during the rampages in Baghdad in May 2003. The secondary sources consist largely of diaries and memoirs, written and published many years after the events they describe. The disadvantage of this material (see Kedourie, 1974) is that it consists to a greater or lesser extent of *pièces justificatives*: it is, for example, only possible to obtain a detailed account of the political infighting of the period from the Abstracts of Police Intelligence, although 'Abd al-'Aziz al-Qassab, Tawfiq al-Suwaydi, 'Ali Jawdat and other politicians and civil servants have written memoirs. Hence these materials have been used only as a supplement to the archives, and have been treated with greater caution.

This study is primarily concerned with British motives, and policy changes; it is possible to follow each new development in detail, because almost every move was documented in detail both in London and in Baghdad. If Iraqi archives were available in similar detail, it would be possible to reconstruct the manoeuvres of the court and the politicians and the growth of the new state in response to the demands of the British authorities and the country itself. I have discussed the published secondary sources in a bibliographical essay which forms the 'Introduction' to C. H. Bleaney and G. J. Roper (compilers), *Iraq: a Bibliographical Guide*, Leiden, Brill, 2004, pp. xi–xxxiv (see also Farouk-Sluglett and Sluglett, 1991).

I(a). UNPUBLISHED MATERIAL Archival Collections:

1. India Office Library (now housed in the British Library)

Letters, Political and Secret, File 10 (LP & S 10)

Used for the period 1914–1921. Correspondence to and from Mesopotamia/Iraq, and interdepartmental correspondence. The Foreign and Political Department of the Government of India was responsible for the administration of Mesopotamia until 1916, when the India Office in London assumed control. The official connection with India and the India Office terminated with the formation of the Middle East Department of the Colonial Office in 1921.

2. Public Record Office

Air Ministry: Air Historical Branch, Series I (Air I).
Used for the period 1914–1918. Papers and reports relating to squadrons of the RFC and RAF: squadron histories and operational narratives.

Air Ministry: Air Historical Branch, Series II Part II (Air 2)
Used for the period 1930–1932. RAF squadron histories and operational narratives. (Follows on chronologically from Air 5).

Air Ministry: Air Historical Branch, Series II, Part I (Air 5)
Used for the period 1921–1930. RAF squadron histories and operational narratives.

Air Ministry: Chief of Air Staff (Air 8)
Policy and planning, 1916–1932. Includes complete records of Cairo Conference.

Air Ministry: Unregistered Papers (Air 20)
Unregistered papers from Air Ministry branches, mostly 1915–1922 relating to policy, strategy, administration, aircraft, British forces in the Middle East, and intelligence services in the Middle East.

Air Ministry: Overseas Commands (Air 23)
1922–1932. Reports and correspondence on operations (Iraq, Indian, Aden, Middle East and Far East Command). Includes war diaries of Air Headquarters, Baghdad, 1923–1930.

Colonial Office: Miscellaneous (CO 537)
1921–1932. Mainly secret despatches and telegrams withheld from the original classes of colony correspondence (i. e. for Iraq, CO 730, CO 732) at the time when they were bound: now declassified.

Colonial Office: Iraq: Sessional Reports (CO 696)
1921–1932. Printed reports from various government departments in Baghdad.

Colonial Office: Iraq (CO 730)
1921–1932. Correspondence between London and Baghdad, and interdepartmental correspondence on Iraq; the principal source for the mandate period.

Colonial Office: Middle East (CO 732)
1921–1932, but mostly (for Iraq) 1921–1922. Correspondence between London, Baghdad, Jerusalem, Aden, etc. and interdepartmental correspondence on the Middle East.

Foreign Office: Commercial (FO 368)
1916–1920. Papers relating to trade with Mesopotamia, the blockade. etc.

Foreign Office: Consular (FO 369)
1925–1940. Consular reports and correspondence from Baghdad and Basra.

Foreign Office: Political (FO 371)
1916–1940. Correspondence between London and Baghdad and interdepartmental correspondence on Iraq: the main source for the post-mandate period.

Foreign Office: Confidential Prints: Eastern Affairs (FO 402)
1900–1914. Reports on Turkey, with sections on Iraq.

Foreign Office: Confidential Prints: Eastern Affairs (FO 406)
1920–1935. Reports, etc. on Iraq.

Foreign Office: Basra Consulate (FO 602)
1900–1914. Correspondence between Basra and London.

Foreign Office: Baghdad Embassy (FO 624)
1921–1945. Mostly after 1932. Most of the locally generated records for the period between 1921 and 1932 are now in the Baghdad High Commission Archive at the National Archives of India (see below).

Foreign Office: Private Papers (FO 800)
1900–1935. Private Papers of Foreign Ministers, Foreign Office officials and members of the diplomatic service: Papers of (Lord) Balfour; Sir Archibald Clerk Kerr, Lord Cranbourne, Sir Lancelot. Oliphant, Sir John Simon, Sir Mark Sykes.

Foreign Office: 'Amara Consulate (FO 838)
1941–1943. Reports on the political situation in 'Amara.

Foreign Office: Lausanne Conference (FO 839)
1922–1923. Miscellaneous papers and reports from Lausanne to London.

National Archives of India, New Delhi
Baghdad High Commission File (BHCF)
In 1941, when an Axis invasion of Iraq seemed likely, the records of the Baghdad

High Commission, covering the period between 1919 and 1932, were removed from the British Embassy in Baghdad and taken to Bombay. The papers were taken over by the Government of India after 1947, and are now in the National Archives of India, New Delhi. This collection, which is of considerable size, contains correspondence between Baghdad and London, and correspondence between the High Commission and British Advisers to Ministries, mostly Interior and Finance. It contains detailed information on local political and economic conditions, the relations between the High Commission, the Court and the Cabinet, and complete series of the weekly *Abstracts* of Police Intelligence (compiled by the CID.) and the fortnightly *Intelligence Summaries*, compiled in the High Commission). Files are divided into subject sections, and subdivided into areas, episodes, persons, etc. e.g. File 6 (Ministry of Finance) 34/34 'Amara Muqata'as: File 27 (Personalities) 411 Salim al-Khayyun.

I (b). Private papers and diaries

These are located either in the Middle East Centre at St. Antony's College Oxford, or in the case of the papers of Balfour and Clayton, in the Sudan Archive at Durham University. (See also Part I (a), Section 2: Foreign Office Private Papers (FO 800).

George. Antonius, F. C. C. Balfour, Sir Edwin Bonham Carter, Humphrey. Bowman, Sir Gilbert Clayton, C.J. Edmonds, S.H. Longrigg, L.S. Nalder, Major-General James Renton, Sir Reginald Wingate, Sir Hubert Young.

Theses and unpublished manuscripts

'Atiyah, G. R, 'Iraq, a Study in Political Consciousness 1908–1921', Edinburgh University Ph.D Thesis, 1968.

Battatu, John, 'The Shaykh and the Peasant in Iraq, 1917–1958', Harvard University Ph.D Thesis, 1960.

Farouk-Sluglett, Marion, 'Der Wandel der Produktions und Machtverhältnisse auf dem Lande im Irak unter der britischen Kolonial Herrschaft 1914–1932', Humboldt University, Berlin Dr.Phil. Thesis, 1974.

Haider, S., 'Land Problems of Iraq', London University Ph.D Thesis, 1942.

Mejcher. H. J. M., 'The Birth of the Mandate Idea and its Fulfilment in Iraq up to 1926', Oxford University D. Phil. Thesis, 1970.

Nadhmi, W. J. O., 'The Political, Social and Intellectual Roots of the Iraqi Independence Movement of 1920', Durham University Ph.D. Thesis, 1974.

al-Nakib, Haifa, 'A critical study of Saiyyid Talib al-Nakib in the setting of his time and environment', Leeds University M.Phil, 1972–1973.

Philby, H. St. J., 'Mesopotage' unpublished manuscript, deposited in the library of St. Antony's College, Oxford, 1939.

Sakai, Keiko, 'Political parties and Social Networks in Iraq, 1908–1920', Durham University M. A. thesis, 1994.

II(a) PUBLISHED MATERIALS: Official Publications

Great Britain

1. Command Papers

Treaties, Commissions of Enquiry, etc. in chronological order

Agreement with Anglo-Persian Oil Company Ltd. with an Explanatory Memorandum and the Report of the Committee of Experts on Their Local Investigations. Cmd. 7419, 1914. (Admiral Slade's Commission).

Report of the Commission appointed to Inquire into the Origin, Inception, and Operations of the War in Mesopotamia, Cmd. 8610, 1917.

Memorandum of Agreement signed at San Remo on 24 April 1920 between M. Philippe Berthelot . . . and Sir John Cadman . . ., Cmd.675, 1920 (San Remo Oil Agreement).

Treaty of Peace with Turkey, signed at Sèvres, 10 August 1920, Cmd. 960, 1920.

Review of the Civil Administration of Mesopotamia from 1914 to the summer of 1920. Compiled by Miss G. L. Bell. Cmd. 1061, 1920. [Bell, *Review*].

Draft Mandates for Mesopotamia and Palestine, Cmd. 1176, 1921.

Franco-British Convention of 23 December 1920, on Certain Points Connected with the Mandates for Syria and the Lebanon, Palestine and Mesopotamia. Cmd. 1195,1921.

Correspondence between H. M. Government and the Government of the United States of America Respecting Economic Rights in Mandated Territories, Cmd. 1226, 1921. (Colby/Curzon Correspondence).

Despatch to H. M. Ambassador at Washington, Enclosing a Memorandum on the Petroleum Situation, Cmd. 1351, 1921.

Final Drafts of Mandates for Mesopotamia and Palestine, Cmd.1500, 1921.

Treaty with H.M. King Faisal, 10 October 1922, Cmd. 1757,1922.

Treaty of Peace with Turkey and Other Instruments signed at Lausanne, 24 July 1923, Cmd. 1929, 1923.

Protocol of 30 April 1923 and Agreements Subsidiary to the Treaty with King Faisal, Cmd. 2120,1924.

Note on the Method of Employment of the Air Arm in Iraq, Cmd. 2217, 1924.

Report of the Financial Mission appointed . . . to enquire into the Financial Position and Prospects of the Government of Iraq, Cmd. 2438, 1925. (Hilton Young Report).

Treaty with King Faisal Signed at Baghdad, 13 January 1926 with an Explanatory Note, Cmd. 2587, 1926.

Treaty between the United Kingdom and Iraq, signed at London, 14 December 1927, Cmd. 2998, 1927.

Policy in Iraq: Memorandum by the Secretary of State for the Colonies, Cmd. 3440, 1929.

Notes Exchanged with the Iraq Prime Minister embodying the separate agreement on Financial Questions referred to in the second exchange of Notes appended to the Anglo-Iraqi Treaty of 30 June 1930, Cmd. 3627, 1930.

Treaty of Alliance between . . . the United Kingdom and Iraq with an Exchange of Notes, Baghdad, 30 June 1930: together with Notes Exchanged Embodying a Separate Financial Agreement, London, 19 August 1930, Cmd. 3797, 1931.

Report of a Committee set up to consider certain correspondence between Sir Henry McMahon and the Sharif of Mecca in 1915 and 1916, Cmd. 5974, 1939.

2. Reports on the Administration of Iraq.

Annual Reports by H. M. Government to the Council of the League of Nations:

October 1920–March 1922, London, His Majesty's Stationery Office (HMSO), 1922.
April 1922–March 1923, London, HMSO, 1924.
April 1923–December 1924, HMSO, 1925.
Thereafter for every calendar year, 1925–1931 inclusive
January–October 1932, London, HMSO, 1933.
Special Report . . . on the Progress of Iraq 1920–1931, London, HMSO, 1931.

3. Semi official Publications

Admiralty Handbook, *Iraq and the Persian Gulf,* 1944.

Woodward, E. L., and Rohan Butler, *Documents on British Foreign Policy.* First Series, Vol. IV (1919), London, H.M. Stationery Office, 1952.

Reports printed in Baghdad for the British occupation authorities and for the government of Iraq have not been listed separately; each document has been accompanied in the footnotes by the number of the file, or the name of the publication, in which it is located e. g. *Muntafiq Report,* 1921, CO 696/4: *Self-Determination in Mesopotamia,* in A. T. Wilson, *Mesopotamia 1917–1920: A Clash of Loyalties,* London, Oxford University Press, 1931, Appendix iii.

League of Nations

Official Journal, (Geneva, 1920–1932).
Records of the Assembly, (Geneva, 1920–1932).
Minutes of the Permanent Mandates Commission, Geneva, 1921–1932).

Books and Articles

'Abdullah, Thabit (2001), *Merchants, Mamluks and Murder: The Political Economy of Trade in Eighteenth Century Basra,* Albany, State University of New York Press.
'Abd al-Jabbar, Falih, see Jabar, Faleh A.
Adams, Robert McCormick (1965), *Land behind Baghdad: a history of settlement on the Diyala Plains,* Chicago, University of Chicago Press.
Adelson, Roger (1995), *London and the Invention of the Middle East,* New Haven, Yale University Press.
Adelson, Roger (1975), *Mark Sykes: Portrait of an Amateur,* London, Cape.
Akrawi, M., and R. D. Matthews (1949), *Education in the Arab Countries of the Near East,* Washington DC, American Council on Education.
Algar, H. (1969), *Religion and State in Iran 1785–1906: The Role of the 'Ulama in the Qajar Period,* Berkeley and Los Angeles, University of California Press.

Andrew, Christopher M., and A.S. Kanya-Forstner (1981), *France Overseas: the Great War and the Climax of French Imperial Expansion 1914–1924*, Stanford, CA, Stanford University Press.

Anon (1906), *Mesopotamien, das Land der Zukunft: seine wissenschaftlische Bedeutung für Mitteleuropa*, Berlin.

Anon (1923), 'Three difficult months in Iraq', *Journal of the Central Asian Society*.

Anon (1924), 'Iraq since the Beginning of the Year', *Journal of the Central Asian Society*, 11, pp. 68–74.

Anon (1926), 'Reflections on the Mosul Problem', *Journal of the Central Asian Society*, XIII, pp. 350–363.

Anscombe, Frederick (1997), *The Ottoman Gulf: the Creation of Kuwait, Saudi Arabia and Qatar*, New York.

Atiyah, Ghassan (1973), *Iraq 1908–1921: A Socio-Political Study*, Beirut, Arab Institute for Research and Publishing.

Baker, Ray S. (1922), *Woodrow Wilson and World Settlement*, 3 vols., Garden City, NY, Doubleday.

Barker, A. J. (1967), *The Neglected War: Mesopotamia 1914–1918*, London, Faber.

Barnes, John, and David Nicholson (eds.) (1980), *The Leo Amery Diaries, Volume I: 1896–1929*, London, Hutchinson.

Batatu, Hanna (1999), *Syria's Peasantry, the Descendants of its Lesser Rural Notables and Their Politics*, Princeton NJ, Princeton University Press.

Batatu, Hanna (1978), *The Old Social Classes and the Revolutionary Movements of Iraq: a Study of Iraq's Old Landed and Commercial Classes and of its Communists, Ba'thists and Free Officers*, Princeton, NJ, Princeton University Press.

Beck, Peter J. (1981), '"A tedious and perilous controversy"; Britain and the settlement of the Mosul dispute, 1918–1926', *Middle Eastern Studies*, 17, pp. 256–76.

Beer, G. L. (1923), 'The Future of Mesopotamia (dated 1 January 1918)' in *African Questions at the Paris Peace Conference, with papers on Egypt, Mesopotamia, and the Colonial Settlement*, New York, Macmillan, pp. 411–29.

Bell, Lady Florence (ed.) (1927), *Letters of Gertrude Bell*, 2 Vols., London, Ernest Benn.

(Bell, G. L.) (1917), *The Arab of Mesopotamia*, Basra, Government Press, (This was published anonymously but Gertrude Bell admits to having written it).

Blaisdell, Donald C. (repr.1966), *European Financial Control in the Ottoman Empire*, AMS Press, New York.

Bowman, Humphrey, (1942), *Middle East Window*, London, Longmans.

Boyle, Andrew (1962), *Trenchard*, London, Collins.

Brown, Kenneth L. (1976), *People of Salé: Tradition and Change in a Moroccan City, 1830–1930*, Manchester: Manchester University Press.

Bullard, Sir Reader William (1961), *The Camels Must Go*, London, Faber.

Burgoyne, Elizabeth (1961), *Gertrude Bell: From Her Personal Papers, 1914–1926*, 2 vols., London, Ernest Benn.

Busch, Briton Cooper (1976), *Mudros to Lausanne: Britain's Frontier in West Asia, 1918–1923,* Albany, State University of New York Press.

Busch, Briton Cooper (1972), *Britain, India and the Arabs 1914–1921*, Berkeley and Los Angeles, University of California Press.

Cell, John W. (1999), 'Colonial Rule', in Judith Brown and Wm. Roger Louis (eds.),

The Oxford History of the British Empire: Volume IV, The Twentieth Century, Oxford and New York, Oxford University Press, pp. 232–254.

Çetinsaya, Gökhan (2006), *The Ottoman Administration of Iraq, 1890–1908*, London, Curzon.

Charlton, Lionel Evelyn Oswald (1931), *Charlton*, London, Faber.

Churchill, W.S. (1923) 'Mesopotamia and the New Government', *Empire Review*, XXXVIII, no. 270, pp. 691–698.

Clayton, Anthony (1999), ' "Deceptive Might": Imperial Defence and Security, 1900–1968', in Judith Brown and Wm. Roger Louis (eds.),*The Oxford History of the British Empire: Volume IV, The Twentieth Century*, Oxford and New York, Oxford University Press, pp. 280–306.

Cleveland, W. L. (1971), *The Making of an Arab Nationalist: Ottomanism and Arabism in the Life and Thought of Sati' al-Husri*, Princeton NJ, Princeton University Press.

Cole, J. R. I. (1986), '"Indian Money" and the shrine cities of Iraq 1786–1850', *Middle Eastern Studies*, 22, pp. 461–480.

Cole, J. R. I. (1986), and Moojan Momen, 'Mafia, mob and Shiism in Iraq; the rebellion of Ottoman Karbala 1824–1843', *Past and Present*, 112, pp. 112–143.

Conway, Agnes (1927), 'Education in Iraq', *Journal of the Central Asian Society*, 14, 334–339.

A Correspondent in Baghdad (1923), 'Three difficult months in Iraq', *Journal of the Central Asian Society*, 10, pp. 68–74.

Cox, J. L. (1985), 'A splendid training ground: the importance to the Royal Air Force of its role in Iraq, 1919–1932', *Journal of Imperial and Commonwealth History*, 13, pp. 157–184.

Cox, P. Z. (1929), 'Iraq', *United Empire*, 20, pp. 132–144.

Crystal, Jill (1995), *Oil and Politics in the Gulf: Rulers and Merchants in Kuwait and Qatar*, Cambridge, Cambridge University Press.

Cumming, H. H. (1938), *Franco-British Rivalry in the Post War Near East; The Decline of the French Influence*, London, Oxford University Press.

Davidson (1932), Sir Nigel, 'Iraq, the New State', *Journal of the Royal Central Asian Society*, 19, 212–233.

Davison, R. H. (1963), *Reform in the Ottoman Empire, 1856–1876*, Princeton NJ, Princeton University Press.

Deringil, Selim (1990), 'The struggle against Shi'ism in Hamidian Iraq: a study in Ottoman counter-propaganda', *Die Welt des Islams,* 30, pp. 45–62.

Dodge, Toby (2003a), 'The social ontology of late colonialism: tribes and the mandated state in Iraq', in Faleh Abdul-Jabar and Hoshem Dawod (eds.), *Tribes and Power: National and Ethnicity in the Middle East*, London, Saqi, pp. 257–282.

Dodge, Toby (2003b), *Inventing Iraq: the Failure of Nation Building and a History Denied,* New York, Columbia University Press.

Dowson, Sir Ernest (1932), *An Inquiry into Land Tenure and Related Questions. Proposals for the Initiation of Reform*, Letchworth, England, Garden City Press.

Edmonds, C.J. (1957), *Kurds, Turks and Arabs; Politics, Travel and Research in North-Eastern Iraq, 1919–1925*, London, Oxford University Press.

Ende, W. (1981), 'Iraq in World War I; the Turks, the Germans and the Shi'ite mujtahids' call for jihad', in R. Peters (ed.), *Proceedings of the Ninth Congress of the*

Union Européenne des Arabisants et Islamisants, Amsterdam, 1978, Leiden, Brill, pp. 57–71.

Eppel, Michael (1994), *The Palestine Conflict in the History of Modern Iraq: The Dynamics of Involvement, 1928–1948*, London, Frank Cass.

Fahmi, A. (1926), *Tahrir hawl al-'Iraq: mabahith 'an tharwat al-bilad wa-iqtisadiyatiha wa halat al-sukkan al-ruhiyah wa-al-ijtima'iyah mustanidan 'ala al-taqrir al-rasmi al-marfu' ila wizarat maliyat al-'Iraq*, Baghdad, al-Maktaba al-'Asriya n.p.

Farouk-Sluglett, Marion, and Peter Sluglett (2007), 'From the politics of notables to the politics of parliamentary government: Iraq 1918–1932', in Hala Fattah and Magnus Bernhardsson (eds)., *Identity, Nation and State in Iraq*, New York, Palgrave Macmillan.

Farouk-Sluglett, Marion, and Sluglett, Peter (2001), *Iraq since 1958: from Revolution to Dictatorship*, 3rd edition, London, I. B. Tauris.

Farouk-Sluglett, Marion, and Peter Sluglett (1991), 'The historiography of modern Iraq', *American Historical Review*, 96, 5, pp. 1408–1421.

Farouk-Sluglett, Marion, and Peter Sluglett (1984), 'The Application of the 1858 Land Code in Greater Syria; Some Preliminary Observations', in Tarif al-Khalidi (ed.)., *Land Tenure and Social Transformation in the Middle East*, Beirut, American University of Beirut, pp. 409–424.

Farouk-Sluglett, Marion, and Peter Sluglett (1983a), 'The Transformation of Land Tenure and Rural Social Structure in Central and Southern Iraq, 1870–1958', *International Journal of Middle East Studies*, 15, pp. 491–505.

Farouk-Sluglett, Marion, and Peter Sluglett (1983b) 'Labour and National Liberation: the Trade Union Movement in Iraq, 1920–1958', *Arab Studies Quarterly*, 5, 1983, pp. 139–154.

Fattah, Hala (1997), *The Politics of Regional Trade in Iraq, Arabia and the Gulf 1745–1900*, Albany, State University of New York Press.

Fernea, Robert A. (1970), *Shaykh and Effendi: Changing Patterns of Authority Among the El Shabana of Southern Iraq*, Cambridge MA, Harvard University Press.

Fiddes, Sir George Vandeleur (1926), *The Dominions and Colonial Office*, London, Putnam.

Fieldhouse, D.K. (2002) (ed.), *Kurds, Arabs and Britons: the memoir of Wallace Lyon in Iraq, 1918–1944*, London, I. B. Tauris.

Fisher, Sir Stanley (1919), *Ottoman land laws: containing the Ottoman Land code and later legislation affecting land, with notes and an appendix of Cyprus laws and rules relating to land*, London and New York, Oxford University Press.

Fitzgerald, Edward Peter (1994), 'France's Middle Eastern Ambitions, the Sykes-Picot Negotiations and the Oil Fields of Mosul', *Journal of Modern History*, 66, pp. 697–715.

Foster, Henry A. (1935), *The Making of Modern Iraq; a Product of World Forces*, Norman OH, University of Oklahoma Press.

Foweraker, Joe, Todd Landman, and Neil Harvey (2003), *Governing Latin America*, Cambridge, Polity Press.

Fulanain, (S. E. and M. E. Hedgecock) (1927), *Hajji Rikkan, Marsh Arab*, London, Chatto and Windus.

Gerig, Benjamin (1930), *The Open Door and the Mandates System; a Study of Economic Equality before and since the Establishment of the Mandates System*, London, Allen and Unwin.

Gilbert, Martin (1975), *Winston S. Churchill, Volume IV, 1916–1922; the Stricken World*, London, Heinemann, 1975.

Gilbert, Martin (ed.) (1966), *Servant of India: the Diaries and Correspondence of Sir James Dunlop Smith*, London, Longmans.

Gowan, C.H. (1938), 'Northern Iraq', *Journal of the Central Asian Society*, 25, pp. 193–203.

Graves, Philip (1941), *The Life of Sir Percy Cox*, London, Hutchinson.

Graves, Robert and B. H. Liddell Hart (1938), *T.E. Lawrence to his biographers, Robert Graves & Liddell Hart*, Garden City, NY, Doubleday.

Haider, S. (1966), 'Land Tenure in the Nineteenth Century', in Charles Issawi (ed.), *The Economic History of the Middle East 1800–1914*, Chicago and London, Chicago University Press, 163–178.

Haldane, Sir James Aylmer (1922), *The Insurrection in Mesopotamia, 1920*, Edinburgh and London, W. Blackwood and Sons.

Hasan, Muhammad Salman (1970), 'The Role of Foreign Trade in the Economic Development of Iraq, 1864–1964: A Study in the Growth of a Dependent Economy', in Michael Cook (ed.), *Studies in the Economic History of the Middle East*, London, Oxford University Press, pp. 346–372.

Hasan, Muhammad Salman (1965) *al-Tatawwur al-iqtisadi fi'l-'Iraq; al-tijara al-kharijiya w'al-tatawwur al-iqtisadi 1864–1958*, Beirut, al-Maktaba al-'Asriya.

Hasan, Muhammad Salman (1958), 'Growth and Structure of Iraq's Population, 1867–1947', *Bulletin of the Oxford University Institute of Economics and Statistics*, 20, iv, pp. 339–352.

al-Hasani, 'Abd al-Razzaq (1933–1940), *Ta'rikh al-wizarat al-'Iraqiyya* (History of the Iraqi cabinets), 4 vols., Sidon : Matba'at al-'Irfan.

Haseeb, K. (1964), *The National Income of Iraq 1953–1961*, London, Oxford University Press.

al-Hashimi, Taha (1967), *Mudhakkirat Taha al-Hashimi 1919–1943 / ma' tahqiq wa-muqaddimah fi tarikh al-'Iraq al-hadith bi-qalam Khaldun Sati' al-Husri*, Beirut, Dar al-Tali'a.

Hay, Sir Rupert (1921), *Two Years in Kurdistan: experiences of a political officer, 1918–1920*, London, Sidgwick & Jackson.

Heussler, Robert (1963), *Yesterday's Rulers: The Making of the British Colonial Service*, Syracuse, N.Y., Syracuse University Press.

Himadeh, Sa'id (1966), 'Taxation in the 1900's' in Charles Issawi (ed.), *The Economic History of the Middle East 1800–1914*, Chicago and London, Chicago University Press, pp. 186–190.

Hinrichs, W. (1914), 'Eine Karawanenreise von Môsul nach Aleppo vom 9. März bis 25. April 1911', *Petermanns Geographische Mitteilungen*, 60, pp. 189–193, 257–259.

Hoepli, Henry U. (1931), *England im Nahen Osten, das Königreich Irak und die Mossulfrage*, Erlangen, Palm und Enke.

Hoffmann, Karl (1927), *Ölpolitik und angelsächsischer Imperialismus*, Berlin, Ring Verlag.

Hogarth, D. G. (1902), *The Nearer East*, London, Heinemann.

Hoisington, William A. (1978), 'Cities in revolt; the Berber *Dahir* (1930) and France's urban strategy in Morocco,' *Journal of Contemporary History*, 13, pp. 443–448.

Holt, P. M. (1961), *A Modern History of the Sudan, from the Funj Sultanate to the Present Day,* London, Weidenfeld and Nicolson.

Hooper, C.A., (1928), *The Constitutional Law of Iraq,* Baghdad, Mackenzie and Mackenzie.

Hoskins, Halford Lancaster (1928), *British Routes to India,* New York, Longman.

Hourani, Albert (1972), 'Revolution in the Arab Middle East', in P.J. Vatikiotis (ed.), *Revolution in the Middle East,* London, Allen and Unwin, pp. 65–72.

Hourani, Albert (1968), 'Ottoman Reform and the Politics of Notables', in W. Polk and R.W. Chambers (eds.), *The Beginnings of Modernization in the Middle East in the Nineteenth Century,* Chicago, Chicago University Press, pp. 41–68.

Hourani, Albert (1962), *Arabic Thought in the Liberal Age, 1798–1939,* London and New York.

Howard, H. N. (1931), *The Partition of Turkey,* Norman, OH, University of Oklahoma Press.

Howell. E. B. (1922), 'The Qanun al-Aradhi of Iraq', *Journal of the Central Asian Society,* pp. 21–39.

Hurewitz, J.C. (1956), *Diplomacy in the Near and Middle East,* Vol. II: 1914–1956, Princeton, NJ, Princeton University Press.

al-Husri, Abu Khaldun Sati', trs. S. Glazer (1966), *The Day of Maysalun; A Page from the Modern History of the Arabs,* Washington, Middle East Institute.

al-Husri, Abu Khaldun Sati' (1967–1968), *Mudhakkirati fi al-'Iraq, 1921–1941,* Vols I & II, Beirut, Dar al-Taliah.

Ireland, P. W. (1937), *Iraq, A Study in Political Development,* London, Jonathan Cape.

Issawi, Charles (ed.) (1986), *The Economic History of the Fertile Crescent 1800-1914: a Documentary Economic History,* Oxford: Oxford University Press.

Issawi, Charles (ed.) (1966), *The Economic History of the Middle East 1800–1914,* Chicago and London, Chicago University Press.

Jabar, Faleh A. (June 2005), 'Nation-Building: Artificial and Natural, the Case of Iraq', unpublished paper presented at the conference on *States and Societies in search of a Future: from Independence until the Present,* Aix en Provence.

Jadirji, Kamil (1970), *Mudhakkirat Kamil al-Jadirji wa-tarikh al-Hizb al-Watani al-Dimukrati,* Beirut, Dar al-Tarliah.

Jamali, Muhammad Fadhil (1934), *The New Iraq: its Problems of Bedouin Education,* New York, Columbia University Press.

Jawdat, 'Ali (1967), *Dhikrayat 'Ali Jawdat 1900–1958,* Beirut, Matba' Wafa'.

Jwaideh, Antoinette (1984), 'Aspects of land tenure and social change in lower Iraq during late Ottoman times', in Tarif al-Khalidi (ed.), *Land Tenure and Social Trans-formation in the Middle East,* Beirut, American University of Beirut, pp. 333–356.

Jwaideh, Antoniette (1965), 'The Sanniya lands of Sultan 'Abd al-Hamid in Iraq', in George Makdisi (ed.), *Arabic and Islamic Studies in honor of Hamilton A.R. Gibb,* Cambridge MA, Department of Near Eastern Languages and Literatures of Harvard University, pp. 326–336.

Jwaideh, Antoinette (1963), 'Midhat Pasha and the Land System of Lower Iraq', in *St. Antony's Papers* Vol. XVI, Middle Eastern Affairs No. 3, pp. 106–137, London.

Karpat, K. H. (1968), 'The Land Regime, Social Structure and Modernization in the Ottoman Empire', in W. Polk and R.W. Chambers (eds.), *The Beginnings of Modernization in the Middle East in the Nineteenth Century*, Chicago, Chicago University Press, pp. 69–90.

Kayalı, Hasan (1997), *Arabs and Young Turks: Ottomanism, Arabism and Islamism in the Ottoman Empire 1908–1918*, Berkeley and Los Angeles, University of California Press.

Keddie, Nikki R. (1966), *Religion and Rebellion in Iran: The Tobacco Protest of 1891–1892*, London, Frank Cass.

Kedourie, Elie (1974), *Arabic political memoirs and other studies*, London, Frank Cass.

Kedourie, Elie (1970), 'The Kingdom of Iraq, a Retrospect', in *The Chatham House Version and Other Middle-Eastern Studies*, London, Weidenfeld and Nicolson, pp. 239–262.

Kedourie, Elie (1956), *England and the Middle East; The Destruction of the Ottoman Empire, 1914–1921*, London, Bowes & Bowes.

Kent, Marian (1993), *Moguls and Mandarins : Oil, Imperialism, and the Middle East in British Foreign policy 1900–1940*, London and Portland, Frank Cass.

Kent, Marian (1976), *Oil and Empire : British Policy and Mesopotamian Oil, 1900–1920*, London, Macmillan.

Khadduri, Majid (1960), *Independent Iraq 1932–1958: a Study in Iraq Politics*, 2nd revised edition, London, Oxford University Press.

Khoury, Dina Rizk (1997), *State and provincial society in the early modern Ottoman Empire: Mosul 1540–1834*, Cambridge, Cambridge University Press.

Khoury, Philip S. (1990), 'The Urban Notables Paradigm Revisited,' *Revue du Monde Musulman et de la Méditerranée*, 55–56, pp. 215–228.

Khoury, Philip S. (1983), *Urban Notables and Arab nationalism: the politics of Damascus 1860–1920,* Cambridge, Cambridge University Press.

Klieman, A. S. (1970), *Foundations of British Policy in the Arab World: The Cairo Conference of 1921*, Baltimore and London, Johns Hopkins University Press.

Kubbah, Muhammad Mahdi (1965), *Mudhakkirati fi samim al-ahdath, 1918–1958,* Beirut, Dar al-Tali'a.

Lambton, A. K. S. (1953), *Landlord and Peasant in Iran*, London, Oxford University Press.

Langley, K. (1961), *Industrialisation in Iraq*, Cambridge MA, Harvard University Press.

Lawrence, T.E. (1935), *Seven Pillars of Wisdom, A Triumph,* London, Jonathan Cape.

Leach, E. R. (1940), *Social and Economic Organisation of the Rowanduz Kurds*, London, Athlone Press, London.

Lees, G. M. (1928), 'Two Years in South Kurdistan', *Journal of the Central Asian Society*, 15, pp. 253–277.

Lewis, Bernard, *The emergence of modern Turkey,* London, Oxford University Press, 1968.

Litvak, Meir (2000), 'A failed manipulation: the British, the Oudh bequest and the Shi'i 'Ulama of Najaf and Karbala', *British Journal of Middle Eastern Studies*, 27, pp. 69–89.

Litvak, Meir (1998), *Shi'i Scholars of nineteenth -century Iraq: the 'ulama' of Najaf and Karbala'* , Cambridge, Cambridge University Press.

Lloyd, H. I. (1926), 'The Geography of the Mosul Boundary', *Geographical Journal*, 68, pp. 104–116.

Longrigg, Stephen H, (1961), *Oil in the Middle East*, 2nd edn., London, Oxford University Press.

Longrigg, Stephen H. (1958), *Syria and Lebanon under French Mandate*, London, Oxford University Press.

Longrigg, Stephen H. (1953), *Iraq 1900–1950; A Political, Social, and Economic History*, London and New York, Oxford University Press.

Longrigg, Stephen H. (1925), *Four Centuries of Modern Iraq*, London, Oxford University Press.

Luizard, Pierre-Jean (2003), 'Le mandat britannique en Irak: une rencontre entre plusieurs projets politiques' in Nadine Méouchy and Peter Sluglett (eds.) *The British and French mandates in comparative perspectives/Les mandats français et anglais dans une perspective comparative*, Leiden, Brill, pp. 361–384.

Luizard, Pierre-Jean (1991), *La formation de l'Irak contemporain : le rôle politique des ulémas chiites à la fin de la domination ottomane et au moment de la construction de l'Etat irakien*, Paris, Editions du CNRS.

Lyell, Thomas Reginald Guise (1923), *The Ins and Outs of Mesopotamia*, London, A.M. Philpot.

Malek, Yusuf (1934), *The Assyrian Tragedy*, Annemasse, Imprimerie Granchamp.

McCarthy, Justin (1981), 'The Population of Ottoman Syria and Iraq 1878–1914', *Asian and African Studies*, 15, 1, pp. 3–44.

Macdonald, A. D. (1936), *Euphrates Exile*, London, G. Bell.

McDowall, David (1996), *A Modern History of the Kurds,* London, I.B. Tauris.

Main, Ernest (1935), *Iraq from Mandate to Independence*, London, Allen & Unwin.

Mann, James Saumarez (ed.) (1921), *An Administrator in the Making; J. S. Mann 1893–1920*, London, New York, Longmans, Green.

Marder, Arthur (1961), *From Dreadnought to Scapa Flow: The Road to War, 1904–1914,* London, Oxford University Press.

Mardin, S. (1962), *The Genesis of Young Ottoman Thought: a Study in the Modernisation of Turkish Political Ideas*, Princeton NJ, Princeton University Press 1962.

Marlowe, John (1967), *Late Victorian: the Life of Sir Arnold Talbot Wilson, K.C.I.E, C.S.I., C.M.G., D.S.O., M.P.,* London, Cresset Press.

Matthews, R.D. and Matta 'Akrawi (1949), *Education in the Arab countries of the Near East: Egypt, Iraq, Palestine, Transjordan, Syria, Lebanon,* Washington D.C., American Council on Education.

Mejcher, Helmut (1976), *The Imperial Quest for Oil, Iraq 1910–1928*, London, Ithaca Press.

Migdal, Joel S. (1988), *Strong Societies and Weak States: State-Society Relations and State Capabilities in the Third World*, Princeton NJ, Princeton University Press.

Mikdashi, Zuhayr M. (1966), *A Financial Analysis of Middle East Oil Concessions, 1901–1965*, New York, F. A. Praeger.

Monroe, Elizabeth (1981), *Britain's Moment in the Middle East 1914–1971*, 2nd edition, London, Chatto and Windus.

Monroe, Paul (1932), *Report of the Educational Inquiry Commission*, Baghdad, Government Press.

Morris, P. (1987), 'Intelligence and its interpretation: Mesopotamia 1914–1916', in Christopher. Andrew and Jeremy Noakes (eds.), *Intelligence and International Relations 1900–1945,* Exeter: Exeter University Press, pp. 77–101.

Nakash, Yitzhak (1994), *The Shi'is of Iraq*, Princeton NJ, Princeton University Press.

Nevakivi, Jukka (1969), *Britain, France and the Arab Middle East 1914–1920*, London, Athlone Press.

Nicolson, Harold (1934), *Curzon, the Last Phase, 1919–1925: a Study in Post-war Diplomacy*, London, Constable.

Nieuwenhuis, Tom (1982), *Politics and Society in Early Modern Iraq: Mamluk Pashas, Tribal Shayks, and Local Rule between 1802 and 1831*, The Hague, Martinus Nijhoff.

O'Dwyer, Sir Michael (1926), *India as I Knew It, 1885–1925*, London, Constable.

Olson, Robert (1991), *The Emergence of Kurdish Nationalism and the Shaykh Said Rebellion 1880–1925*, Austin, TX, University of Texas Press.

Olson, William J. (1980), 'The Genesis of the Anglo-Persian Agreement of 1919', in Elie Kedourie and Sylvia Haim, (eds.), *Towards a Modern Iran: Studies in Thought, Politics and Society*, London, Frank Cass, pp. 185–216.

Omissi, David (1990), *Air Power and Colonial Control: the Royal Air Force 1919–1939*, Manchester, Manchester University Press.

Pannikar, K.M. (1953), *Asia and Western Dominance: a Study of the Vasco da Gama Epoch of Asian History 1498–1945*, London, Allen and Unwin.

Parkinson, Cosmo (1947), *The Colonial Office from Within, 1909–1945*, London, Faber.

Peter, Frank. (2003). 'Dismemberment of Empire and Reconstitution of Regional Space: the Industries of Damascus between 1918 and 1946', in Nadine Méouchy and Peter Sluglett (eds), *The British and French Mandates in Comparative Perspective/ Les mandats français et anglais dans une perspective comparative*, Leiden, E.J. Brill, pp.415–466.

Peterson, Sir Maurice (1950), *Both Sides of the Curtain: an Autobiography*, London, Constable.

Petrie, Sir Charles (1939–1940), *The Life and Letters of the Rt. Hon. Sir Austen Chamberlain, K.G., P.C., M.P.,* 2 vols., London, Cassell.

Polk, W. R., and R. W. Chambers (eds.) (1968), *The Beginnings of Modernization in the Middle East in the Nineteenth Century*, Chicago, Chicago University Press.

Poyck, A.P.G. (1962), *Farm Studies in Iraq*, Mededelingen van de Landbouwhogeschool te Wagenigen, Wagenigen, (Netherlands).

al-Qassab, 'Abd al-'Aziz (1962), *Min dhikrayati,* Beirut, Manshurat Uwaydat.

Quint, Malcolm (1958), 'The Idea of Progress in an Iraqi Village', *Middle East Journal*, 12, 1958, pp. 369–384.

Ranger, Terence (1965), 'African Attempts to Control Education in East and Central Africa 1900–39', *Past and Present*, 32, pp. 57–85.

Al Rasheed, Madawi (2002), *A History of Saudi Arabia*. Cambridge, Cambridge University Press.

Robb, Peter (2002), *A History of India*, London, Palgrave.

Ronaldshay, Lord (1928), *The life of Lord Curzon; being the authorised biography of George Nathaniel, Marquess Curzon of Kedleston,* 3 vols., London, Ernest Benn.

Rondot, P. (1936), 'Les Tribus Montagnardes de l'Asie Antérieure: Quelques Aspects Sociaux des Populations Kurdes et Assyriennes', *Bulletin des Etudes Orientales de l'institut français de Damas.*

Salim, S. M. (1962), *Marsh Dwellers of the Euphrates Delta*, London, Athlone Press.

Sassoon, Sir Philip (1933), 'Air Power in the Middle East', *Journal of the Royal Central Asian Society,* 20, pp. 394–405.

Satia, Priya (2006), 'The Defense of Inhumanity: Air Control and the British Idea of Arabia', *American Historical Review*, 111, i, pp. 16–51.

Seymour, C.S. (ed.) (1926), *The Intimate Papers of Colonel House,* Vols. III–V, Boston and New York, Houghton Mifflin.

Shields, Sarah (2004), 'Mosul Questions: Economy, Identity and Annexation' in Reeva S Simon and Eleanor H. Tejirian (eds.) *The Creation of Iraq 1914–1921*, New York, Columbia University Press, pp. 50–60.

Shields, Sarah (2000), *Mosul before Iraq: Like Bees Making Five-Sided Cells,* Albany, State University of New York Press.

Slater, S.H. (1926), 'Iraq', *The Nineteenth Century and After,* 99, pp. 479–494.

Sluglett, Peter (2005) 'The Urban Bourgeoisie and the Colonial State: the Iraqi and Syrian Middle Classes between the Two World Wars', in Annika Rabo and Bo Utas (eds.), *The Role of the State in West Asia*, Istanbul, Transactions of the Swedish Research Institute in Istanbul, Vol. 14, 2005, pp. 77–90.

Sluglett, Peter (2004a), 'British archival sources for the history of the Middle Eastern mandates', in Peter Sluglett and Nadine Méouchy (eds.), *The British and French mandates in comparative perspectives/Les mandats français et anglais dans une perspective comparative,* Leiden, Brill, 2004, pp. 55–62.

Sluglett, Peter (2004b), 'Introduction', to C. H. Bleaney and G. J. Roper (compilers), *Iraq: a Bibliographical Guide*, Leiden, Brill, pp. xi–xxxiv.

Sluglett, Peter (2002), 'The Resilience of a Frontier: Ottoman and Iraqi Claims to Kuwait, 1871 to 1990', *International History Review,* 24, pp. 783–816.

Sluglett, Peter (1992), 'al-Muntafik in recent times', in *Encylopedia of Islam*, 2nd edition, Leiden, E. J. Brill, Vol. VII, pp. 582–83.

Stafford, R. S. (1935), *The Tragedy of the Assyrians*, London, Allen and Unwin.

Stephens, W.B. (1998), *Education in Britain 1750–1914*, Basingstoke, Macmillan.

Stivers, William (1982), *Supremacy and Oil: Iraq, Turkey, and the Anglo-American world order, 1918–1930*, Ithaca, NY, Cornell University Press.

Storrs, Sir Ronald (1937), *Orientations*, 3rd edn., London, Nicholson and Watson.

al-Suwaydi, Tawfiq (1969), *Mudhakkirati : nisf qarn min tarikh al-'Iraq wa-al-qadiyah al-'Arabiyah,* Beirut, Dar al-Katib al-'Arabi.

Talabani, Mukarram (1969), *Fi sabil islah zira'i jidri f'il-'Iraq*, Baghdad, n.p.

Temperley, H.W.V. (1920), *History of the Peace Conference of Paris*, Vol. VI, London, H. Frowde, and Hodder & Stoughton.

Thesiger, W. (1967), *The Marsh Arabs*, London, Penguin.

Thomas, Bertram (1931), *Alarms and Excursions in Arabia*, London, Allen and Unwin.

Thomson, Lord (1925), 'My Impressions of a Tour in Iraq', *Journal of the Central Asian Society*, 11, pp. 207–225.

Thornton, A. P. (1959), *The Imperial Idea and Its Enemies*, London, Macmillan.

Thornton, T.H. (1895), *Colonel Sir Robert Sandeman: his life and work on our Indian frontier. A memoir, with selections from his correspondence and official writings,* London, John Murray.

Tibi, Bassam (1981), (eds. and trs. Marion Farouk-Sluglett and Peter Sluglett), *Arab Nationalism: a Critical Enquiry*, London, Macmillan.

Townshend, Sir Charles (1920), *My Campaign in Mesopotamia*, London, Butterworth.

Usborne, R. (1974), *Clubland Heroes, a nostalgic study of some recurrent characters in the romantic fiction of Dornford Yates, John Buchan and Sapper*, revised edn., London, Barrie and Jenkins.

Vinogradov, Amal (1972), 'The 1920 revolt in Iraq reconsidered ; the role of tribes in national politics', *International Journal of Middle East Studies*, 3, pp. 123–139.

Visser, Reidar (2005), *Basra, the Failed Gulf State: Separatism and Nationalism in Southern Iraq*, Münster, LIT Verlag.

Walder, David (1969), *The Chanak Affair*, London, Hutchinson.

Waley, S. D. (1964), *Edwin Montagu, a Memoir and an Account of his Visits to India*, New York, Asia Publishing House.

Warriner, Doreen (1969), *Land Reform in Principle and Practice*, Oxford, Clarendon Press.

Warriner, Doreen (1966), 'The Real Meaning of the Ottoman Land Code', in Charles Issawi (ed.), *The Economic History of the Middle East, 1800–1914*, Chicago and London. pp. 72–78.

Warriner, Doreen (1962), *Land Reform and Development in the Middle East: a Study of Egypt, Syria and Iraq*, 2nd edition, London, Oxford University Press.

Warriner, Doreen (1948), *Land and Poverty in the Middle East*, London, Royal Institute for International Affairs.

Whitehead, Clive (2003), *Colonial Educators: the British Indian and Colonial Education Service 1858–1983*, London, I. B. Tauris.

Wigram, W. A. (1929), *The Assyrians and their Neighbours*, London, G. Bell.

Willcocks, Sir W. (1910), 'Mesopotamia; past, present and future,' *Geographical Journal*, 35, pp. 1–18.

Wilson, A. T. (1931), *Mesopotamia 1917–1920: A Clash of Loyalties*, London, Oxford University Press.

Wilson, A. T. (1930), *Loyalties: Mesopotamia 1914–1917*, London, Oxford University Press.

Wilson, A. T. (1921), 'Mesopotamia, 1914–1920', *Journal of the Central Asian Society*, 8, pp. 144–161.

Wirth, E. (1962), *Agrargeographic der Irak*, Hamburg, Selbstverlag des Instituts für Geographie und Wirtschaftgeographie der Universität Hamburg; in Kommission bei Cram, de Gruyter.

Wolpert, S. (1967), *Morley and India, 1906 to 1910*, Berkeley and Los Angeles, University of California Press.

Woodruff, Philip (pseud.) (1953), *The Men Who Ruled India*, London, Jonathan Cape.

Wright, Quincy (1926), 'The Government of Iraq', *American Political Science Review*, 20, pp. 743–769.

Young, Sir Hubert (1933), *The Independent Arab*, London, John Murray.

INDEX OF PERSONS AND PLACES

1. In the brief descriptions attached to the more prominent non-Iraqi individuals, the phrase *in italics* refers to their service in, or related to, Iraq.

2 (Sir) in parentheses means that the individual's knighthood was conferred after his service in Iraq.

3. Arab names are generally sorted by *laqab* (e.g. al-'Askari, Ja'far; al-Gaylani, Rashid 'Ali); Sharif Husayn and his sons appear in the order of their first names (e.g. 'Abdullah, Faysal, Husayn)

INDEX OF SUBJECTS AND THEMES